KAUA'I

Making the Most of Your Family Vacation

by Dona Early and Christie Stilson

P
PRIMA
PRIMA PUBLISHING
PO Box 1260 STI
Rocklin, CA 95677

In affiliation with Paradise Publications

KAUA'I A Paradise Family Guide
Copyright © 1996 Paradise Publications, Portland, Oregon

First Edition: May 1988
Second Edition: May 1989
Third Edition: January 1991
Fourth Edition: October 1995

All rights reserved. No part of this book may be reproduced or transmitted in any form or by any means, electronic or mechanical, including photocopying, recording, or by any information storage or retrieval system without written permission from Prima Publishing, except for the inclusion of quotations in a review.

Illustrations: Janora Bayot
Maps: John Stenersen
Layout & Typesetting: Paradise Publications
Cover Design: Kevin Yee, Dunlavey Studio, Inc.
Cover Photograph: © 1995 Art Brewer / Tony Stone Worldwide

Published By Prima Publishing, Rocklin, California

Library of Congress Cataloging-in-Publication Data

Early, Dona
    Kaua'i: making the most of your family vacation / Dona Early and Christie Stilson.
    -- 4th ed.
      p.   cm.
    Includes bibliographical references and index.
    ISBN 0-7615-0187-8 : $14.95
    1. Kauai (Hawaii)--Guidebooks. I. Stilson, Christie II. Title.

DU628.K3E27   1995   95-20895
919.69'41--dc20   CIP

96 97 98 HH 10 9 8 7 6 4 3 2
Printed in the United States of America

WARNING-DISCLAIMER
Prima Publishing in affiliation with Paradise Publications has designed this book to provide information in regard to the subject matter covered. It is sold with the understanding that the publishers and authors are not liable for the misconception or misuse of information provided. Every effort has been made to make this book as complete and as accurate as possible. The purpose of this book is to educate. The author, Prima Publishing and Paradise Publications shall have neither liability nor responsibility to any person or entity with respect to any loss, damage, or injury caused or alleged to be caused directly or indirectly by the information contained in this book. They shall also not be liable for price changes, or for the completeness or accuracy of the contents of this book.

HOW TO ORDER: Quantity discounts are available from the publisher, Prima Publishing, PO Box 1260BK, Rocklin, CA 95677; telephone (916) 632-4400. On your letterhead include information concerning the intended use of the books and the number of books you wish to purchase.

TABLE OF CONTENTS

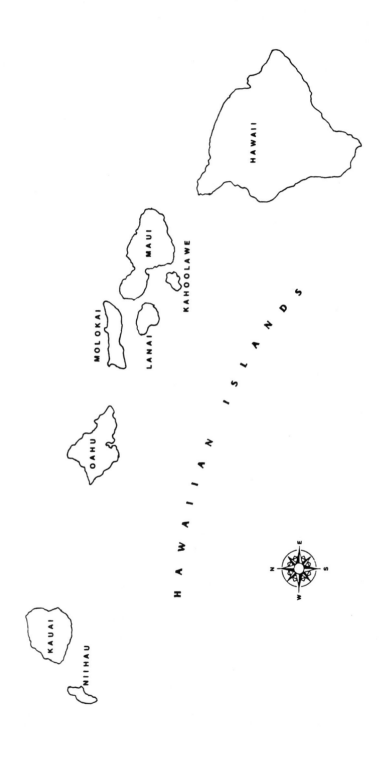

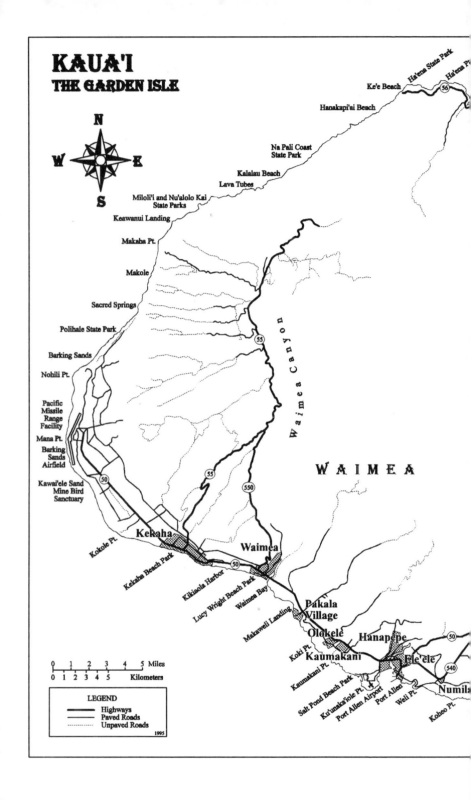

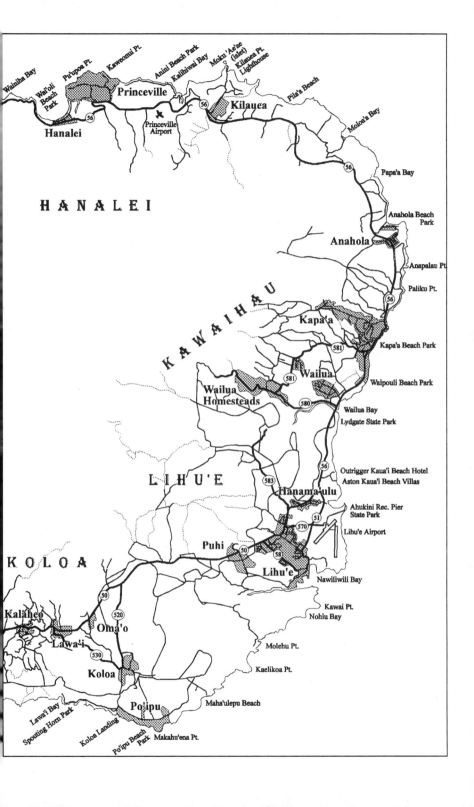

There's an island, across the sea,
Beautiful Kaua'i, beautiful Kaua'i.
It's calling, It's calling to me,
Beautiful Kaua'i, beautiful Kaua'i.

In the mist of Fern Grotto,
Mother Nature made her home,
And the falls of Wailua,
Where lovers often roam.

So I'll return to my isle,
Across the sea,
Beautiful Kaua'i, beautiful Kaua'i,
Where my true love is waiting for me.

By Randy Farden

INTRODUCTION

Kauaʻi is called "The Garden Island," and even to those unfamiliar and unacquainted with this serene and special place, the reasons are obvious and well deserved. It is lush and green, the most verdant of all the Hawaiian Islands. Rich in flora and fauna, it is an "Eden" within a paradise of surpassing natural beauty. There are more waterfalls, more rivers and more birds than on any of the other islands. It is abundant with wild fruit and flowers and provides a loving shelter to many endangered species. Yet it is only within the past decade that the full impact of this nickname has been realized, that Kauaʻi has truly become "The Garden Island."

After two major hurricanes, the island has literally gone back to its roots. It has been replanted, grown back from new seeds and blossomed as much as any living garden. With each devastating hurricane, Kauaʻi has grown and grown back - and grown back again. Like a plant or tree that needs to be pruned so that it will grow and blossom, Kauaʻi has emerged from each disaster stronger and more beautiful than before. With each rebuilding and new growth, its people have become closer together and more appreciative of what they have. Their island has become precious: it is impossible to take nature for granted, whether in its destruction or in its simple beauty. Their lives - and lifestyles - have become precious. Like food, shelter and water, jobs are no longer mere necessities - they have become lifelines never again to be taken for granted.

Tourism, once tolerated and grudgingly acknowledged, was sorely missed and is now seen as a remarkable gift. Because the people of Kauaʻi worked hard to rebuild their island to create its new life, they take particular delight in the opportunity to share, not only with each other, but with those lucky enough to visit their special island. "The Garden Island" has also become "The Welcoming Island" as visitors are embraced with more love, enthusiasm and *Aloha Spirit* than ever before. In fact, the 1994 Conde Nast Traveler Readers' choice awards voted Kauaʻi the most friendly destination in the United States.

So, now that you know you have made the right decision in choosing Kauaʻi for your vacation, you should also know that you have made the right decision in choosing KAUAʻI, A PARADISE FAMILY GUIDE for your companion. From the family values "buzz words" of the 90's we know that "family" can mean anything. *Ohana*, the Hawaiian word for relative or family, is also used for an extended family of friends, neighbors or co-workers. Even visitors who share a common love and respect for the islands are often described as "part of the *ohana*." Your co-authors for this book have felt this "*ohana*" ever since they first visited the islands. In 1983, Dona moved to Maui to live permanently. Christie first visited the islands in 1978, and became so infatuated that she kept returning year after year.

Both your authors are visitors to Kaua'i and look at Kaua'i from a visitor's perspective. As authors who travel in very different modes (Christie, who travels as a family with two children, and Dona as a single adult), we can share our island experiences from different "family" viewpoints. Kaua'i offers the perfect location for a romantic interlude, a vacation with family or a wonderful destination to spend time relaxing with friends. There is plenty of information on traveling with children, as well as older adults who might be a part of your family. (By the way, if you don't have children or seniors to travel with, you might want to consider renting one or two after you read up on some of the freebies and discounts they get!)

You will notice that Kaua'i is divided into three distinct visitor destination areas along the North, South and East coasts of the island. Each area has characteristics uniquely their own, so reading up on them will help you decide just which part of Kaua'i you would like to make your temporary home. The Paradise Guidebooks are all formatted to help you do just that by listing all the accommodations and restaurants by area - section by section - along with sights and attractions particular to that neighborhood. Recreational activities are listed by category - after all, you choose activities by what interests you, not where they are located. General Information is in the front of the book. Overall facts and advice to help you with your vacation plans (as well as your general knowledge) are all in this section, but specific areas of information are emphasized for easy reference. Maps are located throughout the book - see the index for map pages to correspond with the areas you are most interested in.

Because the Hawaiian islands - and especially, Kaua'i - are growing and changing almost daily, it can be difficult to keep up, especially given the particulars of printing and publishing a guide book. Anything can happen in a few weeks or months with the ongoing changes and continuing growth of Kaua'i, and it probably has! Unfortunately, that means that any guidebook is out of date before it is ever in print. However, as a small press, Paradise Publications is able to work up to within weeks of the date this book goes to print. That said, this is one of the most up-to-date and accurate guidebooks on the market and one of the few post-Iniki references that hasn't simply inserted a paragraph about the hurricane into a book of information that is presumed to still be accurate. The fourth edition of this guidebook has been re-written from scratch. Nothing has been left to assumption, everything has been carefully and thoughtfully updated. To further insure that the guidebook is as up-to-date as possible, Paradise Publications also produces *The Kaua'i Update*, a quarterly newsletter to augment the information in this book. Paradise Publications is the only publisher to do so, so as facts in the book change you'll be able to get the latest updates within months.

If your vacation plans include stopovers to one or more of the other islands, Paradise Publications also publishes *Maui, A Paradise Family Guide* by Greg & Christie Stilson and *Hawaii: The Big Island, A Paradise Family Guide* by John Penisten. These guides, too, offer quarterly newsletters. (If you would like more information on either of these titles please see ORDERING INFORMATION at the back of this book.) If you would like a copy of our *Kaua'i Update* newsletter, send a self addressed stamped envelope along with your request and we will be happy to provide you with a sample of the most recent issue.

Of course there are other Kaua'i guidebooks and it doesn't hurt to get a second opinion. Most of the reviews in this book are based on our personal preferences, so you might wish to read others for different points of view or emphasis on other aspects of Kaua'i. We're so confident you'll find this Kaua'i Guide invaluable that we don't mind recommending the competition as well! One of the most current Kaua'i guidebook (prior to this one) is *The Ultimate Kaua'i Book* by Andrew Doughty. Jocelyn K. Fujii has a section on Kaua'i in *The Best of Hawai'i* as does Sean Pager in *Hawai'i: Off the Beaten Path*. Lonely Planet's *Hawai'i: A Travel Survival Kit* and Moon Publications *Kaua'i Handbook* also have varied information with different emphasis.

The primary difference between guidebooks (ours from theirs) seems to be in choosing the information to use. We have tried to list ALL the accommodations, restaurants and activities, not just our favorites or a select few. Of course, with a limited amount of time and resources, we have not been able to review each and every restaurant, recreational activity or restaurant. Those which we have not been able to personally review have plenty of basic facts to assist you in making your decision. To assist you in the selection of your accommodations, restaurant, activity or beach locations, we have added our personal recommendations or "Best Bets" to each chapter of this guide.

We also invite you to please write us with your viewpoints and experiences (they are what make the Paradise Guidebooks and Updates special and uniquely personal) and we will share them with our readers.

We have a few people we would like to thank. Our gratitude to Randy Farden for permission to use his beautiful Kaua'i song lyrics and to the University of Hawai'i Press for use of the poem "Behold." A big hug and special thanks to Maren and Jeff Stilson for their patience while mom spent hours at the computer. A notable thanks to Maren Stilson who is blooming as a budding editor. And a huge heartfelt thanks to John Stenersen for his outstanding work producing the all-new maps for this revised edition.

Aloha!

Dona and Christie

E'Ike Mai

I luna la, i luna
Na manu o ka lewa

I lalo la, i lalo
Na pua o ka honua

I uka la, i uka
Na ulu la 'au

I kai la, i kai
Na i'a o ka moana

Ha'ina mai ka puana
A he nani ke ao ne

Behold

Above, above
all birds in air

below, below
all earth's flowers

inland, inland
all forest trees

seaward, seaward
all ocean fish

sing out and say
again the refrain

Behold this lovely world

Excerpt from *The Echo of Our Song, Chants & Poems of the Hawaiians*. Translated and Edited by Mary K. Pukui and Alfons L. Korn. Reprinted with permission from the University of Hawaii Press.

GENERAL INFORMATION

OUR PERSONAL BEST BETS

BEST FOOD SPLURGE: Champagne Brunch or the Friday evening seafood buffet at the Princeville Hotel.

BEST SUNSET AND COCKTAILS: At the Beach House with free pupus during Happy Hour which is from 4-6 pm. The library lounge at the Princeville Hotel with the sunset over Bali Hai.

BEST SUNSET DINING VIEW: Princeville's Hanalei Cafe.

BEST BEACH SUNSET: From Ke'e Beach with the Na Palis for a backdrop or at the other end of the Na Pali coast at Polihale Beach.

BEST DAILY BREAKFAST BUFFET: Hyatt Regency.

BEST DINNERS IN PARADISE: Gaylord's, A Pacific Cafe, and Roy's.

BEST LUAU VALUE: Check the local Kaua'i newspapers for advertisements listing local luaus that might be held by churches or other organizations as fund raisers -- a great value and you're sure to enjoy some great food!

BEST SALAD BAR VALUE: Sizzler.

BEST ROMANTIC DINING: Tidepools at the Hyatt. The Hanalei Cafe at the Princeville Hotel.

BEST FAMILY DINING VALUES: Barbecue Inn.

BEST FAMILY DINING ATMOSPHERE: Keoki's.

BEST PIZZA: Brick Oven Pizza in Kalaheo. For a gourmet pizza try Tosca's made in their wood-burning pizza oven. Pau Hana wins for unusual toppings.

MOST OUTRAGEOUS DESSERTS: Roy's Chocolate Souffle, Keoki's Hula Pie, and the pies at Green Garden. Camp House Grill has a chewy chocolate chip macadamia nut pie or pineapple cream cheese pie that are both worthy of the calories!

BEST COOL TREATS: Lappert's Ice Cream at one of their many locations. A shave ice at Halo Halo Shave Ice in Lihu'e.

OUTSTANDING FINE DINING VALUE: Gaylord's restaurant or A Pacific Cafe with an entertainment coupon.

BEST TAKE-HOME FOOD PRODUCTS: Fresh papaya salsa from People's Market in Puhi.

BEST SEAFOOD RESTAURANT: Keoki's.

BEST SHOPPING: Kukui Grove Shopping Center.

BEST ALOHA WEAR: Liberty House and Hilo Hattie's.

BEST CHEAP ALOHA WEAR: While not for every traveler, the Salvation Army can be a great place to pick up some Hawaiian clothes to wear on your vacation. A muumuu for less than $5 is great for a beach cover-up or wearing to a luau. There are Salvation Army outlets in Koloa, Lihu'e and Kapa'a that are open Tuesday through Saturday from 9 am - 4 pm. Check the phone book for addresses. Senior discounts on Wednesday and Friday with valid ID.

BEST LEIS: People's Market in Puhi. Also, inexpensive leis can be found at the Honolulu airport or the lei stands outside the Honolulu airport.

MOST SPECTACULAR RESORT GROUNDS: Hyatt.

BEST ROMANTIC ADVENTURE: A trip up the Wailua River to Fern Grotto in a kayak for two. A horse and carriage ride at the Kaua'i Lagoons or Kilohana Plantation.

BEST CHANCE OF GETTING RAINED ON: The Wai'ale'ale Crater, the wettest spot on earth!

BEST EXCURSIONS:
> *Most spectacular* -- a helicopter tour.
> *Most unusual* -- a kayaking trip around the Na Pali coast.
> *Best adventure on foot* -- the first two miles of the Kalalau trail on the Na Pali coast.
> *A world away* -- a helicopter tour of the isolated island of Niihau.

BEST BEACHES:
> *Most scenic* -- Lumaha'i Beach or Ke'e on Kaua'i's northshore.
> *Unspoiled* -- Maha'ulepu, Honapu and Lawa'i Kai.
> *Best for kids* - Salt Ponds, Lydgate Beach Park, or Po'ipu Beach for the protected kiddie wading area.

BEST RECREATION AND TOURS: See the beginning of the RECREATION & TOURS chapter for ideas!

BEST KAUA'I GET-AWAY-FROM-IT-ALL RESORT: Princeville Resort or The Kilauea Lakeside Estate (a private lakefront home).

MOST AFFORDABLE GET-AWAY-FROM-IT-ALL CONDO: Sealodge.

BEST HOTEL VALUE: Kaua'i Coconut Beach with Entertainment coupon.

BEST ACCOMMODATIONS DISCOUNT: *Entertainment Book* coupon discounts continue to offer discounts at several Kaua'i hotels and condominiums. The *Entertainment Book* is printed in most major cities around the country and contains coupons for dining and activities in that area. In addition, they carry discounts for accommodations in other regions of the U.S., including Hawai'i.

You can also check your phone book under Entertainment, Inc. There is a Hawai'i edition which carries coupons for dining and attractions, largely for O'ahu, but the outer islands are included as well. For information contact Entertainment Publications at their Honolulu office at (808) 737-3252 or write them at 4211 Waialae Ave., Honolulu, HI 96816. There is a fee for these books (about $40).

The current edition for Hawai'i lists the following properties on Kaua'i: Colony's Po'ipu Kai, Hanalei Bay Resort and Suites, Hale Moi Cottages, Kaua'i Coconut Beach Hotel, Kaua'i Resort in Wailua, Pali Ke Kua at Princeville, Outrigger Kaua'i Beach in Lihu'e, Plantation Hale in Lihu'e and The Cliffs at Princeville.

Examples: A garden view one bedroom condo at Po'ipu Kai costs $120 high season and $100 low season via the lowest rental agent we could find. Colony quoted us $80-$90 for a garden view unit. Not quite 50 percent savings as advertised, but with a little legwork, you could save a fair piece of change over an extended stay. The best deal was the Kaua'i Coconut Beach Resort with a partial ocean view room priced at less than $60 per night.

Many restrictions apply with limits on availability and categories of rooms. For example, Plantation Hale has a five night maximum stay, excludes Christmas holiday and you must make reservations more than 90 days prior to arrival. They only offer a few rooms at these discounts, so make your travel plans well in advance to take advantage of this vacation bargain!

HIBISCUS & PALM

The beach activities are subject to weather and ocean conditions!

BEST SNORKELING: Beginners -- Poʻipu Beach and Lydgate. Intermediate -- Tunnels (only for strong swimmers).

BEST BODY SURFING: Shipwreck Beach.

BEST SURFING: Waiohai's "Acid Drop," The Beach House, or Hanalei Bay.

BEST WINDSURFING: Beginners -- ʻAnini.
                            Intermediate -- Tunnels or Mahaulapu.

BEST SWIMMING: Poʻipu Beach, Hanalei Bay, Salt Ponds.

BEST FLOWERS: Sunshine Markets around the islands or People's Market in Puhi.

BEST NIGHT SPOTS: Kuhio's and Gilligan's.

UNUSUAL GIFT IDEAS: Fabrics from Kapaia Stitchery. Sunflowers in Hanalei has handcrafted Kauaʻi products. Kauaʻi Tropical Fudge has some unusual and interesting flavors like banana macadamia nut, ginger, pina colada, Kona coffee and cream. Or bring home some tropical scented lotions and soaps from Island Soap Company that are scented with plumeria, torch ginger or pikake and all hand-made in Kilauea using natural ingredients. Available at many local gift shops.

BEST T-SHIRTS: Our favorites are Crazy Shirts, more expensive than the run-of-the-mill variety. However, have great designs.

BEST FREE STUFF:

The Hawaiʻi Visitors Bureau Kauaʻi map.

A tour of the Guava Kai Plantation in Kilauea.

The Kamalani playground at Lydgate Park for kids.

Free movies at the Princeville Hotel for resort guests.

Free camping permits at state parks on Kauaʻi.

The Pacific Whale Foundation sponsors whale slide shows during the winter season. This presentation is complimentary at various locations around the island. Check with the Hanalei Colony at (808) 826-6804 for days, times and location.

A scenic drive along Kaua'i's North Shore.

Free pupus during happy hour from 4-6 pm at the Beach House.

Free introductory scuba lessons at resort pools.

Koloa Plantation Days in July.

Free tour of Moir Cactus Gardens at the Kiahuna Plantation Tuesdays 10 am.

Not quite free, but for a $2 donation we think this counts: Enjoy a hike with an interpretive guide along the many trails of the Koke'e area. Offered during summer months only by the Koke'e Natural History Museum.

Free hula shows at the Coconut Marketplace each Monday, Wednesday, Friday and Saturday at 4:30 pm. The center is located 15 minutes north of Lihu'e between the Wailua River and Kapa'a. For information call (808) 822-3641.

Free keiki hula at Po'ipu Shopping Village on Thursdays at 5:30 pm.

Outrigger Kaua'i Beach Hotel has a "Weekend Wednesdays" hula show each Wednesday at 5:30 pm. Enjoy the performers, then head to Gilligan's for a free movie!

Watch jewelry being designed and created at The Goldsmith's Gallery in the Kinipopo Shopping Village in Wailua.

The Kaua'i Resort Hotel offers free seasonal hula shows, hula lessons and Hawaiian arts and craft sales in their lobby.

The CJM Country Stables in Koloa currently has a complimentary rodeo, held one Sunday a month at 10 am. (808) 742-6096

Events at Borders Books at the Kukui Grove Shopping Center.

Ma's in Lihu'e gives you a free cup of coffee when you order a meal! At the Ohana Bakery on the Northshore at Princeville Center you can also enjoy a free cup of joe with your Danish or breakfast pastry.

On the first Saturday of the month admission is free at the Kaua'i Museum. This monthly event features special family activities. You can obtain a calendar of events by writing 4428 Rice St., Lihu'e, HI 96766 (808) 245-6931.

The Koke'e Natural History Museum offers free guided and trail clearing hikes from June through mid-September. The museum also sponsors a number of environmental and cultural festivals throughout the year. For further information contact them at PO Box 100, Kekaha, HI 96752 (808) 335-9975.

Kaua'i's wilderness areas: Waimea Canyon; Koke'e State Park; Alakai Wilderness Preserve; Na Pali Coast State Park.

A Sunday service in Hawaiian at the Waioli Hui Church in Hanalei or the Waimea Hawaiian Church in Waimea.

Watching the sunset from Ke'e Beach on the North Shore or from Polihale Beach on the western coastline.

The many varied annual events that are offered at no charge.

Free copy of *Kaua'i Update* Newsletter! Send a self addressed stamped envelope to us at Paradise Publications and indicate you'd like the latest copy of our Kaua'i newsletter.

BEST GIFT FOR FRIENDS TRAVELING TO KAUA'I: A copy of *Kaua'i, A Paradise Family Guide* and a subscription to the quarterly *Kaua'i Update* newsletter!

HELICONIA, BIRD OF PARADISE   JANORA BAYOT

HISTORY OF KAUA'I

Although it is not the usual way to begin an historic narrative, this history of Kaua'i must begin with its most recent past and latest chapter: Hurricane Iniki. Its far-reaching impact not only affected you, the visitor, but even the printing of this book! The original fourth edition was already etched into place and ready to roll off the presses in September 1992. The hurricane that struck on September 11 made that new edition of this guide obsolete -- no matter how thorough and extensive the research and updating by the previous authors. It was several years before a new book could even be contemplated, and even now -- when almost all of the island has recovered from the hurricane's devastating effects -- there are still a few hotels not yet open, some restaurants that had to close their doors, and some residents and businesses that just couldn't make it and moved away. But from the destruction sprang new growth and rebirth. Hotels were renovated and remodeled, new restaurants opened and old ones were refurbished and improved.

Hurricane Iniki left a heavy footprint throughout the island in the way it altered physical attributes and geography, the way it impacted important commercial industries like tourism, fishing and agriculture, and the way it affected the attitudes, philosophies, lifestyles and even lives of its people. Many residents left after the second hurricane to hit the island within only ten years. Many others felt that with two hurricanes behind them they could probably face anything and be stronger for it. The facts about Hurricane Iniki were sent out to millions on the international news. Every devastating detail was reported, and we eagerly watched the good and bad news as it unfolded. But now that the day-to-day effects have diminished, and the facts have become historical statistics, they can be neatly and benignly tucked into the section on Weather and its sub-category: hurricanes. That done, let's go back three years plus a few million to the creation of Kaua'i, The Garden Island.

Far beneath the warm waters of the Pacific Ocean is the Pacific Plate, which moves constantly in a northwest direction. Each Hawaiian island was formed as it passed over a hot vent in this plate. Kaua'i, the oldest of the major islands in the Hawai'i chain, was formed first and has since moved away from the plume, the source of the lava, so it is no longer growing. But the ocean that created these islands millions of years ago has all but swallowed them back, leaving only atolls of coral reef. The archipelago known as Hawai'i spans 1523 miles with 132 islands, shoals and reefs that reach as far west as the Aleutian Islands of Alaska. The Big Island is now the youngest in the chain and is continuing to grow. A new island called Lo'ihi (which means "prolonged in time"), southeast of the Big Island, is growing beneath the surface of the Pacific and is expected to emerge from the oceanic depths in about a million years. Except for Midway, which is under the control of the U.S. Navy, all islands other than the major eight come under the jurisdiction of the City and County of Honolulu. The islands we tend to think of as comprising the State of Hawai'i are the eight islands within the 400 southernmost of the island chain: Hawai'i, Maui, Kaho'olawe, Lana'i, Moloka'i, O'ahu, Ni'ihau and Kaua'i.

The northernmost islands of the "eight" major islands, Kaua'i and Ni'ihau, were created together, emerging from the surface of the sea at the same time. They are actually dissected domes separated by the shallow 17-mile wide Kau'lakahi Channel. Lehua to the north and Ka'ula to the south are two tiny uninhabited islets that are part of Ni'ihau and Kaua'i County.

The interpretations of the name Kaua'i prove to be varied. Harry Franck in his 1937 publication entitled, *"Roaming in Hawai'i,"* noted that the translation was "to light upon" or "to dry in the sun." The reason might possibly be because driftwood landed on the shores of Kaua'i more often than on other islands. It lies very much in the track of the trade winds and of ocean currents. He continues: "The more commonly accepted meaning of the name is 'fruitful season or time of plenty,' because in olden times Kaua'i was the only island of the group which never suffered from famine on account of drought. In very ancient times, it was known as Kauai-a-mano-ka-lani-po, which freely translated means 'The fountain-head of many waters from on high and bubbling from below.'"

Kaua'i is young in geological terms, but its birth probably began about 6 million years ago and continued for about 3 million years. It lay dormant for another 1.5 million years before having a resurgence of volcanic activity which created the eastern portions of Kaua'i over the course of more than 1.5 million years. The most recent volcanic activity occurred on the southern shore more than 40,000 years ago. Compared with Maui's most recent volcanic activity which occured only 200 years ago, Kaua'i is the grandfather in the chain of major Hawaiian islands. Kaua'i is much smaller today than when it was first formed. Over eons of time the crashing waves and storms eroded the north shore, reducing the island's diameter from over 30 miles to 25, a small price to pay in return for the dramatic result of the erosion: the splendor and majesty of the incomparable Na Pali Coast. Kaua'i's other phenomenon of nature, Waimea Canyon, was formed when a huge fault broke open and was further eroded by the Waimea River. Kawakini and Wai'ale'ale are the twin peaks of the single shield volcano that formed the island. Mt. Wai'ale'ale is considered the wettest place on earth. Harry Franck in his book, *"Roaming in Hawai'i,"* tells that "in very ancient days the topmost peak was called Ka-wai-kini, 'waters in multitudes' and survey maps still record that appropriate old name. But today it is more familiarly known as Wai'ale'ale (which means 'rippling waters' or 'sparkling waters'), for the surface of the little lake at the summit is never still."

Due to the years of erosion, Kaua'i has many land characteristics unique to the Hawaiian islands. With a total of 136 miles of coastline, Kaua'i has more sandy beaches per square mile than any other of the major islands. The Na Pali coast on Kauai's north shore is another of mother nature's wondrous creations, rising as much as 3,000 feet from the sea. Kaua'i is also home to Hawai'i's only navigable rivers, seven in all. Kaua'i today is a blend of 555 square miles of desert, mountains, beaches and rain forests, making it Hawai'i's fourth largest island.

Life began in the waters surrounding the island in the form of marine creatures. Fish, mammals and microscopic animals found homes under the sea while generations of coral polyps attached themselves to the barren volcanic rock and ultimately created a coral reef. Kaua'i remains on the fringe of the coral reef system. Thus, many of its beaches lack a protective reef and require more caution.

On land, life began slowly, sporadically and quite by accident. Spores of ferns and moss, as well as tiny seeds, were carried by the winds. The few that survived altered the composition of the barren rock by breaking it down into bits of debris and fertile soil. Insects were tossed about by storms and washed ashore on floating debris. Birds blown off course began to colonize, not only populating the island with their own species, but with larger seeds and grasses that they inadvertently carried on their feet, feathers, or in their intestinal tracts.

The introduction of each species of flora or fauna was a rare event, taking thousands of years. With no predators, birds flourished. The only mammals to arrive, without the help of man, were the seal and the bat, and neither provided any threat to the birdlife of the islands. Since the mongoose was never introduced to Kaua'i, the birds continue to flourish here.

Just as the creation of life is explained in two equally valid interpretations -- the scientific and biblical -- the population of the Hawaiian Islands must be explained both by legend and science in equal measures of credibility. Kaua'i was the first home of the Hawaiian volcano goddess, Madame Pele (until her sister drove her out) as well as being the first Hawaiian island populated by the Polynesians.

Although the dates vary greatly, sometime between 200 A.D. to 700 A.D., the first Polynesian explorers came to Kaua'i from the Marquesa Islands. Findings suggest that their ancestors came from the western Pacific, perhaps as far as Madagascar. Centuries later, they were followed by the Tahitians, who came via The Big Island, and from their word manahune (or outcast) came the reality-based legend of the menehune, the Hawaiian leprechaun.

Driven out by her sister, Madame Pele moved to the Big Island taking her fire with her. She now makes her home in the volcanoes of Manua Kea and Mauna Loa and is no longer associated with Kaua'i.

The Polynesians and Tahitians, however, settled on the island between the 11th and 14th centuries and began much of what we know as Hawaiian culture on the island of Kaua'i. The Polynesians brought their double-hulled canoes, laden with the food staples of taro and breadfruit as well as pigs, chickens and dogs (presumably the required quarantine time was more lenient back then), which supplemented their diet of fish. They also introduced a number of plants, including ginger and sugarcane (to name just a few). It was fortunate they arrived so well prepared, as Kaua'i offered them little in the way of edible plants. By the 1700s it is estimated that the Hawaiian population may have risen as high as 300,000 persons, spread throughout the main eight-island chain.

Taro is the root from which poi is made, and it was used not only as a food by early Hawaiians, but as a dye for their tapa cloth and also to seal the lengths of the cloth together. It was used medicinally; rubbing a raw root stock on a wound was said to stop bleeding, the raw leaf stem rubbed on an insect bite was reported to reduce swelling and alleviate pain, and undiluted poi was used as a poultice for skin infections. The root would last for months without spoiling, and at one time more than 300 varieties of taro were found in the islands. Today, fewer than 90 varieties are cultivated.

The Tahitians initiated a class system and the concept of "kapu" or "taboo," which was composed of rigid sanctions and religious laws. However, they also introduced the pleasures of surfing, kite flying, the beauty of leis and the idea and spirit of aloha.

Four principal gods, Kanaloa (the god of the land of departed spirits), Kane (the god of war), Ku (the god who oversaw sacrifices) and Lono (the god of harvest and peace), formed the basis of the Hawaiian religion until the missionaries arrived. The stone foundations of heiaus, the ancient religious temples, can still be found throughout the islands. The governing chief was called the Ali'i, and it was he who kept order by establishing various "kapus." It was kapu, for example, for men and women to dine together. It was not until the death of King Kamehameha that the appointed regent of Hawaii, Ka'ahumanu, broke the kapu system when she persuaded Liholiho, heir of Kamehameha, to eat with her and his mother, Keopulani, in public.

The lower portion of the Wailua River was the sight selected as sacred by the high chiefs and kahunas on Kaua'i. This location, along with another at Waialua on O'ahu, were deemed two of the most sacred places in all the islands. Here you will find remains of seven heiaus where the early Hawaiians worshipped their gods. Future members of the ali'i were born at the sacred birthing stone located here. Rituals were an important part of their life, both in birth and in death. Human sacrifices were sometimes a part of the rituals performed.

Another goddess, Kapo, queen of the lei, is still honored each year on Lei Day. While most leis are made of island flowers, feather leis made with exotic yellow plumage were once reserved for Polynesian royalty.

The all-purpose Hawaiian word "aloha" means both hello and goodbye and encompasses all the principles, subtleties, variations and essence of the word "love."

Where science and legend exist side by side, you will discover some distinct differences about the islands. A business would not consider construction without first receiving a blessing of the land and often several more blessings during the construction. When a business prepares for a grand opening, ti leaves stretched across the threshold are gently untied (never cut), and the kapuna (minister/priest) will enter the building with holy water, words of reverence and gratitude to the creator. This is followed by a welcome to the family and friends. Perhaps this explains the power and strength of the people to rebuild and why these islanders have such hospitable and nurturing spirits. It has a base in reality in the aina -- the land -- and comes out as the spirit of aloha.

The islands were left undisturbed by western influence until the 1778 arrival of Captain James Cook. In search of the Northwest Passage, he first spotted and visited Kaua'i on January 19, 1778. His arrival was heralded by the local people, as his ship was believed to be a heiau for the god Lono. Cook stopped briefly at Ni'ihau and continued on to O'ahu and Maui. He brought with him to the island of Ni'ihau melon, pumpkin and onion seeds. On a later voyage, Cook was killed in a brawl on the Big Island of Hawai'i.

The arrival of Europeans brought not only tremendous changes for the Hawaiian culture, but also the introduction of diseases which killed the Hawaiian people in huge numbers.

One scholarly speculation is rarely spoken of in the history of the Hawaiian islands, but we feel it is at least interesting enough to bear mentioning. The sketches of early Hawaiians show them adorned with their ceremonial cloaks and unusual helmet-shaped headgear. It has been theorized, although rejected by historians, that perhaps Gaetan, a Spanish explorer enroute from the Philippines to Mexico in 1542, may have accidently stumbled across the Hawaiian islands. The headdress of the royal regalia does bear a striking resemblence to helmets worn by the early Spanish conquistadors, and the colors chosen by the Hawaiians for this garb are the royal Spanish colors. Another question this editor would like to address is the apparent knowledge of metal by the early Hawaiians. There are no ore deposits in the Hawaiian islands, yet when Cook arrived on Kaua'i and natives came aboard, they began clamoring for and seizing metal items. In *Kaua'i The Separate Kingdom*, Edward Joesting writes, "The Hawaiians had a knowledge of the importance of metal and eagerly sought these objects (from Cook) in trade for provisions." How did these 18th century Hawaiians know the importance of metal? How had they become introduced to the usefulness of it? Could there be some truth to this theory? Then again, it is perhaps merely coincidence.

Kamehameha the First was born on the Big Island of Hawai'i about 1758. He was the nephew of Kalaiopi, who ruled the Big Island. When Kalaiopi died, his son came to power, only to be subsequently defeated by Kamehameha in 1794. The great chieftain Kahekili was Kamehameha's greatest rival. He ruled not only Maui, but Lana'i and Moloka'i, and also had kinship with the governing royalty of O'ahu and Kaua'i. King Kahekili died in 1794, leaving control of the island to his sons, Kalanikupule. A bloody battle (more like a massacre since Kamehameha used western technology, strategy, and two English advisors) in the Iao Valley resulted in the defeat of Kalanikupule in 1795.

In the early 1790s, when Kamehameha was attempting to gain control of all the islands, The King of Kaua'i, Kaumuali'i, realized he had the advantage of having an island more removed from the rest of the Hawaiian chain. He had no interest in relinquishing his power to Kamehameha. The first attempt to overtake Kaua'i was made by Kamehameha in the spring of 1796. Encountering a storm, many of his soldiers never reached the island, being forced to turn back. Others who reached the island were killed at Maha'ulepu Beach. A later attempt by Kamehameha was thwarted when typhoid struck his soldiers. Without a fight, Kaumuali'i agreed to turn over his island to Kamehameha. Kaahumanu, the widow of Kamehameha I, wishing to further establish the loyalty of Kaumuali'i forced the last King of Kaua'i into marrying her. Still fearful of his allegience, Kaahumanu went a step further. Kealiiahonui, the son of Kaumuali'i, still lived on Kaua'i and his potential power as an opposing force prompted her to take him as her second husband. When the missionaries arrived and found this polygamous practice abhorrent, Kaahumanu released Kealiiahonui from his marriage vows.

The last King of Kaua'i, Kaumuali'i, died on May 28, 1824, on the island of O'ahu, never returning to his home island of Kaua'i. Some histories report that he died on Maui. This information, however, is incorrect. He fell ill, quickly worsened, and died on O'ahu. Following the funeral services, his body was taken to Maui for burial. Kapiolani, royal wife of Kamehameha I, had become close friends with Kaumuali'i. Prior to the death of Kapiolani, an arrangement had been reached that at his death Kaumuali'i would be laid to rest next to her. Thus his burial is in Lahaina on the island of Maui.

Kaua'i was briefly inhabited by the Russians during the reign of Kaumuali'i. The Russian traders erected several forts. The remains of one, Fort Elizabeth, can still be found at the mouth of the Waimea River. Little remains but a few mounds of dirt at Fort Alexander, located on the bluff at Princeville. Another earthen fort in the Hanalei area called Fort Barclay, after a Russian general, has eroded completely away. Georg (with no "e") Scheffer was a German who worked for the Russian American Company. This trading company sent Scheffer to recover goods from one of their vessels that had gone aground off the coast of Kaua'i. When the ship was beached, King Kaumuali'i had seized the shipload of pelts, as well as everything else on board, stating that it now belonged to him.

Georg arrived first on O'ahu where he passed himself off as a botanist and physician. He was both of these and after aiding the royal family when they were ill, he soon had endeared himself to the King. Scheffer reached Kaua'i in the spring of 1816 and expected that he might need force to regain the merchandise held by Kaua'i's King. He was surprised when Kaumuali'i warmly offered to return it. For a number of reasons, Kaumuali'i was eager to be on good terms with the Russians. Gifts were exchanged and Scheffer was later given the entire valley of Hanalei and subsequently bestowed Russian names on the Hanalei Valley, calling it Schefferthal and renaming the Hanapapepe River the Don. King Kaumuali'i figured he could better protect his island from Kamehameha with the Russians as allies. Scheffer promised the King Russian protection. *In Kaua'i: A Separate Kingdom*, Edward Joesting writes, "The co-monarchs of Kaua'i (Kaumuali'i and Scheffer) now plotted the conquering of these islands. On July 1, 1816, they entered into a secret agreement. When Kamehameha learned of this plan in 1817, Scheffer was ordered out of the islands. Interestingly, Georg Scheffer spent his last years in Brazil, having purchased a title for himself. He died Count von Frankenthal in 1836.

Kamehameha united all the islands and made Lahaina, on Maui, the capital of Hawai'i. It remained the capital until the 1840's when Honolulu, on O'ahu, became the center for government affairs.

Liholiho, the heir of Kamehameha I (also known as Kamehameha The Great), ruled as Kamehameha II from 1819 to 1824. Liholiho was not a strong ruler so Kaahumanu, the widow of Kamehameha I, proclaimed herself prime minister during his reign. (While Kaahumanu is said to have been the most favored wife of Kamehameha I, she did not have the bloodline of the ali'i (royalty) and therefore could not be his royal wife.) Kaahumanu ended many of the kapus of the old religion, thus creating a fortuitous vacuum which the soon to arrive missionaries would fill. The first missionaries arrived with their families from New England. On Kaua'i they were welcomed in 1821 and established mission houses around the island.

The missionaries came with good intentions, however, they brought drastic changes to the island with the education of the natives both spiritually and scholastically.

It was the missionaries who set up guidelines that forbade the native women to visit the ships in the harbor. Also, horrified by the bare-breasted Hawaiian women, the missionary women quickly set about to more thoroughly clothe the native ladies. The missionary women realized that their dresses would not be appropriate for these more robust women and, using their nightwear as a guideline, fashioned garments from these by cutting the sleeves off and enlarging the armholes. The muumuu was the result, and translated means "to amputate or to cut short."

HAWAIIAN MUSICAL INSTRUMENTS

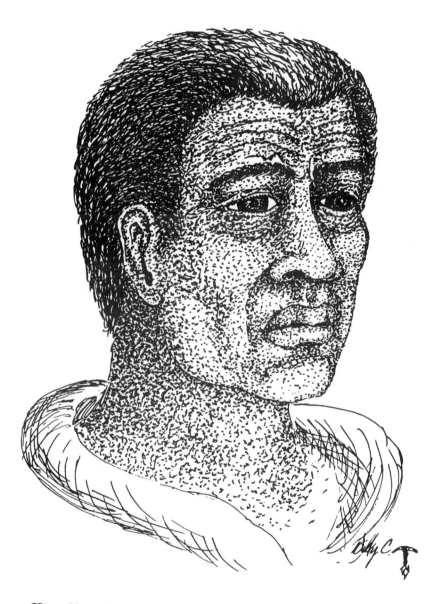

King Kamehameha the First

Many of the missionary descendants became successful planters and the island was blanketed with fields of green sugar cane. Sugar was to prove vital to the economic future of Kaua'i. The Polynesians who migrated from the Central Pacific brought with them the first varieties of "Ko," or sugarcane. The early Hawaiians had many varieties of this grass which was used as a sweetener, as medicine for childbirth, and reportedly as an aphrodisiac. The first successful sugar plantation in Hawai'i was established in Koloa (which means the place of long cane) in 1835 by Ladd & Company. William Hooper, a junior partner in Ladd & Company, established the plantation for that company by leasing 980 acres for $300 a year from King Kamehameha III. During the Civil War, Louisiana's shipping of sugar had been cut off and created a void which Hawai'i would step into. This was also the first sugar to be exported from the islands.

While the first workers in the sugar cane industry were Hawaiians, the increasing development brought workers from the four corners of the globe, which has helped shape much of Kaua'i's history and cultural diversity.

During the next few decades, immigrants began arriving from both Asia and Europe to work in the fields and mills. In 1838 a few Chinese laborers were working for Hooper, but it was not until 1852 that the first contract laborers from China arrived in Hawaii. In 1868 more than 150 Japanese laborers left their homeland to work in the islands. The first Portuguese contract laborers were recruited in the Azores and arrived in 1877. By that year, in the height of the sugar industry on Kaua'i, eight plantations had been established. They included Ele'ele, Grove Farm, Hanalei, Kapa'a, Kawaihau, Kilauea, Koloa, and Lihu'e. Castle and Cooke recruited a group of 629 Norwegian men, women and children who arrived in 1880. Larger groups of Chinese and Japanese immigrants continued to arrive in the 1880's. In 1902 the first Korean laborers arrived and they were followed by laborers from the Philippines in 1906.

A number of various crops have been attempted in Kaua'i, but for a variety of reasons, some of them proved successful, others failed.

The financial adviser to King Kamehameha I, a Spaniard named Don Francisco De Paula Marin, introduced to the islands produce which would soon thrive in the warm tropical climate: limes, guavas, pineapples and mango. Guava, quickly flourished in the islands and today it grows wild around Kaua'i and is also commercially grown. The Guava Kai Plantation operates 480 acres of orchards in Kilaeau and offers a free self-guided tour.

In the 1860's rice cultivation was attempted in Hanalei, Wailua and Kapa'a. Labor proved too expensive and production ceased after only a few years.

Silk production was tried experimentally in Koloa and Hanalei between 1836 and 1845. Exports of raw silk by 1844 were small and the problems of droughts and insect pests caused heavy losses. Another factor was the difficulty in finding skilled labor -- "but G.W. Bates blamed the destruction of the industry upon the religious zeal of the natives, who refused to feed the silkworms on Sunday." (Source: *Hawai'i and It's People* by A. Grove Day.)

A try at tobacco in Hanalei was a failure due to heavy rains. While it proved more successful on the south shore, it was never harvested commercially. One of the other more unusual crops was tapioca, which was attempted in Koloa.

Today, tourism is Kaua'i's major industry, while sugar continues to be the island's largest agricultural crop. Papaya, coffee and guava are also becoming increasingly important as the island diversifies its agricultural economy. Kaua'i has also become well-known on the big screen. The beauty of the island with its spectacular scenery has made Kaua'i play a role in more than 50 movies and full-length television features. Jurassic Park, Uncommon Valor, Flight of the Intruder, Raiders of the Lost Ark, Blue Hawaii, King Kong and South Pacific are only a few. The newest release to reach the "Big Screen" was Outbreak, starring Dustin Hoffman. While filming on the island took three months, the footage shot during the three months on Kaua'i only lasts the first few minutes of the movie!

While visiting the Hawaiian islands, you may never see some of the native species of birds and plantlife. Most of the remaining endangered native species can now only be found in protected areas. The more aggressive species that have been introduced over the past centuries have encroached on these fragile native ones and many endemic varieties have become extinct. Several refuges and botanical gardens on Kaua'i offer the visitor the rare opportunity to see these species at close proximity.

The Hawaiian State Flag was designed for King Kamehameha I in the first part of the nineteenth century. The British Union Jack in the corner acknowledges the early ties the islands had with England. The eight horizontal stripes of red, white and blue signify the eight major islands in the Hawaiian chain. King Kalakaua composed the state's national anthem, 'Hawai'i Pono i'.

A history of Kaua'i cannot be complete without a discussion of the Menehune, which was alluded to previously. An early account in the logs of Captain Cook tells of a people he found in Hawai'i that were smaller in stature and lighter skin-toned than most other Hawaiians. He described them as being a servant class. But are the menehune the stuff of myth or fact?

The folklore says that the Menehune would work at night, creating vast projects such as the Menehune (or Alekoko) Fishpond, (still seen today, located off Nawiliwili Road) and the Menehune Ditches. Among the speculated theories, perhaps the most probable is that the Menehune were people from Tahiti who called themselves Manahune. In earlier times, while still in Tahiti, they had been conquered by warriors from the nearby island of Raiatea. It was theorized that the term Manahune might mean "conquered people" and thus could be construed to mean that they were lower in the social order rather than smaller in size.

A census conducted in the early part of the nineteenth century showed that there were 65 Menehunes living in the Wainiha Valley. Archaeologically, there have never been any bones that indicate a dwarf population was ever present on Kaua'i. While the Menehunes are a part of island storytelling throughout the Hawaiian chain, they seem to have their roots on Kaua'i. If something goes wrong, you can blame it on the Menehunes. So, if you lay down your sunglasses for just a minute, and discover them in the next room a little later, you can figure that the Menehunes must have been up to their mischief. If something is unexplainable, then it probably was the Menehunes. Whatever the facts, the legends of the Menehune are colorful and add much to the richness of the island's folklore.

There are a number of good books that will cover the history of the island and its people. The bibliography lists a number of resources. The most in-depth is *Kauai: The Separate Kingdom* by Edward Joesting, which is well-researched and recommended for those looking for a complete island history. *The Kaua'i Papers*, published by the Kaua'i Historical Society is a collection of historical accounts told by some of Kaua'i's most prominent persons. Between 1914 and 1957 members and invited guests presented 115 papers to the Historical Society. This is the published collection of just some of these papers. The authors were primarily island born and raised. While some are short stories, others are more in-depth coverage of island events. The account of Queen Emmas visit to the Alaka'i Swamp is told by Eric A. Knudsen, and John M. Lydgate recalls the early days of Waimea. A wonderful book that brings the early history of the plantation days on Kaua'i to life. Another book with good general historical background on all the islands is *Hawaii, an Informal History* by Gerrit Judd.

HISTORY OF NI'IHAU

Ni'ihau, located 17 miles west of Kaua'i, continues to be Hawai'i's only privately owned island and visitation is allowed only by special request. The island of Ni'ihau is slightly more than 47,000 acres, with dimensions of 18 miles by 6 miles. The highest elevation is 1,281 feet at Paniau. While Lake Halali'i on Ni'ihau is 841 acres, and the largest inland lake in Hawai'i, it is more a salt flat that becomes a lake with a depth of five or six feet only during heavy rains. Mullet are raised in the lake until the waters recede, then they are caught and sent to market.

The contemporary human history of the island of Ni'ihau began when Mrs. Eliza McHutchenson Sinclair, a widow, relocated from New Zealand. She considered the purchase of a piece of beachfront property on O'ahu, which we now know as Waikiki. However, she visited the island of Ni'ihau in 1863 following a brief rainy spell and found it quite to her liking. She purchased the 46,000 acre parcel from King Kamehameha IV for the price of $10,000 on January 20, 1864. It was not until later that she discovered Ni'ihau suffers from a serious shortage of water, which continues to this day. At the time of Cook's visit, the population may have numbered as many as 10,000 individuals. By the time of the Sinclair purchase, the island had a population of 1,008 individuals. Dogs were raised by the Niihauans for food and the Sinclairs ordered the destruction of all the canines to safeguard the new herds of sheep and cattle. More than 700 kanakas (people) left the island rather than destroy their dogs.

The island offers one paved road, no telephones and power is limited to that supplied by a generator. The town of Pu'uwai is where the local residents live. In the past few years, a helicopter tour began which afforded outsiders their first, albeit small, glimpses of this island. The island population currently numbers in the neighborhood of 230 persons, 95% of whom are Hawaiian, and descendants of the Robinson (whose matriarch was Eliza Sinclair) family speaking Hawaiian and maintaining the customs of old Hawaii. When Eliza Sinclair died at the age of 92, her sole heir was her grandson, Aubry Robinson. Born in 1853 in New Zealand, he had studied law at Boston University before returning to Kaua'i.

It was not only Pearl Harbor on O'ahu that became involved in World War II. Following the attack on Pearl Harbor, a lone Japanese pilot, encountering engine failure, was forced to ditch at Ni'ihau (nearly landing on an outhouse). The pilot was captured by the Niihauans and resident Howard Hawila Kaleohano seized the documents he was carrying. Later these papers would assist in the breaking of the Japanese communication code. While five men made the trip across the channel to Kaua'i for help, apparently the prisoner managed an escape taking with him his machine guns. The spunky Ni'ihau residents, however, after being fed up with this intruder's poor manners, overpowered him. One island resident, Benjamin Kanahele was shot three as times as he tried to convince the pilot to act more civilized. Following the hit by a third bullet, Benjamin became so angry that he promptly grabbed the pilot, throwing him against the wall with such force that he was killed.

Today the island continues to be a working cattle and sheep ranch and Ni'ihau has also become famous for its beautiful shell necklaces. Made from very small shells collected on the island's beaches, the colored strands range in hues from yellow to blue or white. The necklaces are very intricate and it may take hundreds of shells to find one or two that are in perfect condition. The price of these necklaces range from hundreds to thousands of dollars. Look for them on display at gift and jewelry stores and appreciate the craftsmanship of these fine pieces of Hawaiian art.

For more information on this remote island, an excellent resource is *Ni'ihau: The Traditions of an Hawaiian Island* by Reriorterai Tava and Moses K. Keale, Sr., Published by Mutual Publishing in 1989. It is an outstanding account of the history of the island and its people from ancient to modern times.

TARO

31

KAUA'I NAMES AND PLACES

AHUKINI - altar (for) many (blessings)

ALAKA'I - to lead

'ELE'ELE - black

HA'ENA - red hot

HANAKAPI'AI - bay sprinkling food

HANALEI - crescent bay

HANAPEPE - crushed bay (due to landslides)

HA'UPU - recollection

KAHANA - cutting

KA-HOLUA MANU - the sled course (of) Manu

KA-LA-HEO - the proud day

KA-LALAU - the straying

KA-LAMA - the torch

KA-LIHI KAI - seaward Kalihi (the edge)

KA'LIHI WAI - water Kalihi

KANAKA-NUNUI-MOE - sleeping giant

KA-ULA-KAHI - the single flame (streak of color)

KA-UMU-ALI'I - the royal oven

KA-WAI-KINI - multitudinous water

KE-KAHA - the place

KIKI A OLA - container (acquired) by Ola

KI-LAU-EA - spewing, much spreading (referring to volcanic eruptions)

KILOHANA - lookout point or best, superior

KOKE'E - to bend or to wind

KOLOA - place of long cane, the word "Ko" means sweet sugarcane grass

KO'OLAU - windward

LIHU'E - cold child

MANA - arid

MILO-LI'I - fine twist (as sennit cord)

NA-MOLO-KAMA - the interweaving bound fast

NA'PALI - the cliffs

NA-WILIWILI - the wiliwili trees

NIU-MALU - shade (of) coconut trees

NOUNOU - throwing

POI'PU - completely overcast or crashing (as waves)

POLI-'AHU - garment (for the) bosom (referring to snow)

POLI-HALE - house bosom

PUHI - blow

PU'U KA PELE - the volcano hill

WAI'ALE'ALE - rippling water or overflowing water

WAI-LUA - two waters

WAI-PAHE'E - slippery water

For more information on Hawaiian place names consult Place Names of Hawaii by Mary Kawena Pukui, Samuel H. Elbert and Esther T. Mookini.

ISLAND FACTS AND FIGURES

While the islands are known as Hawaii, the largest single island in the chain is also dubbed Hawaii. Confusing to say the least! The islands as a total unit have their own nickname, state flower, bird, tree and fish. However, each island also has their own unique identity. Here is a little background on each.

THE HAWAIIAN ISLANDS

Nickname: The Aloha State
State Flower: Hibiscus
State Tree: Kukui
State Bird: Nene Goose
State Fish: Humuhumunukunukuapuaa
State Mammal: The Humpback Whale
State Capitol: Honolulu

KAUA'I

Nickname: The Garden Island
Island color: Purple
Flower: Mokihana (fragrant berry)
County Seat: Lihu'e
Area: 550 sq. miles
Length: 33 miles
Width: 25 miles
Coastline: 90 miles
Population: 52,000
Highest point: 5,243 ft. Kawaikiki

O'AHU
Nickname: The Gathering Place
Island color: yellow/gold
Flower: Ilima
County Seat: Honolulu
Area: 595 sq. miles
Length: 44 miles
Width: 30 miles
Coastline: 112 miles
Population: 850,000
Highest point: 4,003 feet Ka'ala Peak

NI'IHAU
Nickname: The Forbidden Island
Island color: white or brown
Flower: None
Emblem: Pupu shells
Main Town: Pu'uwai
Area: 73 sq. miles
Length: 14 miles
Width: 16 miles
Coastline: 40 miles
Population: 250
Highest point: 1,281 feet at Paniau

MAUI
Nickname: The Valley Isle
Island Color: Pink
Flower: Lokelani (cottage rose)
County Seat: Wailuku
Area: 729 sq. miles
Length: 48 miles
Width: 26 miles
Coastline: 40 miles
Population: 92,000
Highest point: 10,023 ft. Haleakala

KAHO'OLAWE
Nickname: Lonely Island
Island Color: Gray
Flower: Hinahina
Area: 45 sq. miles
Length: 6 miles
Width: 10 miles
Coastline: 20 miles
Population: currently only goats
Highest point: 1,477 ft. Moa'ulanui

MOLOKA'I
Nickname: Friendly Island
Island Color: Green
Flower: White Kukui Blossom
Main Town: Kaunakakai
Area: 260 sq. miles
Length: 38 miles
Width: 10 miles
Coastline: 88 miles
Population: 6,717
Highest point: 4,961 ft. Kamakou

LANA'I
Nickname: The Private Island
Island Color: Orange/gold
Flower: Kaunaoa
Main Town: Lana'i City
Area: 140 sq. miles
Length: 18 miles
Width: 13 miles
Coastline: 47 miles
Population: 2,426
Highest point: 3,366 ft. Lana'ihale

HAWAI'I
Nickname: The Big Island
Island color: Red
Flower: Red Lehua
(flower of the Goddess Pele)
County Seat: Hilo
Area: 4,038 sq. miles
Length: 93 miles
Width: 76 miles
Coastline: 266 miles
Population: 120,000
Highest point: 13,796 ft. Mauna Kea

HAWAIIAN STILT

The Hawaiian language was first written down by American missionaries. Using the written language they created an alphabet with only twelve letters, five of which are vowels. The key to the language is to remember to pronounce each letter, except for some vowels which run together as one. Substitute the "v" sound when "w" appears, in some cases. The "'" symbol you see is a glottal stop and instructs you to say each letter separately (such as ali'i). Also, pick up a copy of *Instant Hawaiian*, this small handy guide will have you speaking like a kama'aina in no time!

Following are some of the more commonly used Hawaiian words that you may hear:

HAWAIIAN WORDS AND THEIR MEANINGS

ali'i (ah-lee-ee) chief
aloha (ah-loh-hah) greetings
hale (Hah-lay) house
hana (HA-nah) work
hana hou (ha-nah HO) to do it again
Heiau (heh-ee-ah-oo) temple
haole (how-lee) a caucasian
kai (kye) ocean
kahuna (kah-HOO-nah) teacher, priest
Kamaaina (Kah-mah-ai-nuh) native born
kane (kah-nay) man
kapu (kah-poo) keep out
keiki (kayee-kee) child
lanai (lah-nah-ee) porch or patio
lomi lomi (loh-mee-LOH-mee) to rub or massage
luau (loo-ah-oo) feast
makai (mah-kah-ee) toward the ocean
malihini (mah-lee-hee-nee) a newcomer or visitor
mauka (mah-oo-kah) toward the mountain
mauna (MAU-nah) mountain
mele (MAY-leh) Hawaiian song or chant
menehune (may-nay-hoo-nee) Hawaiian dwarf or elf
moana (moh-ah-nah) ocean
nani (NAH-nee) beautiful
ono (oh-no) delicious
pali (PAH-lee) cliff, precipice
paniolo (pah-nee-ou-loh) Hawaiian cowboy
pau (pow) finished
poi (poy) a paste made from the taro root
pua (POO-ah) flower
puka (POO-ka) a hole
pupus (poo-poos) appetizers
wahine (wah-hee-nay) woman
wiki wiki (wee-kee wee-kee) hurry

WHAT TO PACK

When traveling to paradise, you won't need too much. Comfortable shoes are important for all the sightseeing. Sandals are the norm for footwear. Dress is casual for dining. A few restaurants require men to wear sport shirts with collars. Clothes should be lightweight and easy care. Cotton and cotton blends are more comfortable for the tropical climate than polyesters. Shorts and bathing suits are the dress code here! A lightweight jacket with a hood or sweater is advisable for evenings and the occasional rain showers. The only need for warmer clothes is if your plans should include hiking at higher elevations or visiting the Koke'e area. Tennis shoes or hiking shoes are a good idea for longer hikes. Sunscreens are a must and we recommend you toss in a bottle of insect repellent. A camera, of course, needs to be tucked in and perhaps your video camera. A hat with a brim is a good idea for protecting the head and neck from the sun while touring or just sitting on a beach. Binoculars are an option and may be well used if you are traveling between December and April when the whales arrive for their winter vacation, or used to enjoy the incredible sea and land birds found on the Garden Isle. Special needs for traveling with children are discussed in the next section. Anything that you need can probably be purchased once you arrive. Don't forget to leave some extra space in those suitcases for goodies that you will want to take back home!

TRAVELING WITH CHILDREN

Traveling with children can be an exhausting experience for parents and children alike, especially when the trip is as long as the one to Kaua'i. Unfortunately, there are currently no direct flights from the mainland to Kaua'i. Your trip to the island will include a stopover on O'ahu and a transfer to one of the outer island airlines.

Packing a child's goody bag for the long flight is a must. A few new activity books or toys that can be pulled out enroute can be sanity saving. Snacks (boxes of juice are a favorite with younger children) can tide over the little ones at the airport or on the plane while awaiting your food/drink service. The new squeeze-it juice drinks are also very portable and can be frozen in their plastic bottle, providing a cool drink when the need arises. A thermos with a drinking spout works well and is handy for use during vacations. A change of clothes and a swim suit for the little ones can be tucked into your carry-on bag. (Suitcases have been known to be lost or delayed.) Another handy addition is a small nightlight, as unfamiliar accommodations can be somewhat confusing for little ones during the bedtime hours. Disposable diapers are a real travel convenience, but are very expensive in the islands. You might wish to fill up any extra space in that suitcase with these! And don't forget a strong sunscreen!

Young children may have difficulty clearing their ears when landing. Many don't realize that cabins are pressurized to approximately the 6,000 foot level during flight. To help relieve the pressure of descent, have infants nurse or drink from a bottle, and older children may benefit from chewing gum. If this is a concern of yours, consult with your pediatrician about the use of a decongestant prior to descent.

CAR SEATS: By law, children 3-4 years of age must have seat belts unless they are in a federally approved car seat. Federally approved car seats are required for all children birth up to three years.

While some rental agencies do have car seats for rent, you need to request them well in advance as they have a limited number. The one, and only, car seat we have rented had seen better days, and its design was only marginal for child safety. Prices run about $25 per week, $36 for two weeks or $6 per day. After that single experience, we always brought our own car seats with us. Several styles are permitted by the airlines for use in flight, or it may be checked as a piece of baggage.

BABYSITTING: There are no full-time childcare services on Kaua'i. Arrangements for childcare can be made through your hotel concierge and the front desk at most condominiums will be able to assist you. Service is expensive and will run you about $9-10 per hour for a single child, $10-12 per hour for two. As you can easily figure from the rates, spending much time away from your children can be costly. Consider the feasibility of bringing your own sitter, it may actually be less expensive, and certainly much more convenient. This has worked well for us on numerous occasions. Grandmothers work well too!

CRIBS: Most condominiums and hotels will be able to provide you with a rental crib. There are many new folding, very portable, cribs that can be packed into a large duffle bag. They weigh under 20 pounds and can be purchased for less than the price of a 10 day rental.

Ready Rentals (808) 823-8008 or 1-800-599-8008 has cribs, car seats, high chairs, strollers and more for rent on a daily or weekly basis.

EMERGENCIES: The main hospital in Kaua'i is found in Lihu'e. G.N. Wilcox Memorial Hospital is located at 3420 Kuhio Hwy., Lihu'e. Phone (808) 245-1100.

The following provide general out-patient health services to persons requiring health care:

> Garden Island Medical Group-Koloa Clinic, PO Box 238, Koloa, HI 96756 (808) 742-1677.
>
> Garden Island Medical Group-Ele'ele Clinic, PO Box 188, Ele'ele, HI 96705. (808) 335-3107.
>
> Garden Island Medical Group-Waimea Dispensary, PO Box 669, Waimea, Hi 96796 (808) 338-1645.
>
> Kaua'i Medical Group, 3420-B Kuhio Highway, Lihu'e, HI 96766. (808) 245-1500.

See the section on Helpful Information for additional numbers. Calling 911 will put you in contact with local fire, police and ambulances.

DINING: You'll soon discover, if you have not already, that a children's menu is often referred to as a "Keiki Menu."

A few restaurants that offer menus for the young traveler (or child-size portions) include TomKat's, LaGriglia, Green Garden, Brennecke's, The Beach House, Barbecue Inn, Camp House Grill, Planters, Bali Hai, and The Bull Shed. A Pacific Cafe will serve any item on their menu at half size for half price. Be sure to ask for children's menus or prices wherever you dine.

BEACHES - POOLS: Another precaution on the beach that is easily neglected is the application of a good sunscreen; always reapply after swimming. It is easy to forget that in the cool pool or ocean, you are still getting those strong rays of sun.

There is a natural kiddie wading pool at Poʻipu Beach Park that is ideal for toddlers and very young swimmers. The nearby handy access to bathrooms can be a plus for the traveling family, too! To the west of Poʻipu Beach is a small protected cove known as Baby Beach. This can be accessed from Spouting Horn Road to Hoʻome Road. Good swimming locations for the younger set might also be found at Lydgate Beach Park and at Salt Beach Park. At both locations you'll find an ocean pool made from boulders. Several beaches do have lifeguards on duty. Unfortunately, many people underestimate the power of the ocean and drownings occur far too often on Kauaʻi. Beaches are generally not posted with flags, as on some other islands, if the surf is creating conditions which are unsafe. Most beaches only have a generic warning sign posted. If the surf is up, choose a different activity that day, or just enjoy a picnic on the beach. Some beaches are fine for children in the summer, but are definitely NOT an option during the higher surf of winter.

There is a Kamalani playground at Lydgate Beach Park which will give your lively young ones a chance to expend some of their energy.

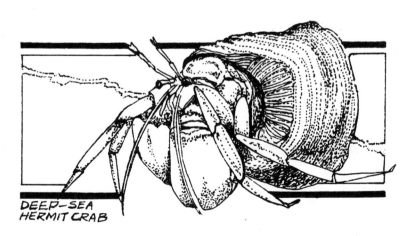

DEEP-SEA
HERMIT CRAB

Few resorts have pools with the very young traveler in mind. The Point, a south shore condominium, has a toddler pool. The Outrigger Kaua'i Beach also has a keiki pool as does Kaua'i Beachboy Hotel.

We recommend taking a life jacket or water wings (floaties). Packing a small inflatable pool for use on your lanai or courtyard may provide a cool and safe retreat for your little one. Typically resorts and hotels DO NOT offer lifeguard services.

CHILDCARE PROGRAMS: Some of these youth programs are seasonal, offered just summer, spring and Christmas holidays. A few are available year round. Generally, only resort guests can partake of these childcare programs.

Camp Hyatt offers a program for children of resort guests. The program is for youths ages 3 - 12 years and begins with 9:15 registration and runs until 4 pm. The charge is $45 per child per day and includes lunch, Camp Hyatt T-shirt and activities. Reservations are required. Night Camp is available from 6-10 pm with advance reservation. The cost is $5 per hour and does not include meals or a T-shirt. Activities vary with the group size, age, interest and weather, but might include cave exploring, nature hike, koi fish feeding, munchkin tennis, swim and slide, face painting and arts and crafts.

At the Princeville Hotel the Keiki Aloha program is offered from mid-June through the end of August and also during the Christmas holidays for youth aged 5-12 years. This program is offered complimentary to hotel guests and includes special excursions and Hawaiian arts and crafts. The program is Monday through Saturday from 9 am - 3 pm and is also offered sometimes on Friday evening. During off season, care is available for $35 per child per day for the first child and $25 for additional children plus a lunch fee. They need 24 hours notice to accommodate your request.

The Kiahuna Keiki Klub at the Kiahuna Plantation is for registered hotel guests and is offered Monday through Friday 9 am until 3 pm. A maximum of 15 children per day ages 5 - 12 years. A daily fee of $25 includes lunch and a KLUB T-shirt.

MOVIE THEATERS: The Coconut Marketplace is one of the best all around family malls on Kaua'i. Lots of small shops ensure that there will be something for every member of the family. While mom visits the art galleries, fashion and jewelry stores, the younger members will enjoy Kaua'i Magic or High As A Kite. If everyone wants something different for lunch, it shouldn't be a problem. There's the Fish Hut, Zack's Famous Frozen Yogurt, Aloha Kaua'i Pizza or Big Mel's Deli, to name a few. Don't like to shop? Then take in a movie at the adjoining double screen cinema. Shopping Center phone 822-3641. The Coconut Cinemas theater phone 822-9391.

Gilligan's at the Outrigger has free movies each Wednesday that were filmed on or are associated with Kaua'i. Phone 245-1955.

There is also the Kaua'i Film Festival, call the County Information office at 245-2313 for upcoming schedule.

Kukui Grove Cinemas has two screens in their theater which is across the street from the Kukui Grove Shopping Center. Phone 245-5055 to hear a recording.

OTHER ACTIVITIES WITH KIDS:

Children will enjoy the hourly tour of the Kaua'i Lagoons. Board an Italian-crafted motor launch to tour the 40 acres of waterways. The captain will give a narration of the many exotic animals, from kangaroos to monkeys, which inhabit the many man-made islands. Cost is $12 for adults, $6 for children 12 and under. Phone (808) 245-2222 or 1-800-367-2914.

Older children will enjoy a luau. The Kaua'i Coconut Beach has a program which currently offers a free luau for each child with an accompanying adult on Saturday evenings.

The free hula show at the Coconut Marketplace often features child performers. The younger children in your traveling family might enjoy this casual, outdoor performance.

There are two miniature golf courses on Kaua'i, one in Lawa'i is Mustard's Last Stand (332-7245). The kids will like the hot dogs here too! Near Kukui Grove Shopping Center in Lihu'e is Wally World (245-5252) with an 18 hole miniature course, splash and bash motorized bumper cars and a video arcade. They may soon be adding batting cages.

You'll find a Fun Factory game arcade at the Kuku'i Grove Shopping Center and another at the Waipouli Town Center next to Foodland.

Joe-Jo's Clubhouse at 9734 Kaumaulii Hwy. in Waimea is a small store, but fun and festive. A good place to take the kids after the scenic wonders of Waimea Canyon. Joe-Jo's has yummy waffle boats, shave ice with over 50 flavors, nachos, and hot dogs. Open 10 am - 6 pm daily. 338-0056.

Borders Bookstore in the Kukui Grove Shopping Center has thoughtfully created a play corner. They also have a very extensive children's book section and a large Hawaiian book section. They schedule events from storytelling to clown visits. And it's all free!

The CJM Country Stables in Koloa currently has a complimentary rodeo, held once a month on Sundays at 10 am. As always, we suggest you phone to confirm this activity. 742-6096.

The Hyatt Regency has a new guide for traveling youngsters. The brochure describes suggestions for five activity-filled days perfect for families. These self-guided tours, which include a variety of cultural and outdoor activities, are designed to assist family vacationers in experiencing the best Kaua'i has to offer. Hiking, biking to a hidden beach, lei making, and exploring a lagoon with exotic wildlife are among the many suggestions. Families of all ages can enjoy one or all of the "Five Days of Family Fun," which includes: "A Day in the Neighborhood" which outlines suggestions in the Poʻipu area or "neighborhood" of the Hyatt. Suggestions include the use of mountain bikes, available at the tennis center, bass fishing at one of the nearby reservoirs or horseback tour of the beach and sand dunes. "The Wildlife Adventure" begins with a trip to the Kilauea Lighthouse, a drive north to Hanalei to visit the Waioli Mission House and continuing north to the Na Pali coast State Parks with stops at the unusual wet and dry caves. "The Family Safari" is a trip that begins at Spouting Horn and then heads North to Nawiliwili Bay for a tour of the lagoons of the Marriott aboard a Venetian mahogany launch and finishing up the day at the Kamalani Playground. "The Old West" heads to Hanapepe, Kauaʻi's biggest little town and then continues to Waimea and Kokeʻe. The last is "A Day at Home" with suggestions for enjoying the many varied activities at the Hyatt property. The guide is free of charge and is available through the hotel's concierge desk. Parents who may be planning trips can also receive a copy of the guide by calling Hyatt Regency Kauaʻi reservations at (808) 742-1234.

EXCURSIONS: Kauaʻi abounds with natural beauty that will be enjoyed by the traveler of any age.

Waipoʻo Falls is a good and fairly easy hike for families. Kayaks are available for two, so pair up with one of the kids and enjoy the scenic wonders on one of Kauaʻi's navigable rivers. The Wailua River trip is picturesque and affords a chance to hear the Wedding Song performed when the tour boats arrive at Fern Grotto. Stay around after the tour boat leaves and enjoy the silent beauty of this unique location.

Older children will enjoy horseback riding, or trying their skills at boogie boarding at Poiʻpu Beach Park next to the kiddie pool.

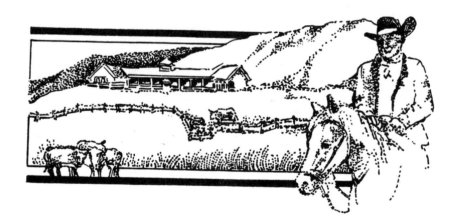

TRAVEL TIPS FOR THE
PHYSICALLY IMPAIRED

Make your travel plans well in advance and inform hotels and airlines when making your reservations that you are handicapped. Most facilities will be happy to accommodate. Bring along your medical records in the event of an emergency. It is recommended that you bring your own wheelchair and notify the airlines in advance that you will be transporting it. Other medical equipment rental information is listed below.

Additional information can be obtained from the State Commission on Persons with Disabilities on Kaua'i at 3060 Eiwa St. Room 207, Lihu'e, HI 96766 (808) 241-3308 which can provide general information on accessibility for private and public facilities on Kaua'i. For information on accessibility features and technical assistance regarding access standards contact the Commission on Persons with Disabilities, 500 Ala Moana Blvd. #5-210, Honolulu, HI 96813. (808) 586-8121 or inter-island toll free 1-800-468-4644.

Contact Parents with Special Keikis c/o Easter Seal Society of Hawaii, Kaua'i Service Center 4-1991 Kuhio Highway, Kapa'a, HI 96746. (808) 823-0092. They provide support, education and advocacy groups for parents of children with disabilities.

ARRIVAL AND DEPARTURE: On arrival at the Lihu'e airport you will find the building easily accessible for mobility impaired persons. Parking areas are located in front of the main terminal for disabled persons. Restrooms with handicapped stalls (male and female) are also found in the main terminal.

TRANSPORTATION: The only public transportation is The Kaua'i Bus which charges riders $1 per ride. Monthly bus passes are available for $25 which provide unlimited rides. A monthly pass for senior citizens, students, and persons with disabilities runs $12.50. Caregivers traveling with eligible individuals will not be charged a fee. For additional information phone the County Transportation Office at 241-6428.

Public transportation for the disabled is available by reservation. Call 241-6410 at least 24 hours in advance and they can reserve as far as two weeks in advance. You do need special ID from home and it is on a space available basis.

ACCOMMODATIONS: Each of the major island hotels offer one or more handicapped rooms including bathroom entries of at least 29" to allow for wheelchairs. Due to the limited number of rooms, reservations should be made well in advance. Information on condominium accessibility is available from the State Commission on Persons with Disability on Kaua'i at (808) 241-3308.

Victoria Place B&B and Po'ipu B&B Inn are a few of the bed and breakfasts that have a handicapped accessible room.

ACTIVITIES: Call Easter Seals of Hawai'i on Kaua'i regarding other activities.

MEDICAL SERVICES AND EQUIPMENT:

A.B. Medical Inc., 2952-1 Kress St., Lihu'e, HI 96766 (808) 245-4995. They rent and sell medical equipment and supplies, including appliances and access devices. 24-hour emergency service is available.

American Cancer Society, 3115 Elua St., Lihu'e, Hi 96766 (808) 245-2942. They provide equipment including hospital beds, walkers, wheelchairs, etc. on loan without charge for home use, with priority to persons with cancer.

Garden Island Oxygen Supplies, 4330 Kaua'i Beach Drive #G23, Lihu'e, Hi 96766. (808) 245-1767. Rents, sells and services oxygen tanks and ancillary equipment.

Home Infusion Associates 4473 Pahee, St., Suite I, Lihu'e, HI 96766. (808) 245-3787. Rents and sells medical equipment including wheelchairs.

Ray Thomas of CHP Medical rents a variety of medical equipment. (808) 246-9550.

GINGER &
ANTHURIUMS

WEDDINGS - HONEYMOONS

With tropical waterfalls, lush gardens and idyllic beachfront settings, a wedding ceremony on Kaua'i can meet all your dreams.

While the requirements are simple, here are a few tips (based on current requirements at time of publication) for making your wedding plans run more smoothly. We advise you to double check the requirements as things change!

Both bride and groom must be over 18 years of age. Birth certificates are not required, but you do need a proof of age such as a driver's license or passport. You do not need proof of citizenship or residence. If either partner has been divorced, the date, county and state of finalization for each divorce must be verbally provided to the licensing agent. If a divorce was finalized within the last three months, then a decree must be provided to the licensing agent. The bride will need to have a rubella blood test and must bring proof of the screening test from her state of residence. However, the test is not required if the female has had rubella immunization, has had rubella in the past, has had sterilization, is past menopause or has other reasons for inability to conceive. A health certificate attesting to one of these reasons for not having the test is required. There is no blood test required for the groom.

A license must be purchased in person in the state of Hawai'i. The Department of Health can give you names of the licensing agents on the island. You need to make appointments with these licensing agents. Both bride and groom must appear in person before the agent. At the present time there are agents at five locations on Kaua'i. If you have questions, the local registrar on Kaua'i can be contacted at 241-3495. The fee is currently $16. There is no waiting period once you have the license, but the license is valid for only 30 days.

One wedding agency informed us that your personal vows for a Catholic wedding require special arrangements between your home priest and the Kaua'i priest. If both bride and groom are practicing Catholics, the Church requires that you marry within the church building, unless you are granted special permission from the Bishop in Honolulu.

Check with the Chamber of Commerce on Kaua'i, 2970 Kele St. Room 201, PO Box 1969, Lihu'e, HI 96766 (808-245-7363) for information regarding a pastor. Many island pastors are very flexible in meeting your needs, such as an outdoor location, etc.

For copies of current requirements and forms, write in advance to the State of Hawaii, Department of Health, Marriage License Section, PO Box 3378, Honolulu, HI 96801. 808-586-4545.

WEDDING BASICS:

The Hyatt Regency and other island hotel resorts frequently offer "honeymoon" or "romance" packages. Since these vary seasonally, inquire with the property when making your reservations.

Weddings & Honeymoons

Wedding Chapels:
Aloha Church, Assembly of God, 245-6593

Kaua'i Lagoons Chapel By the Sea, Lihu'e. Indoor or outdoor weddings are available. 241-6021

Koloa Church, founded in 1835, is located at 3269 Po'ipu Rd. Outdoor weddings also available. 742-9956

Formal wear rentals:
Your Special Day offers tuxedo rentals and also sells wedding and bridesmaids dresses. 245-2292

Catering:
Heavenly Creations, custom catering and a personal chef. 828-1700

Video tape services:
Hawaiian Creative Video   822-5784
I DO Video Productions   823-6130

Photographers:
Islandwide Photograph 823-0200
Linc Rydell Photograph 822-2520
Rainbow Photograph 822-7372 (by appointment only)
The Wedding Photographer   245-2866

WEDDING COMPANIES:

A basic wedding package costs anywhere from $300 - $450. Add a few extras and the price will boost to $500-1000. Although each company varies the package slightly, a basic package will probably include assistance in choosing a location (public or private), getting your marriage license, selecting a minister and a varying assortment of amenities such as champagne, a small cake, or leis. Video taping, witnesses, or music are available for an extra charge. There are a variety of beautiful public facilities at which you may be married. However, wedding companies do have a variety of private locations which may be rented for an additional fee ($50-$150).

American Hawaii Cruises offers a wedding package on board one of their cruise ships. The package includes the services of a minister/judge, a Hawaiian lei and haku (floral hairpiece) for the bride and a lei or boutonniere for the groom, a chilled bottle of champagne, two dozen 5 x 7 photos in an album, live music performed by Hawaiian musicians and a wedding cake for two. The package is $595. Weddings may be performed onboard in Honolulu prior to departure. Only one wedding is scheduled per ship, per sailing and specific times for ceremonies are given at the time of bookings. For an additional fee, a private wedding reception may be arranged as well. To obtain a wedding license, both the bride and groom must appear in person before the marriage bureau in Hawai'i. The marriage license bureau is open from 8 am - 4 pm Monday through Friday. To ensure plenty of time to obtain the license prior to the ceremony, a two-night pre-cruise weekday hotel stay is recommended.

Hawaiian Weddings, PO Box 3306 Princeville, HI 96722, (808) 826-5157. They offer weddings at a private estate or at a secluded bay by a Hawaiian minister. Their basic package "Hangloose" includes the marriage ceremony, leis for bride and groom and a keepsake wedding certificate $295. Their Hawaiian Contemporary Marriage Ceremony includes photography, champagne, Maile Lei for the groom and a tropical flower lei for the bride, $595. Other amenities include hula dancers, limousine, flowers, wedding cake, and a soloist.

Island Weddings, PO Box 603, Kilauea, HI (808) 828-1609. A "Simple and Special" wedding begins at $250. Their "Aloha Wedding Special" includes a wedding ceremony, witness, tropical outdoor location, two leis, and 24 photos for $450. They offer non-denominational as well as religious ceremonies.

Kaua'i Aloha Weddings, 356 Likeke Place, Kapa'a, HI 96746. (808) 822-1477, FAX (808) 822-7067. This Hawaiian owned and operated company offers couples the opportunity of having their marriage performed by ordained ministers in the Hawaiian language.

Kaua'i Fantasy Weddings, PO Box 3671, Lihu'e, HI 96766.(808) 245-6500. Photo packages or wedding packages available from $275-1250. Hans Hellriegel has been a photographer for twenty-five years. He says each wedding is unique and he always falls a little in love with each bride. He has taken wedding couples to the beach, up into the mountains, to a church, with ceremonies held at sunrise, at sunset or during the day. They may be arranged for weddings involving twenty attendants or with just the couple.

Kaua'i Lagoons Weddings, PO Box 3330, Lihu'e, HI 96766. (808) 241-6020. FAX (808) 241-6075. This wedding company uses a single location, the beautiful Chapel by the Sea at Kaua'i Lagoons. Weddings are scheduled 4 times daily. The use of the chapel, floral arrangements, lei or bouquet, minister and solo musician runs $1000. An outdoor ceremony runs $750. Photography package (24 prints) runs $275, video $375. Add a ride in a private white wedding carriage for $400.

NAUPAKA KAHAKAI

Kilohana, 3-2087 Kaumuali'i Hwy (mailing address: PO Box 3121, Lihu'e, HI 96766.) (808) 245-9593, FAX (808) 245-7818. A basic wedding package begins at $550 and includes your choice of setting, a non-denominational minister and a one hour use of a wedding carriage. They can arrange for intimate or large receptions.

Mohala Wedding Service, PO Box 1737, Koloa, HI 96756. (808) 742-8777, 1-800-800-8489, FAX (808) 742-8777. Jona and Jim Clark work as a team to put together your wedding package. Jim is an ordained minister who performs the ceremonies. A Japanese Garden, a beachside wedding, a sunset ceremony on the Kilauea estate on the North Shore with Bali Hai as a back drop or choose a gazebo with a waterfall. Packages run $285 - $920. Private locations run slightly more.

Smith's Motor Boat Service, Inc. offers wedding packages in the Fern Grotto and in the Smith's own gardens. Wedding times for the Grotto are currently only 8:30 am, 11:30 am and 4 pm. As for ceremonies in their gardens, the hours are more flexible. They do not do ceremonies on Sundays or holidays. Fern Grotto Packages run $575-$925 (with optional video $235-295). It includes your own private boat with entertainers, minister, photography, leis and assorted extras. Wedding packages in the Smith's Tropical Paradise Gardens run $185-$465. 174 Wailua Rd., Kapa'a, HI 96746. (808) 822-7405, FAX (808) 822-4520.

Wedding Fantasies (808) 822-7997. This company utilizes only ministers affiliated with a church and the ceremony is always part Hawaiian. Charlene O'Brien can arrange a basic wedding package including minister, flower leis, beach or garden setting, and witnesses (if needed) for $275. Other options, including Hawaiian soloists, photography and video taping, can be arranged as a package or with each item priced a la carte.

Weddings in Paradise, PO Box 1728, Lihu'e, HI 96766. (808) 246-2779 or 1-800-733-7431. A non-denominational minister and a choice of locations begins at $295. Basic packages run about $655 and include photography, leis, musician and flowers. They provide a set of photographs with their brochure which gives a good feeling for their location selections. Wedding sites include "A Terrace Wedding in the Limahuli Valley," "A Fern Grotto Wedding" (basic package $900), "Pakala Beach," the "Japanese Garden in Kukuiolono" or a private white sand beach. Other options include photography, leis, videography, music.

Weddings on the Beach, PO Box 1377, Koloa HI 96756. (808) 742-7099 1-800-625-2824. Judy Neale, wedding coordinator, offers ocean view or ocean front weddings from $275. For the more adventurous, how about an ocean adventure wedding where you cruise to your wedding site? The two hour cabin cruiser adventure wedding runs $1,500 or a four hour cabin cruiser wedding with Na Pali Coast Tour for $2,300. Or, if you prefer to be above the sea, select an air adventure wedding where you fly to a privately owned site. With this air option, priced at $3,300, there is room for the wedding couple and just one guest. Limousine service, food and beverages, musicians, flowers and photography services are available.

PARTIES/RECEPTIONS

Kilohana offers an assortment of "theme parties" available for business or personal celebrations. A Paniolo Hoedown, a Garden Party, a Murder Mystery, a Kilohana Luau, South Pacific, Polo or Rock Around the Clock are among the possibilities available. For information contact Kilohana, PO Box 3121, Lihu'e, HI 96766. (808) 245-5608.

ESPECIALLY FOR SENIORS

More and more businesses are beginning to offer special savings to seniors. RSVP booking agency offers special rates for seniors who book their accommodations through them. They are listed in the Rental Agents section of our accommodations chapter.

Whether it is a boating activity, an airline ticket or a condominium, be sure to ask about special senior rates. And be sure to travel with identification showing your birthdate.

Check the yellow pages when you arrive on Kaua'i for the senior discount program logo. Look for a black circle with white star in the ads.

The County of Kaua'i, Office of Elderly Affairs at 4193 Hardy St., Lihu'e, HI 96766 (808) 241-6400 provides advocacy to elderly persons and their families. Senior discounts available to persons 65 and older.

Kaua'i Senior Centers, 4491 Kou Street, Kapa'a, HI 96746. (808) 822-9675. They sponsor centers in Kilauea, Kapa'a (main office), Lihu'e, Koloa, Kalaheo, Hanapepe and Waimea. They provide programs for persons who are elderly or persons with elderly disabilities.

Remember that AARP members get many travel discounts for rooms, cars and tours.

The Salvation Army can be a real treasure trove for the adventurous shopper. A muumuu for a couple of dollars is perfect for that luau. On Wednesdays and Fridays seniors receive an extra discount (with valid ID). Locations of the Salvation Army are scattered around the islands, open Tuesday through Saturday 9 am - 4 pm.

A number of airlines have special discounts for seniors. Some also have a wonderful feature which provides a discount for the traveling companion that is accompanying the senior. Coupon books for senior discounts are also available from a number of airline carriers.

The local Kaua'i Bus offers discounts for senior citizens.

HELPFUL INFORMATION

FREE INFORMATION: Racks located at the shopping areas can provide helpful information and lots of brochures! Some of them have coupons, which if it was something you were planning on doing anyway, may save you a few dollars. The Hawai'i Visitors Bureau-Kaua'i and the County of Kaua'i have compiled an *Illustrated Pocket Map.* You can pick them up at these free racks. It is a nicely done island map that gives a lot of in-depth information.

The Kaua'i Hotline, begun after Hurricane Iniki to keep visitors apprised of the recovery process, continues its services. This offers live tourism industry updates, directly from Kaua'i. The phones are staffed by local volunteers and the number is good for all the U.S. and in Canada. 1-800-262-1400, 6 am - 6 pm daily Hawaiian standard time. Or send them your fax 1-800-637-5762.

HAWAI'I VISITORS BUREAU-KAUA'I: 3016 Umi, Room 207, Lihu'e, Kaua'i, HI 96766 (808) 245-3971, FAX (808) 246-9235.

Other sources for information include:

Kaua'i Coconut Coast Visitors Bureau, PO Box 1178 Kapa'a, HI 96746 (808) 823-6122.

Po'ipu Beach Resort Association, PO Box 730, Koloa, HI 96756. (808) 742-7444. FAX (808) 742-7887.

Kalapaki Bay Resort Association, 4180 Rice St. #6, Lihu'e, HI 96766. (808) 246-0766.

Information on Po'ipu Beach is now also available on Internet. Their e-mail address is: info@poipu-beach.org. Hawai'i OnLine's Internet home pages are located at: http://www.aloha.net.

'ILIMA

TELEVISION: We anticipate that you'll be much too busy enjoying the island to do much television viewing. The KVIC station on either channel 3 or channel 18 (depending on your area of the island) will have on-going programs aimed at you, the tourist. It's a guided tour from your room that might offer you a little more insight at something you had not planned on doing.

The following are channels on basic cable service.

2 KHON (NBC)
3 KFVE or KVIC (Visitor Information Channel)
4 KITV (ABC)
8 PEG (Government Access)
9 KGMB (CBS)
10 PEG (Educational Access
11 KHET (PBS)
12 PEG (Public Access)
13 KHYNL
14 TBS (Turner Broadcasting Systems)
15 L/O (Local Origin)
18 KVIC (Visitor Information Channel)
20 QVC
21 CSPN
23 ESPN
24 TDC (The Discovery Channel)
25 TLC (The Learning Channel)
26 USA
27 CNN
28 HN (Headline News)
29 AMC (American Movie Classics)
30 MTV (Music Television)
31 VH-1 (Video Hits One)
32 TNN (The Nashville Network)
33 COM (Comedy Central)
34 Life
35 TNT
36 NICK (Nickelodeon)

PERIODICALS: The Garden Island Newspaper is published six days a week. They can be reached at 3137 Kuhio Hwy., PO Box 231, Lihu'e, HI 96766 (808) 245-3681. Subscriptions are available by mail. The other island newspaper, the Kaua'i Times, was purchased in 1995 by The Garden Island Newspaper. The new publication, sort of a two for one arrangement, includes The Island Times which comes out on Saturday and The Kaua'i Times which comes out on Wednesday. The Kaua'i Times subscription runs $7 per month (808) 245-6325 for information. The Honolulu Star Bulletin and Advertiser can be contacted at PO Box 3110 Honolulu, HI 96802.

If you are considering a relocation to the islands, a copy of the Kaua'i phone book is a handy resource. Call GTE on Kaua'i at (808) 643-3458 and for a small fee ($3 when we called) they'll mail you a copy.

A helpful publication for the individual considering a move to the islands is the KAUA'I DATA BOOK available from the Chamber of Commerce. An island overview is provided including information on population, employment, cost of living, education, the tax system, utility costs, gas prices, drivers license information, weather and job searching. Kaua'i Chamber of Commerce can be reached at (808) 245-7363.

As mentioned previously, there are a number of free publications, small booklets that are available at racks around most visitor areas. Most of these free publications offer lots of advertising. However, they do have coupons which will give you discounts on everything from meals to sporting activities to clothing. It may save you a bit to search through these before making your purchases.

SUN SAFETY: The sunshine is stronger in Hawai'i than on the mainland, so a few basic guidelines will ensure that you return home with a tan, not a burn. Use a good lotion with a sunscreen, reapply after swimming and don't forget the lips! Be sure to moisturize after a day in the sun and wear a hat to protect your face. Exercise self-control and stay out a limited time the first few days, remembering that a gradual tan will last longer. It is best to avoid being out between the hours of noon and three when it is the hottest. Be cautious of overcast days when it is very easy to become burned unknowingly. Don't forget that the ocean acts as a reflector and time spent in it equals time spent on the beach.

FOR YOUR PROTECTION: Do not leave valuables in your car, even in your trunk. Many rental car companies urge you to not lock your car as vandals cause extensive and expensive damage breaking the locks.

ISLAND FAUNA: There are few dangerous land and sea creatures in Hawai'i. And not to be alarmists, it makes common sense to use good judgment about them.

Mosquitoes were the gift of a ship called the Wellington, which arrived on Maui in 1826. They soon spread to the other islands and can be most irritating in the wetter, forested areas. It is worth packing a bottle of repellent.

The only other insect that is to be avoided is the centipede. One guidebook we read said that you'll almost never encounter one. We have seen them on several occasions, right at a condominium. Generally they show up only when the landscape crews are trimming the palm trees and they are knocked to the ground. One groundskeeper told us that if you step on one end they can swing up the other end around your sandal and inflict a sting. If you see one; avoid it, the sting is extremely painful.

Hawai'i has no snakes and it is with very serious concern that a snake or two has been seen, caught and destroyed in the islands over the past decade. Great care is taken to ensure that none come to the islands unintentionally as part of cargo and dogs are even trained to sniff them out. The brown tree snake is among the most feared, for on Guam it has virtually destroyed their wild bird population.

The bufo toad is a very friendly fellow that can be found all around the islands, but generally is more noticed after a heavy rain, or unfortunately flattened on a road. In 1932 this frog was brought from Puerto Rico to assist with insect control. They don't mind being held, and can be turned over and seem to love having their stomachs rubbed. However, on the bufo toad you will notice a lump behind their head which carries a poison. The poison awaits a sharp blow or puncture to cause it to squirt out. A handy defense for this amphibian and dogs or cats quickly learn not to bother them. The poison can cause them to become seriously ill or can be fatal. We have also been told their body secretions can be irritating to the skin, especially eyes, and we suggest you just enjoy watching them instead.

On Kauaʻi you'll see no mongoose, the only major Hawaiian island without these animals which prey on birds and their eggs. Consequently, Kauaʻi is blessed with more birdlife than other islands.

The other Hawaiian creature that cannot go without mention is the gecko. They are finding their way into the suitcases of many an island visitor, in the form of tee-shirts, sunvisors and jewelry. This small lizard is a relative of the chameleon and grows to a length of three or four inches. They dine on roaches, termites, mosquitos, ants, moths and other pesky insects. While there are nearly 800 species of geckos found in warm climates around the world, there are only about five varieties found in Hawaii. The house gecko is the most commonly found, with tiny rows of spines that circle its tail, while the mourning gecko has a smooth, satiny skin and along the middle of its back it sports pale stripes and pairs of dark spots. The mourning gecko species is parthenogenic. That means that there are only females which produce fertile eggs, and no need for a mate!

The stump-toed variety is distinguished by its thick flattened tail. The tree gecko enjoys the solitude of the forests, and the fox gecko, with a long snout and spines along its tail, prefers to hide around rocks or tree trunks. The first geckos may have reached Hawaiʻi with early voyagers from Polynesia, but the house gecko may have arrived as recently as the 1940s, along with military shipments to Hawaii. Geckos are most easily spotted at night when they seem to enjoy the warm lights outside your door. We have heard they each establish little territories where they live and breed so you will no doubt see them around the same area each night. They are very shy and will scurry off quickly. Sometimes you may find one living in your hotel or condo. They're friendly and beneficial animals and are said to bring good luck, so make them welcome.

Birdlife abounds on Kauaʻi, and no doubt the first you will note are the chickens! Wild chickens? Yes! The wild chickens that you may see in the area of Kokeʻe and the lodge are descendants from the ones brought by the Polynesians, but you will find chickens just about everywhere you turn on Kauaʻi these days. Hurricane Iwa, and to a greater extend Hurricane Iniki, caused a number of domesticated chickens to escape and they are obviously proliferating in paradise. Those descendants of the Polynesians have now inter-mixed with the domestic varieties that you will see many diverse colorations, particularly on the roosters. The roosters can be a bit of a nuisance in rural areas, where their alarm wake-up calls are not always appreciated!

The songbirds of Hawai'i owe a great deal of credit to Mrs. Dora Isenberg. The New York Herald Tribune, September, 1938, edition carried the following historical background: "Thanks to the efforts of one woman, the Hawaiian Islands are now the home of thousands of gaily colored songbirds from all parts of the world. Mrs. Dora Isenberg began her hobby of importing songsters forty years ago in celebration of Hawaii's joining the United States [as a territory]. After permitting them to get acclimated in her garden on Kaua'i Island, Mrs. Isenberg gave the birds their freedom. Her first attempts were unsuccessful when fourteen larks from the Orient were released and never heard of again. But, undismayed, Mrs. Isenberg continued her efforts, and many other people took up the hobby, with the result that today the islands boast thousands of such imported birds as the Peko thrush, African ringneck dove, Mongolian thrush, Chinese thrush, Bleeding Heart dove, meadow-lark, tomtit, and cardinal."

The goats found in the Koke'e area are descendants of those brought to the islands by Captain Cook. They have done significant damage to the vegetation and hunting for them is allowed. A pair of binoculars, or even a sharp lookout at one of the Waimea Canyon viewing areas and you might spot one or more. They blend in so well that we almost failed to spot one goat that was within a few hundred yards.

AQUATIC SAFETY: Drinking of fresh water from streams, waterfalls and/or pools is not safe at any location. While there are many micro-organisms and parasites that can wreak havoc with your system, one of the most dangerous is Leptospirosis. This finds its way into rivers and streams in the urine of rodents and cattle and can be fatal. The symptoms are flu-like and because they do not result until 1 - 4 weeks after contamination, people who are infected may not connect their illness with a possible contamination weeks earlier. It can also be contracted through the skin if there are open sores or cuts. Be sure to pack your own drinking water should you do any hiking.

As for cautions you should use in and around the ocean, please refer to our chapter on Beaches.

COMMON 'AMAKIHI

HELPFUL PHONE NUMBERS:

EMERGENCY: Police - Ambulance - Fire 911

NON-EMERGENCY POLICE:
Non-emergency requests 241-6711
Police: Crime Stoppers 241-6787
Weather Conditions 241-6789
Poison Control 1-800-362-3585
Sexual Assault Crisis (YWCA) 245-4144
YWCA Shelter 245-6362
Helpline (suicide & crisis center) 245-3411
Consumer Protection 241-3365
Kaua'i County of Elderly Affairs 241-6420
Transportation for Elderly or Handicapped 241-6420
Transportation: Airports Division 246-1401
Transportation: Highway Division 241-3461
HELPLINE Kaua'i 245-3411
Kaua'i Chamber of Commerce 245-7363
Po'ipu Beach Resort Association 742-7444
Kalapaki Beach Resort Association 245-5050
DIRECTORY ASSISTANCE:
    Local .... 1+411
    Inter-island 1-808-555-1212
    Long distance outside area code .... 1+ area code+555-1212
HOSPITALS:
    Wilcox Memorial in Lihu'e: 245-1100
    Kaua'i Veterans Memorial Hospital in Waimea 338-9431
Kaua'i Visitors Bureau 245-3971
Time of Day 245-0212
LAND AND NATURAL RESOURCES:
    Division of State Parks
    State Parks Camping Permits 241-3444
    Main Office 241-3446
    Koke'e 335-5871
    Wailua Marina 822-5065
    Division of Aquatic Resources 241-3400

The Aloha pages in the front of the phone book has various hotline numbers to call for community events, entertainment, etc on Kaua'i. While the call is free, the companies pay to be included, so information is biased.

COMMUNICATION: With the tremendous growth in the cellular phone industry, it is no surprise that rental cellular phones are a vacation option. At Alamo car rental, a phone will run you $4.95 per day, with calls charged at $1.60 per minute and additional $.45 per minute additional charge for calls to the mainland. A pricey arrangement if you plan on using it frequently, but given certain situations, it might be a worthwhile investment for peace of mind!

GETTING THERE -- *AIRLINES AND MORE*

The best air prices on major air carriers can generally be arranged through a reputable travel agent who can often secure air or air with car packages at good prices by volume purchasing. Prices can vary considerably so comparison shopping is a wise idea. Always ask about senior citizen and companion fare discounts.

Another alternative is to book a package trip through one of several agencies which specialize in Hawai'i travel. While Creative Leisure uses major airlines (we were quoted on United), the other two use charter services. Airfare only is available through both Suntrips and Pleasant Hawaiian Holidays. However, be advised that Suntrips currently only departs from San Francisco, San Diego, Ontario, Sacramento and San Jose. Days of departures may be limited and therefore restricting on both Suntrips and Pleasant Hawaiian Holidays. Here's the bottom line on some package air/land/car operations based on a Portland, Oregon, to Lihu'e excursion.

Pleasant Hawaiian Holidays 1-800-242-9244, in the news with their great low airfare only rates, may need to extend their phone hours. They may be a great deal, but they are no deal at all if you can't get through the phone lines. I finally got through very early one Saturday morning. They were discontinuing their American Trans Air service out of Portland at the time I called to inquire, which meant a shuttle service to Seattle. Some of their flights go by way of Maui, so for me it would mean Portland to Seattle to Maui to Honolulu to Kaua'i. A very circuitous route that would have meant an entire day of travel. Pleasant Hawaiian previously only had package deals, but by breaking up their packages it allows a great many more possibilities.

Suntrips at 1-800-786-8747 had a operator that was cordial enough, but obviously didn't know the island. A little disconcerting when they stumble over and mispronounce the names of the towns and rental properties. Their bottom line, however, was tough to beat. Nine nights at the Kaua'i Sands for double occupancy ran about $670 per person. Keep in mind this is a very meager accommodation. They do have a selection of moderate and expensive accommodations as well. Hanalei Bay for the same number of days ran $1400. Also, as mentioned previously they leave out of California airports, so if you have to pay a high price to get airfare to that destination, it may not be the best deal.

The least expensive option with *Creative Leisure* at 1-800-426-6367 was Plantation Hale arriving via a United Airlines flight with all taxes included and a 4 door Hertz compact for about $2100 for two persons. A refundable cancellation policy was available at $35 per person. The package for Po'ipu Kai was about $2650 for a 1 Bedroom, 1 Bath. Anna, the agent I spoke with at Creative Leisure, was obviously knowledgeable about properties and when queried I discovered that they sent their agents over to familiarize them. Customer service is a high priority with them, and it showed!

Suite Paradise ★ is a condominium rental agency which specializes in the "Best of Po'ipu." In addition to accommodations they offer very attractive rates on car/condo packages. They are also able to arrange ticketing on regularly scheduled airlines (United and Hawaiian) at discounts with their air ticketing affiliate. Contact Suite Paradise at 1-800-745-6144 to request information on all their vacation options. They have a wonderful, helpful staff that greet your arrival on the island with a tropical fruit drink or a mai tai. Suite Paradise also has an air affiliate which they report can provide exceptional airline discounts. Contact Suite Paradise to receive information on contacting the airline.

Strangely enough, after all my calling to these package agencies and even checking the local paper which quoted Hawaiian Air as having the lowest rates at the present time, I stopped by my local United Airlines. I inquired as to the cost of a round trip Portland to Kaua'i and was quoted a price of $611. Slightly more than the price for Hawaiian Air at $589. But then I had her calculate the airfare to Honolulu only and because of a special promotion for a few months during the spring of 1995, the rate was an unbelievable $301. From Honolulu you can purchase airfare to neighbor islands for about $35-$79 one way, less if one of the local airlines is doing a special. Adding in the neighbor island airfare, it still came in at far less than what the local paper stated was the lowest rate.

The moral of this story? A little leg work pays off. Sometimes the best deal may be through one of these agencies, but do a thorough investigation and you may be pleasantly surprised. I was!! Always make sure you let them know if you are flexible on your arrival and departure days. You may be able to squeeze into some window that offers an even better value on your flight dollar. I was inquiring for rates in April, which is one of those in-between times when they may have special deals.

Kaua'i has two airports. The main one is in central Kaua'i, at Lihu'e, and a smaller commuter airport is located in Princeville on the north shore.

FLIGHTS TO THE ISLANDS

The major American carriers that fly from the mainland to The Honolulu International Airport on O'ahu, Hawai'i are:

AMERICAN AIRLINES - 1-800-433-7300. In Honolulu 808-523-9376. On Kaua'i dial the 800 # as there is no local phone.

AMERICA WEST AIRLINES - 1-800-235-9393. They offer service to Honolulu through its major mainland hubs of Las Vegas and Phoenix with connecting service to over 67 cities nationwide.

CANADIAN AIRLINES INTERNATIONAL - 1-800-426-7000. Eighteen weekly flights from Vancouver to and from Honolulu. Then connecting inter-island carriers to Kaua'i.

CONTINENTAL AIRLINES - 1-800-525-0280. In Honolulu phone 808-836-7730. Flights to Honolulu with connecting service to Kaua'i.

DELTA AIR LINES - 1-800-221-1212. They fly out of Atlanta, stopping in Los Angeles, then onto Honolulu. They also have one flight direct from Dallas-Fort Worth to Honolulu.

GENERAL INFORMATION
Getting There

HAWAIIAN AIRLINES - 1-800-367-5320; in Honolulu, 808-838-1555; on Kaua'i 808-245-1813.

NORTHWEST AIRLINES - 1-800-225-2525; in Honolulu, 808-955-2255. No local Kaua'i number.

PLEASANT HAWAIIAN HOLIDAYS - 1-800-242-9244. We were recently informed by one of our readers that they saved over $150 per ticket (over the lowest rate quoted by another airline) using an "airfare only" package from Pleasant Hawaiian. They tell us it was as good, if not better, than the service they've had on United. They even had a separate audio channel oriented towards small children. They added that the seat configuration on the L-1011 is 3-4-3 and they recommend tall people staying away from the middle 4 seats, which seemed to have less leg room.

TWA - 1-800-221-2000.

UNITED AIRLINES - UAL Reservations 1-800-241-6522. Flight information 1-800-824-6100. Their Honolulu number is 808-547-2211. Kaua'i phone 245-9533. United has more flights to Hawai'i from more U.S. cities than any other airline.

INTER-ISLAND FLIGHTS

Hawai'i is unique in that its intrastate roads are actually water or sky. For your travel by sky, there are several inter-island carriers that operate between Honolulu and Kaua'i. If you plan on doing frequent inter-island excursions, some allow you to purchase a coupon book of six or so tickets that work out to being a small discount per ticket over a single ticket purchase.

Travel agents schedule at least an hour and a half between arrival on O'ahu and departure for Kaua'i to account for any delays, baggage transfers, and the time required to reach the inter-island terminal. The flight time from O'ahu to Lihu'e on Kaua'i is just 25 minutes. A flight from O'ahu to Princeville Airport is 50 minutes. The Princeville Airport is served by IslandAir, a commuter air service.

Traveling from the main carrier to the inter-island terminal can be rather exhausting and confusing. You will probably need to take one wiki wiki bus to a drop-off point and then pick up another to take you to the inter-island terminal. The exception is for the new kid on the block, Mahalo, which is another adventure in itself. See Mahalo, on the next page, for that saga!

If you do arrive early, check with the inter-island carrier. Very often you can get an earlier flight which will arrive on Kaua'i in time to get your car before returning to pick up your luggage when it arrives on your scheduled flight.

If you are traveling "light" and have brought with you carry-on luggage only, be advised that what is carry-on for the major airlines may not be carry-on for the inter-island carriers. For example, those new small suitcases with wheels and long handles that extend out to pull along behind you MUST be checked by many of the inter-island carriers. Knowing this in advance, you may be able to pack those items that are more fragile in a smaller tote bag.

ALOHA AIRLINES ★ - They fly only jets - mostly 737s. 1-800-367-5250 U.S., 1-800-663-9471 Canada. Their Honolulu number is 808-484-1111, on Kaua'i 808-245-3691. Aloha offers First Class service, Drive-Thru Check-In at Honolulu and non-stop service between Kaua'i and Maui on two of their flights. This airline also has more respect for its schedule than the others and they continue to have one of the lowest passenger complaint records of all U.S. Airlines. They fly over 1,200 flights weekly with their fleet of fifteen Boeing 737s. They also offer weekly charter service to Christmas Island and long range charters upon request.

ISLAND AIR - The sister airline to Aloha (formerly called Aloha Island Air) specializes in serving Hawai'i's smaller community and resort destinations. On Kaua'i they offer exclusive service to Princeville Airport, very close and convenient for those staying on the Northshore. Their fleet consists of eight 18 passenger twin engine De Havilland Dash 6 Twin Otters (Turbo-prop) aircraft. From Hawai'i, the toll free number is 1-800-652-6541 or locally on Kaua'i it is (808) 826-7969 at Princeville Airport. From the U.S. Mainland call 1-800-323-3324.

HAWAIIAN AIRLINES - They offer an hourly shuttle service to Kaua'i. Toll free 1-800-367-5320. (808) 245-1813.

MAHALO AIR - This is the new kid on the block. Begun in December, 1994, they might be worth a call to check on prices. The newest inter-island carrier generally sets the pace for the air wars! When we checked the price was half what it was for the standard fare on Aloha ($35 versus $70). All their flights go through Honolulu. Currently operating 9 flights per day to and from Honolulu and Lihu'e, they fly ATR 42, which seat 48 passengers. It takes only about an extra five minutes to reach Kaua'i. There is no beverage or other service on board during the brief flight. The amusing portion of this saga is that you may have difficulty finding a wiki wiki bus to take you to the Mahalo terminal on O'ahu. It is not at the main inter-island terminal and the traveler who contacted us reported that he had to ask four wiki wiki drivers before he found one that would take him "way out there." The rest replied that it was just "too far." It is actually a short walk from the inter-island terminal. On Kaua'i, you won't have a problem, as Mahalo flies out of the Hawaiian Airline portion of the Lihu'e airport. O'ahu (808) 833-5555, neighbor islands 1-800-277-8333. U.S. Mainland 1-800-4-MAH-ALO.

LIHU'E AIRPORT:
Congratulations! It has been a long day of travel, but now you're here! Most visitors to Kaua'i will arrive at the island's major air terminal. The Lihu'e Airport covers 804 acres and is located on the southeast coast of the island of Kaua'i, about 1 1/2 miles from the town of Lihu'e. The new airport terminal opened in February of 1987. The airport operates two runways and offers passenger and cargo transportation. Currently the runway length does not allow direct international or overseas domestic air service by large aircraft.

DISTANCES FROM THE LIHU'E AIRPORT TO OTHER AREAS:
From the Lihu'e airport it is a 10 minute drive to Kapa'a, 25 minutes to Po'ipu, 50 minutes to Hanalei, 65 minutes to Ha'ena and 70 minutes to the Waimea Canyon, barring traffic tie ups.

GENERAL INFORMATION
Getting There

One pleasant way to see the Hawaiian islands is aboard one of the *American Hawai'i Cruise* ships, the *Independence* or *Constitution*. These comfortable 700-foot (800 passenger) ships provide comfortable accommodations and friendly service during the seven day sail around the islands. In 1993, American Hawai'i Cruises was acquired by The Delta Queen Steamboat Co. and they initiated some interesting new on-board programs. Hawaiian costumes, hands-on Hawaiian museum exhibits, cabins with Hawaiian names, traditional Hawaiian church services, menus filled with Hawaiian specialties, and tropical flowers in every room are among the changes which bring the essence of Hawai'i on board. American Hawai'i has also added Kumus (Hawaiian teachers) to teach passengers about the culture and history of Hawaii. A Kumu's Study with historic artifacts is located off the central lounge. The Sports Deck Solarium, on the Independence, has been converted into top-of-the-line passenger suites. Fully handicap-accessible suites were created in the renovations. Direct cellular telephone service is provided from each cabin.

The S.S. Independence departs Honolulu on Saturdays, the S.S. Constitution from Honolulu on Tuesdays. They travel a seven day route from Honolulu to Kona and Hilo on the Big Island, then to Lahaina on Maui, and finish up with a stop at Nawiliwili on Kaua'i. The S.S. Constitution will be in dry dock beginning July 1995 and will be returned to service, fully upgraded and refurbished in July of 1996.

Also available on both ships are a number of "Theme Cruises" which range from Big Band cruises to one which combines with the island's Aloha Festival. The ships come into port at each of the major islands for a day (or in some cases two) for touring.

Currently each ship visits Kaua'i one day each week. The Independence arrives on Friday and the Constitution on Monday.

Wedding ceremonies can be performed aboard both of American Hawaii's ships with the purchase of a special $595 wedding package. The package includes a minister/judge fee, a Hawaiian lei and haku for the bride and matching lei or boutonniere for the groom, 24 photos in an album, live Hawaiian music and a wedding cake for two. Anniversary couples can arrange to renew their vows in a ceremony performed by the Captain himself. See Weddings & Honeymoons in this chapter for information on tests and licenses.

American Hawai'i has added new shore excursions which include opportunities for passengers to discover the "hidden" Hawaii. Trips include the opportunity to relax in an authentic Polynesian-style outrigger canoe as a personal tour guide paddles through tropical landscapes and by exotic wildlife, or you can hike through a rain forest to discover a hidden waterfall.

The idea of a cruise is to give you a taste of each of the islands without the time and inconvenience of traveling by plane in-between islands. In fact, it would be impossible to see all the islands in a week in any other fashion.

For additional information write American Hawai'i Cruises, Two North Riverside Plaza, Chicago, Illinois 60606. (312) 466-6000. FAX (312) 466-6001.

There are other cruise lines that visit the Hawaiian islands on a less frequent basis. Check with your travel agents regarding those that depart from the Mainland U.S., visit Hawai'i, and either return to the mainland or go beyond.

GETTING AROUND

We pause here with a brief aside. It seems most appropriate in the category of "getting around" the island, in general, to make note of this interesting fact. The street addresses may easily confuse you as you are trying to locate a particular establishment. You may see a number such as 3-5920 next to 5924, as an example. The number in front of the dash stands for the area of the island. 0-1 is Waimea, 2 is Koloa, 3 is Lihu'e, 4 is Kapa'a and 5 is Hanalei. That seems fairly clear, but it can get a little confusing as to where the cut off point is for each of those areas. Another problem is some people use the first number and the dash and some do not. So, all we can say is, good luck!

FROM THE AIRPORT: After arriving, there are several options. Taxi cabs, because of the distances between areas, can be very costly, i.e., $31 from Lihu'e to Po'ipu. That would pay for your economy rental car for the first day!

LOCAL TRANSPORTATION: If you don't choose a rental car, you will find Kaua'i Bus does service island-wide.

ABC Taxi of Kaua'i 822-7641
Aloha Taxi 245-4609
Hanamalulu Taxi 245-3727
Kaua'i Cab Service 246-9554
Paradise Taxi/Kaua'i Shuttle Service 742-2528
North Shore Cab & Tours 826-6189
Scotty's Taxi 245-7888 or cellular 651-8493

GREAT FRIGATE BIRD   JBAYOT

RENTAL CARS AND TRUCKS: Given the status of public transportation on Kaua'i, a rental car is still the best bet to get around the island and, for your dollar, a good buy. Prices per day are approximated as follows: Vans $80-110, Jeep $60-110 (only Alamo, Avis and Dollar had any currently available), Mid-size $34-66, Compacts $34-63. In every category, Alamo came in with the best prices and Dollar was the highest. Note that some rental car agencies are discussing the reinstitution of mileage charges of 25 cents a mile or more. Be sure to inquire!

An aside here is to point out that probably the first person who will greet you on Kaua'i is the car rental company agent. It is unfortunate that "Jolly" John at Alamo could not be synthesized and reproduced in mass. He was funny, patient, helpful, and spent time explaining a few extra directions and places to eat. He wasn't at all hurried and he made sure that we had all our questions answered. He was not aware that our business was travel writing! Alamo gets a plus for having such a bonafide Aloha spirited employee!

On Kaua'i there are currently no companies which rent camping equipment. Vans are available from a number of agencies, but camping in them is not encouraged.

The policies of all the rental car agencies are basically the same. Most require a minimum age of 21 to 25 and a maximum age of 70. All feature unlimited mileage with you buying the gas ($1.60-$1.70 per gallon). Hanamalu Shell station has gas a few cents cheaper and the folks that work there are nice too! You might consider filling up before you return your car, the rental companies charge between $1.63 (Alamo) up to $2-2.50 (Hertz, National, et.al) per gallon to do it for you. A few require a deposit or major credit card to hold your reservation. Please note that there are limited gas stations located on the north shore!

Insurance is an option you may wish, which can run an additional $10 a day. A few agencies will require insurance for those under age 25. Most of the car rental agencies strongly encourage you to take the additional insurance coverage. Hawai'i is a no-fault state and without the insurance, you are required to take care of all the damages before leaving the island. We suggest you check with your own insurance company before you leave to verify exactly what your policy covers. Some credit cards now provide insurance for rental cars if you use that credit card to charge your rental fees (usually a practice with Gold Cards). Add to the rental price a 4% sales tax and a $2 per day highway road tax.

Rental companies prohibit cars on any unpaved roads, like Polihale. The rental agencies will provide you with a map showing restrictions. Should you travel on these roads they will hold you responsible for any damage.

Discounts are few and far between. You might be able to use some airline award coupons or entertainment book coupons, but they are often very restrictive. If you are a member of AAA you can receive a discount on rental cars. During our checking, Alamo had by far the best rates. Remember that weekly rates are always a better value, even if you're only there for six days. The rental booths are at the Lihu'e airport and pick-up and return areas are conveniently located to the airline terminal and easy to find. Preferred customers get only a slight advantage by picking their cars up at the airport. The rest of the companies offer a convenient shuttle bus to travel the short distance to their rental office.

At the Princeville Airport you will only have the choice of Hertz or Avis.

RENTAL CAR LISTING:

ALAMO RENT A CAR ★
1-800-327-9633
Lihu'e 246-0645

AVIS
1-800-331-1212
Hyatt Regency:
742-1627

Princeville Airport:
826-9773

BUDGET
1-800-527-0700
Lihu'e: 245-1901

DOLLAR
1-800-367-7006
Lihu'e: 245-3651

HERTZ
1-800-654-3131
Lihu'e: 245-3356
Princeville:
826-7455

NATIONAL
1-800-227-7368
Lihu'e 245-3356

SEARS RENT A CAR
contracts w/ Budget
1-800-451-3600

TOOLMASTER HAWAII
Pickup & Truck rentals
246-1111

WESTSIDE U-DRIVE
332-8644

WILIWILI

63

GROCERY SHOPPING

Grocery store prices may be one of the biggest surprises of your trip. While there are some locally grown foods and dairies, most of the products must be flown or shipped to the islands. The local folks can shop the advertisements and use the coupons, but it isn't so easy when traveling. To give you an idea of what to expect at the supermarket, here are some grocery store prices. Bread $1.65 and up, bananas $.99 /lb., strained baby food 2 jars for $1, chicken $1.29 /lb., hamburger $1.99 /lb. and up, mayonnaise $1.99, Starkist Tuna $1.33, disposable diapers 12 count $5.99, 32 oz. ketchup $2.49, skim milk $3.79 a gallon.

Look for the Sunshine Market, an outdoor farmer's market held at different locations around the island. We suggest a call to the Hawai'i visitors Bureau to check on their schedule, but currently they run: Monday-Koloa Ball Park at noon; Tuesday-Kalaheo Neighborhood Center at 3:30 pm; Wednesday-Kapa'a New Town Park at 3 pm; Thursday-Kilauea Neighborhood Center 4:30 pm; Friday Vidinha Stadium parking lot in Lihu'e at Hoolako Street 3 pm; Saturday-Kekaha Neighborhood Center 9 am.

If you are a devoted ad shopper (even on vacation), check the Wednesday paper for grocery specials. On the South Shore you can shop at Big Save in Koloa. On the East shore there is a Big Save in Kapa'a and a Safeway at Kaua'i Village. In Lihu'e you'll find a Big Save and in the Kukui Grove a Star Market. In Waipouli you'll find a Foodland that has a full service Bank of America in the store, not just an ATM! On the West side there is a Big Save in Waimea and in Ele'ele. On the North shore you can chose between a Big Save in Hanalei or a Foodland in Princeville. All major stores accept Visa or Mastercard. These larger stores offer the same variety as your hometown store and the prices are better than at the small grocery outlets.

The best part of shopping for food in Hawai'i are the interesting specialty markets. You find wonderful fresh fish, fruit, vegetable and pupu markets in all the towns. "Health" foods can be tracked down at Papaya's in Kapa'a.

BREADFRUIT

ANNUAL KAUA'I EVENTS

JANUARY
- Brown Bags to Stardom at Kaua'i War Memorial Convention Hall. 245-4355. A talent competition for top finalists from area high schools.

FEBRUARY
- Hanapepe Raft Run sponsored by the Garden Island Road Runners. 338-1475.
- Mirage Pro-Am Golf Tournament at Princeville. 826-3580.
- Chinese New Year Celebrations around the island.
- Celebration in Waimea, usually the third weekend in February. A Friday night and Saturday event featuring a fun run and amusements. 338-9957.

MARCH
- Prince Kuhio Run in Po'ipu, 742-9391.
- Prince Kuhio Festival in Po'ipu. Commemorative service at Prince Kuhio Park. Canoe regatta, Holoku pageant and royal ball. 245-3971.
- March 26 - Prince Kuhio Day - State Holiday.

APRIL
- Polo season begins and runs through September. Sundays at 'Anini Polo Field, 3 pm.
- Annual Businessmen's Canoe Race, Wailua Beach to Kalapaki Beach.

MAY
- May 1st, Lei Day, various programs around the island
- Ke Ola Hou Hawaiian arts and crafts Spring Festival at Hanapepe Town Park. 335-5765.
- Pooku Hanalei Stampede at Pooku Stables. Rodeo, music, and dancing. 826-6777.
- Annual Banana Poka Festival celebrating "Earth Day" at Koke'e Museum. 335-9975.

JUNE
- King Kamehameha Day celebrations around the state.
- Obon Season: June - August, Buddhist tradition in which spirits of ancestors are welcomed with prayers, offerings and dance. Fri. & Sat. nights at various Buddhist temples around the island.

JULY
- King Kong Ultra Triathalon. 826-4393.
- Koloa Plantation Days. 332-9201.
- Annual Na Hula o Ka'ohikukapulani, hula exhibition. 335-6466.
- Concert in the sky at Vidinha Stadium with fire-works, 4th of July celebration, crafts, and food. A fundraiser for Kaua'i Hospice. 245-7277.
- Annual Chili Cook Off to benefit Kaua'i Humane Society (at Kaua'i Village).
- Tahiti Fete, Kukui Grove Shopping Center Pavilion. Cultural exchange festival with Tahiti.

AUGUST
- Hanalei Stampede - the biggest rodeo event on Kaua'i at Po'oku Stables.
- August 21 - Admission Day, a state holiday.
- Trout season opens in Koke'e State Park.

SEPTEMBER
- Labor Day Weekend - Farm Fair at the Warm Memorial Convention Hall in Lihu'e.
- Mokihana Festival, annual musical event featuring Kaua'i Composers Contest, folk arts workshops, flowerless lei contests and ukulele jam. 822-2166.

OCTOBER
- Kaua'i Renaissance Faire at the Kilohana Estate in Puhi. 245-6684.
- Aloha Festivals, third week of the month, featuring the Aloha Spirit around the island.
- Triathalon - Begins and ends in Hanalei. 825-9343.
- Annual "Eo e emalani i Alakai Festival" commemorating Queen Emma's journey to Koke'e and the Alakai Swamp with hula and music at the Koke'e Lodge. 335-9975.
- Hanalei Taro Festival, Hoolaulea in Hanalei with taro tasting, craft fairs, music, and dancing. 826-6522.

NOVEMBER
- 5-10KM Marathon, begins in Kapa'a at Sheraton Coconut Beach Hotel.
- Hawaiian International Film Festival.
- PGA Grand Slam - Po'ipu Bay Resort Golf Course.

DECEMBER
- Kilohana Craft Fair at the Kilohana Estate in Puhi.
- Kaua'i Museum Christmas Craft Fair.
- December 31: Annual Christmas Bird Count and potluck. Koke'e Natural History Museum. 335-9975.

For the exact dates of many of these events, write to the Hawai'i Visitors Bureau, 2270 Kalakaua Avenue #801, Honolulu, HI 96815, and request the Hawai'i Special Events Calendar. The calendar also gives non-annual information and the contact person for each event. A more complete listing for Kaua'i events can be obtained from the Kaua'i Visitors Bureau at 3016 Umi, Room 207, Lihu'e, Kaua'i, HI 96766 (808) 245-3971, FAX (808) 246-9235. Check the local papers for dates of additional events. The *Kaua'i Update* newsletter will also advise you on current events!

WEATHER

When thinking of Hawai'i one visualizes bright sunny days cooled by refreshing trade winds, and this is the weather at least 300 days a year. What about the other 65 days? Most aren't really bad - just not perfect. Although there are only two seasons, summer and winter, temperatures remain quite constant. Following are the average daily highs and lows for each month and the general weather conditions.

January	80/64	May	84/67	September	87/70
Feb.	79/64	June	86/69	October	86/69
March	80/64	July	86/70	November	83/68
April	82/66	Aug.	87/71	December	80/66

Winter: Mid October through April, 70 - 80 degree days, 60 - 70 degree nights. Tradewinds are more erratic, vigorous to none. Kona winds are more frequent causing wide-spread cloudiness, rain showers, mugginess and even an occasional thunderstorm. 11 hours of daylight.

Summer: May through mid October, 80 degree days, 70 - 80 degree nights. Tradewinds are more consistent keeping the temperatures tolerable, however, when the trades stop, the weather becomes hot and sticky. Kona winds are less frequent. 13 hours of daylight.

Summer type wear is suitable all year round. However, a warm sweater or light-weight jacket is a good idea for evenings and trips such as to Koke'e.

If you are interested in the types of weather you may encounter, or are confused by some of the terms you hear, read on. For further reference consult *Weather in Hawaiian Waters*, by Paul Haraguchi, 99 pages, available at island bookstores.

Average water temperature ranges between 74 degrees in February to a warm 80 degrees by October. For additional information on surf conditions on Kaua'i call the Surf Report at 335-3611.

TRADE WINDS: Trade winds are an almost constant wind blowing from the northeast through the east and are caused by the Pacific anti-cyclone, a high pressure area. This high pressure area is well developed and remains semi-stationary in the summer causing the trades to remain steady over 90% of the time. Interruptions are much more frequent in the winter when they blow only 40 to 60% of the time.

KONA WINDS: The Kona Wind is a stormy, rain-bearing wind blowing from the southwest, or basically from the opposite direction of the trades. It brings high, rough surf to the resort side of the island - great for surfing and boogie-boarding, bad for snorkeling. These conditions are caused by low pressure areas northwest of the islands. Kona winds strong enough to cause property damage have occurred only twice since 1970. Lighter non-damaging Kona winds are much more common, occurring usually 2 - 5 times almost every winter (Nov-April).

KONA WEATHER: Windless, hot and humid weather is referred to as Kona weather. The interruption of the normal trade wind pattern brings this on. The trades are replaced by light and variable winds and, although this may occur any time of the year, it is most noticeable during the summer when the weather is generally hotter and more humid, with fewer localized breezes.

KONA LOW: A Kona low is a slow-moving, meandering, extensive low pressure area which forms near the islands. This causes continuous rain with thunderstorms over an extensive area and lasts for several days. November through May is the most usual time for these to occur.

RAIN: Paradise would not be paradise without it! However, parts of Kaua'i receive more than an equal share. With the Northeast Trade Winds reaching the North Shore of Kaua'i first, they deposit a greater share on this coastline. The Hanalei/Princeville area receives up to 45 inches per year. The East side fares better, receiving only 30 inches per year. The south and western coastlines receive between 5 and 20 inches per year. And then there is Mt. Wai'ale'ale, possibly the wettest place on earth with a record 665.5 inches of rain falling in 1982. More average years will result in 450-475 inches of rain fall on this, Kaua'i's second highest peak.

HURRICANES: Hurricanes (called typhoons when they are west of the 180 degree longitude) have come near enough to do serious damage to the Hawaiian islands on several occasions. The storms which affect Hawaii usually originate off Central America or Mexico and most of the threatening tropical cyclones have weakened before reaching the islands, or have passed harmlessly to the west. Their effects are usually minimal, causing only high surf on the eastern and southern shores of some of the islands. At least 21 hurricanes or tropical storms have passed within 300 miles of the islands in the last 33 years, but most did little or no damage. Hurricane season is considered to be July through November. Hurricanes are given Hawaiian names when they pass within 1,000 miles of the Hawaiian islands.

In August of 1950 Hurricane Hiki went to the north of Kaua'i, but still brought 70 mile per hour winds to the island. In 1957, Kaua'i felt the force of two hurricanes which also passed nearby. Both Hurricane Della (in September of that year) and Hurricane Nina (which followed in early December) skirted a mere 100 miles from the southwestern shore of Kaua'i, bringing high winds and high surf.

Hurricane Dot struck the island in August of 1959, with winds nearing 100 miles per hour. In this decade before much development, major damage was restricted to crops.

Hurricane Iwa of November 1982 passed between Ni'ihau and Kaua'i causing extensive damage to crops and property with winds gusting to 100 miles per hour.

Hurricane Iniki (which means piercing wind) struck Kaua'i with incredible force in September 1992. Strangely it was within weeks of Hurricane Andrew's blow to Florida. As Iniki traveled across the Atlantic, crossing into the Pacific, it had time to develop winds that blew at 165 miles per hour with one gust at Na Pali on the Makaha Ridge which recorded a speed of 227 miles per hour.

Iniki was considered a Category Four hurricane. Trees were uprooted, homes were destroyed, property damage was extensive and island wide. Power and phone lines was down for weeks. Due to the remoteness of the island, help was slower to arrive to Kaua'i than to Florida. While the news media continued to focus on Florida for weeks following Hurricane Andrew, after a few days of coverage, Kaua'i was almost forgotten. Today Kaua'i residents refer to Iniki (and Iniki Day) as 911. A little pun since it occurred on September 11th, 9-11!

Kaua'i has been much slower to recover from this latest natural disaster. Only two major resorts, the Hyatt Regency and Princeville had reopened within two years following the hurricane. The former Westin Kaua'i reopened in July of 1995 under the Marriott hotel chain. Other hotels sit and wait as insurance settlements have yet to be agreed upon.

Even good things can result from tragedies. Within hours of Hurricane Iniki, Kaua'i residents were pulling together to begin to normalize their lives. They began with neighbors helping neighbors. No one was untouched, but those with dwellings suffering more minor damage were welcoming neighbors into their homes. We were told that Stephen Speilberg, just finishing up his Jurassic Park filming, offered his private helicopter to bring in much needed medical personnel. Kaua'i continues to rebuild and grow stronger because of Iniki. Government agencies have begun to work in closer harmony, to make plans for the safety of the population of Kaua'i should any other disaster strike the island and its people.

TSUNAMI: A tsunami is an ocean wave produced by an undersea earthquake, volcanic eruption, or landslide. Tsunamis are usually generated along the coasts of South America, the Aleutian Islands, the Kamchatka Peninsula, or Japan and travel through the ocean at 400 to 500 miles an hour. It takes at least 4 1/2 hours for a tsunami to reach the Hawaiian Islands. A 24-hour Tsunami Warning System has been established in Hawai'i since 1946. When the possibility exists of a tsunami reaching Hawaiian waters, the public will be informed by the sound of the attention alert signal sirens. This particular signal is a steady one minute siren, followed by one minute of silence, repeating as long as necessary. Immediately turn on a TV or radio; all stations will carry CIV-Alert emergency information and instructions with the arrival time of the first waves. Do not take chances - false alarms are not issued. Move quickly out of low lying coastal areas that are subject to possible inundation.

The warning sirens are tested throughout the state on the first working Monday of every month at 11 am, so don't be alarmed when you hear the siren blare! The test lasts only a few minutes and CIV-Alert announces on all stations that the test is underway. Since 1813, there have been 112 tsunamis observed in Hawai'i with only 16 causing significant damage.

Tsunamis may also be generated by local volcanic earthquakes. In the last 100 years there have been only six, with the last one November 29, 1975, affecting the southeast coast of the island of Hawaii. The Hawaiian Civil Defense has placed earthquake sensors on all the islands and, if a violent local earthquake occurs, an urgent tsunami warning will be broadcast and the tsunami sirens will sound.

A locally generated tsunami will reach the other islands very quickly. Therefore, there may not be time for an attention alert signal to sound. Any violent earthquake that causes you to fall or hold onto something to prevent falling is an urgent warning, and you should immediately evacuate beaches and coastal low-lying areas.

There have been two tsunamis in recent history which struck Kaua'i doing serious damage to property and taking human life. In 1946 and in 1957 the tsunami did the most destruction to the North Shore of Kaua'i. A tsunami alert is taken seriously, but fortunately the most recent (1995) tsunami generated a wave of only 2 inches.

For additional information on warnings and procedures in the event of a hurricane, tsunami, earthquake or flash flood, read the civil defense section located in the forward section of the Kaua'i phone book.

TIDES: The average tidal range is about two feet.

SUNRISE AND SUNSET: In Hawaii, day length and the altitude of the noon sun above the horizon do not vary as much throughout the year as at the temperate regions because of the island's low latitude within the sub-tropics. The longest day is 13 hours 26 minutes (sunrise 5:53 am, sunset 7:18 pm) at the end of June, and the shortest day is 10 hours 50 minutes (sunrise 7:09 am and sunset 6:01 pm at the end of December). Daylight for outdoor activities without artificial lighting lasts about 45 minutes past sunset.

SPINNER DOLPHINS

WHERE TO STAY --
WHAT TO SEE

INTRODUCTION

In the fall of 1994, Kaua'i offered 2,687 hotel rooms, 2,714 condominium units, 12 cabins, and 230 bed & breakfasts and inns. This was prior to the opening of several major hotels, which will add a substantial number of rooms to the inventory. The island can easily be divided into three main areas, with perhaps some sub-areas: Princeville and Hanalei -- North Shore; The East/Central region; and the third which we have grouped into one area that includes the south and west shores. This last area covers Po'ipu Beach and the Koloa areas, and continues to the west side to include the accommodations in the Waimea and Koke'e areas. This chapter contains a list of essentially all of the condominiums that are in rental programs as well as the island's hotels.

Bed & breakfasts are a booming business and an alternative that has become increasingly popular over the years. Kaua'i, in particular, seems to have more prominently listed B & B units than the other islands. This again can probably be traced to Hurricane Iniki. When businesses were closed or destroyed, many whose homes needed to be rebuilt and renovated anyway looked into a B & B as a way to create their own jobs and/or additional income. Now that tourism is back in business, they are too, and there are dozens of new B & B's that are ready, able (and happy), to welcome guests.

Traditionally B & B means a room in a private home (usually with a shared entrance) and those range from $45 a night. Condos, cottages and studios with private entrances and/or baths range from $55 to $200 a night. Bed & breakfast homes are sprinkled around the island and we have listed them within the areas of the island where they are located.

Also included at the conclusion of this chapter are several of the Bed & breakfast agencies which handle many more homes than we have been able to include in this volume. *Bed & Breakfast Hawai'i* is run by Evie Sands. Her directory "Bed & Breakfast goes Hawaiian," which is co-authored by Al Davis, and sells for $12.95. It lists B & Bs throughout the state with additional information on area restaurants, events and activities. *Pacific Hawai'i Bed & Breakfast* has over 20 units on Kaua'i. All of their properties require a three night minimum stay. *Bed & Breakfast Kaua'i* is run very personably and efficiently by Liz Hey. She specializes in finding just the right place for your individual needs. A bed & breakfast is quite often a matter of matching personalities and interests. You can also try *All Islands Bed and Breakfast.*

71

Note that very few bed and breakfast facilities accept any type of charge cards. Some do not allow children.

Remember when calling Hawai'i to adjust for the time difference. Most offices are open during business hours Hawai'i standard time and some only weekdays. Bed & breakfast homes would no doubt really appreciate calls during the day or evening (Hawai'i time).

HOW TO USE THIS CHAPTER: For ease in locating information, the properties are first indexed alphabetically following this introduction. In each of the three distinctly different geographical areas, we have divided the condominiums and listed them in order of price and then alphabetized them for quick reference.

Keep in mind that in providing directions, we may refer to the Hawaiian terms of mauka, which means towards the mountains and makai, which means towards the ocean. On these islands it is much less cumbersome to utilize this form of indicating direction than the standard north, east, south and west!

Often the management at the property takes reservations, but some do not. In some cases there are several rental agents handling units in addition to the on-site management and we have listed an assortment of these. We suggest that when you determine which condo you are interested in that you call all of the agents. Be aware that while one agent may tell you they have no vacancy, another will have several. The prices we have listed are generally the lowest available (although some agents may offer lower rates with the reduction of certain services such as maid service on check in only - that means your room is clean when you arrive, rather than daily maid service). You may find that one of the package air/condo-/car options will be an all-around better value than booking each of these separately.

Prices are listed to aid your selection and, while these were the most current available at press time, they are subject to change without notice. As island vacationers ourselves, we found it important to include this feature rather than just giving you broad categories such as budget or expensive. After all, one person's "expensive" may be "budget" to someone else!

For the sake of space, we have made use of several abbreviations. The size of the condominiums are identified as studio (S BR), one bedroom (1 BR), two bedroom (2 BR) and three bedroom (3 BR). The numbers in parentheses refers to the number of people that can occupy the unit for the price listed and that there are enough beds for a maximum number of people to occupy this unit i.e. 2 BR (max 4. The description will tell you how much it will be for additional persons over two, i.e. $10/night. Some facilities consider an infant as an extra person, others will allow children free up to a specified age. The abbreviations o.f., g.v., and o.v. refer to oceanfront, gardenview and oceanview units.

Some of the prices may be listed with a slash dividing them. The first price listed is the high season rate, the second price is the low season rate. More and more properties are going to a flat all-season rate. A few include the summer months as high season, and a few others have complicated matters by having a three season fee schedule.

All listings are condominiums unless specified as a (Hotel). Condos are abundant, and the prices and facilities they offer can be quite varied. We have tried to indicate our own personal preferences by the use of a ★. We felt these were the best buys or special in some way. However, it is impossible for us to view all the units within a complex, and since condominiums are privately owned, each unit can vary in its furnishings and its condition.

WHERE TO STAY: As for choosing the area of the island in which to stay, we offer these suggestions:

SOUTH SHORE: Along the south shore you'll find it generally sunnier in the Poi'pu area with perhaps the best beach conditions. During the winter months the south shore beaches are generally safer.

NORTH SHORE/HANALEI: If you want incredible scenery, lots of lush green vegetation and are eager to get just a little further away from civilization, then Princeville may be for you. With varied accommodations you can choose between luxury and moderate. During the winter months, high surf can make the north shore ocean conditions very dangerous.

EASTERN SHORE: Affectionately known as the Coconut Coast, you'll find the best selection of affordable accommodations. Centrally located, you can easily drive to either the south or north shore for the many varied activities they offer.

HOW TO SAVE MONEY: Kaua'i has two price seasons. High or "in" season and low or "off" season. Low season is generally considered to be April 15 to about December 15, and the rates are discounted at some places as much as 30%. Different resorts and condominiums may vary these dates by as much as two weeks and a few resorts are going to a flat, year-round rate. Ironically, some of the best weather is during the fall when temperatures are cooler than summer and there is less rain than the winter and spring months. (See GENERAL INFORMA-TION - Weather for year-round temperatures).

For longer than one week, a condo unit with a kitchen can result in significant savings on your food bill. While this will give you more space than a hotel room and at a lower price, you may give up some resort amenities (shops, restaurants, maid service, etc.). There are several large grocery stores around the island with fairly competitive prices, although most things at the store will run about 30% higher than on the mainland. (See GENERAL INFORMATION - Shopping.)

Most condominiums offer maid service only on check-out. A few might offer it twice a week or weekly. Additional maid service may be available for an extra charge. A few condos still do not provide in-room phones or color televisions, and a few have no pool. (A few words of caution: condominium units within one complex can differ greatly and, if a phone is important to you, ask!) Many are adding microwaves to their kitchens. Some may offer free local calls while others will tack on an extra $1 per local call. Some units have washers and dryers in the rooms, while others do not. Most have coin-operated laundry facilities on the premises.

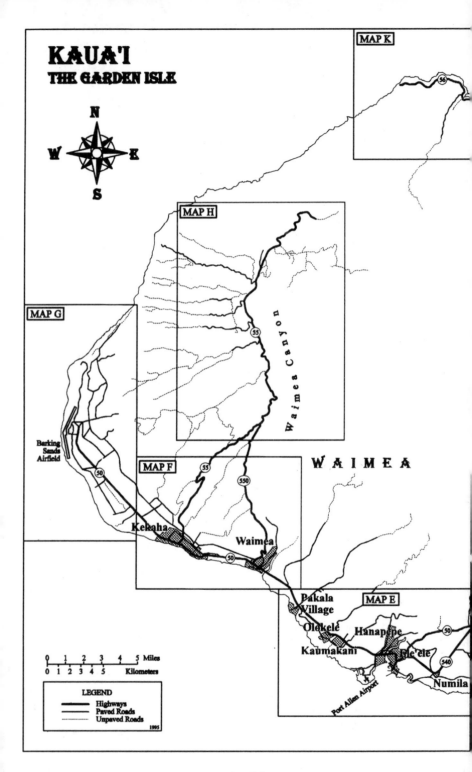

KAUA'I
THE GARDEN ISLE

MAP K

MAP H

MAP G

Waimea Canyon

Barking
Sands
Airfield

MAP F

WAIMEA

Kekaha

Waimea

Pakala
Village

MAP E

Olokele

Hanapepe

Kaumakani

'Ele'ele

Numila

Port Allen Airport

```
0   1   2   3   4   5 Miles
0 1 2 3 4 5  Kilometers
```

LEGEND
Highways
Paved Roads
Unpaved Roads

1995

74

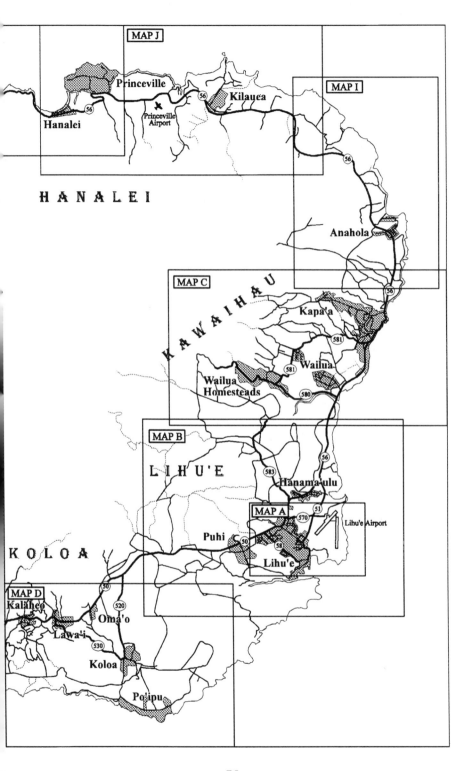

MAP J

Princeville

Kilauea

Hanalei

Princeville
Airport

HANALEI

MAP I

Anahola

MAP C

KAWAIHAU

Kapa'a

Wailua

Wailua
Homesteads

MAP B

LIHU'E

Hanama-ulu

MAP A

Puhi

Lihu'e Airport

Lihu'e

KOLOA

MAP D
Kalaheo

Oma'o

Lawa'i

Koloa

Po'ipu

75

Travel agents will be able to book your stay in the Kaua'i hotels and also in most condominiums. If you prefer to make your own reservation, we have listed the various contacts for each condominium and endeavored to quote the best price generally available. A little phone work can be very cost effective! Rates vary between rental agents, so check all those listed for a particular condominium. We have indicated toll free 800 numbers for the U.S. when available. For additional Canadian toll free numbers, check the rental agent list at the end of this chapter. Look for an 808 area code preceding the non-toll free numbers. You might also check the classified ads in your local newspaper for owners offering their units for rent, which may even be a better bargain.

Although prices can jump, most go up only 5-10% per year. Prices listed do not include the sales tax which is over 9%.

GENERAL POLICIES: Condominium complexes require a deposit, usually equivalent to one or two nights stay, to secure your reservation and insure your room rate against price increases. Some charge higher deposits during winter or over Christmas holidays. Generally a 30 day notice of cancellation is needed to receive a full refund. Most require payment in full either 30 days prior to arrival or upon arrival, and some do not accept credit cards.

The usual minimum condo stay is 3 nights with some requiring one week in winter. Christmas holidays may have steeper restrictions with minimum stays as long as two weeks, payments 90 days in advance and heavy cancellation penalties. It is not uncommon to book as much as two years in advance for the Christmas season. ALL CONDOMINIUMS HAVE KITCHENS, T.V.'S, AND POOLS UNLESS OTHERWISE SPECIFIED. Most condominiums have ceiling fans, but many have no air conditioning.

Monthly and oftentimes weekly discounts are available. Room rates quoted are generally for two. Additional persons run $8 to $15 per night per person with the exception of the high class resorts and hotels where it may run as much as $25 to $35 extra. Many complexes can arrange for crib rentals. (See GENERAL INFORMATION - Traveling with Children.)

We have tried to give the lowest rates generally available, which might not be through the hotel or condo office, so check with the offices as well as the rental agents. Variations in prices may be due to the amenities of a particular unit or the general condition of the condo. When contacting condominium complexes by mail, be sure to address your correspondence to the attention of the manager. The managers of several complexes do not handle any reservations and we have indicated to whom you should address reservation requests. If two addresses are given, use the P.O. Box rather than street address for your correspondence.

CONDOMINIUM AND HOTEL INDEX

GINGER

CENTRAL/EASTSIDE

Kapa'a - Lihu'e - Nawiliwili - Wailua

In this section we will begin at Lihu'e and travel up the west coast in a northerly direction to Hanamaulu, Wailua, Waipouli, and Kapa'a.

INTRODUCTION

Kaua'i's main airport is located in Lihu'e, so this is probably the first place you'll see. It's not exactly the garden spot of the Garden Isle, but it is the least touristy and most "normal" area. This is the county seat where all the government and business offices are located and the place to find everyday necessities like the post office, discount shopping, banks, churches and a library. It also offers the best selection of inexpensive local restaurants.

Hotels, motels and condos in Lihu'e are inexpensive and convenient to the airport, but with the exception of only two resort areas, accommodations are very basic. Even if you stay at another property for the duration of your stay, they are worth considering for a night if you have a late evening arrival or an early morning departure. And don't worry about being too far away from the "good stuff," the Anchor Cove and Pacific Ocean Plaza shopping centers are very close, as is the Kaua'i Museum, and there are plenty of restaurants in the area - from funky local dining and ethnic places to fine dining selections. The Outrigger Kaua'i Hilton Hotel & Beach Villas and the newly opened Kaua'i Marriott Resort & Beach Club (the old Westin which was the older Kaua'i Surf) are the only two resorts with the Outrigger and Aston Villas slightly north of the general area.

Along the central or royal coconut coast are an abundance of affordably priced hotels and condominiums and there is plenty of wonderful natural beauty to be enjoyed as well.

WHAT TO SEE

LIHU'E

The word Lihu'e means "open to chill" and according to the Kaua'i Talking Guidebook the town was named in 1837 by the Governor who relocated from the Big Island. His home town there, Lihu'e had a cooler climate and was a more appropriate name than here on Kaua'i.

Because of our unusual island-state, mayors in Hawai'i govern counties which consist of one or more islands rather than areas of land. The island of Kaua'i (along with Ni'ihau) is a county of the state of Hawai'i and Lihu'e is the county seat. The historic county building was built in 1913 and, with its sprawling lawn and tall palm trees, it is a focal point of Lihu'e. Although government agencies are not usually high on one's list of visitor attractions, you may find the need to visit one or more while you're here on Kaua'i.

The *Hawai'i Visitors Bureau* is always a good place to start to pick up some brochures and ask for information. It is located in the State Building which also houses the *Parks and Recreation Department* - a place you will need to go to if you plan on doing any camping, hiking, or generally any nature-oriented trips. Here you will be able to pick up your permits. (Phone 241-3444 Division of State Parks - Camping permits.)

Just past the Pacific Ocean Plaza you can turn from Rice onto Hardy to reach the *Kaua'i War Memorial Convention Hall* and the Regional Library. The library has an excellent selection of Hawaiian titles, many of which are now out-of-print. If you are a Hawaiiana buff, you might like to include this on your itinerary! (The Kaua'i Community College also has a fairly good Hawaiiana section in their library).

If you spend any time at all in Lihu'e you'll become quite familiar with Rice Street. It seems this single road can get you anywhere you want to go. Continue on Rice Street past the Pacific Ocean Plaza to the Rice Shopping Center. It houses the island's only bowling alley, a Philippine bakery and a couple of local style eateries. A bit further is the Hawai'i Visitors Bureau and continuing up Rice you'll find the Kaua'i Museum next to the Lihu'e Shopping Center and across the street is the post office.

The *Kaua'i Museum* ★ is a great place to get acquainted with the island's history. It is located at 4428 Rice Street in the Wilcox Building that was originally constructed in the 1920's as the first public library. Mrs. Emma Mahelona Wilcox offered $74,000 in February of 1922 for the construction of a permanent library in memory of her husband, Albert Spencer Wilcox. The building, designed by Hart Wood, was dedicated on May 24, 1924. In 1954 work began to create a Kaua'i Museum and it officially opened on December 3, 1960. In 1969 the adjacent Albert Spencer Wilcox Library building became the central building of the Kaua'i Museum Complex. The original museum building was named after William Hyde Rice. The museum offers a combination of permanent and changing exhibits. Enjoy exhibits that tell the story that begins with the island's volcanic

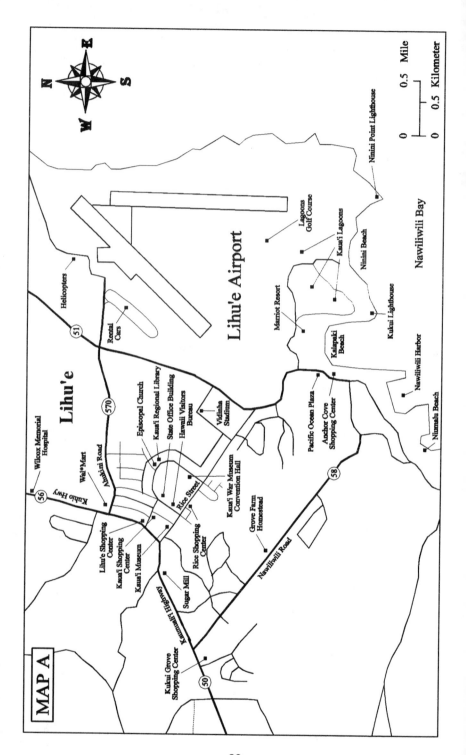

MAP A

Lihu'e

Lihu'e Airport

Nawiliwili Bay

Wilcox Memorial Hospital

Helicopters

Rental Cars

Kuhio Hwy

Wal*Mart

Ahukini Road

Episcopal Church

Kaua'i Regional Library

State Office Building

Hawaii Visitors Bureau

Vidinha Stadium

Lihu'e Shopping Center

Kaua'i Shopping Center

Kaua'i Museum

Rice Street

Rice Shopping Center

Kaua'i War Museum Convention Hall

Grove Farm Homestead

Sugar Mill

Kaumali'i Highway

Kukui Grove Shopping Center

Nawiliwili Road

Pacific Ocean Plaza

Anchor Cove Shopping Center

Marriot Resort

Kalapaki Beach

Kukui Lighthouse

Nawiliwili Harbor

Niumalu Beach

Lagoons Golf Course

Kaua'i Lagoons

Ninini Beach

Ninini Point Lighthouse

0   0.5   Mile

0   0.5   Kilometer

56

51

570

50

58

82

creation while other displays explain the role immigrants have played in creating the multi-cultural community that exists here today. The ancient people and their culture, discovery by Captain Cook, missionary occupation, royal families, and agricultural history are all explored. Their 30 minute aerial film tour of Kaua'i provides a great base for planning your island excursions. Art, music, dance, religion, language, farming, surfing, healing and the move from royalty to statehood are all covered. The Kaua'i Museum has quite possibly the best selection of Hawaiian titles as well as some wonderful handcrafted gift items. There is no admission charge if you wish to visit only the gift store, tell them at the front counter, just advise them at the front counter. The museum is free to all on the first Saturday of each month. They have periodic special presentations and family activities. Open weekdays 9 am - 4:30 pm, Sat. 9 - 1 pm, closed Sun. (808) 245-6931.

If you are hot after a day of sightseeing and shopping, take a short detour to Halo Halo Shave Ice. It is part of *Hamura Saimin* and is just off Rice Street.

Just past the Lihu'e Shopping Center, Rice Street meets the Kuhio Highway. If you turn north onto Hwy. 50 you will find the newest addition to Kaua'i, a branch of the national chain, *Walmart*. This drug and sundry store has most things you might have forgotten to pack. Although we still like the comfortable feeling of a Long's Drug Store, Walmart does have clothes and a larger selection of most items. Hilo Hatties, just up the street, is a mainstay for the traditional aloha wear. In addition to clothing they sell an assortment of candies and giftware items.

Heading south, a short drive will take you to the *Kukui Grove Shopping Center*. This area is known as Puhi and was once a plantation town. This is the largest shopping center and is the location for island's two major department stores, Penney's and Liberty House. There is also a Penthouse outlet which is the discount store for clearance and special order Liberty House merchandise. Pick up a pair of sunglasses for $5 or a pair of sandals on clearance. There are several restaurants and eateries to be found in the mall, but better and more reasonable dining will be found back in the town of Lihu'e. The Kaua'i Products store has a lovely selection of locally made quilts, muumuus, jewelry, lotions, and keiki clothing.

The *Borders Books and Music* by the Kukui Grove Center, next to Kmart, is worth a stop. This is a bookstore chain, but it offers a terrific selection of books, music, and videos as well as the drifting scent of espresso! They offer special events (free!) and their children's corner is a nice touch for the traveling family. 4303 Nawiliwili Rd., Lihu'e, HI 96766. (808) 246-0862.

Across the road from the Kukui Grove Shopping Center, on the same side of the road as Kaua'i Community College, is a viewing area. This is a good location to pull alongside the road and glance at the Hoary Head Mountain Range which appears beyond and behind the Kukui Center. Look closely and you will see the *profile of Queen Victoria*. Her head is slightly tipped back and she has a crown perched on the top of her head. A finger is pointing up as if she is reprimanding someone in the distance beyond. This area is what we would call a suburb of Lihu'e. The town is called Puhi and was once a plantation town. The old plantation store in Puhi stood until it was destroyed in 1991 by the hurricane.

Also on Nawiliwili Rd. is the ***Grove Farm Homestead***. Kaua'i's history can be traced to the beginnings and growth of the sugar plantations. A visit to the Grove Farm Homestead in Lihu'e provides visitors with a fascinating look into the island's past. Grove Farm, one of the earliest sugar plantations, was founded in 1864 by George Wilcox, Gaylord's uncle. Today, this historic museum showcases the old sugar days and Hawai'i's politics from the monarchy to statehood. A two-and-one-half hour tour takes visitors through the original home, which was enlarged in later years to accommodate a growing family. The property, which includes the gracious old Wilcox home and the cottage of the plantation laundress, is situated amidst tropical gardens, orchards and rolling lawns. The tours are small and intimate and the guides knowledgeable about the island's sugar industry and its history. This living legacy was left by Miss Mabel Wilcox, the last surviving niece of George Wilcox, who wanted her family home to be preserved. She lived here until the time of her death in 1978. The property opened to the public in October of 1980. Most visitors miss touring the Grove Farm Homestead because reservations have to be booked weeks in advance. This tour is worth a phone call ahead as you plan your island itinerary. This is quite possibly Kaua'i's best cultural experience. Cost is $5 per person with tours available on Mon., Wed. and Thurs. Reservations are required and can be made up to three months in advance. (808) 245-3202, PO Box 1631, Lihu'e, HI.

Kilohana ★ is reminiscent of the grandeur and elegance of an earlier age. At the time when sugar was king on the island and prosperity reigned, plantation owners would build luxurious homes. One of the grandest on Kaua'i was the home of Gaylord Parke Wilcox and is known as Kilohana. Built in 1935, this 16,000 square foot Tudor mansion was designed by a British architect named Mark Potter. The property was named for the large cinder cone which is located above and behind the property. The grounds are carefully landscaped and inside furniture came from the exclusive and expensive Gump's in San Francisco. In addition to the gift shops, galleries, and Gaylord's Courtyard Restaurant, you'll find several tour options for this 35-acre estate.

The Canefield Tour is a step back into the history of sugarcane on Kaua'i. A wagon ride returns you in time to 1835 with historical background on the property. Our guide, Doug, was interesting and informative and nonplussed by the rain showers as our wagon, drawn by two Clydesdales, navigated through the fields. In 1865 the second sugar plantation, the Lihu'e Plantation, was established along the Wailua River. It was the first to bring immigrant workers and to use stone grinders in the processing of the cane. George Norton Wilcox, the son of island missionaries returned to the island in 1864 following his studies at Scheffield (Yale) in engineering. He purchased 900 acres of wasteland for $10,000. When he broached the subject of irrigation, others thought he was crazy. He proceeded to dig a ditch 11.2 miles in length to bring water from Mt. Wai'ale'ale. The ditch, dug by hand, took two years to complete. His introduction of foreign immigrants from Japan, Philippines, Germany, Australia, and elsewhere began the cultural diversity of the islands of today. George was concerned that most of the workers would chose to return to their homelands following their contract. He approached them inquiring what would entice them to remain. Their answer resulted in Grove Farm providing single family, 300 sq. ft. homes for the workers. These camp houses were designed after those used in logging camps in Oregon and Washington. These camp houses were sent to Hawai'i in ready-to-assemble units.

The only differences between these cabins and those in the Pacific Northwest logging camps were the lanai's which were added to the front and the use of tin for the roofs. Because of the cane burning and risk of flying cinders, a wooden roof would have been a fire hazard. He also introduced chemical fertilization, developed hybrid strains of cane, and when the depression struck the country, George diversified. He died in 1933 at the age of 89 leaving everything to his nephew Gaylord. Gaylord built the 16,000 sq. ft. Kilohana home for his wife Ethel. Gaylord continued management of the company and ensured its continued success to this day. This sugar cane tour takes about an hour, but may not be a lively enough experience to keep the interest of youth. Those interested in a deeper background on the Wilcox family might enjoy the more lengthy tour at the Grove Farm Homestead. The carriage ride is a shorter, more romantic excursion around the grounds. Carriage rides are available Monday to Saturday 11 am - 6:30 pm and Sundays 11 am - 5 pm. Horse dawn Sugar Cane Tours are set up by advance reservations, 246-9529. Admission to Kilohana and its grounds is free, carriage rides are $7 adults/$4 children. Sugar Cane Tours are $18 adults/$10 children. Kilohana and the shops open daily at 9:30 am. Gaylord's serves brunch Saturday and Sunday 9:30 am - 3 pm, lunch Monday to Friday 11 am - 3 pm and dinner from 5 pm. Located just outside Lihu'e, travel east along Kaumualii Highway, Route 50. Kilohana is on your left just before the town of Lihu'e. If you are arriving from the north or east, travel Kuhio Hwy., Route 56 south and west through Lihu'e. Bear right at the traffic light at the end of Kuhio Hwy. Kilohana will be 1.4 miles down Kaumualii Highway on your right. Kilohana (808) 245-5608.

NAWILIWILI

Following Nawiliwili Road past Kukui Grove and the Grove Farm Homestead will take you toward the harbor. The route we will travel is through scenic Lihu'e following Rice Street, Hwy. 51, down past the new Kaua'i Marriott Resort toward the harbor.

HORSE AND CARRIAGE

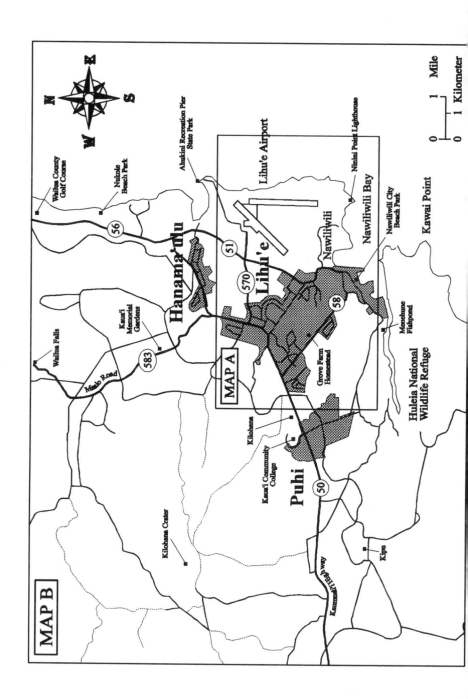

MAP B

MAP A

N
W E
S

Waiha County
Golf Course

Niɡole
Beach Park

Wailua Falls

Kauaʻi
Memorial Gardens

Maalo Road

583

56

Hanamaʻulu

51

570

Lihuʻe

Aliikini Recreation Pier
State Park

Lihuʻe Airport

Nawiliwili

58

Nawiliwili Bay

Ninini Point Lighthouse

Nawiliwili City
Beach Park

Kawai Point

Grove Farm
Homestead

Menehune
Fishpond

Huleia National
Wildlife Refuge

Kilohana

Kauaʻi Community
College

Kilohana Crater

Puhi

50

Kaumualii Highway

Kipu

0   1   Mile
0   1 Kilometer

86

The new *Kaua'i Marriott Resort & Beach Club*, formerly the Westin Maui and prior to that the Kaua'i Surf, opened in the summer of 1995. It is located above the Nawiliwili Harbor at Kalapaki Bay. Following serious damage from Hurricane Iniki, the hotel sat vacant for several years before Marriott chose to take over the property and convert it into a combination timeshare and hotel. They have done major renovations converting the European style of this lavish resort to one with a Hawaiiana atmosphere. The changes have much improved the property and made it more fitting to the style of the islands. This hotel is the tallest building on the island. Following the construction of the Kaua'i Surf Hotel, zoning laws changed building codes so that no building on Kaua'i may be taller than a palm tree.

The Lagoons suffered far less damage than the Westin Kaua'i. Former employees of the Lagoons joined forces to reopen and continue operations. South Sea Tours continues to offer hourly tours of the 40 acres of waterways at *Kaua'i Lagoons* aboard Italian crafted motor launches. The captain gives an interesting narration of the many exotic animals, from kangaroos to monkeys, that inhabit the different man-made islands. Cost of the tour is $12 adults, $6 children 12 and under. Wedding services are available on the grounds or in their romantic gazebo.

Moving back down toward the Nawiliwili Harbor, you will pass the Anchor Cove Shopping Center and the Pacific Ocean Plaza. The Pacific Ocean Plaza has several boutiques along with the Cafe Portofino Restaurant, Tokyo Lobby and Kaua'i Chop Suey. At Anchor Cove you will find a Crazy Shirts outlet, a Wyland Gallery, and J.J.'s Broiler.

Nawiliwili was named for the abundant wiliwili trees that once thrived in this area. Nawiliwili Harbor became Kaua'i's main deep water harbor upon its completion in 1930. Following the completion of the harbor, Lihu'e became the island's major city. The Nawiliwili Beach Park was refurbished early in 1995. A cement foundation destroyed by Hurricane Iniki was removed and play areas, barbecues and picnic tables were added. If you have some recreational time to take out from your island tour, consider stopping by the kayak rental at Nawiliwili's small boat harbor which offers half day trips up the river past the Menehune Fish Ponds. (Refer to recreation chapter for specifics.)

The *Menehune Fish Pond* is another spot you may easily miss. Follow Highway 51 toward the Nawiliwili Harbor and look for the Wilcox Rd sign. Follow it left onto Niumalu Road. Then turn right onto Hulemalu Road where a sign (the last time we checked) indicated the Menehune Fish Ponds. From this turn-off it is another 6/10 of a mile to the lookout which will be on your left. The fish ponds appear to be just a small pond adjacent to the Huleia River (or Huleia Stream, depending on the map you follow). Portions of Raiders of the Lost Ark were filmed along this waterway. Again, no historical background exists about the building of this pond, but legend tells that it was done by the menehunes who were interrupted during their nighttime work and quit, leaving the pond unfinished with pukas (holes) in it! Some years ago a family tried to rebuild the gates to make the fish pond once again a working proposition, but plans or events changed and it was never made operational. The only way to see this up close is to do it by kayak along the Huleia River. Tours up the river are available from a company called Kaua'i by Kayak which begin near the Nawiliwili small boat harbor.

The access road to the pond is posted as No Trespassing and while that doesn't stop some people from venturing beyond, we prefer to let the property owners maintain their legal rights.

Located along the Huleia River is the ***Huleia National Wildlife Refuge***, which is home to the endangered koloa duck. In 1973, 241 acres were purchased to provide a habitat for water birds. The lands, once taro and rice fields, are now breeding and feeding grounds for a variety of waterfowl. The refuge is located in a relatively flat valley along the Huleia River which is bordered by a steep wooded hillside. There are 31 species of migratory birds which inhabit the area, 18 of which were introduced. A special permit is issued annually to a commercial kayaking business for access through an upland portion of the refuge. The refuge is adjacent to the Menehune Fish Ponds is not open to the public. However, a view of it from the Menehune overlook along the road is possible. Continue exploring the roads beyond the Menehune Ponds. There are some nice vistas of the Huleia Wildlife Refuge and we found a little fruit stand that had piles of papaya. The papayas were each labeled with a black marker indicating the price. We picked out the one, dropped the money in the can, and were on our way. Oh wondrous Kaua'i!

WHERE TO SHOP

Anchor Cove and Pacific Ocean Plaza are visitor-oriented shopping areas located within blocks of each other on Rice Street as you head towards Nawiliwili.

If you plan to be on Kaua'i for a while, especially if you are staying in a condo and plan to make some of your own meals, check out the Holsum/Orowheat Thrift Store at 4302A Rice Street (at the corner of Rice and Hardy) for great bargains on bread and packaged baked goods. (People always ask how people can afford to live in Hawai'i when groceries are so expensive. This is one of the ways!) They are open Monday - Saturday from 8 am - 4 pm. Try to go on a Wednesday when day-old products (or those nearing their expiration date) are further discounted for mo' bettah bread bargains. Call 245-8983. There is also a Loves Bakery at 4100 Rice St. with discounted bread and specials for seniors on Tuesdays and Fridays. Open 9 am - 4:30 pm and Sunday 9 am - 2 pm.

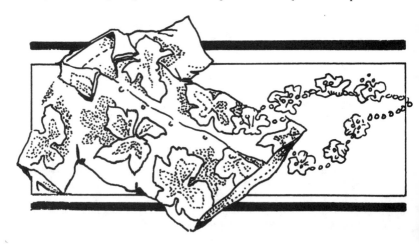

Just south on Highway 50 is the ***Kukui Grove Shopping Center***. Located at 3-2600 Kaumualii Highway, it is the largest shopping center on Kaua'i. This mall offers Liberty House, J.C. Penney's, Woolworth's (a must stop for sundry items and souvenirs as well), Long's Drug Store (a great place to pick up souvenir items), Sears, Kmart, a Borders Bookstore (to pick up that favorite paperback for the beach) and some small specialty shops and restaurants. For the young at heart there is the Fun Factory (a game arcade), Wally's World Miniature Golf, as well as a double screen cinema.

Following Hwy. 583 toward Kapa'a you pass the ***Kapai'a Stitchery***, just before it meets with Highway 56. This shop will be of interest to anyone who enjoys sewing, especially quilters. They have a large selection of brightly colored fabrics, Hawaiian quilt squares and supplies, plus a variety of craft items. Needlepoint fanciers will appreciate the beautiful hand-painted canvases of local settings. The store is open 10:00 am to 4:30 pm Monday through Saturday.

Just beyond Kapai'a Stitchery there is a fork in the road. A sign indicates the direction onto Ma'alo Road, also labeled Hwy. 583. This is a rather narrow, rutted road that winds through cane fields. At slightly more than three miles from the turn-off onto Ma'alo Road you will arrive at ***Wailua Falls***. There is parking where the road dead ends. A picturesque camera shot can be taken at this vista. There is a path which leads down to the base of the falls. The trail is dangerous, steep and slippery. Many have been seriously or fatally injured and we suggest you enjoy the falls from the lookout above. Wailua, whose name means "two waters," was once actually two rivers which have merged into one. The river below is the largest navigable river on the island of Kaua'i and should definitely be explored during your Kaua'i stay.

Retrace your route back down to Highway 56 and continue northward. At mile marker #2 along Highway 56 you will be in ***Hanamalulu*** where you'll find the Planters Restaurant, Hanamalulu Restaurant and the Shell Gas Station which usually has gas at a few cents less per gallon than anywhere else on the island. Back in 1875, Hanamalulu was a plantation camp. Cane was transported by oxen to Lihu'e until a mill was built in town, and it continued to operate until 1918.

The ***Kaua'i Fruit and Flower Market*** on the makai side of the road has a spot for shooting your own photo with a human size pineapple.

The ***Outrigger Hotel*** just beyond has several popular evening activities including free movies and a comedy club. Near mile marker #4 is the Wailua Golf Course. Green fees on this municipal course are $25 weekdays and $35 weekends for eighteen holes of play.

The golf course runs into the ***Lydgate Park*** area where you will find the Kaua'i Resort and the Aston Kaua'i Beach Villas. This is one of the island's safest beaches with two pools made of lava rock. One very shallow, the other slightly deeper. There is also a lifeguard on duty. The fish are able to swim into the pools and are very tame. You might like to pick up a bag of fish food at one of the dive shops, or check Safeway. This is a great place to give those want-to-be snorkelers a chance to try out this sport. The Kamalani Playground was recently completed and is a terrific spot to let the kids burn off those extra calories.

WAILUA

This area is a three-mile length along the Kuhio Highway. This region was of special religious importance to the kahunas and ali'is of ancient times. In fact, it is considered to be one of the two most sacred spots in all of the Hawaiian Islands. The *Wailua River* cuts back into a verdant valley with many splendors to be shared. The name Wailua means "two waters" as the Wailua River was originally two rivers.

A river cruise up to *Fern Grotto* is an excellent way to learn how Hawaiian royalty lived. The river and its surrounding land were once part of the royal grounds. Boat cruises run upriver daily to this natural rock cavern filled with maidenhair ferns. Boats depart every half hour from 9:30 am to 4:00 pm. Smith's boats have musical entertainment on board. With a $10 charge, it is certainly a pleasantly affordable way to spend an hour and a half. The Fern Grotto gift shop was one of the few places we found that had authentic Hawaiian plant starts packaged to pass through customs.

You may wish to rent a one or two person kayak at the mouth of the Wailua to enjoy this lovely river at your own speed.

The 30-acre *Smith's Botanical Gardens* is situated alongside the Wailua River and provides a wonderful opportunity to learn the names of the island's flowering trees and plants. Peacocks, ducks, colorful bantam roosters, and other birds inhabit the gardens too. Bird food is available, and carrying a sackful is almost certain to attract an entourage. Smith's meandering pathways will take you onto a Japanese island, through a sweet-smelling hibiscus garden, into a bamboo forest, and past a variety of fruit and nut trees. Along the way you'll see a replica of an Easter Island statue and grass huts representing several island cultures. The gardens are fairly empty in the mornings; they open at 8:30 am and close at 4 pm. A luau is held here Monday through Friday evenings.

The *Coco Palms* had a free historical visitor center on their property prior to Iniki. It is hoped that if and when this property is renovated and reopened, the museum will be reopened as well. This area of palms was once the dream of a German plantation owner who, in the early 1800's, hoped to raise coconuts and sell copra, or dried coconut meat, to the mainland. From the copra, coconut oil can be made. His dreams were dashed but the tall and elegant trees remain. The future of the Coco Palms resort is not yet known. As it has been sitting idle for several years following the hurricane, the possibility of restoring the original structures becomes more and more bleak. Due to new zoning codes, the old structures would have to have such major renovations, such as new sprinkler systems, that it may not be feasible to ever restore this landmark. Sadie Thompson was filmed here and the scene where Tatoo on Fantasy Island goes flying by in the jeep was also filmed in this coconut grove. Should you see the ghost of Elvis around, it is because he was also here during a portion of his filming of the movie Blue Hawai'i.

Turn at the Coco Palms onto Kaumo'o Road for a short, but interesting, detour. Where the *Wailua River* meets the sea, was in ancient times the place where Kings were born. Located along the Wailua River and following up toward Mount

Wai'ale'ale are a series of seven heiaus. Located on a part of Lydgate State Park is the *Hauola O' Honaunau,* or *Temple of Refuge.* The refuge and the Hikina Heiau are distinguished by a low wall which encircles them. It was at this site that kapu breakers were sent to atone for their deeds. Following this punishment, they could then return forgiven. Six of these religious sites are located within a mile of the mouth of the Wailua River. Some are easily spotted, while one is more difficult to view since it is located in an abandoned sugar cane field. The Malae Heiau is located in the corner of a canefield on the left side of the road just prior to the Wailua Bridge. It is somewhat hidden by a clump of trees and so over-grown that exploring it is nearly impossible. This is the largest heiau on the island, measuring 273 feet x 324 feet.

At 2/10 of a mile past the Coco Palms is a heiau that is actually mislabeled and information in publications has continued the erroneous details. Don and Bea Donohugh, authors of the first three editions of this Paradise Guide, enlisted an archeologist to visit the site to confirm their suspicions. The archeologist verified that the site marked as the Holoholoku heiau was actually the location of an old pig pen. The heiau itself no longer exists, but its location would have been at the cemetery located on the top of the hill. Some books on Kaua'i say that the heiau was converted to a pig pen, but this would seem inaccurate given the archeological investigation.

If a kapu (a rule or law) was broken, the penalties were stiff. Often death was the penalty for just having your shadow cast on an ali'i. However if you could reach a special heiau, like the Holoholoku, it would be a place of refuge and you could return forgiven. Behind the pig pen is the birthing stone, the spot where royalty were born. The early Hawaiians tried to improve their royal line and it was not uncommon for a brother to marry a sister. As the years progressed, due to diseases and other causes, the numbers of ali'i diminished. A common woman could be chosen to give birth at this special and sacred site and her child would then become an ali'i.

2.7 miles on the left is the *Wailua River State Park* and the *Poli'ahu Heiau.* An interpretive center along the scenic bluff explains the importance of the Wailua River Valley to the Hawaiians in earlier times. Wailua was a center for the Hawaiian ali'i (royalty) and kahuna (priests). The fertile valley soil and plentiful supply of fresh water were ideal for supporting the large Hawaiian population which once inhabited this region. Adjoining the overlook is the Poli'ahu Heiau. The stones were brought from the bluffs to build this religious site which was used for ceremonies until the traditional ways were abolished in 1819. This is named after Poliahu, the goddess of snow and a sister to Pele. This is also believed to be a luakini heiau, which means a place of human sacrifice. An undesirable person was preferably: a prisoner of war, a person who had broken a kapu or sometimes a slave, but never a woman. They were generally killed in their sleep and then placed as an offering upon the altar. A large enclosure of black lava rock can be viewed which had been the personal temple of Kaua'i's last king, Kaumuali'i. This temple was reportedly built by the menehune. You will see a dirt road just before the interpretive center. While very unimproved and rutted, the road is marked by a sign indicating the way to the *Bell Stone.* You will find two large rocks which appear to be a gateway. By following the path to the end you will be treated to another lovely view of the Wailua Valley. You will have to experiment to discover which of these stones made a resonant sound when struck. At the birth of a royal child, the stone was pounded to signal the arrival of a new member of the ali'i.

Just beyond at 2.8 miles is the *Opaeka'a Falls* lookout on the right of the road and the Wailua River lookout on the left. Both are easily accessible and there is a paved parking lot with restrooms. The Opaeka'a Falls lookout affords a wonderful opportunity to see this 40 foot waterfall. This lovely waterfall has multiple cascades and flows year round. After walking the viewpoint trail, you can cross the highway for a view of the Wailua River and the Kamokila Hawaiian Village.

The family-owned and operated business, *Kamokila Hawaiian Village*, in Wailua, sustained serious damage from Hurricane Iniki. They have been busy recreating the original site of Kamokila and you can visit ruins and petroglyphs. Nineteen huts were destroyed and they have been rebuilt. All are different and each has a different cultural significance. For instance, there are the medicine huts, assistant chief's, canoe, etc. Visitors can watch them make poi or try samples, make haku leis and watch salt making (like that done at the salt ponds.) The taro fields have been refurbished and there are fifteen peacocks on the grounds along with a new road to the village and a boat shuttle. Located opposite Opaeka'a Falls, the Kaumo'o Road entrance is just past the Wailua Bridge. Admission is $5 adults, $3 children.

WAIPOULI

The Waipouli area of Kaua'i offers some excellent hiking opportunities. A section on hiking from Craig Chisholm's *Kaua'i Hiking Trails* is included under hiking in the recreation chapter of this guide.

The lush tropical region of this area is synonymous with Kaua'i. As a backdrop for this region is *Sleeping Giant Mountain*. In her book, *Legends of Old Hawai'i*, Betty Allen retells the legend of the Sleeping Giant. To summarize it, this tale began long ago in Kapa'a where a fisherman and his wife lived. This fisherman always caught the largest of fish and one day when he pulled in his net he found the biggest fish he had ever caught. When the fish began to cry he realized it was no ordinary fish, but an akua (good or evil spirit) and took it home to his wife. The only thing that kept the fish from crying was when they fed him poi. His appetite was enormous, so people from all around came to feed him. The fish then transformed into a young giant that grew larger and larger as they continued to feed him poi and sweet potatoes. He grew so large that he could no longer walk and he lay down. They sent for a kahuna who told them that they needed to sing to the giant, but he would not reveal which song should be sung. The villagers began to sing to the giant, but to no avail. A small girl named Pua-nai was nearby looking at the rocks on the ground. Suddenly she began to sing a song she had never heard before and the giant miraculously changed to stone. They say that the giant sleeps yet today.

Continuing up Kamao'o Road 4.8 miles, you will pass an Agricultural Research Station. Continue on to the Wailua Reservoir which is one of several fresh water fishing areas on Kaua'i. Several hiking trails have their trail heads in this area.

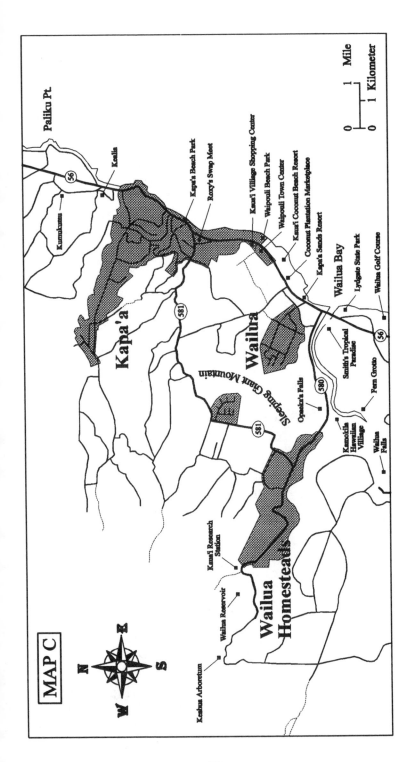

MAP C

Paliku Pt

Keālia

Kumukumu

56

581

Kapa'a

Kapa'a Beach Park
Roxy's Swap Meet

Kaua'i Village Shopping Center
Waipouli Beach Park
Waipouli Town Center
Kaua'i Coconut Beach Resort
Coconut Plantation Marketplace
Kapa'a Sands Resort

Wailua Bay

Lydgate State Park
Wailua Golf Course

Wailua

Sleeping Giant Mountain

Opaeka'a Falls

580

Smith's Tropical Paradise

Fern Grotto

56

Kamokila Hawaiian Village

Wailua Falls

581

Kaua'i Research Station

Wailua Homesteads

Wailua Reservoir

Keahua Arboretum

N W S E

0   1   Mile
0   1 Kilometer

At 5.45 miles you will enter the Hawaii State Forest Reserve. If you plan a day of hiking, the location of the **Kuilau Ridge Trail** head is at 5.5 miles and just beyond is the **Keahua Arboretum**. The Arboretum has suffered from hurricanes and neglect, but still offers a quiet retreat for a picnic. Several streams cross the road from here on in and, depending on the waterflow and your rental car, you may choose not to proceed further.

As you retrace your path down the road look off to the left side, just beyond the Agricultural Research Station, for a small pull out. A view of the reservoir with Sleeping Giant Mountain behind is a fine reward.

Back down to the Highway and the Coco Palms Resort, reset your odometer at zero and continue northward. Another 6/10 of a mile and you will pass the largest shopping center on the east coast of Kaua'i.

The **Coconut Marketplace** has something for everyone. Located between the Wailua River and Kapa'a, it is open daily from 9 am - 9 pm. Phone (808) 822-3641. This is one shopping center the kids may enjoy more than most with shops such as Kaua'i Magic, High As A Kite, the Gecko Store, Crazy Shirts and plenty of inexpensive eateries. A selection of jewelry and art galleries as well as a two-screen movie theater are also found here. The photo stand out on the highway side of the center has several "theatrical sets" that could make any lady appear to be swooning in the arms of Tom Selleck. Or perhaps you would prefer to show folks back home a photo of yourself parading a huge marlin that you (apparently) just caught or riding that big tube wave. A single polaroid runs $8, photo postcards run 5 for $17. Other packages also available. Two of the more interesting shops are operated by Patrick and Mary Dunn. Their Parrot Walk shop is a bird store and you can pay for a handful of feed to share with some of the colorful parrots and macaws. Their other shop, Collectors Corner, specializes in Hawaiiana articles from decades ago. Old ukeles, Aloha shirts, Hawaiian ceramics and prints make interesting perusing. New items included Hawaiian rubber stamps, seashells and gift items as well. A free hula show is featured Mondays, Wednesday, Fridays and Saturdays at 4:30 pm. The restaurants remain open after the shops close.

PARROTS

At 1.3 miles past the Coco Palms begins the row of strip malls that line the highway between Wailua and Kapa'a. The first is the ***Waipouli Town Center***, not to be confused with the other two "Waipouli" malls. Here you will find Foodland Market as the center of interest, and there is also a Fun Factory (video arcade), Block Buster (video rentals) and the popular Waipouli Restaurant. The neighboring McDonald's and a small stream divides this center from the next.

Kaua'i Village in Kapa'a, is an eight-acre shopping center featuring over 30 stores and restaurants. Tenants include Long's Drug Store, Waldenbooks, Crazy Shirts, and a variety of locally owned boutiques, jewelry stores, gift shops and other businesses. The restaurants at Kaua'i Village range from fast food to fine dining including A Pacific Cafe. The shopping village is distinguished by its turn-of-the century plantation architectural design, landmark three-story clock tower, garden courtyard, and two Whaling Wall murals by internationally-known environmental artist Wyland. The courtyard features a garden of indigenous Hawaiian plants labeled with names and historical information. There is plenty of room in the open air courtyard graced with a ten foot waterfall and a series of landscaped ponds and streams to relax while other members of your group are off shopping. The village also has a Hawaiian Garden with indigenous (without human aid) and endemic (found only in Hawaii) plants growing with plaques which label them.

Only 1/10 mile ahead is the next in a string of malls and mini-malls. ***Waipouli Plaza*** is the location of King & I and Dragon Inn restaurant. ***Waipouli Complex*** is another 2/10 of a mile and is the location for the Aloha Diner and the K.C.L. Barbecue Drive Inn restaurants. This is the last mall before the town of Kapa'a.

KAPA'A

Kapa'a was a center for rice cultivation until sugar cane replaced it as the major agricultural industry in the 1920's. Life went along peacefully for this quiet town on Kaua'i's western shore until tourism discovered Kapa'a in the 1970's.

The ***Hongwanji Temple*** is located across the street from the Big Save Market. Behind it is a Salvation Army Thrift Store, where the adventurous can try their luck. A little further, turning onto Waikomo Road, is the Jodo Mission.

There are several roads which travel into the island to follow and/or cross the Kapa'a Stream and lead to Ho'opi'i Falls. Along Hwy. 56, Kawaihau Road is the first option. Follow this road which then intersects with Hauaala Rd. Just outside of Kapa'a, turn onto Mailihuna Road, which also connects with Hauaala Road. Hauaala Road meets Kealia Road and if you follow it northeast you will reach the Kaneha Reservoir.

WHERE TO SHOP

As you leave the malls, you enter the town of Kapa'a. A small town gone tourist, it is still a very pleasant place to dine or shop. Roxy's Swap Meet is held on Saturdays. Look for the tents, and depending on the season, this swap meet can be just a booth or two or quite a few sellers of tourist wares. Sometimes you can pick up good deals on tee-shirts and jewelry.

Bo Ku Ma Rue, next to Michelle's Cafe in Kapa'a town, has some interesting gauze clothing, dresses and coverups. Because many of the styles are one-size-fits -all, the prices are very reasonable.

BEST BETS

Garden Island Inn - convenient and inexpensive. *Outrigger Kaua'i Beach Hotel* and *Aston Kaua'i Beach Villas* - resort surroundings and amenities in a separate coastal area, yet close to the airport and downtown Lihu'e. *The Kaua'i Coconut Beach* - this may be the best travel bargain with the use of an Entertainment discount card. The *Kaua'i Marriott Resort & Beach Club* - a little more expensive, but a lovely and luxurious atmosphere. *Bed & Breakfast* - Try Rosewood B&B - it is simply wonderful!

BED AND BREAKFASTS

ALOHILANI BED AND BREAKFAST INN
1470 Wanaao Rd., Kapa'a, HI 96746 (808) 823-0128 or 1-800-533-9316. Hosts Sharon Mitchell and William Whitney offer their home which takes its name from the Hawaiian words meaning "Bright Sky." Located above Kapa'a town, their rates include breakfast of fresh squeezed juices, tropical fruits, and home baked breakfast breads and muffins. Their Guest Suite has a fully equipped kitchen and is set apart among the trees. Rates are $95 per night, $595 weekly, for two. Their Guest Suite has ocean and mountain views, a king-size bed and a living room area with sleeper sofa at $85 per night, $535 weekly. Their Pa'ana a ka la (Sunshine Atrium) has wide French glass doors which open onto a lanai with a valley view. A queen size bed and a sleeper sofa are included along with a small refrigerator and microwave. *$85 per night, $535 weekly.*

CANDY'S CABIN
5940 Ohe St., Kapa'a, HI 96746. (808) 822-5451. Located in the Wailua Homesteads. A studio apartment with a king-size bed, living area, private bath, lanai and refrigerator. Very roomy and adequate for a family. If you choose breakfast, you'll find some home baked goodies. Stroll around the grounds and visit the family of mallard ducks that visit from the nearby stream. Located 15 minutes from the Lihu'e airport. *Rates for two vary, but run $65 per night for two with breakfast, $60 per night without. Each additional adult is $10, discounts for stays of 5 nights or longer. No minimum stay.*

HALE KAHAWAI BED & BREAKFAST
185 Kahawai Place, Kapa'a, HI 96746. (808) 822-1031, FAX (808) 823-8220. Four rooms from which to select include a daily tropical breakfast. This B & B is located on Kuamo'o Ridge overlooking the Wailua River Gorge. A guest lounge is equipped with a 35" screen stereo cable TV. Your host at Hale Kahawai is Gary Gordon. Three night minimum stay. Visa and Mastercard accepted. *Room rates for a private apartment run $60-90 single, $70-90 double occupancy.*

HOUSE OF ALEVA
5509 Kuamoo Rd., Kapa'a, HI 96746. (808) 822-4606. They offer two upstairs rooms with a bath to share. A single room downstairs has a private bath. *$55 per night per couple, $40 per night single.*

KAKALINA'S B & B

6781 Kawaihau Rd., Kapa'a, HI 96746. (808) 822-2328, FAX (808) 823-6833. Located on a three-acre tropical flower farm in the foothills of Mt. Wai'ale'ale. Their Hale 'Akahi unit is two rooms on the ground floor with a private entrance featuring king-size beds, shower, deep bath for soaking, and kitchenette. The Hale 'Elua unit is a ground floor studio with queen size bed, ceiling fan and private bathroom with shower and full-size kitchen. Each unit has color TV, microwave oven, refrigerator and laundry facilities.

Room rates run $70-75 with discounts for weekly stays.

KAY BARKER'S BED & BREAKFAST

PO Box 740, Kapa'a, HI 96746. (808) 822-3073. 1-800-835-2845. Visa and Mastercard are accepted. Located in Wailua Homesteads, this B & B began in 1983. Kay's son, Gordon, now takes charge of the business. Four separate rooms, each with a private bath. A two-room cottage suite is also available. All rooms have ceiling fans. Mornings begin with a continental breakfast. Beach towels, beach mats, ice chests and boogie boards are available for use. Smoking acceptable. Gordon not only bakes, but he'll even be happy to assist by washing clothes. Local calls are free. It is a large house with many original paintings. The view is wonderful, very pastoral with meadows and horses. The long, large living room and lounge offers guests the use of two televisions. The rooms and separate cottages are homey, and the environment feels like that of a friend.

Single occupancy $35-$60, double occupancy $45-70. A 15% discount for stays over 6 days.

KEAPANA CENTER

5620 Keapana Rd., Kapa'a, HI 96746. (808) 822-7968, 1-800-822-7968. Located on six acres. Rates include continental breakfast use of jacuzzis. They also offer space for small group retreats. The "yurt" is a 24' round structure that can accommodate 3 persons. There is a limit of 12 persons in the house.

Room with shared bath $55 double, $40 single; room with private bath $70 double, $55 single.Exclusive use of the house accommodations, 5 BR without breakfast is $300 per night, an extra $60 per night for the yurt.

LAMPY'S BED & BREAKFAST

6078 Kolopua Street, Kapa'a, HI 96746. Phone or FAX (808) 822-0478. Located 5 minutes from Wailua Bay. Each of three bedrooms are furnished with country decor and offers a private entrance and private bath. Tom and Lampy Lowy retired to Kaua'i in 1987 after 30 years as residents in Las Vegas, Nevada. After the decision was made to build a wing on their home for a B & B they opened in March of 1989. While Lampy's suffered moderate damage from Hurricane Iniki, they were still able to house 14 neighbors whose homes were uninhabitable following the hurricane. GTE Hawaiian Telephone crews were housed in the Lowy's home for several months during the post-Iniki reconstruction.

Single rates are $50 nightly - double rates $55 nightly. Extra persons $10 additional and weekly rates are available.

MOHALA KE OLA

5663 Ohelo Rd., Kapa'a, HI 96746. Phone or FAX (808) 823-6398. A "Bed & Breakfast Retreat" you can choose between the Kamaaina room $50; Garden patio room $70; or the pool view room $85. 10% discount for 7 days or longer. Mohala Ke Ola offers a pool and jacuzzi, private bathrooms and a private entrance. Extended patio offers a spectacular view of Opaeka'a Falls and canyon. Quiet and peaceful surroundings, but congenial and friendly atmosphere. Host Ed Stumpf will great you at the airport or assist if you need some shopping help. He also speaks fluent Japanese and is very knowledgeable about sightseeing and activities. Arrangements for shiatsu, acupuncture, lomi-lomi massage or reiki is available.

ROSEWOOD BED & BREAKFAST ★

872 Kamalu Rd., Kapa'a, HI 96746. (808) 822-5216, FAX (808) 822-5478. This home, located in Wailua Homesteads, was formerly an old Macadamia Nut Plantation Home. The area is rural with rolling pastures with grazing cattle framed by a wide mountain range with Mt. Wai'ale'ale in the center. After a nighttime shower, many waterfalls are visible with vivid rainbows.

Since they moved to the islands 17 years ago, Rosemary and Norbert Smith have been restoring their home. A second cottage with two bedrooms, designed after the main house is called the "Victorian Cottage." A smaller one is designed with an Hawaiian look is called the "Thatched" and a third option is their "Bunkhouse" which has proven popular with European visitors and hikers. The one-acre grounds include two ponds with small waterfalls, and lots of fruit and flowering trees and bushes. "Thatched" is a one bedroom cottage with a king-size bed, screened lanai, kitchenette with hot plate, microwave and small refrigerator. The toilet and sink are indoors, but the hot/cold shower sits outside enclosed in the garden and surrounded by native plants. The "Victorian Cottage" offers two bedrooms and one bath, also an outdoor hot/cold shower. The master bedroom is downstairs with a Queen bed, upstairs is a loft bedroom with two twin beds. A sofa opens into a sleeper bed. The kitchen is full sized and includes a dishwasher, and a washer/dryer. The unit has a television and telephone with fax. The two "traditional" units in the main house each have a private bath. They have a king bed, which can be converted to two twins. Breakfast is left in the cottages, and for main house guests is served in the kitchen. The bunkhouse has three separate rooms and a shared outside shower. Each room has its own sink, toaster, coffee maker and small refrigerator. The larger room offers a microwave. Bunkhouse #1 has twin bunk beds, Bunkhouse #2 has a sofa bed that opens to a queen plus a queen bed in the loft. Bunkhouse #3 consists of a Queen bed in the loft. None of the bunkhouse units include breakfast or maid service. Breakfast may be provided for an additional $5 per day per person. All units are non-smoking. Conveniently located just four miles to beaches, shopping and restaurants.

Victorian $115; Thatched $85; Traditional $65; Bunkhouse #1 and #3 $40 per day; Bunkhouse #2 $50 per day.

WAILUA COUNTRY BED & BREAKFAST

505 Kamalu Road, Kapa'a, HI 96746. (808) 822-0166, FAX (808) 822-2708. Located on the east coast of Kaua'i behind Sleeping Giant Mountain. All units have ceiling fans and separate bathrooms. Cottages and studios have kitchens or

kitchenettes. Main residence suite offers king-size bed, TV, refrigerator, micro-wave, sitting and dining area, and private bath with jacuzzi. $50 single or double. Private apartment with queen size bed, sleeping couch, full kitchen and bath. $70 single or double, children ten or under add $10 per night. Studio apartment includes a queen size bed, day bed, private bath and mini kitchen. $60 single or double, children under ten $10 per night. Two bedroom cottage includes one queen and one full bed, as well as one bath, a full kitchen, dining room and a living area that has sleeping sofa for a small child. *Double $80 night, 3-4 persons add $25 per night. Breakfast is served upon request for an extra charge.*

BUDGET

HALE LIHU'E MOTEL
2931 Kalena St., Lihu'e, HI 96766. (808) 245-3141/245-2751. Twenty two one-bedroom units, some with kitchenettes and air conditioning. Inexpensive and spartan two-story, frame building located near the main business area of down-town Lihu'e. Walking distance to local restaurants, government offices, churches and banks. Rates including tax are the cheapest in an already inexpensive area. A little unkempt and rundown, and not really what you'd envision paradise to be.

Single, double or triple occupancy $22.80/$26.00/$31.20; with kitchenette and air conditioning single $31.20, double $41.60. Weekly and monthly discounts available.

KAUA'I INTERNATIONAL HOSTEL
4532 Lehua St., Kapa'a, HI 96746. 1-800-858-2295. The hostel has forty beds, full kitchen facilities, baths and showers. One week maximum stay. No alcohol allowed. Daily hikes and excursions for $10 per person explore waterfalls, beaches and off-the-beaten-trek places. Located in the heart of Kapa'a across the street from the beach and park. Private rooms available. *$15 per night plus tax.*

MOTEL LANI
4240 Rice St. (PO Box 1836) Lihu'e, HI 96766. (808) 245-2965. At the corner of Rice and Hardy, the center of the Lihu'e business district. Then have ten units, each with shower and one double or two twin beds. Wall fans, no air condition-ing. Like Hale Lihu'e, inexpensive and very basic: "A place to sleep," *Rates are $30-48 per night, two night minimum.*

INEXPENSIVE

BANYAN HARBOR CONDOMINIUMS
3411 Wilcox Road, Lihu'e, HI 96766. 1-800-422-6926 or (808) 245-7333. Located in the Kalapaki Bay area. RENTAL AGENT: Prosser Realty 1-800-767-4707. 149 units on a hilltop location near Kalapaki Beach, some have a view of the Nawiliwili Harbor. Pool, shuffle board and tennis court. Shops and restaurants nearby. Telephones in all units. Newly (1995) renovated exterior face lift. Two bedroom units all with TV, telephones and washer/dryers. A good value. *Rates from Prosser Realty are slightly lower than through the front desk: 2 BR 2 BTH $75. Front desk g.v. $95-105; o.v. $105-116.*

GARDEN ISLAND INN

Located in Nawiliwili. 3445 Wilcox Rd., Lihu'e, HI 96766. 1-800-648-0154 or (808) 245-7227. Recently renovated 21-room hotel with tropical decor and a cheery cottage-feel to each of the rooms. Wilcox Road has been closed to through-traffic so the property is now on a quieter cul-de-sac (though there is still a lot of activity during the day). Owners Steve and Susan Layne live on the property and will be happy to help you with sightseeing recommendations. They'll also provide golf clubs, camping and beach equipment and you can help yourself to bananas and tangelos from the trees on the property. A short walk to the Kaua'i Marriott, Kalapaki Beach and Anchor Cove Shopping Center (with J.J.'s Broiler)and just across the road to Nawiliwili Beach Park. All rooms have refrigerators, wet bars, TV, microwaves and coffeemakers. Studio and one-bedroom suites on the third floor. Comfortable, friendly and cheap, too!

Std. $55, std. w/ balcony & o.v. $65; 1 BR suites $75-85.

HOTEL CORAL REEF

1516 Kuhio Hwy., Kapa'a, HI 96746. 1-800-843-4659, (808) 822-4481. The main building opened early in 1995 following restoration as a result of Hurricane Iniki. Ground floor rooms are tiled, upstairs rooms are carpeted. Good, clean rooms with limited views. The oceanfront building offers beach views and is equipped with refrigerators and a choice of single or double beds. Beachfront is not suitable for swimming. Pay telephone and television in lobby. Daily maid service. Grocery store and restaurants nearby. Located within walking distance of a public swimming pool. Room and car packages available.

Main building o.v. and g.v. rooms range from $45-70; two m.v. suites $70-85. Senior citizen discounts available. Oceanfront building $80 single or double occupancy, $10 each additional person.

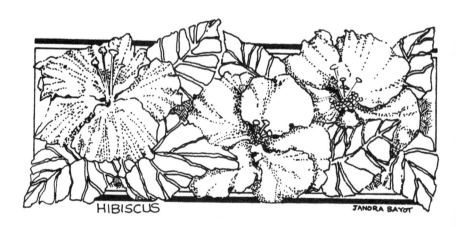

HIBISCUS   JANORA BAYOT

KAUA'I COCONUT BEACH (HOTEL) ★

PO Box 830, Kapa'a, HI 96746. (808) 822-3455; FAX (808) 822-1830. 1-800-22-
ALOHA. This is a Hawaiian Hotels & Resorts Property, also known as Pleasant
Hawaiian Holidays. Located on 10.5 acres at Waipouli Beach. The resort was built
in 1978, Ed & Lynn Hogan purchased the property in 1985, ITT Sheraton
continued to manage it until January 1992. Renovated and rededicated in January
1995, the redecoration project included new hand-carved custom furniture for
many of the resort's 311 rooms. The rooms are in pastels and reflect the plantation era. One hundred of the economy rooms also sport new bath fixtures,
wallpaper, carpeting, new televisions and fresh paint. The resort features a
swimming pool/jacuzzi, three tennis courts, coin laundry and a restaurant on the
property. Rooms feature lanai, refrigerator, coffeemakers with free coffee, air
conditioning, and a handicapped room is also available. Demonstrations of
Hawaiian crafts are given daily and a nightly traditional torch-lighting ceremony
is performed. There is a complimentary summer children's program. On the down
side, the parking area, while large, can be very crowded and make finding a spot
a little difficult at times. The hallways have poor lighting, making them very dark.
The proximity to nearby Kaua'i Shopping Village (with a Safeway) and just a few
blocks to the Coconut Marketplace make it ideally situated. Children under age
17 may stay free in rooms with their parents when using existing bedding. All in
all a good value, especially if they continue to maintain the quality of their rooms
and grounds. Be sure to check the Entertainment book for half price coupons on
your stay. The discount makes this a recommended accommodation! A buffet
breakfast is served at their Voyage Room Restaurant and is included with some
of their room packages. The restaurant also serves a la carte and buffet lunches.
Dinner is served at the Flying Lobster Restaurant. Nightly entertainment is at
Cook's Landing Lounge. Their twice weekly luau and Hawaiian revue received
the Hawai'i Visitors Bureau Kahili Award.

*Hawaiian Holidays now offers separate land/car packages as well as air/land/car
alternatives. Rooms with a car and complimentary daily buffet breakfast: g.v. $95;
partial o.v. $115; o.v. $135; o.f. $170. Rooms have two double beds or one king.*

KAUA'I KAILANI

856 Kuhio Hwy., Kapa'a, HI 96746. RENTAL AGENT: Hawai'i Kailani, 119 N.
Commercial, Suite 1400, Bellingham, WA 98225, (206) 676-1434, FAX (206)
676-1435. Kaua'i Kailani consists of two properties, KK1 and KK2, for short. A
total of fifty seven, two bedroom apartments that offer kitchens, maid service and
two swimming pools. Walking distance to Kapa'a town.
Rates are $60-$65 for 1-4 persons.

MOKIHANA OF KAUA'I

796 Kuhio Hwy., Kapa'a, HI 96746. RENTAL AGENT: Hawai'i Kailani, 119 N.
Commercial, Suite 1400, Bellingham, WA 98225, (206) 676-1434, FAX (206)
676-1435. Seventy-nine studio apartments with maid service. Located at Waipouli.
Swimming pool.
$55 for studio apartment, max. 3.

TIP TOP MOTEL
Located in downtown Lihu'e. PO Box 1231, Lihu'e, HI 96766. (808) 245-2333.
These air conditioned rooms are spartan and basic. In operation since 1916, well
not exactly: they actually moved to their present location in the early '60's.
Maybe that is why they note on their brochure that they are "Kaua'is Newest
Motel." The restaurant and cocktail lounge are still here, and although the famous
bakery closed at the end of 1994 it has reopened and is now run by Kilauea
Bakery. These no frills accommodations are stark, very basic and, of course,
cheap! All units are air conditioned.
Single or double $44 (includes tax) plus $10 key deposit.

MODERATE

COCO PALMS (HOTEL)
(808) 823-0760. They have announced a late 1995 reopening date. We will keep
you posted as renovations progress in our Kaua'i Update newsletter.

HALE MAKANA VACATION COTTAGE
PO Box 3671, Lihu'e, HI 96766, (206) 242-4866 (Seattle, WA) or (808) 245-
6500 (Kaua'i). The guest cottage features 750 sq. feet with two bedrooms and one
bathroom. One bedroom is equipped with a queen size bed, the other has twins.
A microwave, dishwasher, range, refrigerator and basic cooking utensils are
supplied in the kitchen.
$600 per week, $100 per day with three night minimum.

ISLANDER ON THE BEACH ★
484 Kuhio Hwy., Kapa'a, HI 96746. (808) 822-7417, 1-800-847-7417, FAX (808)
822-1947. RENTAL AGENTS: Maui & All 1-800-663-696-6962. Total units 196
in three story buildings. A small understated lobby is tasteful and reminiscent of
a simple, old fashioned Hawaiian plantation. Very pleasing grounds and rooms
and an excellent value for your vacation dollar. The hotel features an outdoor pool
and spa, restaurant and lounge on the property. All rooms offer king or two
double beds, air conditioning, wet bar, refrigerator, microwaves in oceanfront
units and suites, color TV and in-room coffee makers. Laundry facilities. Rooms
have all been newly renovated, however, they are on the small side. Third and
fourth persons are charged $10 per person per night. No charge for children 17
and under when sharing parents room. Room and car packages available. Located
on one of the best beaches on the eastern shore of Kaua'i. Located on 6.5
oceanfront acres, next to the Jolly Roger Restaurant, and across from the Coconut
Marketplace.
Units g.v. $95; partial o.v. $105; o.v. $115, o.f. $125, Junior Suite $165.

(ASTON) KAHA LANI
4460 Nehe Rd., Lihu'e, HI 96766 (808) 822-9331. Located next door to Wailua
Golf Course and walk next door to Lydgate Park. RENTAL AGENT: Managed
by Aston Resorts 1-800-922-7866. Prosser Realty 1-800-767-4707. Maui & All
1-800-663-696-6962. Two and three story buildings with a total of 74 units. Pool,
BBQ area and tennis court. Next door to golf. Located on beachfront at Lydgate
Park, one of the islands better beaches. The Kamalani playground at Lydgate Park

will amuse the children in your party for hours! Units have full kitchens, ceiling fans, laundry facilities, lanais, daily maid service.
1 BR g.v. $115, o.v. $132, o.f. $142; 2 BR g.v. $146; o.v. $165, o.f. $178; 3 BR o.v. 242.

KAPA'A SANDS
380 Papaloa Rd., Kapa'a, HI 96746 (808) 822-4901, 1-800-222-4901, FAX (808) 822-1556. The postal address is Kapa'a, but they are located in Wailua. Minimum maid service daily with full linen change every fourth day. Twenty-four individually owned studio and two bedroom condominiums. Conveniently located behind Kinipopo Shopping Village which is just a short walk for shops and restaurants at the Coconut Plantation Marketplace. Swimming pool, laundry facilities, and attractive lanai's and grounds. Located on a pleasant beachfront. If you are up early in the morning (and sometimes in the afternoon) you can watch sea turtles feeding off the reef just in front of the property.
Studio o.v. $75 (max 2); studio o.f. $85 (max 2); 2 BR o.v. $99 (max 4); 2 BR o.f. $109 (max 4). Extra charge of $10 per night for the 5th person in a 2 BR unit.

KAPA'A SHORE
4-0900 Kuhio Hwy., Kapa'a, HI 96746. 1-800-827-3922, FAX (808) 822-1457. Maui & All 1-800-663-696-6962. Eighty-one units, three story buildings. Three night minimum stay, seven night minimum over Christmas holidays. Weekly and monthly discounts. Rollaways and cribs are $7 per night, $5 per night for five days or longer. Laundry facilities, some rooms have ceiling fans. Pool, tennis courts and jacuzzi.
1 BR partial ocean $100/85; o.v. $110/95; o.f. $125/110
2 BR partial ocean $120/105; o.v. $115/100; o.f. $145/130

(ASTON) KAUA'I BEACHBOY HOTEL
4330 Kaua'i Beach Drive, Lihu'e, HI 96766. (808) 822-3441. RENTAL AGENT: Aston Hotels & Resorts 1-800-922-7866. Maui & All 1-800-663-696-6962. 243 units in three stories. Pool, tennis courts. Rooms have air conditioning, television and lanais. No kitchens, but they do have a bar size refrigerator. Daily maid service. Located next door to Marketplace at Coconut Plantation. The beachfront here is strewn with drift wood and not recommended for water recreation. A nice plus is that they have a keiki pool as well as an adult pool. Complimentary coffee is served mornings in the lobby for resort guests. Additional persons $12 per night. No charge for children under 18 using existing beds. A new Host Marriott restaurant opened here in the summer of 1995. In early 1995 they also launched a Hawaiiana program. Guests can enjoy ancient games, song, dance and arts & crafts of Old Hawai'i at no charge. Hawaiian dance lessons are available several times each week and on view at various times each week is a collection of Ni'ihau Shell leis and other Hawaiian crafts. They also have a Hawaiiana library with books available to check out.
Standard hotel room g.v. $98 (1-2); o.v. $118 (1-2), o.f. $128 (1-2). 1 BR 1 BTH Suite with kitchen o.v. $145; o.f. $165.

(ASTON) KAUA'I BEACH VILLAS
4330 Kaua'i Beach Drive, Lihu'e, HI 96766. (808) 245-7711. RENTAL AGENT: Managed by Aston Properties 1-800-922-7866. Maui & All 1-800-663-696-6962.

150 units, three floors (no elevator) located on 13 acres. These condominiums, along with what is now the Outrigger Hotel, once comprised the Kaua'i Hilton. They share the resort amenities - beach, pools, tropical landscaping and waterfalls, jet spa, four tennis courts, putting green, BBQ grills, but are managed and run separately. Condominium guests check-in at the Villas, but have signing privileges at the adjacent Outrigger's bars and restaurants. Complimentary parking. The Villas were refurbished just before the 1992 hurricane and most of the 150 rooms weathered the storm to remain open and relatively untouched. TV, phone, kitchens, lanais, and daily maid service in all units; air-conditioning in bedroom suites only.
SBR with kitchen $139/119 (max 2); 1 BR $170-180/160-180 (max. 4); 2 BR g.v. $245/225, 2 BR o.v. $295/275

KAUA'I RESORT HOTEL
3-5920 Kuhio Hwy., Wailua, HI 96746. (808) 245-3931, FAX (808) 822-7339. RENTAL AGENT: Hawaiian Pacific Resorts 1-800-367-5004. Castle Resorts & Hotels (808) 591-2235, FAX (808) 596-0158, 1-800-367-5004. 242 room resort. Room amenities include air conditioning, phone, refrigerator, and TV. Microwave ovens in suites, studios and kitchenette units have refrigerator, coffee maker and toaster. Daily maid service, laundry facilities. Two swimming pools, spa, tennis courts on property. Restaurants and lounges include the Pacific Room, Pikake Terrace and Lobby Bar. Also meeting facilities available. Ask about their room and car packages. Rooms are pleasantly decorated in pastel hues, they have a good location on Lydgate Park and free shuttle service to shopping center.

The Kaua'i Resort Hotel was auctioned to the highest bidder in late October of 1994. However, the highest bidder happened to be the only bidder who purchased the resort for the minimum asking bid of $4.5 million in cash. The Bankruptcy Court in San Diego handled the auction of the property. Maruko Inc. had purchased the Kaua'i Resort Hotel in 1988 for $27 million and due to high debts was forced to put it up for sale. New owners tell us they plan on changes including brighter, more tropical rooms and restaurants with a more tropical menu.

Economy Cabana $75; standard $99; g.v. $145; studio with full kitchen $150; dlx o.v. $155; 1 BR w/kitchenette $160; studio o.v. with full kitchen $169; 1 BR suite w/ kitchenette $200.

KAUA'I SANDS
420 Papaloa Rd., Kapa'a, HI 96746. (808) 822-4951. RENTAL AGENT: Sand & Seaside Hotels, 1-800-367-7000 U.S., 1-800-654-7020 Canada, Local (808) 922-5333. This Americanized Japanese complex has Hawaiian/Japanese decor. The black and white exterior could be painted more attractively. The rooms don't get much sun, but this keeps them cool and keeps the dark-colored spreads and carpets from fading - they look brand new. Self-service laundry. They are on a beachfront, but it is better for sitting and ocean watching than for swimming and sunbathing. Rooms are air conditioned. Aldon's Restaurant over looks the ocean. Located in Wailua, it is located between Papaloa Road and the Coconut Plantation Marketplace.
Economy $80, Superior garden $85, deluxe poolview $90, kitchenette poolview $95, Jr. suite with kitchen o.f. $130.

LAE NANI
410 Papaloa Rd., Kapa'a, HI 96746. (808) 822-4938. Located adjacent to the Coconut Market Place in Kapa'a. RENTAL AGENT: Village Resorts, 1-800-367-7052, (808) 822-4238, FAX (808) 822-1022. Kaua'i Vacation Rentals 1-800-367-5025. Maui & All 1-800-663-696-6962. 84 units in three story buildings. 1 BR units are 800 sq. ft., 2 BR 2 BTH units are 1,072 sq. ft. These apartments are spacious with nice island-style decor and furnishings, light colors with cane and bamboo accents. Amenities include swimming pool, daily maid service, bbq/picnic area. All units have full kitchens and private lanais. Some units have microwaves. Laundry facilities. This property has seven acres of grounds of lovely grounds. The rocky promontory along the beach is a remnant of an early heiau. A small man-made rock pool along the bay has been created.
1 BR g.v. $175/150; o.v. $195/175; o.f. $205/185 (max. 4)
2 BR g.v. $220/200; o.v. $250/225; o.f. $275/250 (max. 6)

OUTRIGGER KAUA'I BEACH (HOTEL)
4331 Kaua'i Beach Drive, Lihu'e, HI 96765. (808) 245-1955. Outrigger Hotels Hawai'i 1-800-733-7777 US & Canada, 0014-800-125-642 Australia, FAX 1-800-456-4329, Direct 808-926-0679. RENTAL AGENT: Maui & All 1-800-663-696-6962. 350 units in five story building. This property opened the day after Hurricane Iniki struck the island and has had continuous service ever since. Located on 25 acres of oceanfront property, three miles north of Lihu'e on Nukoli'i Beach (which means the beach of the kole fish). It provides a secluded setting for sunbathing, swimming and snorkeling (with free scuba lessons available through the resort) but the beach can be unsafe for water activities at times. Three swimming pools (2 adult, 1 keiki) and spa amid lush tropical gardens and rockscaped waterfalls. The hotel and adjacent Villas (now managed by Aston) used to be the Hilton. Four tennis courts (two lighted), lobby shops, activity desk and fitness club. Wailua Golf Course nearby. Meeting and banquet space. Units have TV, telephones, air conditioning, refrigerator, and private lanais. Although the furniture is accented with bamboo, the beige and "hot" coral decor is somewhat more modern than Hawaiian. Rooms tend to be a little damp during rainy season, but black-out curtains and particularly comfortable beds are conducive to a good night of sleep. Hale Kipa Restaurant is open for breakfast, lunch and dinner and offers specialty buffets on selected nights. Snacks and light lunches are available poolside at Cascades or in the Lobby Lounge which also offers nightly entertainment. Cocktail lounge. Gilligan's disco becomes a comedy club on Thursdays, but "Weekend Wednesdays" offer a free Polynesian Show (poolside) followed by a free movie (all filmed on or particular to Kaua'i) at Gilligan's and the restaurant has both a steak and seafood special and a Paniolo Buffet. A variety of arts & crafts classes and twice weekly "coffee clatches" are just some of the activities that were started to entertain guests in the aftermath of Hurricane Iniki when there was little to do off-property. They proved so popular that they've been kept on ever since. The rooms have daily maid service, air conditioning, refrigerator, television and direct dial phones. No laundry facilities. Additional persons $20 per night, Children 17 and under free when sharing with parent in existing beds.
1 BR o.v. $170/160, partial o.v. $145/135, pool/lagoon view $135/125, m.v. $125/115, suites $220-750.

PALI KAI COTTAGES
Five units on a bluff at Kukui'i Point that overlooks Nawiliwili Harbor and Kalapaki Bay. AGENT: Kaua'i Vacation Rentals 1-800-367-5025, Surrounded by the Marriott complex and lagoons and on a bluff overlooking Kalapaki Bay. 1 & 2 bedrooms, all have two baths and sleep four. $160-320.

PLANTATION HALE
484 Kuhio Highway, Kapa'a, HI 96746 (808) 822-4941, 1-800-775-4253. RENTAL AGENT: Outrigger Hotels Hawai'i 1-800-733-7777 US & Canada, 0014-800-125-642 Australia, FAX 1-800-456-4329, Direct 808-926-0679. Maui & All 1-800-663-696-6962. A total of 151 rooms in ten two-story buildings, located in the Coconut Plantation, across the street from the beach. All units are one bedroom with kitchenettes and refrigerators. No dishwashers. In 1995 they completed renovations on guests rooms and the property. Renovations included refurbishment of all guests rooms and they now sport pastel hues of greens, blues and mauves. They have installed new carpeting, drapes and bedspreads. Additionally, all of the entry ways, bathrooms and kitchens were re-tiled. A new spa and pool deck were also installed. Three pools, BBQ area and laundry facilities. Air conditioning and daily maid service. Non-smoking rooms available. Second floor units have balconies, first floor have patios. A one block walk to the beach. The location of this property is between the road leading to the Coconut Beach Hotel and the highway. A few of the oceanside rooms have limited oceanviews. Those rooms on the highway side are subject to street noise. The same problem affects the pools which are along the highway side and while they are well screened, the traffic noise is a bit unpleasant. Request a room on the side farthest from the highway! There are televisions in both the living room and bedroom to help ease any program disputes! Check your Entertainment book for discounts at this property. *1 BR $120/104 (1-4)*

PONO KAI RESORT
1250 Kuhio Hwy., Kapa'a, HI 96746. RENTAL AGENT: Marc Resorts Hawai'i 1-800-535-0085, toll free FAX 1-800-633-5085, local (808) 922-9700. Maui & All 1-800-663-696-6962. Amenities include pool, jacuzzi, sauna, BBQ area. Weekly discounts. Units have ceiling fans, telephones, lanais, full kitchens including microwaves. Located on the edge of Kapa'a town.
1 BR g.v. $145; 1 BR o.v. $160; 1 BR of $190; (max 4)
2 BR g.v. $190; 2 BR o.v. $215; 2 BR of $235. (max 6)
Extra person $15 per night.

ROYAL DRIVE COTTAGES
147 Royal Dr., Kapa'a, HI 96746. (808) 822-2321. Bob Levine offers two guest cottages that can be arranged with two twin beds or made up as a single king-size. A kitchen offers the convenience of a refrigerator, microwave, and other serving and dining essentials. A private bath and ceiling fans. With plenty of fruit trees in the garden, there may be ripe papayas or bananas to sample.
Cottage rates run $60 single or $80 double. Extra person using a futon $10 each. Discount for stays of a week or longer.

WAILUA BAY VIEW

320 Papaloa Rd., Kapaʻa, HI 96746. (808) 822-3651. Located overlooking Wailua Bay. RENTAL AGENT: Prosser Realty 1-800-767-4707. Maui & All 1-800-663-696-6962. These apartments are lengthwise, so the living room is at the end facing the ocean and as the name implies, providing a beautiful bay view. Full kitchens, microwaves (in some units) dishwasher, washer and dryers. Some units air conditioned. King or queen beds. Sleeper sofa in living room. Swimming pool and BBQ area. Walking distance to shopping and restaurants. No laundry facilities. Daily maid service. Located on beachfront. Tennis courts across the street.
1 BR $100-$120 (1-4, max. 4)

EXPENSIVE

HALE AWAPUHI

Only nine units at this complex with an oceanfront pool. RENTAL AGENT: Kauaʻi Vacation Rentals 1-800-367-5025. *2 BR 2 BTH $250/210; 2 BR w/loft $320/280.*

KAUAʻI MARRIOTT RESORT & BEACH CLUB ★

3610 Rice Street. 1-800-228-9290 or (808) 245-5050. Located on 51 acres overlooking Kalapaki Bay, the Kauaʻi Marriott Resort & Beach officially opened in June of 1995. The property consists of 356 hotel rooms, the Kauaʻi Marriott, and a community of 232 one and two bedroom Vacation Ownership villas named Marriott's Kauaʻi Beach Club. The villas feature living rooms, dining areas, master bedrooms and baths, kitchenettes, color TVs and private lanais overlooking Kalapaki Beach and Nawiliwili Bay.

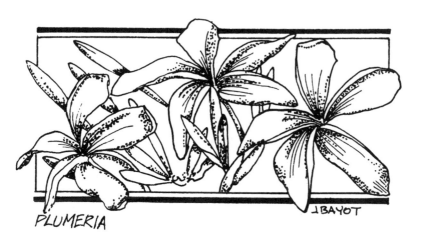

PLUMERIA

The Kaua'i Surf was the original property on this location which in the late 1980's was redesigned by Chris Hemmeter and reopened as the Westin Kaua'i. The Westin was designed with a heavy European influence and a style that many felt was out of place on Kaua'i. Hurricane Iniki's devastation on this property was massive and the hotel remained closed until Marriott stepped in to take over operation. They have chosen a new approach, combining time share with a hotel property. The $30 million renovation of the Kaua'i Marriott began in September 1994, with a team of designers incorporating Hawaiian history and culture into the new interior design, while keeping within the existing architectural elements and scale of the buildings. The most significant design element has been the transformation of the former Palace Court, with its marble fountains that were reminiscent of Versaille in France, into a Garden Court, featuring a lush tropical garden, lagoon, and waterfall. The Marriott, we are happy to say, is much improved over the Westin. It is not nearly as ostentatious or garish, much more reflecting the tropical elegance of Kaua'i. The most significant change was the replacement of the Roman pool in front with a much more subtle lagoon and more natural landscaping. This single element has made a big difference. The pink and beige color scheme is warmer and less showy, but the property is still luxurious, just in a more appropriate way. Of course much of the Westin structures remain, the marble columns and such, but they have made an effort to make them less focal.

The villas will feature a total of four restaurants and one lounge when they are all fully open. Casual poolside dining will be available at the Kalapaki Grill, and Kukui's as well as lunches and dinners at Duke's Canoe Club or the Japanese Edo Mae restaurant featuring a courtyard garden view. Aupaka Terrace offers daytime refreshments or evening specialty cocktails, featuring an espresso and garden island ice cream bar. The resort amenities include Hawaii's largest swimming pool, and a 20,400 square foot retail shopping center.

There are eight tennis courts and nearby are two outstanding golf courses designed by Jack Nicklaus. Adjoining the resort, the Kaua'i Lagoons also offers miles of lagoons and inland waterways upon which outrigger canoes and 35-passenger and 10 passenger mahogany launches carry guests through a series of six islands which serve as habitats for exotic wildlife. Guests can disembark from canoes and explore one of the islands on foot. The islands offer a collection of wallabies, flamingoes, African cranes, gazelles, rhea, and a variety of pheasants, monkeys, llamas, a kangaroo and a zebra.

Garden View $225; ocean/pool view $265; ocean view $325; deluxe ocean view $375; Suites $575.

LANIKAI
390 Papaloa Rd., Kapa'a, HI 96746. RENTAL AGENT: Windward Properties (808) 822-7700, 1-800-755-2824. Two, three story buildings offer eighteen units, half of these are in the rental program. These ocean-front condominiums with large lanais, full kitchens and daily maid service. Property amenities include pool, bbq area. Located near to Wailua State Park Beach.
2 BR $230 per night.

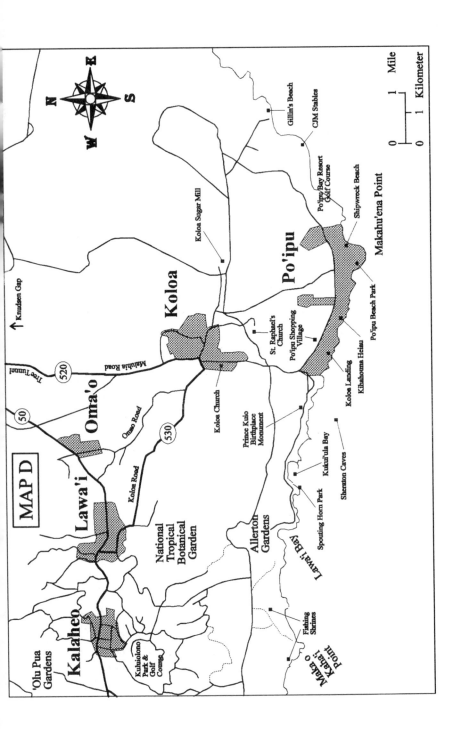

MAP D

'Olu Pua Gardens

Kalaheo

Kukuiolono Park & Golf Course

Lawa'i

National Tropical Botanical Garden

Oma'o

Allerton Gardens

Lawa'i Bay

Māke'e o Kāka'i Point

Fishing Shrines

Spouting Horn Park

Sheraton Caves

Kukui'ula Bay

Koloa Road

530

Omao Road

Prince Kuio Birthplace Monument

Koloa Church

520

50

Tree Tunnel

Maluhia Road

Knudsen Gap

Koloa

Koloa Sugar Mill

St. Raphael's Church

Po'ipu Shopping Village

Koloa Landing

Kihahouma Heiau

Po'ipu

Po'ipu Beach Park

Makahu'ena Point

Shipwreck Beach

Po'ipu Bay Resort Golf Course

Gillin's Beach

CJM Stables

N
W   E
S

0   1   Mile
0   1   Kilometer

109

SOUTH SHORE TO WEST SHORE -- INTRODUCTION

Koloa-Poiʻpu-Lawaʻi-Port Allen-

Hanapepe-Waimea-Kekaha-Kokeʻe

WHAT TO SEE/WHERE TO SHOP

This portion of accommodations and sights to see will begin as we head down Hwy. 50 from Lihuʻe through Puhi then Hwy. 520 (the tree tunnel) to Koloa, continuing down to Poiʻpu and Lawaʻi, then following back up to Hwy. 50 (via 530, Lawaʻi) eastward to Port Allen, Hanapepe, Waimea, Kekaha, and finally offering a course to the Waimea Canyon State Park and Kokeʻe State Park.

As you follow Hwy. 50 toward Koloa, you will turn left onto Hwy. 520. You will not be able to miss the stunning stand of trees which line the road on either side. Walter Duncan McBryde was landscaping his homestead at the turn of the century when he discovered he had an excess of eucalyptus trees. He donated five hundred eucalyptus (also known as swamp mahogany) to the county and they were planted along Hwy. 520. This famed Eucalyptus Grove, known as the *Tunnel of Trees*, has recovered substantially since the hurricane, but a little more time will be required for mother nature to rebuild the canopy effect. In the days before the construction of the Kaumualii Hwy., the tree tunnel was three times longer than its current size. Construction of the highway resulted in the removal of some of the trees, but others remain on their original site along the dirt road through the canefields on the left side as you head to Lihuʻe.

KOLOA

The last volcanic eruptions occurred on Kauaʻi in the Koloa area some one million years ago. Traveling around the area you will see cinder cones still dotting the landscape.

The word Koloa has several meanings, but the most common translation is "place of long cane." The town of Koloa developed along the Waikomo Stream which provided not only fresh water, but power for the first sugar mills. In 1835, Ladd and Company established the first successful sugar plantation in Hawaiʻi here. King Kamehameha III leased 980 acres to a Bostonian, William Hooper, for $300 a year. The first mill was built in 1836 in an area known as Green Pond. The mill used large koa logs to grind the cane juice. The second mill was built in 1838 in the same location, but used much improved iron rollers. Ladd and Company built the third mill in 1841 near the confluence of the Omao and Waikomo Streams. The mill was powered by water and firewood fueled the boilers. The chimney stack at the park across the street from the monkey pod tree in Koloa is all that remains of this third mill which was used until 1913. The monument represents the many varied ethnic groups which contributed their labors to the sugar cane industry. The "new" mill was built in 1913 and continues in production for the Koloa Sugar Company. From its inception in 1835 and then continuing for 21 years, this was the only sugar cane plantation in the Hawaiian islands.

The quaint plantation feel of this town continues to this day. A small strip of shops line the town of Koloa. Tomkats restaurant and the Koloa Broiler are adjacent to several art galleries. One has some interesting old Hawaiiana prints and reprints.

The large monkey pod tree was planted in 1925 and lends its shade to the Crazy Shirts store. This building was originally built by Mr. Yamaka who ran a hotel in the back until the mid 1920's when the Yamamoto family began their store at this sight. Behind this is a small mall area with the Koloa Museum. This small, free, museum depicts the development of the sugar industry in this area. The hours it is open seem to be sporadic.

The best deal in town is behind Sueoka's grocery. The small "snack shop" is reminiscent of the Azeka's snack shop on Maui. Walk up to the window and order your grinds. Open just for lunch, it is worth the drive back from Po'ipu Beach to pick up a meal!

The Waita Reservoir on the east side of Koloa is the largest reservoir in Hawaii. This man-made body of water was built on marshlands between 1903 and 1906 and covers 370 acres.

The *Koloa Church*, located on Po'ipu Road, was established in 1835. However, this pristine white church was not built until 1859. The design reflects a traditional New England style, typical of the missionary influence in early Hawai'i.

In Koloa you will find one of Kaua'i's notable historic religious landmarks. More than 150 years ago, in 1841, *St. Raphael Catholic Church* opened its doors on Kaua'i. The island's first Catholic church was damaged by Hurricane Iniki, but

KOLOA

fortunately was repairable. Other buildings on the property had to be torn down or still await major repairs. The original church had walls that were thickly built. A mortar was made by burning sand into lime and it was then mixed with pounded coral. This was used to hold together the rocks that constituted the walls. A reporting of the church's construction was published in a centennial celebration held in 1941: "The gathering of coral was a saga itself. The men and women swam out to the reef from Koloa beach and there dived under water to break off huge slabs of coral. They would then swim with the slab back to the beach, tie it onto their shoulders and trudge the three miles across the plain to the church." Changes to the original church over the years included the addition of more arched windows and a steeple was added in 1933. St. Raphael was originally a parish school and offered instruction for many years. While the main church seats only 150 persons, you may find three times that many in attendance on Sundays. So, in addition to the rebuilding efforts, the church also has plans for expansion. You might also visit the Lady of Lourdes shrine, built of lava rocks which is in a secluded spot at the back of the property.

Koloa Landing, on the edge of town, was the state's third largest whaling port in the 1800's and was also used for the exporting of raw sugar and sweet potatoes. An inter-island ferry would traverse between the islands, bringing passengers to this port on Kaua'i. The landing as a port sight was abandoned in 1928. Today you can still see the remains of the old mill and nearby is a sculpture that depicts the history of the area and the various ethnic groups that made their mark on Kaua'i's sugar industry.

PO'IPU

While Poi'pu has no definitive town center, it is none-the-less a wonderful Kaua'i vacation destination. Located on the south shore, there are several excellent accommodations. Po'ipu Beach is located in front of the Kiahuna Plantation. This is one of the island's best all-around beaches for family activities, except during high seas. The Hyatt Regency is located on Keoneloa Beach, fondly referred to as Shipwreck Beach for a long-since-gone wreck that once was beached on this stretch of coastline.

The *Po'ipu Shopping Center* is the largest and only real shopping center in this area. You will find Roy's Restaurant which recently opened, along with La Griglia Restaurant, Keoki's restaurant, Crazy Shirts and some other touristy shops. Many of the shops and kiosks still remain vacant since Hurricane Iniki. With so many of the major hotels in this area so slow to open, the resulting effect has meant that the once bustling shops at this village are also awaiting the return of tourism.

Prince Kuhio Park is located on Lawa'i Beach Road. Prince Kuhio was the youngest son of Kaua'i's chief David Kahalepouli Piikoli and the grandson of Kaumuali'i, the last King of Kaua'i. His aunt was Kapiolani and Prince Kuhio was adopted by Queen Kapiolani and grew up in the royal household in Honolulu. The monument at this park marks the birth site of Prince Jonah Kuhio Kalaniana-ole.

Prince Jonah was known as the "People's Prince" because of his achievements for his Hawaiian people. You can see the foundation of Kuhio's parent's home, royal fishpond, shrine, Hoai Heiau where the kahuna (priests) meditated and lived, and a sitting bench that faced the grounds. He was born in 1871, and elected in 1902 as a delegate to Congress, where he served until his death on January 7, 1922.

Located just to the east of Po'ipu Beach there is a lava rock outcropping known as *Spouting Horn*. It is named for the shooting geyser of sea water that appears during high tide. The spouting results from the surf washing into the lava tube and being sucked up through a hole in the coastal rock. The geyser reaches heights of as much as 60 feet. This popular tourist attraction is open to the public at no charge. It is easy to find, follow Hwy. 520 to Lawa'i Rd. (also known as Spouting Horn Rd.). Heed the posted signs which caution about the dangerous rocks. Continuing on along Lawa'i Road will lead you to the mouth of the Lawa'i Stream.

If you haven't already, take time to backtrack along Lawa'i Road to Po'ipu Road, head north to the charming town of Koloa. Old Koloa Town offers lots of interesting historic sights and quaint shopping opportunities.

If you'd like to experience a little of the pleasures of Robinson Crusoe or Swiss Family Robinson, plan an excursion to Maha'ulepu Beach. It was here that King Kamehameha I made his attempt to conquer the island of Kaua'i in 1796. Unfortunately, a storm forced a retreat, but the advance forces of Kamehameha's troops arrived on the island unaware of the order to retreat and were quickly killed. This is the beach site where George C. Scott portrayed Ernest Hemingway in the movie "Islands in the Stream." Maha'ulepu Beach is actually a collection of smaller beaches. Bones of ancient and now extinct flightless birds have been found in the caves in this area. The beaches offer a diverse assortment of aquatic activities including fishing, surfing, bodyboarding, body surfing, kayaking, windsurfing, snorkeling and swimming. The three areas along this beachfront are Gillin's Beach, Kawailoa Bay and Ha'ula Beach. Gillin's was named for the supervisor of Grove Farm Company, Elbert Gillin, who arrived in the islands in 1912 and relocated to Kaua'i in 1925 where he built his home. He was the supervisor of the Ha'upu Range Tunnel. Following two hurricanes, all that remains is Gillin's chimney. Several feet below this beach are the Rainbow Petroglyphs. Discovered in January of 1980 when a severe storm took out as much as six feet of beachfront, the petrogylphs were suddenly exposed. Working in reverse, the sea soon chose to cover them up once again. Currents at Kawailoa Bay make it unsafe for swimming or snorkeling. To reach Ha'ula Beach you may park on the east side of Pa'o'o Point and travel to the shore by trail. This area is the south shore's most dangerous beach.

The first beach, Gillin's, on occasion may be good for the experienced snorkeler during calm surf. Ha'ula Beach, since it requires a bit more effort to reach, may be the perfect place to sit on the beach and watch the ocean all by yourself. Access is a little tricky since it is over private land. You must pass a guard house and sign a release. To get to the guard house you need a release from the McBryde Sugar Company. You can pick one up at their main office Mon.-Fri. 3-10 pm, Sat. and Sun. 7 am-10 pm. The information number for McBryde Sugar is (808) 335-5111. You can also call and request that they mail you a form, but do so a month prior to your arrival. Then you'll need to stop at the guard house to sign a release with the Grove Farm. Since access could be denied at any time, it is requested that you take all your litter with you and be respectful of the right to use these gorgeous beaches of Kaua'i. From Weliweli Rd. in Koa the road connects with a dirt road by the sugar mill, follow it mauka. Or, take the dirt road at the end of Po'ipu Rd. and turn right at the cane road. Be aware of cane hauling trucks. There are no facilities here, so bring your own water and snacks. Parking is limited to along the roadside.

This area of **Maha'ulepu** is important geologically as well as archaeologically. Many of the early Hawaiian archeological sites were destroyed when the land was cleared for sugar cane. However, scientists have enough information to speculate that this area was heavily populated in pre-contact times. (Referring to the period prior to the arrival of Captain Cook.) The area offered the early Hawaiians excellent fishing grounds and a fertile valley making it a very suitable living environment. It was noted by Captain George Vancouver that from this area the glow of numerous campfires could be seen as he sailed past. Further confirmation was found by the many burial sites located in the sand dunes here. Geologically the area lies below Mt. Ha'upu, which is now only an eroded caldera. The sand dunes have born other rich geological treasures including the fossils of extinct birds. They have identified a flightless bird called a rail, several species of geese and a long-legged owl. John Clark's, *Beaches of Kaua'i* notes that, "Several caves in the vicinity contain two extremely rare insects, one a blind wolf spider and the other a blind terrestrial amphipod."

LAWA'I

Leaving Koloa and heading on Hwy. 530 eastward, you'll travel to Lawa'i. Little is known of early Lawa'i. According to an account by David Forbes in his book, *Queen Emma and Lawai*, the early maps and photographs show that the valley was cultivated in taro and later in rice. Queen Emma, the wife of Kamehameha IV, probably first saw Lawa'i during her visit in 1856, but returned for a more lengthy stay during the winter and spring in 1871. On arrival she found the area rather desolate, and compared with the busy life in Honolulu, it must have seemed so. In her correspondence with her family on O'ahu she requested many items to be sent, including plant slips. With these plant starts she began to develop one of the finest gardens in the islands. Queen Emma leased the Lawa'i land to Duncan McBryde for a span of fifteen years in 1876, however, she reserved her house lot and several acres of taro patch land. According to Forbes, "In 1886, after the Queen's death, Mrs. Elizabeth McBryde bought the entire Ahupuaa for $50,000 The upper lands were planted to sugar cane, and the valley was apparently leased to Chinese rice growers and taro planters." In 1899, Alexander McBryde obtained the land and with a love of plants, he continued to enlarge and cultivate the gardens which had been begun by the queen. Alexander McBryde died in 1935 and the land was sold to Robert Allerton and his son John in 1938. They continued to enlarge the gardens, searching out plants from around South East Asia. Today Lawa'i is a horticulturist's dream, with an outstanding collection of tropical plants.

The *National Tropical Botanical Garden* is a nationally-chartered non-profit organization that is actually made up of five separate gardens. Three are on Kaua'i, one is on Maui and another is located in Florida. Each of the gardens has an individual name, however, they are sometimes incorrectly referred to as simply the "National Tropical Botanical Garden."

The Lawa'i Garden (National Tropical Botanical Garden Headquarters Garden) is located on Kaua'i's southern shore in the lush Lawa'i Valley, and was the first garden site to be acquired by the National Tropical Botanical Garden. The NTBG headquarter facilities are located adjacent to the Lawa'i Garden. The headquarters complex includes a scientific laboratory, an herbarium housing nearly 30,000 specimens of tropical plants, an 8,000 volume research library, a computer records center, an educational center, and offices for staff and visiting scientists. *Lawa'i Garden* is a research and educational garden comprised of 186 acres. The garden's extensive collections include tropical plants of the world that are of particular significance for research, conservation, or cultural purposes. Special emphasis is given to rare and endangered Hawaiian species and to economic plants of the tropical world. *Three Springs* is at the interior of the Lawa'i Garden (makai or toward the mountains). This 120-acre area was acquired as a bequest to the Garden. As yet undeveloped, it will eventually be designed as an additional garden section, emphasizing the beautiful natural land and water features.

The nearby *Allerton Garden* is located oceanfront at Lawa'i-Kai, adjacent to the Lawa'i Garden. The new visitor entrance will be at Spouting Horn. This was formerly a private 100-acre estate. The beautifully designed garden is managed by the National Tropical Botanical Garden pursuant to an agreement with the Allerton Estate Trust. The gardens developed by Queen Emma were lovingly developed and expanded over a period of 50 years by Robert Allerton and his son John. The sculpted gardens contain numerous plants of interest, outstanding examples of garden design and water features, as well as Queen Emma's original summer cottage. The cottage was severely damaged by Hurricane Iniki and plans for restoration are underway. Reservations are required for tours of the Lawa'i and Allerton Gardens. Tour fee is currently $25. For information on scheduled tours and reservations, call (808) 332-7361. PO Box 340 Lawa'i, HI 96765.

NIGHTBLOOMING CEREUS

KALAHEO

The town of Kalaheo was home to many Portuguese immigrants at the turn of the century. The name translates to "the proud day." As you enter into the town of Kalaheo you will pass Brick Oven Pizza, thought by many to serve the best pizzas on the island, so if you're in the mood for a pizza pie stop by. Also in town is Paradise Sportswear Factory Outlet. Depending on what you might need, you may find a good value here. To take a short and worthwhile detour you need to turn left onto Papalina Road and head for Kukuiolono Park. An interesting note here is that many of the street names are Hawaiian words for parts of the body. Glimpse off to your left as you climb the winding road and, if you are fortunate, you'll see a rainbow hanging over Poi'pu. The three huge satellite dishes on the right will warn you that your turn is just ahead. A small white sign on the right is too small and too near the turn off to prepare you for the U turn onto Puu Rd. Enter Kukuiolono Park through the huge rock archway with iron gates into the park grounds. *Kukuiolono Park* is a series of gardens with sweeping Pacific and Lawa'i Valley views. This park was built by Walter McBryde, a founding father in the island's sugar industry. This beautiful, scenic public park is a popular location for wedding ceremonies. There is also a Hawaiian garden which displays some interesting ancient stone artifacts. There are huge rock bowls and a stone with a shape resembling the island called "Kaua'i iki" or Little Kaua'i. It is said by some if you haven't seen Little Kaua'i, then you haven't seen Kaua'i. The public golf course located here is the best deal on the island! They are open 6:30 am - 6:30 pm. No tee-offs allowed after 4:50. This is the best golf value on the island with 9 picturesque holes costing $6. Because of the value it may be crowded, but if you tee-off late in the day and don't have time to finish, it may be well worth the green fees. You might like to stop at the Kalaheo Coffee and Cafe, just past the Papalina Rd. intersection and pick up some of their huge sandwiches to enjoy as a picnic up at the park.

Just past Kalaheo is the *Olu Pua Gardens*, another splendid botanical wonderland. Olu Pua, which means "floral serenity" is a 12-acre garden of shade paths with a hibiscus garden, palm garden, edible plants and a lush jungle garden. There is also a pond shaped like a hibiscus. Founded in the 1900's as the Kaua'i Pineapple Company's plantation manager's estate, the center now has an on-going collecting program to expand the diversity of plantings including tropical vegetation from around the world. Located in Kalaheo, narrated tours are offered daily at 10:30 am, 12:30 pm, and 2:30 pm. Cost is $10 adults, $5 children.

ELE'ELE and PORT ALLEN

Just beyond mile marker 14 on the right is a scenic overlook of the Hanapepe Valley. It is a strikingly beautiful vista with the sheer canyon walls in hues of amber, ocher and red. You will first travel through Ele'ele and Port Allen before reaching the town of Hanapepe, so we'll describe it later.

As you continue toward Waimea, you will note a series of substantial looking electrical poles bordering the road on both sides. These were put in following the devastation caused by Hurricane Iniki and we were told they should withstand wind forces up to 120 miles per hour. As the road curves downhill you will reach the area of Ele'ele. The most notable landmark is the Ele'ele Shopping Center.

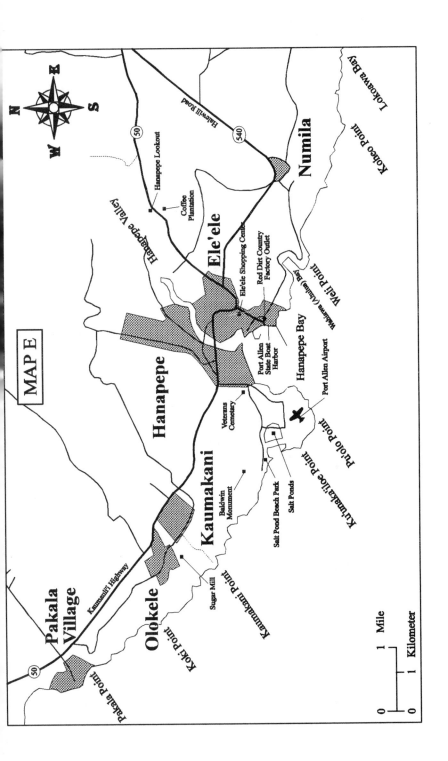

MAP E

Pakala Village

Olokele

Kōkī Point

Kaumakani

Kaumualiʻi Highway

Sugar Mill

Baldwin Monument

Kaumakani Point

Salt Pond Beach Park

Salt Ponds

Kuʻumakaʻōleʻō Point

Hanapepe

Veterans Cemetery

Puʻolo Point

Port Allen Airport

Hanapepe Bay

Port Allen State Boat Harbor

Red Dirt Country Factory Outlet

Eleʻele Shopping Center

Eleʻele

Wahiawa (Achiu) Bay

Weli Point

Hanapepe Valley

Coffee Plantation

Hanapepe Lookout

Halewili Road

50

540

Numila

Koheo Point

Lōkoawa Bay

N W E S

0   1 Mile

0   1 Kilometer

Daylight Donuts and Deli, a Big Save and the Port Allen Bar & Grill is here. Turn down toward Port Allen to see one of Kaua'i's seaports. The coast guard has boats here and some are "drones" or target ships. They warn "Target Drone, Stay Clear" in large bold letters. Obviously these in the harbor have either not had a turn at being bombed, or they just got lucky with some misses!

You may have noticed that the dirt has become redder as you proceed around the southern coastline. This area has been in sugar cultivation, but much of the iron still remains in the soil. A very clever entrepreneur has taken advantage of this red clay which has a natural property for staining anything that it comes in contact with. Port Allen has just recently become the "Home of the Red Dirt Shirt." You may have seen them in various shops around the island. It is here in Port Allen that you will find their factory and factory outlet. While it did not seem to this editor that the prices were any better than other shops for these same shirts, the selection was definitely more varied. In the back you might see one of the workers putting dirt, which has been blessed by a Hawaiian minister, through a sifter and in the back room they are running the silk screening. The dying itself is done at home as sort of a cottage industry, Call 335-5670. If you can't wait to visit, you can order by mail. Paradise Sportswear, PO Box 1027, Kalaheo, HI 96741. Tanks and shirts are $20. Kids sizes $16, plus $3 for shipping and handling. Send for a copy of their catalog which depicts their many varied styles.

HANAPEPE

Hanapepe, which means crushed bay, was Kaua'i's largest town back in the 1820's. Two decades later, however, the population had dwindled significantly. The area was rediscovered by the Chinese immigrants who began to grow rice in the area. Hanapepe was once again one of Kaua'i's busiest towns from World War I through the early 1950's. During the second World War, this coastal village was alive with thousands of GIs and sailors who were sent from the mainland and the rest of Hawai'i to train for Pacific Theater duty and to shore up Kaua'i's defenses. Hanapepe boasts that it is the biggest little town on Kaua'i. Unfortunately, or perhaps fortunately, Hanapepe feels like a step back in time with its plantation era buildings and slow pace. When the highway was widened it was decided to by-pass the town of Hanapepe and it was probably at that time that Hanapepe began to fade into despair. The opening of the Kukui Mall in Kapa'a was another blow to shopkeepers who just could not compete. It is a quaint town that has potential for being a wonderful little artisans gallery or such. You may recognize this town for scenes from the made-for-television movie, Thornbirds. Many of the buildings damaged by Hurricane Iniki have not, and may not ever, be repaired. The Taro Ko Chips factory is on the edge of town, and you might catch them when they are open. Mr. and Mrs. Nagamine started this business following their retirement and they cook up chips made from taro grown in fields nearby.

The Hanapepe Bookstore and the Aloha Angels Gallery are two of just a few shops to visit. A number of new art galleries have been springing up in recent months, optimistic that perhaps this artisan community will soon be discovered by more and more visitors exploring Kaua'i's western shore. Yoshiura's General Store operated as Mikado until World War II and is a classic. By 4 pm the town

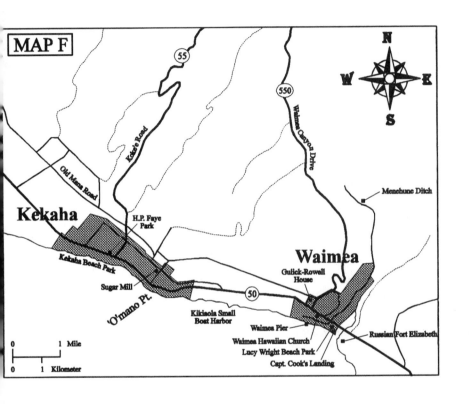

MAP F

Kekaha

Waimea

55

550

Waimea Canyon Drive

Kōkeʻe Road

Old Mana Road

Menehune Ditch

H.P. Faye Park

Kekaha Beach Park

Gulick-Rowell House

Sugar Mill

'O'mano Pt.

50

Kikiaola Small Boat Harbor

Waimea Pier

Waimea Hawaiian Church

Lucy Wright Beach Park

Capt. Cook's Landing

Russian Fort Elizabeth

0   1 Mile
0   1 Kilometer

is pretty well closed up. The Green Garden Restaurant on the edge of town has been hopping since 1948 when the GI's would stop by for a meal and a piece of their wonderful pie. Sinaloa, a popular Mexican restaurant, is also located here.

One of the most fascinating natural sites in Hanapepe is the salt ponds at Salt Pond Beach. The natural flats along this beach have been used by Hawaiians for generations. Today, this site continues to be used for traditional salt making. The resulting product is used for salting meat and for medicinal purposes. In late spring the wells, or puna, are cleaned and the salt making process runs through the summer months. Mother nature has been kind enough to create a ridge of rock between the two rocky points at Salt Bond Beach, resulting in a large lagoon area that is fairly well protected, allowing swimming and snorkeling, except during times of high surf. Popular for surfing and windsurfing as well. This park is popular, because of its protected swimming area, for families and children. A lifeguard is generally on duty. Because this part of the island is often sunny and warmer, even when there is rain on the south and east shore, Salt Pond Beach can be a great day-long excursion. There are picnic areas, restrooms, a rinse off shower, and generally a lifeguard on duty. Camping is permitted with a county permit. To reach the park, turn mauka off Kaumualii Hwy. on Lele Rd. then go past the Veterans Cemetery on Lokokai to parking area. (Follow the signs to the Humane Society.)

WAIMEA

Waimea is best known in the history of Kaua'i as the location where Captain James Cook first landed in the Hawaiian islands in January 1778. In later times rice was cultivated in this area, but when irrigation was introduced to the area, it was converted to sugar cane.

It is a wonderfully quaint town and with its location on the eastern coastline, often provides better weather conditions than in other areas of the island. You can stop by the library, located at Ola Road, across the road from the high school and pick up a free walking tour of the island. However, the librarian advised us that the information was rather dated, having been compiled in 1987, and some of the buildings have been destroyed and others are awaiting renovation from the hurricane. There are no immediate plans to update the listing. The library has limited hours of operation, Monday and Wednesday noon until 8 pm, Tuesday, Thursday and Friday 9 am - 5 pm, and closed Saturday and Sunday.

Just before you reach Waimea, before crossing the river, is **Fort Elizabeth** (also known as the Russian Fort). Built on the mouth of the Waimea River in 1817 by a German doctor, Georg (that's right, no "e") Anton Scheffer, who was employed by the Russian Fur Company of Alaska. When he began to fortify his fort the native chiefs grew concerned and notified the king who in turn ordered the Russians out of Kaua'i. There are restroom facilities located here. Across the river on the other side of the mouth is the Lucy Wright State Park. This beach sight was named for a school teacher who taught in Waimea for more than thirty-five years, Lucy Kapahu Aukai Wright. She was born August 20, 1873 in Anahola.

Just past the Waimea River turn right onto Menehune Road. Follow the road up 1.3 miles to the cliff on the left. You will note the cactus which drapes down over the cliff face. Caverns in the cliff are said to be sacred burial sites of the early Hawaiians. Kiki'aolo'a or the *Menehune Ditches* extend 25 miles up the Waimea River. The construction of it is of unknown origin, and there is some question that the early Hawaiians had the talents to build in this "dressed lava" stone fashion. A much simpler explanation is the legend that it was built in one night by the menehune to irrigate taro patches for the people in Waimea. Today, you can still see a two-foot-high portion of one of the walls that is marked by a plaque. Frankly, the ditches are not as interesting as one might expect. A picturesque sight formed by the lovely stream and the swinging rope that dangles above it is quite pleasant. If you are in luck you will see the local people fording the stream to the other side, or perhaps meet the enormous long-haired boar that goes for a walk and a bath in the stream with her owner.

Take a walking tour of the town of Waimea and visit its historic sights. Several continue to be under repair from the hurricane.

The *Gulick Rowell House* was begun in 1829 by the Reverend Peter Gulick, but was not finished until 17 years later by missionary George Rowell. This is one of the oldest surviving examples of early missionary structures in Hawaii. The 24 inch thick walls provided natural cooling.

The *Waimea Foreign Church* was built about 1859 by Reverend George Rowell. According to John Lydgate in a speech given in the early 1900s, the church was built of sandstone blocks cut from a mile or so away near the beach. They were soft when cut, but hardened when exposed to the air. They were transported by bullock-carts and secured with lime mortar. Pieces of the reef were broken off by divers and a 20-foot lime kiln pit was dug. Workers dragged lehua wood down from the mountains with teams of oxen for the woodwork used in the structure.

The **Waimea Hawaiian Church** was built around 1865 by Reverend Howell when he had a falling out with the Waimea Foreign Church. It was seriously damaged by Hurricane Iniki. They had on-going reconstruction for many months. You might wish to visit a Sunday morning church service which is conducted in Hawaiian.

The monument to **Captain Cook** is found in the center of town. It was placed there in 1928 in celebration of the 150th anniversary of Captain Cook's discovery of the islands and his first landing in the islands at Waimea. The statue was placed in Waimea by the state in 1978 commemorating the 200th anniversary of Cook's discovery at Hofgaard Park and in 1987 was moved to its present location.

At Waimea Highway 550 turns north and heads up to Koke'e and the Waimea Canyon. A description of this area follows. For now, we will proceed northwest along the Kaumualii Hwy, Highway 50, to Kekaha and you can travel up to Waimea Canyon by that route and then return down via Hwy. 550.

KEKAHA AND POLIHALE

On a clear day from the coast near Kekaha, you can enjoy a clear view of Ni'ihau. There is another small island farther to the north called Lehua. It is uninhabited. There appears to be a lower island just beyond Ni'ihau. This, however, is part of the island of Ni'ihau.

Kekaha Beach Park is a 30-acre stretch of beach with plenty of parking along the highway and restroom facilities. The weather on this part of the island is generally drier, so if you are looking for some sun, visit the western coast. Refer to the beaches chapter for more information on safety conditions for shorelines in this area.

If you continue northward you will reach the area of the Barking Sands Airfield and the *Pacific Missile Range*. This is a naval base with testing facilities which runs along the Mana shore.

A huge monkeypod tree in the road with a very unofficial sign will advise you that you are almost to Polihale. You may see some cars parked here. If you choose to do so, also be careful your wheels don't become mired in the sand! Then proceed by foot over the dunes to a unique natural formation. Known as *Queen's Pond,* this is a lagoon protected within the reef. It can be safe for a cool dip, but only when the surf is calm. It is said in ancient times a king of Kaua'i was killed at Barking Sands, and that today the sand still groans when you rub the pieces between your hands. We tried it, maybe you will have better luck! Some say that merely walking on the dry sand will cause the same effect.

It is another few bumpy and dusty miles along the dirt road before it ends at Polihale State Park. (See the beaches chapter for recreational opportunities afforded along the Mana coastline of West Kaua'i.) This beach is unsafe for any water activity, but strolling along the shoreline you should look closely to be fortunate enough to find some of the very small shells like those that scatter the coastline of Ni'ihau.

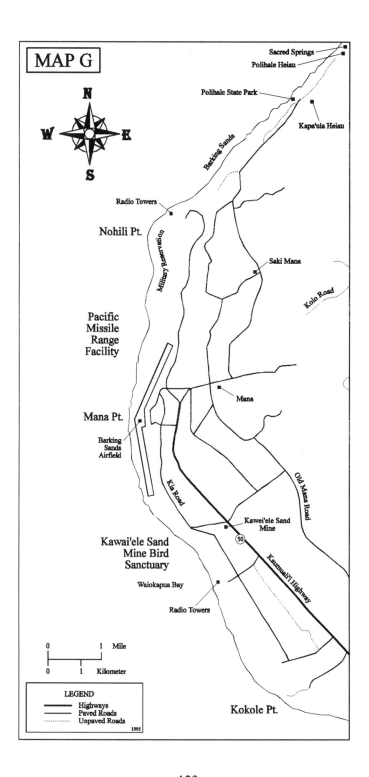

MAP G

Sacred Springs
Polihale Heiau

Polihale State Park

Kapaʻula Heiau

Barking Sands

Radio Towers

Nohili Pt.

Military Reservation

Saki Mana

Kolo Road

Pacific
Missile
Range
Facility

Mana

Mana Pt.

Barking
Sands
Airfield

Old Mana Road

Kia Road

Kawei'ele Sand
Mine

50

Kaumuali'i Highway

Kawai'ele Sand
Mine Bird
Sanctuary

Waiokapua Bay

Radio Towers

0   1   Mile
0   1   Kilometer

LEGEND
———— Highways
———— Paved Roads
.... Unpaved Roads
1995

Kokole Pt.

123

Choosing either Hwy. 550 from Waimea or Hwy. 55 from Kekaha you can follow the road as it slowly winds up to *Waimea Canyon*. We would recommend you go to Kekaha and follow Hwy. 50 from Kekaha up to Waimea Canyon and take the other, Hwy. 550, down from the canyon. This offers an opportunity to enjoy some dramatically different scenery. You might want to take this opportunity to check your gas gauge.

You may wish to bring along that sweater, sweatshirt or lightweight jacket you packed in your bag. The slightly higher elevation can drop the temperature down a few pleasantly cool degrees. While the weather topside may appear overcast from below the mountain, it can also blow through quickly. However, you might wish to call ahead to the National Guard Station at 335-6556 to check on weather conditions.

The Kokeʻe Road from Kekaha, Hwy. 55, was built in 1911, but is in fact a better road than the newer road from Waimea and is hence used by the tour bus drivers. The Waimea Canyon Road, while newer, is much steeper. After about seven miles. you will reach the sign for Waimea Canyon State Park. Another 1/2 mile and the Kokeʻe Rd intersects with the Waimea Canyon Rd. Just before the road mile marker 9 is the Kukui Trailhead. This is one of many trails which riddle the area and offer outstanding day hiking opportunities. Many are reached by main roads, some are accessible by smaller dirt roads. Another 2 1/2 miles and the road fork will advise you of the turn-off to either Kokeʻe Park or Waimea Canyon.

Waimea Canyon State Park provides unsurpassed opportunities for exploration. Follow Waimea Canyon Drive as it winds its way up 12 miles into the interior of the island, hugging the rim of the canyon for a dramatic panorama. The view of the 3,000-foot deep canyon is staggering. Hues of orange and red are splashed against the tropical green of 1,866 acres of parkland. Mark Twain aptly described this as the *"Grand Canyon of the Pacific."* Contiguous with Waimea Canyon is Kokeʻe State Park.

Waimea Canyon Lookout is the first of several lookouts. At an elevation of 3,120 feet, this is a stunning canyon vista.

Puu Ka Pele Lookout is the next stop as you continue to climb. It offers picnic tables and another, slightly different, view of the canyon. Puu Hinahina is another vista, viewing out toward Niʻihau.

Near the entrance to Waimea Canyon Park is the trailhead to the *Iliau Nature Trail*. This is a good family hike which follows a short .3 mile trail with an overview of the canyon and the waterfall on the far side of the crater. A relative of the silversword plants found on Maui at Haleakala National Park and the Big Island of Hawaii grows only here on Kauaʻi. The iliau is an unusual plant which, like the silversword, blooms with a profusion of blossoms which marks the end of its life.

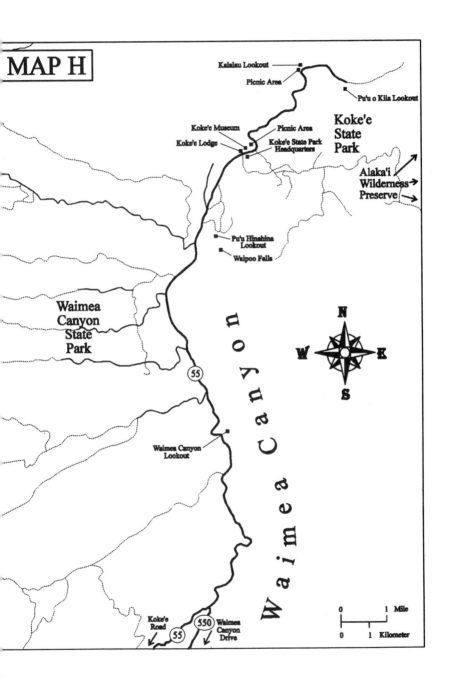

MAP H

Kalalau Lookout

Picnic Area

Pu'u o Kila Lookout

Koke'e Museum   Picnic Area

Koke'e Lodge

Koke'e State Park
Headquarters

Koke'e
State
Park

Alaka'i
Wilderness
Preserve

Pu'u Hinahina
Lookout

Waipoo Falls

Waimea
Canyon
State
Park

W a i m e a   C a n y o n

55

Waimea Canyon
Lookout

N

W   E

S

0   1 Mile

0   1 Kilometer

Koke'e
Road

550 Waimea
Canyon
Drive

55

KOKE'E

The ***Koke'e Museum*** offers displays about the park's natural history, flora and fauna, and the adjacent gift store offers a chance to purchase your own selection of books about Hawai'i's wildlife. ***Koke'e State Park*** offers 45 miles of named hiking trails. The Canyon Trail leads to the east rim of Waimea Canyon and offers a breathtaking view into its depth. The main canyon stretches for 12 miles and drops 3,000 feet. This is an easy trail for even the novice hiker, traversing 1.4 miles. Poomau Canyon Lookout Trail heads through a native rainforest and a series of Japanese plum trees. Awaawapuhi Trail leads through a forest to a 2,500-foot high vista which overlooks cliffs and the ocean. Halemanu-Koke'e Trail offers stunning views of the Na Pali Coast including Honopu Valley and the Valley of the Lost Tribe. Hikers on the Iliau Nature Loop will catch a glimpse of many endemic plant species. The Nature Trail begins at Koke'e Museum and passes through a koa forest. The Alakai Wilderness Preserve encompasses the Alakai Swamp and is adjacent to Koke'e State Park. The swamp is 10 miles long and two miles wide and spans the basin of the caldera. There are pristine nature trails and a new boardwalk over the boggy terrain for viewing some of Hawai'i's rarest flora and fauna. The Alakai Swamp Trail passes through bogs and rain forests to the Kilohana Lookout above Hanalei Bay.

Continue up Koke'e Road another couple of miles and you will reach the Kalalau and Puu o Kila lookouts. Kalalau Beach, which lies below along the coast, is that part of the Na Pali which requires an eleven mile hike to reach. On a clear day, this is perhaps the most picturesque location on Kaua'i. The valley falls below for 4,000 feet and is splashed by waterfalls. *Kaua'i, A Separate Kingdom,* as well as a tale by Jack London, portrays the saga of Ko'olau, his wife and young son. During the days when leprosy was scourged by forcing the infected victims to be confined to Moloka'i without their family, Ko'olau fled to this valley area. Several others fled as well, but they were eventually tracked down. Ko'olau's son, Kalei, succumbed first to the disease, and later Ko'olau also died from the affliction. His wife, Piilani, buried him in the wilderness. Never infected with this tragic disease, Piilani, returned to Waimea after the death of her husband and son and remarried.

'OHI'A LEHUA

BEST BETS

Po'ipu Kai - large property with some nice accommodations that are value priced. *Hyatt Regency* - a lovely, tropical resort. *Whaler's Cove* - a more expensive condominium, but an ideal location. *Embassy Vacation Resort at Po'ipu Point* - spacious and elegant with all the amenities of a resort and a condominium combined. *Kiahuna Plantation* - Well located, this is a beautiful upscale property with plenty of amenities. *Waimea Cottages* - Just what you'd imagine a Hawaiian home to be. For B&B's we would recommend *Gloria's Spouting Horn* - lovely, but pricey! Also *Marjorie's* and *Po'ipu Inn B&B*.

BED & BREAKFASTS

CORAL BY THE SEA B & B
PO Box 820, Waimea, HI 96796. 1-800-337-1084. Hosts Fred and Sharon offer guests a fully equipped unit with queen-size bed and sitting room, private bath with shower, cable tv. Within one block of sandy beaches. *$65 double occupancy.*

GLORIA'S SPOUTING HORN B & B
4464 Lawa'i Rd., Lawa'i, HI 96765 (808) 742-6995. Located on the same property, but after completely renovating following Hurricane Iniki, they now have an all new custom-designed beachhouse featuring spacious oceanfront guest rooms, and Hawaiian rock baths. Each of the five units includes a telephone, TV/VCR, wet bar with sink, refrigerator and microwave, along with a coffee and popcorn maker. One room offers a unique twig canopy bed. There are complimentary snacks and liquor, beach towels, and mats. The buffet breakfast offers fresh fruits, breads and cereal. The rooms are beautifully appointed. They have now raised the rates to $140, and while it may be worth it, this does make it a high end option. Since children are allowed only ages 14 and above, it is restrictive for families with young children. While it rates a star for quality, we can't give it a star for value. But if you can splurge, look into this one! Rates higher over Christmas holiday. *$140 per night single or double occupancy.*

HALE KEOKI BED & BREAKFAST
PO Box 1508, Koloa, HI 97656. (808) 332-9094. Located in Lawa'i, George and Susan Czetwertynski began their B & B in the fall of 1994. Their studio cottage has 1 queen bed, kitchen, TV, VCR, and microwave. Panoramic views of coffee and sugarcane fields plus ocean and mountain views. Outdoor spa. *$65 per night.*

HALE KUA
4896-E Kua Rd., PO Box 649, Lawa'i, HI 96765. (808) 332-8570. Two units available, one located above the garage and the other is in a guest house behind the main house. Each features a queen-size bed, full bath, kitchen, queen sleeper sofa in living room. television, telephone and washer/dryer. Breakfast is optional. Views of the ocean, Lawa'i Valley and the mountains, including Mount Kahili. Breakfast is optional. *Room rates $65-70.*

ISLAND HOME
1707 Kekaukia St., Koloa, HI 96756. (808) 742-2839. Two units, both with private entrances, microwaves and compact refrigerators. No children. Swimming privileges at nearby resort pool. *Single or double occupancy $65-$75.*

MARJORIE'S KAUA'I INN ★

PO Box 866, Lawa'i, HI 96765. 1-800-717-8838 from 8 am-1 pm Mon.-Fri. Hawaiian time. In Hawai'i (808) 332-8838). This classifies as an "inn" rather than a B & B since it does not include breakfast. The units have a mini-kitchen and on the first night you'll receive a basket with fruits, homemade banana bread, juice in the refrigerator and coffee with coffeemakers. Each room is a mini studio apartment with a private entrance. (She also has a single room with private bath at $45). The unbelievable breathtaking panoramic view of the Lawa'i Valley is truly spectacular. There is a hot tub in a gazebo at the end of the property and that, too, overlooks the valley. Marjorie Ketcher has travel agency experience and is very knowledgeable about activities. At $45-70 per night this B & B is a good value with a superb view as a benefit.

PO'IPU BED & BREAKFAST INN ★

2720 Hoonani Rd., Koloa, HI 96756. 808) 742-1146 (FAX) 742-6843, 1-800-22-POIPU. Dottie Cichon is host of these four bed and breakfast units located in this 1933 plantation inn. All units have private baths, most with whirlpool tub and separate shower, king bed, cable TV and VCR, wicker and pine antiques. Some units have a kitchenette or the option of twin beds. A honeymoon suite features ocean views, private lanai and whirlpool tub for two plus air conditioning. In fact there is a deep, luxurious whirlpool tub (and a shower) in almost all the rooms. Afternoon tea is a wonderful touch of hospitality and breakfast on the oceanfront lanai (or in bed by special request) is a pleasant selection of fresh fruits, fresh fruit smoothies, assorted breads and homemade pineapple or blueberry pancakes. Guests also have membership privileges for tennis and the pool at the nearby Kiahuna Tennis Club. A handicapped accessible room is also available. This property has lots of pleasant amenities and little extras. The collection of carousel horses is distinctive and adds extra charm. Prices run $110-$140. Oceanfront unit runs $175. Also available through the owners is a unit at Whaler's Cove and cottages at Kalaheo. Lovely accommodations, but too expensive to earn a star.

SOUTH SHORE VISTA

P.O. Box 1025, Kalaheo, HI 96741 (808) 332-9339 or (808) 332-9201, FAX (808) 332-7771. Located on the hillside of Kalaheo, this one-bedroom apartment has an ocean view and is located only two blocks from a public golf course and park. The unit features a queen-size bed, living area with full-size fold out couch, kitchenette with microwave, oven and utensils, a private deck and separate entrance. Coffee, tea and oatmeal provided in the unit. Breakfast provisions stocked in the kitchen for an extra fee. $69 double occupancy; $10 for an extra person. One night stay has $15 surcharge.

VICTORIA PLACE

3459 Lawailoa Lane, PO Box 930, Lawa'i, HI 96765. (808) 332-9300. Three guest rooms and a studio apartment offer a choice of your B & B options. The three main rooms are all charming and look out onto the pool deck. The single room is a little smaller. The sitting area is pleasant with plenty of books and lots of helpful information on touring and dining on Kaua'i. Host Edee Seymour is very knowledgeable and eager to share her opinions. Raindrop Room, single occupancy only $55-65; Cala Lily Room with queen bed $65-75; Shell Room with twin beds or king-size is handicapped accessible $75. A studio apartment with private entrance, king bed and day bed, kitchen $95-100.

INEXPENSIVE

KOKE'E LODGE CABINS

PO Box 819, Waimea, HI 96796 (808) 335-6061. Located at an elevation of 3,600 feet the Lodge is located in Hawai'i's 4,345 acre Koke'e State Park. A dozen housekeeping cabins furnished with refrigerators, stoves, hot showers, cooking and eating utensils, linens, towels, blankets and pillows. Size of units vary from one large room which sleeps three, to two-bedroom cabins that sleep seven. Maximum stay is five days and pets are not permitted. Full payment is required for confirmation. *$35-$45 per cabin.*

KOLOA LANDING COTTAGES

2704-B Hoonani Rd., Koloa, HI 96756. (808) 742-1470 or (808) 332-6326. FAX (808) 332-9584. The cottages are set in a tropical garden across the street from the beach. All cottages and studios include microwave, telephone, color cable TV and full kitchens. Coin operated laundry facilities are on premises. Studios have queen bed. Cottages include one queen bed and one set of twins. The studios can accommodate 2 persons, the cottages sleep four people, with room for 2 extra persons at $10 each sleeping on futons. One time cleaning fee of $20-$60.
Large cottage $100; Cottages 1-2 persons $70, 3-4 persons $85, studio 1-2 persons $50.

PO'IPU PLANTATION

1792 Pe'e Rd., Koloa, HI 96756. (808) 742-6757. 1-800-733-1632. FAX (808) 822-2723. One and two bedroom units. Air conditioned. Laundry room. Outdoor BBQ area and hot tub.
1 BR g.v. $80; 1 BR lower o.v. $85; 1 BR upper o.v. $90; 2 BR lower o.v. $100 double ($10 each additional person). 2 BR upper o.v. $105 double, add $10 each additional person.

PRINCE KUHIO

Mailing address: PO Box 3284, Lihu'e, HI 96766. (808) 245-9337. 1-800-3ALOHA3. Inter-island toll free 1-800-325-6423. RENTAL AGENTS: Prosser Realty 1-800-767-4707, Kaua'i Vacation Rentals 1-800-367-5025. Studio, one and two bedroom units. All have microwave ovens, full-size refrigerators, cable TV and telephones. Guest laundry facility on the ground floor. BBQ, pool. Located next to Prince Kuhio Park in Lawa'i area of Po'ipu. *Studio $69/59; 1 BR $79/69; Two BR penthouse $125/115.*

MODERATE

ALIHI LANI

2564 Hoonani Rd., at Po'ipu Beach. 1-800-742-2260 (808) 742-7299. This property has a total of six complexes. Po'ipu Realty rents a 2 BR 2 Bath unit at this oceanfront location for $175. Po'ipu Connection 1-800-742-2260 has rental units for $165. These units include a complete kitchen (even stir-fry woks), full-size washer and dryers. Outside is a private swimming pool and sunning deck. The six unit complex is located on a rocky oceanfront location.

CLASSIC VACATION COTTAGES

2666 Puuholo Rd., Koloa, HI 96756, (808) 742-6717. RENTAL AGENT: 2687 Onu Place, PO Box 901, Kalaheo, HI 96741. (808) 332-9201, FAX (808) 332-7645. The sea cliff cottages are located on a small ocean inlet where the Waikomo Stream meets the ocean overlooking historic Koloa Landing. These are ocean view units. The Hale Waipahu cottages feature open beamed ceilings. A queen bed on the upper main floor and twins on the lower. Four nights deposit required. Also Bed and Breakfast units $58-$68.

Sea Cliff Cottages:
1 BR $113/102; 1 BR dlx $140/130; 2 BR 2 BTH (1-4 persons) $184/177; studio with bath and lanai $90/85.

Hale Waipahu:
Suite $140/130 1-2 persons and $174/160 for 3-4 persons; Large studio $81/76

GARDEN ISLAND SUNSET VACATION RENTALS

Rental Agent: Kaua'i Vacation Rentals, 1-800-367-5025. Oceanfront, this new (1994) 4-plex offers wonderful sunsets and views of Ni'ihau. A short walk to Waimea Town. All units are 2 bedroom, one bath, sleep four.
$130/110, weekly rates $650/550.

HALE HOKU

4534 Lawa'i Rd., Koloa, HI 96756. (808) 742-1509. This two bedroom, two bathroom unit provides a full kitchen, washer/dryer, cable TV. Outdoor pool, outdoor shower and BBQ.
2 BR 2 BTH $230/180.

LAWA'I BEACH RESORT

5017 Lawa'i Rd., Koloa, HI 96756. (808) 742-9581. FAX (808) 742-7981. RENTAL AGENTS: Suite Paradise 1-800-367-8020. This property has turned into timeshare, but a few units are still in the vacation rental program. Cable TV with HBO, private phone, washer/dryer. Pool, jacuzzi, BBQ grill, limited maid service. Coin-op laundry. Telephones. *1 BR $161/133-148; 2 BR 180/ $149-165.*

MAKAHUENA RESORT CONDOMINIUMS

Located in Poi'pu. Mailing address: 1661 Pe'e Rd., Koloa, HI 96756. 1-800-367-8022 (808) 742-7555. RENTAL AGENT: R&R (808) 742-7555, 1-800-367-8022. Maui & All 1-800-663-6962. 79 2 BR condominiums. Resort includes pool, tennis court, jacuzzi and BBQ area. Units have ceiling fans, full kitchens, and television, washer/dryer. *2 BR $129/117*

NIHI KAI VILLAS

Located up the hill from Brennecke's Beach. 1-800-325-5701. (808) 642-1412. RENTAL AGENTS: Grantham Resorts 1-800-325-5701 (they currently manage the front office.) R&R (808) 742-7555, 1-800-367-8022. Prosser Realty 1-800-767-4707. Suite Paradise 1-800-367-8020. Garden Island Rentals 1-800-247-5599. Seventy units one, two and three bedroom. Phones, TV, microwave, full kitchens, washer/dryer. Many oceanview. Ocean front swimming pool, tennis courts and paddle tennis court. Nearby beach is popular for body surfing.

1 BR 2 BTH g.v. $120/100 (1-4); 1 BR 2 BATH o.v. $130/100 (1-4); 2 BR 2 BTH g.v. $199/140 (1-6); 2 BR 2 BTH o.v. $150/$129 (1-6); 2 BR 2 BA superior o.v. $160/139 (1-6); 3 BR 2 BTH super ocean $180/$149 (1-6); 3 BR 2 BTH o.f. $230/230 (1-6).

PO'IPU CRATER

2330 Ho'ohu Rd., (808) 742-7260. RENTAL AGENT: R&R (808) 742-7555, 1-800-367-8022. Suite Paradise 1-800-367-8020. Grantham Resorts 1-800-325-5701. Thirty condominiums in a garden setting. Each two bedroom, two bath bungalow is furnished with telephone, cable TV, VCR, microwave, washer/dryer and full kitchen. Located near Brennecke's Beach. Resort features tennis, swimming pool, sauna, BBQ. *Rates with Grantham: 1 BR 2 BTH g.f. $110/89 (1-4); 2 BR 2 BTH g.v. $120/$99 (1-6)*

PO'IPU KAI

1941 Po'ipu Rd., Koloa, HI 96756 (808) 742-6464. Managed by Colony Resorts. 1-800-777-1700. OTHER RENTAL AGENTS: R&R (808) 742-7555, 1-800-367-8022. Prosser Realty 1-800-767-4707. Suite Paradise 1-800-367-8020. Colony Hotels and Resorts 1-800-777-1700, Grantham Resorts 1-800-325-5701. Maui & All 1-800-663-696-6962. Po'ipu Connection (808) 742-2233. Three hundred and fifty condominium units. Seven resorts within a master resort. The privately owned condominiums include Po'ipu Sands, Manualoha, Makanui, Kahala and The Regency. Lanai Villas and Bayview offer private homes. Shop around, prices vary greatly depending on rental agent, as can quality of the unit. Colony charges $175 for their g.v. 1 BR unit here. Prices may reflect location in resort. Prices as low as: *1 BR 1 BTH g.v. $120/100; 2 BR 2 BTH o.f. $160/139.*

PO'IPU KAPILI

2221 Kapili Rd., Koloa, HI 96756. RENTAL AGENT: Po'ipu Ocean View Resorts 1-800-443-7714, FAX (808) 742-9162. Sixty one and two bedroom condominiums featuring a traditional Hawaiian plantation architecture. Kitchens fully equipped including microwave ovens. Laundry facilities are available on the property, but two bedroom units have their own washer and dryer. Oceanview pool, and tennis courts lighted for night play. The property is very private and the attractive and well cared for grounds add to the appeal. Christmas holiday rates are higher than the high season rates which follow. As nice as some other units costing much more. *1 BR o.v. $160/150; 1 BR o.v. dlx $175/165; 1 BR superior $195/185; 2 BR o.v. $215/200; 2 BR o.v. dlx $250/235; 2 BR superior $275/260.*

PO'IPU MAKAI

1677 Pe'e. Small swimming pool. Located overlooking ocean. RENTAL AGENT: Prosser Realty 1-800-767-4707. Po'ipu Connection (808) 742-2233. 15 units. Each unit fronts the ocean. *1 BR $140*

PO'IPU PALMS

1697 Pe'e Rd., at Po'ipu Beach. (808) 245-4711. RENTAL AGENT: R&R (808) 742-7555, 1-800-367-8022. Prosser Realty 1-800-767-4707. Po'ipu Connection (808) 742-2233. There are 12 units in this complex which are small two bedroom, two bath units. The pool remains inoperative. Located oceanfront. *2 BR 2 BTH $135-$125*

PO'IPU SHORES
1775 Pe'e Rd. Koloa, HI 96756. 1-800-869-7959, (808) 742-7700. RENTAL AGENT: Castle Resorts and Hotels (808) 591-2235, FAX (808) 596-0158, 1-800-367-5004. Thirty-three oceanfront condominiums one, two and three bedrooms. All suites feature fully-equipped kitchens, color TV, washer/dryer and private lanai. Both the living room and bedroom have oceanviews. *1 BR ov $150/130; 2 BR $175-200/165-175; 3 BR $230/185-225.*

SUNSET KAHILI
1763 Pe'e Road, Koloa, HI 96756. 1-800-82-POIPU, (808) 742-7434. RENTAL AGENT: Maui & All 1-800-663-696-6962. 36 condominiums in a five story building. Pool. Full kitchens, television, telephones, ceiling fans, washer/dryer, lanais, and swimming pool. One block to Brennecke's Beach. *1 BR $85-90/$83-88 2 BR $125/115*

WAIKOMO STREAM VILLAS
Located in Po'ipu. RENTAL AGENT: Grantham Resorts 1-800-325-5701. Sixty one and two bedroom units in tropical setting. Units have private lanais and are equipped with kitchen telephone, cable TV, VCR, microwave, washer and dryer. Free tennis, BBQ area and an adult and children's swimming pool are amenities. *1 BR 1 BTH g.v. $110/89 (1-4); 2 BR 2 BTH g.v. $120/99 (1-6); 2 BR 2 BTH "distant ocean" $130/109 (1-6)*

WAIMEA PLANTATION COTTAGES
PO Box 367, Waimea, HI 96796. (808) 338-1625. 1-800-9-WAIMEA. Visa and Mastercard accepted. Each of their cottages has been fully restored and updated. Located in a lovely grove of palms, these individual houses are just what you'd expect a Hawaiian home to be.

Their information sheet includes the following history: "In 1884, Hans Peter Faye, a Norwegian engineer and farmer, secured a lease from Kalakaua, King of Hawai'i, for about 200 acres of Mana swamp land, where he successfully grew sugar cane. He and nearby planters combined their lands to form the Kekaha Sugar Company in 1898, one of Hawai'i's most profitable cane producers. By 1910, W.P. Faye, Limited had privately purchased the neighboring Waimea Sugar Mill Company. Today, Faye's descendants manage Waimea Sugar Mill lands as Kikiaola Land Company, Ltd."

The Alan E. Faye Manager's Estate is a two story house circa 1900. This five bedroom home is 4,000 sq. ft. H.P. Faye's first home, originally in Mana, 20 miles away, was relocated to the entryway where it now serves as the front desk. On site is the Grove Dining Room, open for lunch and dinner as well as brunch on Sunday. The property is divided into several areas: Seaside, Historic Mill Camp, Hanawai Courtyard and Coconut Grove. They also have a 1916 two story beach house and cottage located on the shore of Hanalei Bay available for rent.

Seaside:

Manager's estate --	5 BR, (max 9) weekly rental only $2,625.
Director's Cottage --	3 BR, (max 6) $220 night/$1,470 week.
Field Supt. "B"& "C" --	2 BR, (max 4) $200 night/$1,260 week
Hale Iki "G" --	1 BR, (max 2) $130 night, $840 week.

Historic Mill Camp:
Garden setting 1, 2 and 3 BR (2-5 persons) $125-$150
One and two bedroom units, o.f. sleep 2-4 persons. $150-175 night.

Hanawai Courtyard:
2 BR o.f. (max 4) $175
E.K. Bull House "68" 2 BR, (max 4) $180
J.B.F. "58", 4 BR, (max 8) $230
Cottage "55", 1, 2 and 3 BR (sleeps 2-5) $140-180.

Faye Hanalei Cottage, 1 BR (max 3) $170
Faye Hanalei House, 6 BR (max 12) $2,625 per week.

EXPENSIVE

EMBASSY VACATION RESORT - PO'IPU POINT ★ (HOTEL)

1613 Pe'e Rd., Koloa, HI 96756. Reservations: 1-800-92-ASTON. 218 units. This is another very pleasant luxury property with architectural style like that of the Moana Hotel on O'ahu. The decor is reminiscent of an English country estate with dark greens accented by antique floral patterns. The bathrooms are spacious with big showers and deep tubs. The units have a full kitchen with washer/dryer, microwave, dishwasher and compactor. Two TVs, two phones, stereo, VCR, and iron. Coffee in rooms with complimentary breakfast in the Club Room by the pool. Breakfast includes assorted juices, fresh fruit and breads. The landscaped pool area and whirlpool are surrounded by sand with lawn chairs around the border. One bedroom suites have a king bed and sleeper sofa. The two-bedroom suites have a king bed and two twin beds plus a sleeper sofa in the living room. Health Club features workout equipment, steam and sauna baths. Toddler pool. With all these amenities, you may never leave the property!
1 BR g.v. (max 4) $250; 1 BR partial o.v. $290; 1 BR o.v. $325; 1 BR o.f. $390.
2 BR g.v. (max.6) $300; 2 BR partial o.v. $360; 2 BR o.v. $425; 2 BR o.f. $500.

HYATT REGENCY ★ (HOTEL)

1571 Po'ipu Rd., Koloa, HI 96756. (808) 742-1234, FAX (808) 742-1557. Hyatt Reservations 1-800-233-1234. This Hyatt, while not on as grand a scale as some other Hawai'i Hyatt properties, still has a grand feeling. This property is located on fifty oceanfront acres in the Po'ipu Beach District. The property opened in November 1990.

The classic traditional Hawaiian architecture is reminiscent of the 1920s and 1930s. Very open and elegant, while maintaining a regal, Hawaiiana look. Even during high occupancy, this resort doesn't feel crowded. A pleasant surprise are the pools, which are heated. With lagoons, bridges, jacuzzis plus an adult swimming area near the bar, you may decide to never leave the property while visiting Kaua'i. The Dock offers poolside coffee, beverages and snacks. The Seaview Lounge is living room like, very open and airy with a beautiful view. The Stevenson's Library is a cruise ship-type bar area, a combination gaming room, library and bar, although very un bar-like. The Kuhio Nightclub will keep you going until the wee hours of the morning. Dondero's is their fine dining Italian restaurant.

While the beachfront is pleasant, the winds and surf can come up and make it unsafe for swimming. The Hyatt does post flags advising people of the ocean safety. The guest rooms are light and bright with plantation-style furnishings. As with many Hyatt properties, they offer the Regency Club which are special floors offering special guest amenities such as complimentary breakfast, beverage service, and late afternoon hors d'oeurvres. While damaged from Hurricane Iniki, their restoration was completed and the resort reopened in seven months.

Room rates are single/double occupancy. No charge for children 18 and under when sharing their parents room using existing bed space. For additional persons 19 and older, $25 charge per night; $45 per night for the Regency Club. Maximum four adults or two adults and two children per room.

Garden accommodations $275; Lagoon accommodations $295; Golf/Mountain Accommodations $295; Ocean Accommodations $355; Deluxe Ocean Accommodations $395; Regency Club Accommodations $465. Suites range $425-$2,500.

KIAHUNA PLANTATION ★
Located in Po'ipu. Mailing address: 2253 Po'ipu Rd., Koloa, HI 96756. 1-800-367-7052 from the U.S. and Canada, (808) 742-6411, FAX (808) 742-7233. RENTAL AGENT: Maui & All 1-800-663-6962. 330 units in two and three story buildings. Kiahuna is the largest resort condominium on Kaua'i with 333 units set on 35-acres of lush gardens and expansive lawns which were once part of Hawai'is first sugar cane plantation. The historic manor house was originally the home of the plantation manager. Today the resort's front desk and restaurant are located there. This is what might be called "classy Hawaiian." The rooms are very attractively decorated and have the feel of a comfortable beach home. They have high ceilings and are nicely decorated with wicker and wood with the bedroom set off in a cozy nook of its own. The kitchens have coffee makings and a microwave with complimentary microwave popcorn. The property has plenty of amenities as well, free hula on Wednesday and Saturday, the Kiahuna Keiki Club, crafts and Hawaiian activities and free tours of the grounds. The comforts of a condo and the amenities and convenience of a hotel earn this property a star.

BOUGAINVILLEA   J.BAYOT

One and two bedroom units have various garden view, ocean view and oceanfront categories. All units include living room and dining room, private lanai, fully equipped kitchen, color TV, video tape player and ceiling fans. Daily maid service, laundry facilities, complimentary beach chairs and towels, gas BBQs. Pool and ten tennis courts. Excellent location on Po'ipu Beach.
1 BR $141-249; 2 BR $258-399.

STOUFFER WAIOHAI BEACH RESORT
2249 Po'ipu Road, Koloa, HI 96756. Rumor has it that this property may be turned into a time share. For now, it remains as it was left by Hurricane Iniki.

WHALER'S COVE ★
Located in Po'ipu. Mailing address Koloa Landing at Po'ipu, 2640 Puuholo Rd., Koloa, HI 96756. (808) 742-7571. Village Resorts 1-800-367-7052. RENTAL AGENTS: Suite Paradise 1-800-367-8020. Garden Island Rentals 1-800-247-5599. Maui & All 1-800-663-696-6962. Thirty-eight units. Oceanside pool. Full kitchen including microwave and dishwasher. Located on a promontory overlooking the ocean. Years ago whaling ships anchored at this cove to unload passengers and cargo. Swimming beach one mile away. The cove fronting the property offers very good snorkeling. Rooms have private jacuzzis and patio/lanai are spacious and private. Discounts for longer stays. Garden Island has one 1 BR unit for $165, and a 2 BR unit for $195 plus cleaning fee.
1 BR g.v./o.v. $225 (max 2), 1 BR o.f. $275 (max 2); 2 BR g.v./o.v. $275 (max. 4); 2 BR o.f. $325 (max 6), 2 BR o.f. dlx. $375 (max 6), Ali'i Suite $550 (max. 2)

135

NORTH SHORE

Anahola-Kilauea-Princeville-Hanalei-Haena-Na Pali

INTRODUCTION

The picturesque beauty of the North Shore is unsurpassed in the Hawaiian Islands. Most of the attractions on this side of Kaua'i revolve around the sights provided by mother nature. From botanical gardens to postcard perfect sunsets on the beach, here you can ignore the hustle and bustle and simply relax!

KEALIA

At mile marker 10 you'll see a long stretch of beach that looks pleasant enough, but the water conditions are not safe. The rip currents along this beachfront are very strong. Kealia was another old plantation town and you may still see some of the old plantation buildings remaining. The word Kealia means "salt encrusted" and it was to this beach that the early Hawaiians gathered salt that had evaporated along the beachfront. From Kealia the road moves inland slightly as you continue around toward Kaua'i's north shore.

ANAHOLA

Five miles from Kapa'a and just prior to mile marker 14 is what most visitors see of Anahola. This is, in our opinion, the best place to get a burger on Kaua'i. Duane's Ono Burgers are REALLY onolicious! Across the street is a chicken BBQ restaurant with plate lunches running $4-5 and shave ice for $2.

Historically, the hole in the mountain above on the seaward side of Anahola carries a legend. It tells that the hole was made by an early Hawaiian giant's spear. The giant threw it at the King of Kaua'i and missed him, piercing the mountain and leaving the hole. And, of course, another version says it was another chieftain who opposed the king and that Kamehameha threw the spear, which went entirely through the rock behind him.

In more recent history, Anahola suffered the effects of a severe flood in late 1991. The heavy rainfall during the night caused the stream to swell and the subsequent flooding came as a surprise to the residents. Not only property, but lives were lost as well.

To reach the beaches between Anahola and Kilauea, Ka'aka'aniu Beach (Larsen's) and Wa'iakalua, will require parking and a short walk to reach. Neither is safe for water activities.

The road moves past dairy farms nestled along the foothills. Signs warn that the roads may flood if there are heavy rains.

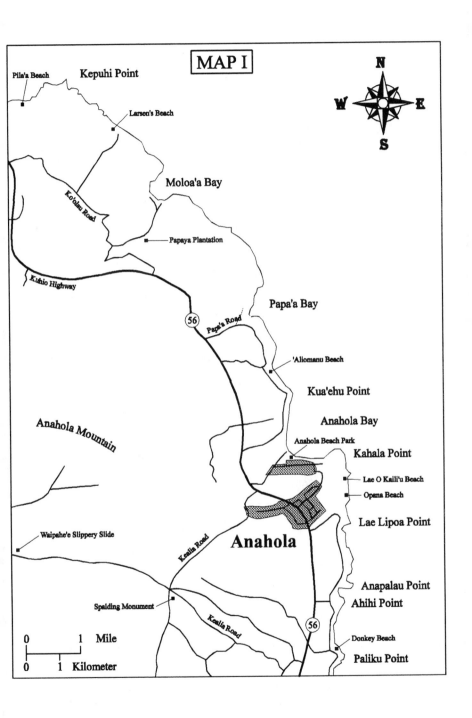

MAP I

Pila'a Beach
Kepuhi Point
Larsen's Beach
Ko'olau Road
Moloa'a Bay
Papaya Plantation
Kuhio Highway
Papa'a Bay
56
Papa'a Road
'Aliomanu Beach
Kua'ehu Point
Anahola Bay
Anahola Mountain
Anahola Beach Park
Kahala Point
Lae O Kaili'u Beach
Opana Beach
Lae Lipoa Point
Waipahe'e Slippery Slide
Kealia Road
Anahola
Anapalau Point
Ahihi Point
Spalding Monument
Kealia Road
56
Donkey Beach
Paliku Point

0   1   Mile
0   1   Kilometer

KILAUEA

The next stop on the map is Kilauea. You can turn right onto Kolo into town or go a little farther and turn right on Kilauea Road, which happens to be the LAST gas station on the north shore. If you travel down Kolo Rd., turning at Mango Mama's, you will see the Christ Memorial Episcopal Church. This small church has beautiful stained glass windows which were sent from England and Mrs. William Hyde Rice designed the hand carved altar. While the church had its origins many years ago, the current structure only dates to 1941.

A bit further you will pass by *St. Sylvester's church* with its unusual octagonal architecture. Either way you'll reach Kilauea Road and continue down to the lighthouse. But first you may wish a brief respite at the *Kong Lung Center* in Kilauea. They offer a variety of shopping opportunities. The Kong Lung Company is an emporium housed in a restored historic building. Products include a wide variety of unique, "essential luxury" items. They opened in 1978 and were closed for a year following Hurricane Iniki. They offer Kong Lung's own T-shirts and backpack-style tote bags, swimwear, tableware, and lamps. The Kong Lung Co.'s structure dates back to 1860, in a building which once housed the Kilauea Plantation General store, which was originally a two-story wooden building. In about 1918 the Kilauea Sugar Company's plantation manager tore down the old wooden structure. In the early 1940's the plantation rebuilt the structure using a fieldstone construction method which is unique to Hawai'i and the Chew "Chow" Lung store reopened as the new Kong Lung Store. In the early 1970's the Kilauea Sugar Company closed and the Kong Lung Center was purchased by local businessmen. Following the damage caused by Hurricane Iniki, the decision was made to restore the Kong Lung Co. to the authentic, plantation-style architecture and design that makes the building historically significant. In August 1993 is was placed on the National Register of Historic Places. During the year-long remodel, an old floor-safe was discovered in what is now used as a dressing room. The original butcher's freezer, dating to 1943, is now a large private dressing room. Open 9 am - 6 pm Monday through Saturday and 10 am - 5 pm on Sundays. Phone (808) 828-1822, FAX (808) 828-1227.

The Kilauea Bakery and Pau Hana Pizza at the *Kong Lung Center* is popular with visitors and local residents alike. They opened in July of 1991 and their signature items include Na Pali brown bread, guava fermented Hawaiian sourdough bread, tropical fruit layer cakes with whipped cream icing, "Big Blue" pizza with smoked mahimahi, capers and lemon. They have a limited number of seats inside and a courtyard with a few tables outdoors. Tom Pickett, formerly a pastry chef with the Sheraton Princeville, and his wife Katie, opened their business as only a bakery. Adding the pizza business was a natural progression as their popularity increased. Open from 6:30 am-9 pm, Monday through Saturday. Phone (808) 828-2020.

A new store in the back of the center is worth a peek for those ladies who love a good deal. Reinventions is an assortment of new and gently used clothing. It opened in the spring of 1995. While some items are used, others are new and include the clearance items from the neighboring Kong Lung Store. (828-1125). The Casa Di Amici restaurant at Kong Lung has closed. No announced plans of reopening.

Continuing onto the lighthouse, we will begin with a bit of history of the area geographically, the lighthouse, and the wildlife refuge.

Kilauea Point is a remnant of the former Kilauea volcanic vent that last erupted 15,000 years ago. Today, there is only a small "U" shaped portion of the vent that remains, which allows for a spectacular view from the 570 foot ocean bluff.

The history of the *lighthouse* began in 1909 when the property was purchased for a one dollar token fee from the Kilauea Sugar Plantation Company. The location for the lighthouse was perfectly suited, for this grass covered bluff was surrounded by pounding surf on three sides. Winter swells of twenty feet or more were not uncommon. We hope you have packed that pair of binoculars! Work began on the lighthouse in 1912 and was completed in May, 1913, with a light shining to ships 21 nautical miles away. The light house is today on the National Register of Historic Places. The visitor center adjacent to the lighthouse will have displays explaining the seabirds and their sanctuaries when they reopen.

The *Kilauea Point National Wildlife Refuge* was established in 1974 and is recognized as Hawai'i's largest seabird sanctuary, a place that is home to more than 5,000 seabirds. This refuge is a nesting site for the red-footed booby, wedge-tailed shearwater, Laysan albatross and many other species of Hawaiian seabirds. The acquisition of land has continued ever since with this sanctuary now encompassing 203 acres. The refuge was struck hard by Hurricane Iniki. Not only was there much damage to the birdlife and vegetation, but the famous lighthouse was also seriously affected. At Kilauea Point, they reported that about 80% of the native plants suffered damage. On Crater Hill, at least 25% were lost and an additional 50% damaged. Mokolea Point vegetation suffered little damage. Kilauea Point lost the most birds and suffered the worst damage to the habitat. The Kaua'i Natural Wildlife Refuge complex lost 12 of their 20 buildings. There was also damage to the lighthouse visitor center and bookstore, storage buildings, fences, and the water delivery system.

KILAUEA LIGHTHOUSE

When the lighthouse and support facilities were transferred from the U.S. Coast Guard on February 15, 1985, Kilauea Point became the 425th National Wildlife Refuge. The adjacent Kilauea Point Humpback Whale National Marine Sanctuary was established in 1994. Over 250,000 visitors enjoy the Kilauea Point National Wildlife Refuge visitor center and wildlife viewing areas each year. As many as 1,000 visitors per day may tour the facility over the Christmas holiday. There is an on-going habitat management program that includes water development, native plant propagation, volunteer conservation group and service club, and nursery activities. Over 200 volunteers donate hours to a variety of refuge projects. Of the 203 acres, 183 acres are owned, and another 20 acres are conservation easement.

Kilauea Point, PO Box 87, Kilauea, Kaua'i, HI 96754, is open to the public Monday through Friday 10 am - 4 pm. (808) 828-1413. Admission, when fully opened, will be $2.

Back on the Highway and continuing toward Princeville, you'll pass Banana Joe's. A landmark you will definitely want to visit if you have a thirst for a fruit smoothie!

On the left as you head toward Princeville, just past mile marker 23, you turn onto Kuawa Road on the mauka side of the Highway, and follow it up to Guava Kai Plantation. There are 480 acres of guava orchards under commercial cultivation at the *Guava Kai Plantation* in Kilauea, which is considered the Guava Capitol of the world. Visit the plantation's visitor center and discover how guava is grown and processed into a variety of treats. Guava has fewer calories and more vitamin C than oranges, and it is also a good source of vitamin A, potassium and phosphorus. Guava is actually not a citrus, it is a berry with a fleshy seed cavity and a thick skin. The guava can survive in dry or very tropical conditions. The Kilauea orchards receive 100 inches of rainfall each year with temperate 65-80 degree weather that is very agreeable to this crop. During dry months each tree receives up to 75 gallons of water per day. The seedlings were planted in this orchard in 1977 and began producing fruit in 1979. The first commercial yield was in January of 1980 with 2,000 pounds per acre harvested. Today the yield is 5,000 pounds per acre or about 400 pounds of fruit per tree per harvest cycle. The fruit at this plantation is hand-picked and harvested year round on a full-scale crop cycling system. The fruit meat can vary from white or yellow to orange or pink. The variety grown at the Guava Kai Plantation is a hybrid developed by the University of Hawai'i's College of Tropical Agriculture and has a bright pink flesh and an edible rind. The color in your glass of juice is all natural. The guava was a native of South America and introduced to the islands in 1791 by the Spaniard Don Francisco de Paula Marin, who was an advisor to Kamehameha I. The guava flourished and many now grow wild in Hawaii. There is a self-guided tour that includes a view of the orchard and of the processing plants as well as an informative eight minute video. There is a man-made fish pond and an assortment of native Hawaiian plants. The snack bar, only open in the summer months, sells ice cream, juice, breads and other bakery items made with guava. There are free samples of guava juice, jams, jellies and coffee. Since they are owned by Maunaloa, they also sell their products at slightly lower rates than retail outlets. Guava Kai Plantation is open 9 am - 5 pm. (808) 828-6121.

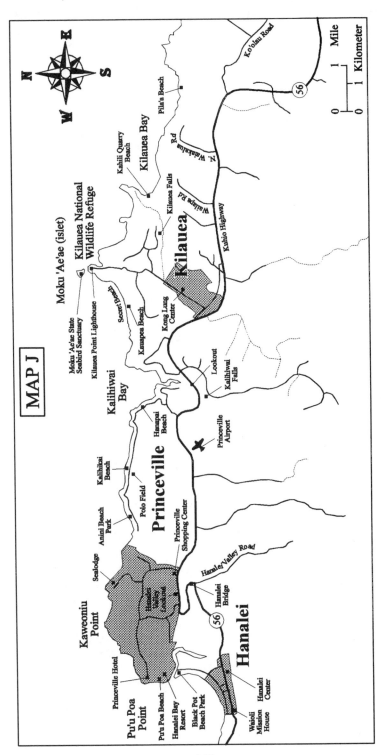

MAP J

141

At mile marker 25 is a scenic lookout for ***Kalihiwai Falls***. The valley is visible on the makai side of the road and it is a cautious vacationer who must venture down the bridge and over to the other side to view the falls. During the 1957 tsunami, the original bridge was actually lifted up off the foundation and moved 50 - 100 feet up stream. The Kalihiwai Falls is actually two falls, accessible by hike, kayak or horseback.

Between mile markers 25 and 26 take Kalihiwai Road down to ***'Anini Beach***. This is a popular windsurfing location and can be good for snorkeling during calm surf. Across the road from the beach they have polo matches each Sunday beginning in late April and running through the early fall. There is another birthstone located here.

Just before mile marker 26 you will pass the airport on your left (mauka) and the Princeville Golf Club will be on the makai side (your right). Even if you aren't a golfer, you might be interested in their health club or restaurant.

The Pooku Stables up the road a short distance and on your left, will take you to see the beauty of this area up close from horseback. Breathtaking vistas offered by the Princeville course or your right may tempt even the non-golfer. Suddenly the entrance to Princeville appears on your right and access to the hotels and condominiums is all off of this road. The Princeville Center is located at this intersection as well.

Continuation along the highway will lead to the Hanalei area and that will be discussed following the Princeville portion.

PRINCEVILLE

It was in late January of 1815 that the Behring went aground at Waimea Bay. The Behring, owned by the Russian-American company, was headed toward Sitka with a load of seal skins. Kaua'i's king, Kaumuali'i, confiscated the cargo. In 1816 a German named Georg (that's right, no "e") Anton Scheffer was selected by the manager of the Russian-American Company, Alexander Andreievich Baranov, to head to Kaua'i to claim their load of pelts. He arrived in November of 1815 and arrived in Kaua'i in May of 1816. While Georg and his forces were prepared to take back their cargo by force, the king returned the cargo as a show of good faith. The King had hopes of an alliance with the Russian Empire. Schaffer had ideas that were slightly different, with plans to take over the entire island chain for the Russian Empire. He constructed a fort at Waimea Bay in September of that year and named it after the Russian Empress Elizabeth and ordered two additional two forts to be built, one at Hanalei and another in Princeville. His fort on top of Pu'u Poa in Princeville was named Fort Alexander for Tsar Alexander I. After King Kamehameha learned of his plans to overthrow the government, Georg was ordered to depart from the islands. Georg made his stand at Pu'u Poa, but failed in his attempt and shortly thereafter he sailed to Honolulu and then fled the islands. The grassy area just outside of the porte cochere for the Princeville Hotel has only a few rocky outcroppings, for little remained of a fort made of dirt and clay. A kiosk with an interpretative center sits beyond the plateau and also offers an panoramic view of the Pacific Ocean.

A Scottish physician, Robert Crichton Wyllie came to Kaua'i and in the 1844 after making a fortunate as a merchant in South America. He had not planned on staying in the islands but was persuaded to accept an appointment by King Kamehameha III as minister of foreign affairs, a post he held for 20 years. He desired a manor with the opulence and elegance as those found in his homeland in Scotland and selected Hanalei as the site. In early days, taro was raised here. When Wyllie purchased the property it was a coffee plantation he converted to a cattle ranch. Later rice was grown in the area and now it has returned to taro cultivation. In fact fifty percent of all of Hawai'i's poi comes from the taro root grown here.

The name *Princeville* was given in the 1860's when Kamehameha IV and his wife Queen Emma visited Wyllie's home and plantation along with their young son, the prince. Upon his death in 1865, Wyllie bequeathed the estate to a nephew. However the estate was deeply in debt and the young fellow was so overwhelmed that he committed suicide. In 1867 the lands were auctioned off. The area later became a cattle ranch and was then sold in 1968 for resort development. Today the Princeville Resort Community occupies 9,000 acres and is a mix of private homes, condominiums, golf courses and several hotels. The Princeville airport is served by IslandAir, a commuter airline. Approximately 4,000 acres are zoned conservation.

In 1969, the first major development of the Princeville Resort area began with the State of Highway reclassifying 995 acres from agricultural to urban. 532 acres of these were zoned for single and multi-family housing and hotel development, the remaining 463 acres would become the Makai Golf Club. The 27 hole golf course opened in July 1971 and by 1973, Golf Digest had already selected this course as one of "America's greatest 100 courses." In 1976 the Princeville Airstrip was completed and since then it has provided daily flights from Princeville to neighbor islands. By 1983 the Princeville Shopping Center had expanded to 66,000 square feet and construction began that same year on the Sheraton Princeville Hotel. The resort opened in September 1985. In 1987 the first nine holes of the Prince Golf Course officially opened and by July 1990 the full 18-holes of the course were complete. Between 1989 and 1991 renovations and improvements were made to the Sheraton Princeville Hotel. Following Hurricane Iniki in September 1992, the hotel was closed for restoration and resumed operation in October 1993.

The Princeville Resort is worth stopping by to view. With a European flare, this outstanding resort is located on a picture perfect location in Princeville. Enjoy afternoon tea in their lobby lounge or plan on splurging for Sunday brunch or the Friday evening seafood buffet at their Cafe Hanalei restaurant. See the review of this property under the accommodations section which follows.

In 1865 a small volume was published in Boston. Author Mary E. Anderson had visited the Hawaiian Islands with her grandmother and shared her experiences in print. Stepping back into time, it is a glimpse of the North Shore of Kaua'i, over 130 years ago.

"We arrived at Hanalei, Kauai, about twelve on Tuesday, and were met on the beach by the missionaries, Messrs. Johnson and Wilcox, who escorted us on horseback to the house of the former gentleman. The next morning we breakfasted at Mr. Wilcox's, then at twelve had a meeting in the church, where a goodly number of natives were assembled; among them Kanoa, the governor of Kauai, who afterwards dined with us.

At three o'clock Mr. Wyllie sent down a boat for a party to take us to his estate called Princeville. It was a delightful row up the river, the foliage on either bank was the richest and most luxuriant we had seen. There was hardly a ripple on the water and no sound was to be heard but the gentle dip of the oars.

First, we visited the sugar-mill, which is the finest and most expensive in the islands. There we witnessed the whole process, from the grinding of the cane to the grained sugar. After that we went up to the agent's house, and were cordially welcomed by his family, and shown over the beautiful garden surrounding the house. There was a hedge of lovely roses, with a profusion of fragrant blossoms....The view from the piazza is exquisite. Mountains rise peak above peak in the distance, while a beautiful valley, with its meandering stream, lies at your feet. Tropical trees and lovely flowers are all around you. I do not wonder that Mr. Wyllie is proud of Kikiula Valley, with its waving fields of sugar-cane. He called his estate Princeville after the young Prince of Hawaii, who is now dead.

On Thursday morning, bright and early, we started on our travels again. The roads of Kauai are better than on any of the other islands. Several members of the party started a little before the others, and rode up Kikiula Valley through Princeville. After a ride of about two and a half miles, we dismounted and ascended a little eminence. What a scene was before us! Far below was the river with its rapids, the course of which we could trace down the valley for some distance. Around us were mountains, on the left a bluff, and before us the Twin Peaks, with cascades in the distance. We galloped back, and soon overtook our cavalcade...We lunched at the house of a German, who kept a small store, and then rode on several miles to Kealia Park, the residence of Mr. Krull, a kind German gentleman, who hospitably entertained us overnight. Mr. Krull has a large dairy which in part supplies the Honolulu market with butter....The grounds about the house are prettily laid out, with two walks leading to a picturesque summerhouse called "Bellevue" from which one looks over an extensive plain to the sea. We slept in a nice grass house, with matting on the side instead of paper. Familiar engravings adorned the walls, and the beds, with their pretty muslin mosquito-curtains, looking inviting enough to the weary traveler."

Disney has a magic touch and they are thinking of casting their wand toward Kaua'i. Recent reports indicate **Walt Disney Corporation** has made an offer to purchase a property on the North Shore. Plans are to develop it into a resort-type vacation club, possibly time-share, albeit without Mickey. The property, located in Hanalei, was once the location of a Club Med and Princeville Corporation is currently the owner. After a statewide search, Disney felt Kaua'i had the most to offer for their proposed resort.

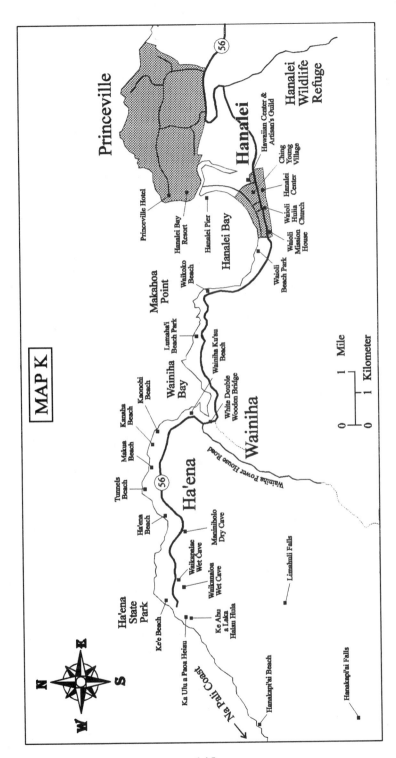

MAP K

Princeville

Hanalei

Hanalei Wildlife Refuge

Hawaiian Center & Artisan's Guild

Ching Young Village

Princeville Hotel

Hanalei Bay Resort

Hanalei Pier

Hanalei Center

Waioli Huiia Church

Waioli Mission House

Hanalei Bay

Waioli Beach Park

Waikoko Beach

Makahoa Point

Lumahai Beach Park

Wainiha Ku'au Beach

Wainiha Bay

Keonohi Beach

White Double Wooden Bridge

Wainiha

Kanaha Beach

Makua Beach

Wainiha Power House Road

Tunnels Beach

Ha'ena

Ha'ena Beach

Waikapalae Wet Cave

Maniniholo Dry Cave

Waikanaloa Wet Cave

Limahuli Falls

Ha'ena State Park

Ke'e Beach

Ke Ahu a Laka Halau Hula

Ka Ulu a Paoa Heiau

Na Pali Coast

Hanakapi'ai Beach

Hanakapi'ai Falls

0   1   Mile
0   1   Kilometer

N E S W

HANALEI

Just past the entrance to Princeville Resort area is the *Princeville Center*. Several restaurants, a great bakery, Foodland grocery, a medical center and assorted shops make for interesting strolling. Foodland has a very good deli with hearty sand-wiches to take along on your picnic lunch. Also of special merit at this shopping mall is the Ohana bakery and don't be surprised if the line is out the door. Hale O'Java serves up a great espresso. As you pass the shopping center you are at mile marker 28 on Hwy. 56, which now switches to mile marker 0 as you suddenly change to highway 560. Just past this on the left is the scenic lookout for the Hanalei Wildlife Refuge.

The *Hanalei Wildlife Refuge* was established on 917 acres in 1972 and is located in the Hanalei Valley. Unique to many refuges, taro is allowed to be commercially farmed on a portion of the property and one permit is granted for cattle grazing. Administered by the U.S. Fish and Wildlife Service as a unit of the National Wildlife Refuge System, they actively manage habitat to provide wetlands for endangered Hawaiian waterbirds. Historic farming (taro) and grazing practices are compatible with the refuge's objectives and thus permitted to a limited degree. There are 49 species of birds, including the endangered Hawaiian black-necked stilt, gallinule, coot, and duck that make their home here. Of the 49 species, 18 are introduced. There are no native mammals, reptiles, or amphibians, except possibly the Hawaiian bat. The refuge is not open to the public, but an interpretive overlook on the state highway just north of the refuge allows an excellent photo opportunity. Hurricane Iniki caused major damage to the facilities and habitat of this refuge and recovery continues.

The road winds down and you can glimpse buffalo grazing in the meadows below. As you cross the one-lane bridge into the Hanalei Valley you can imagine why Peter, Paul and Mary chose this magical place for their enchanted dragon, Puff, although they distorted the name slightly, no doubt for better lyrical flow. Look off to the mountains for the many small waterfalls which glisten down the cliffs.

The first stop in Hanalei town are a couple of shops which merge with the Hanalei Dolphin, one of the areas more popular restaurants. Koko's and Kai Kanes offer some interesting selections of aloha wear for ladies and gentlemen and the adjoining Ola's has glassware and other unusual gift items.

Tahiti Nui is a long time favorite for local fare and also presents a twice weekly luau. The Wake Up Cafe is a little hole in the wall, but offers perhaps the best French toast in Hawai'i.

Hanalei means "lei shaped." *The Hanalei Pier*, is a scenic location, and one you'll no doubt remember if you saw the movie South Pacific. The wooden pier was constructed in 1892 and then 30 years later was reinforced with concrete. It was used by the local farmers for shipping their rice until it was closed in 1933. In 1979 the pier joined other landmarks in the National Register of Historic Places. As a result of age the pier was condemned prior to Hurricane Iniki and was rebuilt following the Hurricane. To reach the Hanalei Pier and the parking areas along Hanalei Bay turn right on Aku Rd or on Malalo Road. Both take you down to Weke Road which runs parallel to the bay.

Continuing through the town of Hanalei is an assortment of restaurants and shops to meet most of the visitors needs. Several shops offer sea excursions along the Na Pali coast.

At the *Ching Young Center* you'll find a variety store, natural foods store, pizza, Subway and a Big Save Market.

Across the street, the old Hanalei school has been converted to art and clothing shops and the Hanalei Gourmet Deli. The school, built in 1926, is listed in the National Register of Historic Places. Adjoining is the Hanalei Center with Toscas Restaurant, the Hanalei Coffee Company, The Wishing Well (for shave ice!), and Bubba Burgers. Perhaps the most interesting shop is *Yellowfin Trading*. Tucked in the back next to Toscas, it is a little harder to find, but worth the hunt. They have Hawaiiana collectibles and antiques along with some unusual gift items.

Following the road through town, you will pass the green Waioli Church and the Wai'oli Mission House. *Wai'oli Mission House* is open to the public Tuesdays, Thursdays and Saturdays. Listed in the National Register of Historic Places, the home is open between 9 am and 3 pm. The original coral church was built in 1837 with Reverend William Alexander the first clergyman on the North Shore. In 1846, Abner and Lucy Wilcox arrived here as missionaries and while the church was founded in 1834, the present green and white *Wai'oli Church* was not built until 1921. The Wilcox family established themselves on the north shore and it was Abner and Lucy's three grand-daughters that initiated the restoration of the church in 1921. The half-day guided tour is taken on a walk-in basis with donations welcomed at the end of the visit. Sunday services performed in English and Hawaiian are fascinating. To tour the property for groups of 12 people or more, please write or call in advance. (808) 245-3202.

WAI'OLI MISSION HOUSE

The next few miles are dotted with one lane bridges. Just past the second is a Farmers Market which has produce for sale each week. Currently they set up on Tuesday at 2 pm.

Several more one lane bridges must be traversed before mile marker 5 and the lookout to Lumahai Beach. The east end of Lumaha'i Beach, Kahalahala (which means pandanus trees), is where Mitzi Gaynor filmed her famous "wash that man right out of my hair" scene. At mile marker 5 there is a very small pullout along the road that offers an unbeatable photo opportunity.

The *Lumaha'i Valley* was once populated with Hawaiians, later by Chinese and finally Japanese, who farmed first taro and then later immigrants cultivated rice. The 23 square mile area is now used for cattle grazing.

Wainiha Beach is a known shark breeding ground and not recommended for swimming or water activities. Pass the Wainiha store and pick up a cold drink or sandwich. It was in this valley in the 19th century that 65 persons reported their ethnicity as "menehune." A few miles beyond Wainiha Beach is Powerhouse Road; just before mile marker 7, turn off to climb inland through the valley. The road travels through some beautiful, not-to-be-missed scenery and ends at the Powerhouse. Built in 1906, it served to provide irrigation for the McBryde Sugar Company.

HAENA

Now you are entering the Haena area of Kaua'i. *Camp Naue*, a four-acre camp operated by the YMCA, is located between the 7 and 8 mile markers. More information on lodgings and accommodations will follow under rental information.

Here is the last vestige of civilization. The *Hanalei Colony Resort* is a quiet get-away and it adjoin's Charo's restaurant. The food at this ideal beachfront location does not live up to the view, but it is a terrific place to stop for a cool beverage.

Mile marker 8 indicates you have reached *Makua Beach*. You will probably see cars parked alongside the road and on a short sandy side road. Makua is one of the most popular beaches on the North shore and is commonly referred to as Tunnels Beach. You can also park down at Haena Beach Park and walk down to Tunnels. While this is among the safest beaches on the north shore and offers fair snorkeling, there can be strong rip currents even during small surf. You may note that many of the tour boats and zodiacs will come here to have their tour group snorkel along the reef for an hour or so. On the day we took a boat trip, the surf was fairly calm, but one member from our group on the boat, a stocky young man, was caught up in the rip current and struggling with a face mask which had a broken strap, had to be pulled into shore by one of the crew members. Always use caution on Kaua'i's many beautiful beaches. Beauty can be deceptive and we don't want any of our readers to become a statistic!

You will notice many of the houses are up on concrete stilts. This area has been struck hard by the tsunamis of 1946 and 1957. The stilts makes it a long walk up to deliver the groceries, but gives the homeowners the added benefits of obtaining limited home owners insurance. Whether this precaution will serve its purpose should another tsunami strike the area, will hopefully never be tested. *Haena Beach Park* is a five-acre park maintained by the County of Kaua'i. The foreshore here is steep and therefore the dangerous shorebreak makes it inadvisable for swimming or bodysurfing. Although you may see some bodysurfing done here, it is not for the novice.

Across the road from Haena Beach Park is *Maninolo Dry Cave*. This lava tube, was a sea cave in earlier centuries when the sea was higher. You can travel several hundred yards and emerge at the other end. We were told that the cave was larger before it was filled in with sand by the tsunami that hit the island in 1957. Maninolo Dry Cave, according to one legend, was created by the menehunes who had caught a great quantity of fish. There were too many fish to take them all home in one trip, so they carried as much as they could to their home in the mountain planning to return later for the rest of their catch. When they returned they discovered the remaining fish had been stolen. The menehunes noticed a small hole in the mountain which was a clue to path that the fish thieves had taken. The menehunes proceeded to dig out the thieves and the result was this dry cave. Another legend credits the goddess Pele who traveled along the Na Pali coast searching for fire in the earth. She fell in love with the high chief of Kaua'i, Lohiau, however the couple could not be together until Pele found fire beneath Kaua'i, so she began to dig in search of it. She was unsuccessful and left Lohiau to go to the island of Hawai'i. The caves were the result of her efforts. In actuality, it is a lava tube. It is said that the inner room was used as a meeting chamber by chieftains.

Following another 2/10 of a mile past Haena State Park and just beyond Limahuli Steam are the *Waikapala'e Wet Caves,* accessible by a short hike up and behind the gravel parking area. One of the caves has a fresh water pool and a unique phenomena. The Waikapala'e (the name is commonly thought to mean water of the lace fern) Wet Cave has a cool shady cave known as the blue room. It requires a venture into the chilly waters and, depending on the water height, possibly an underwater swim through a submerged tunnel. This is one adventure we have yet to try, but we are told it is an inspiring experience. Apparently the reflection of the light through the tunnel causes the incredible blue effect on the cavern walls. Jim Borg, editor of Hawaii Magazine, wrote a humorous account of his excursions into the blue cave in the June 1995 issue. The second wet cave, the *Waikanaloa Cave*, is located roadside. This cave is salt water and not suitable for swimming. Slightly east of Ke'e, and not far beyond the "Blue Cave" is the area that in the 1960's became the *Taylor Camp*, owned by the brother of Elizabeth Taylor. The beach chapter has this tale of the island's flower children.

Limahuli Gardens is the newest of the three gardens on Kaua'i which are a part of the National Tropical Botanical Gardens. These gardens are situated on the north shore of Kaua'i, near the end of the highway in Haena. This magnificent site, surrounded by towering mountains and breathtaking natural beauty, receives an annual rainfall of 80 to more than 200 inches. Within Limahuli Valley are two important ecosystems -- the lowland rain forest and the mixed mesophytic forest. Together these two ecosystems are the natural habitat of over 70% of Kaua'i's, and 59% of Hawai'i's, endangered plant species. Thus, Limahuli Garden is vitally important as a botanical and horticultural resource. The Garden emphasizes rare and endangered plants of Hawai'i, as well as plants of ethno-botanical value.

Limahuli Gardens is also a part of an archaeologically significant site known as the Limahuli complex. The entire area has a rich history, and a series of ancient stone terraces, believed to be well over 700 years old, are visible at the garden. Limahuli Gardens encompass 15 acres, and was gifted to the NTBG by Juliet Rice Wichman in the mid 1970's. An additional 990 acres behind the garden are set aside as a natural preserve. In 1994 the gardens were opened up to tours on a limited basis. In the future there is the possibility that they may open up a trail to the 800-foot Limahuli Falls. Guided tours are currently available only on Tuesdays at 1 pm and Sundays at 10 am, the cost is $15 per person. Self-guided tours are offered for $10 per person each Tuesday at 10 am, Wednesday at 10 am and 1 pm, Thursday at 10 am and 1 pm, and Sunday at 1 pm. Parking area and restroom facilities are available. Picnic lunches are prohibited. Advance reservations are required for both the guided and the self-guided tours. (808) 826-1053.

When you reach Ke'e Beach, you've come to the end of the road. Remnants of ancient Hawaiian villages and the Kaulu o Laka Heiau can be found here. This sacred altar is set among the cliffs of Na Pali and was built for Laka, the goddess of hula. It is one of the dramatic sites on the island with views of the cliffs and ocean. The heiau is still used today by hula halaus.

Ke'e Beach is the end of your scenic drive (mile marker 10) and beyond is the Na Pali Coast, 11 miles of which are accessible by foot along the ***Kalalau Trail***. See the recreation chapter for a brief description of this scenic trail. While some have remarked that this is the most beautiful trail in the world, be forewarned that the Sierra Club rates the 11 mile hike to the Kalalau Valley as a "ten" on their scale of difficulty. The shorter hike to Hanakapi'ai is a partial day hike and more suited to the recreational hiker. Ke'e Beach currently has a lifeguard (but talk is that the service will be discontinued) and dangerous water conditions. Swimming and snorkeling is only recommended during very calm conditions and then using common sense. Above the beach, a walk of about 5 or 10 minutes will take you to remnants of ancient Hawaiian villages and the Kaulu o Laka Heiau. This sacred altar is set among the cliffs of Na Pali and was built for Laka, the goddess of hula. It is one of the dramatic sites on the island with views of the cliffs and ocean. The heiau is still used today by hula halaus. Ke'e Beach is the end of your road, but a great place to begin an evening sunset!

BEST BETS

Princeville Resort - elegantly wonderful, what an ideal way to enjoy Paradise. ***Sealodge*** - affordable and an incredible view of the Kilauea lighthouse. ***Hanalei Bay Resorts and Suites***

BED & BREAKFASTS

The following are just a few of the bed and breakfast options offered on the North Shore. See the end of this chapter under Rental Agents for companies that offer a wide range of properties around the island.

HALE 'AHA ★

3875 Kamehameha, PO Box 3370, Princeville, HI 96722 Phone (808) 826-6733, FAX (808) 826-9052. Toll free 1-800-826-6733. This is the only B & B overlooking the Princeville Golf Course. The upstairs house is reserved for guests; the living room is pretty and pastel with a cozy fireplace and dining area set up for breakfast. Rooms are cushy and comfy, everything is very homey, especially the hospitality of Ruth and Herb. Breakfast is at 8:00, but Herb gets up at 6:30 to put on the coffee for early risers who might want it with a muffin or cereal on the run. But if you wait, you'll be treated to a full spread that includes hot homemade bread (with guava butter), muffins, fresh fruit, granola or cereal; a tropical smoothie, fresh fruit, steamed brown rice with brown sugar, crushed almonds, raisins and fruit plus a baked apple with whipped cream! Rooms have TV's, mini refrigerators, bathroom amenities and extra towels and pillow. Guests are entitled to substantial golf discounts at the course. They take Visa and MC, but sorry, they don't take children. They provide a brochure that is very detailed and informative. The penthouse suite is the top floor of the property with 1,000 square feet of room, separate living area, large whirlpool tub and washer and dryer. Three night minimum stay. *Double occupancy from $85 up to penthouse suite at $210.*

HALE HO'O MAHA

PO Box 422, Kilauea, HI 96754. (808) 828-1341, 1-800-851-0291. Located in a country farm-like setting (in fact a bull lives just down the road), surrounded by ponds and streams with the ocean and bay just a bit further. The decor is whimsical and eclectic with lots of wood and wood artifacts and an aquarium in the living room. Each room has a personality of its own: the Pineapple Room has a round bed with pineapple bedspread, rugs and knick-knacks, and the romantic guava room has a canopy bed with sheer, wispy draping. Breakfast includes Anahola Granola (made just a few miles away), muffins and a plate of fresh fruit that not only offers papaya, pineapple, bananas and grapes, but rambutans, too! (They are like lichees with spikes!) Located on 5 acres, this home is within walking distance to two beaches. $20 per night charged for additional person. A 50% deposit is required to confirm your reservation for each room. Visa or mastercard accepted. Your hosts are Toby & Kirby Searles. *They offer four varied accommodations from $55-$80 per night, double or single occupancy.*

MAHINA KAI BED & BREAKFAST

Box 699, Anahola, HI 96703. (808) 822-9451. An Asian-Pacific style home located on a terraced hillside overlooking Anahola Bay. The bed and breakfast rooms rent for $95 single, $115 double with breakfast included. Also available is a 2 bedroom apartment that can sleep up to six persons. Rates are $150 for two, $175 for four, and $200 for six. Also on property is a tea house and two large meeting areas, with a capacity for 12-14 persons, this property could be geared for a small retreat. Cost to rent the entire facility is $600 per night. Breakfast would be included and other meals could be served by arrangement. Three night minimum stay is requested.

MAKAI FARMS

PO Box 93, Kilauea, HI 96754 (808) 828-1874. Located just outside the town of Kilauea, this small family farm specializes in the growing of orchids. This Bed & Breakfast is located in a building separate from the main house, with ocean and mountain views from the upper level. There is a king-size bed and a sleeper sofa.

Downstairs is a kitchen and bathroom. Breakfast fixings are provided and include fruits grown on the farm and freshly laid eggs. *$74 per night single or double occupancy, extra persons add $10 each. Children are welcome and no extra charge for those under age 14. A two-night minimum is requested.*

NORTH COUNTRY FARMS
PO Box 723, Kilauea, HI 96754, (808) 828-1513. North Country Farms is an organic vegetable, fruit and flower farm surrounded by horse farms. Their redwood guest cottage includes a kitchen for snacks and meals. *$85 per night.*

RIVER'S EDGE
PO Box 382, Kilauea, HI 96754. (808) 828-1582. Your hosts, Barbara and Gerry Johnson invite you to their North Shore home. *$65 single/double. Each additional person $10 per night.*

TASSA HANALEI
PO Box 856, Hanalei, HI 96714. (808) 826-7298 phone or FAX. Tassa Hanalei means Cup and Saucer Hawaiian Style, named after Tassajarra Hot Springs, a Buddhist retreat in California. Tassa Hanalei offers three cottages in an ethereal garden setting. The proverbial babbling brook runs right along the front and there are bottles of shampoo (biodegradable) within easy reach if you want to wash your hair in the clear and natural water. There are fresh flowers in the rooms, mini-kitchens with coffee makers and a mini-refrigerator, but the bathrooms are down the garden path next to the outdoor jacuzzi. (Bathing suits are optional in both the stream and the jacuzzi). Breakfast of fresh fruit and homemade pastry is brought to your room in a basket. The gardens are lush, the whole setting natural and tranquil. If it weren't for the outdoor privies, this would rate a star for its unique surroundings and retreat-like experience.
Three suites begin at $65 single/$85 double. Their King Kamehameha suite, with full kitchen and three sleeping areas runs $125 per night per family or $150 for a group of six.

INEXPENSIVE

(THE) FISH SHACK
Anahola. RENTAL AGENT: Prosser Realty 1-800-767-4707. In an ever continuing effort to give our readers the most options available, we felt it necessary to include this property. Located right on the edge of reef-protected Anahola Bay near the end of a dead-end road. Their flyer notes that this is a studio "for one or two who like each other." A "vacation" kitchen and full-size bed along with outdoor bamboo shower. *Rental rate: $50*

HALE MOI
5300 Ka Haku Rd., PO Box 899, Princeville, HI 96714. (808) 826-9602. Maui & All 1-800-663-696-6962. Forty units in two story buildings. Hotel rooms, studio suites with kitchens, 1 1/2 bedroom suites with kitchens. Mountain and garden views. Full kitchens except in hotel room units. Washer/dryer except in hotel units. Additional person $13 per night includes rollaway. Children 18 and under no charge when using existing bedding.
Hotel $76/62, studio $94/74; 1 BR 2 BTH $105-$125/ $65-95.

PANIOLO
Princeville. RENTAL AGENT: Hanalei Aloha 1-800-487-9833. Studio and 1 BR 2 BTH units. Swimming pool. Short walk to shopping and beach. *Studio and 1 BR units $105-125/$65-95.*

SANDPIPER VILLAGE
Located in Princeville. RENTAL AGENTS: Kaua'i Paradise Vacations 1-800-826-7782. This property offers hotel rooms, 1, 2 or 3 bedroom units. Pool and hot tub. Not all rooms have phones. Some 2 bedrooms have loft. Some have washer/dryer. *Hotel Room $50; 1 BR & loft $110, full unit $150.*

SEALODGE ★
Located in Princeville. RENTAL AGENTS: Carol Goodwin rents her J-7 unit with a fabulous view of the Kilauea Lighthouse (415) 573-0636. Kaua'i Paradise Vacations 1-800-826-7782. Oceanfront Realty 1-800-222-5541. Blue Water Vacation Rentals 1-800-628-5533. Hanalei North Shore Properties 1-800-488-3336. Ocean view units located along the bluff at Princeville. Sealodge took a heavy blow when Iniki swept through, but on the positive side much of the interiors of the condominiums, as well as the exteriors are sparkly and new. The exterior is cedar shake which is reminiscent of accommodations on the Oregon beachfront. While each unit has a different view, those on the farther eastern end have a spectacular view of the Kilauea lighthouse and Pacific coastline. Watch the waves come in over the extensive reef, enjoy the seabirds frolicking in the air currents or during the winter enjoy this outstanding viewpoint from which to watch whales. Just make sure you pack your binoculars! The trail down to the beach is marked by a "use at your own risk" sign and is steep and very slippery when muddy and recommended only for the hale and hearty. The trail ends on a rocky shore and you will need to clamor over the rocks to your left to reach the crescent shaped stretch of white sand beach that is the length of a football field. Because of the enormous 'Anini reef, this piece of coastline is fairly well protected all year from high ocean swell and surf.

With all the comforts of home, and outstanding vista, and value priced, you could hardly do better on the North Shore. Carol Goodwin offers the lowest rate for her beautiful J-7 unit:
1 BR 1 BTH $80; 2 BR, 2 BTH $100. Discounts for stays of two weeks or longer.

MODERATE

ALII KAI I
Located in Princeville. RENTAL AGENTS: Kaua'i Paradise Vacations 1-800-826-7782. Oceanfront Realty 1-800-222-5541. Blue Water Vacation Rentals 1-800-628-5533. Two bedroom, two bath units, some ocean front. Depending on the owners, units may be furnished with two double beds, a queen or one king. Most units have sleeper sofas. Some units with full-size washer/dryer. Units have ocean or mountain views. Pool *2 BR 2 BTH $140-150/120-130.*

ALII KAI II
Located in Princeville. On property management 1-800-648-9988. RENTAL AGENT: Kaua'i Paradise Vacations 1-800-826-7782. Some units with ocean view others to Bali or the mountain. Activity desk. Most units 1100 sq. ft. and recently

redecorated. Most include microwave, TV, many with VCR and washer/dryer. Pool and hot tub. *2 BR 2 BTH $125/$110.*

CLIFFS
Located in Princeville. RENTAL AGENTS: Kaua'i Paradise Vacations 1-800-826-7782. Blue Water Vacation Rentals 1-800-628-5533. Maui & All 1-800-663-696-6962. Studios, 1 BR 2 BTH, 2 BR 2 BTH and even 4 BR 4 BTH units available through some rental agents. Amenities include pool, 4 tennis courts, two jacuzzis, sauna, BBQ area and a recreation pavilion. Units have ceiling fans, lanais, full kitchens. Daily maid service. Beach nearby. *SBR $85, 1 BR 2 BTH $125, 2 BR 3 BTH $150, 3 BR 3 BA $200, 4 BR 4 BTH $250.*

HANALEI COLONY RESORT
Rental Agent: Hanalei Colony Resort, PO Box 206, Hanalei, HI 96714, (808) 826-6235, FAX (808) 8260-9893, 1-800-628-3004. Located on 4.5 acres of beach front, this village of condominiums offers accommodations with 2 bedrooms and twice weekly maid service. Situated just prior to the end of the road at Na Pali. The rooms are decorated island-style and they are open and airy with fabulous views and the beach in your backyard. This is truly a place to get away from it all because they don't have TV's, stereos, or phones (although there is a telephone by the pool where guests can make complimentary local phone calls). They do offer a complimentary breakfast poolside with tea, coffee and juice and a selection of fresh fruits and freshly baked pastries. Charo's Restaurant is located next door. Hotel amenities also include pool and jacuzzi. The first price listed is high season, generally the Christmas holidays and over summer. Car and condo packages available. Prices are for 1-2 days, discounts for 3 or more days. Weekly discount includes one night free. *2 BR g.v. $135/$115; o.v. $160/140; o.f. $190/170, premium ocean $210/$190.*

KAMAHANA
Located in Princeville. RENTAL AGENTS: Oceanfront Realty 1-800-222-5541. Kaua'i Paradise Vacations 1-800-826-7782. Blue Water Vacation Rentals 1-800-628-5533. One and two story condominiums overlooking the golf course. Pool. Located next to Sealodge. Bluewater rents *2 BR 2 BTH $140/125.*

MAKAI CLUB AND MAKAI CLUB COTTAGES
Located on the first fairway of Princeville's golf course. The Makai Club features one bedroom condo suites with full kitchens, washer/dryers, lanai, TV and VCR. The Makai Club Cottages are two bedroom cottages with two self-contained master suites, full kitchens, lanais with ocean, golf or mountain views. *An 8 day 7 night two bedroom cottage runs $1199 and sleeps six. Weekly rate for a one bedroom condo is $599.*

PALI KE KUA
5300 Ka Haku Rd., PO Box 899, Princeville, HI 96714. (808) 826-9066. Located at Princeville. RENTAL AGENTS: Marc Resorts Hawai'i 1-800-535-0085, toll free FAX 1-800-633-5085, local (808) 922-9700. Kaua'i Paradise Vacations 1-800-826-7782. Oceanfront Realty 1-800-222-5541. Maui & All 1-800-663-696-6962. Blue Water Vacation Rentals 1-800-628-5533. Hanalei North Shore Properties 1-800-488-3336. Ninety eight units in two story buildings, this property

has an ultra-modern exterior. 1 BR units are 763 sq. ft., 2 BR are 1,135 sq. ft. Amenities include pool and jacuzzi. A short walk to a small beach. Located on the cliffs at Princeville. Adjacent to the Princeville Golf Courses. Weekly maid service. NOTE: This is an example of the call around and check prices theory. Below are the standard rates we found, however, Kaua'i Paradise Vacations offers hotel room units as low as $70 and "posh" units 1 BR $130-140, 2 BR 150-160. *1 BR dlx o.v. $169; 1 BR dlx o.f. $199; (max 4)*
2 BR dlx mt.v. $189; 2 BR dlx o.v. $219; 2 BR dlx o.f. $249; (max 6)

PUAMANA
Located on golf course in Princeville. (808) 826-9768. RENTAL AGENTS: Oceanfront Realty 1-800-222-5541. Prosser Realty 1-800-767-4707. Blue Water Vacation Rentals 1-800-628-5533. Two bedroom, two bath units, many with ocean views. Swimming pool. *Blue Water Rentals units priced: 2 BR 2 BTH $125/105. Prosser Realty offers a 3 BR 3 bath home at Puamana with a golf course view for $125 for 2. $10 each additional person.*

WAIOLI VACATION RENTAL
PO Box 1261, 5539 Weke Rd., Hanalei, HI 96714. (808) 826-6405. Claudia Herfurt offers an 800 square foot apartment which is on the lower level of her home. It has a living room, separate bedroom, and outside patio and bbq. Located across the road from the beach. *$600 per week. 3 day minimum stay.*

EXPENSIVE

HANALEI BAY RESORT AND SUITES ★ (HOTEL)
Located in Princeville. RENTAL AGENT: Castle Resorts & Hotels (808) 591-2235, FAX (808) 596-0158, 1-800-367-5004. Maui & All 1-800-663-696-6962. The Hanalei Bay Resort has combined with what was formerly Embassy Suites Resort and is the Hanalei Bay Resorts and Suites. The property is now one resort managed by Castle Resorts.

Built in 1979 and completely renovated in 1994, the former Hanalei Bay Resort offers three floors with a total of 153 rooms. The former Embassy Suites portion added another 75 one two and three bedroom suites on three floors. No elevators.

Suites are equipped with a full kitchen offering a full-size refrigerator, stove/oven, dishwasher and coffee maker. One bedroom suites are 1091 sq. ft with two televisions. Two bedroom suites are 1622 sq. feet with two bathrooms and three televisions. Three bedroom suites are 2085 sq. ft with three bathrooms, four televisions and service for eight guests.

There are a lot of free activities for guests: slide presentations, scuba lessons or a tennis clinic. The on site Bali Hai restaurant has a spectacular view and a hula presentation by Halau 'O Hanalei every Sunday evening. Sunday afternoon there is Jazz in the Happy Talk Lounge. The pool and jacuzzi are built in a natural lagoon setting with an island in the middle. It almost looks like it was there before and the hotel was built around it. The bathrooms are unusually decorated with a

Victorian look: a flowered patterned rug, green tile and floral decor make it more homey and a lot less sterile than most hotel bathrooms. Resort amenities include an over size swimming pool and eight tennis courts (some lighted for night play) on the property. Rooms feature air-conditioning, telephones, balcony, and daily maid service. Non-smoking rooms available on request. Hotel rooms are 521 sq. ft. and studios are 570 sq. ft. Conference facilities available. Eight complimentary tennis courts are on the property. Tennis school available during the summer months. The Princeville Makai and Prince Golf Courses are adjacent to the property (a total of 45 holes) and golf shuttle service. Conference facilities available.

Hotel rooms with mt.v., o.v., g.v. (1-2) $135-$230; Studio with kitchenette mt.v., g.v., o.v. (1-2) $150-240. Additional persons $20. Ask about room and car packages.

1 BR Suite mt.v. $250, o.v. $270 (1-4); 2 BR Suite mt.v. $350, o.v. $460 (1-6); 3 BR Suite o.v. $650 (1-8). Additional person $20. Also available are 1, 2 and 3 bedroom prestige suites, all ocean view $500-$1000.

PRINCEVILLE RESORT ★ (HOTEL)
PO Box 3069, Princeville, HI 96722. 1-800-826-4400 from the US & Canada, locally (808) 826-9644, FAX (808) 826-1166. For reservations call their toll-free number 1-800-325-3535.

The Sheraton Princeville Hotel opened their 252-room resort in September 1985. The hotel was closed following Hurricane Iniki in September 1992 and reopened in October 1993. Readers of the Conde Nast Traveler voted the Princeville Resort the eighth best tropical resort in the world and the best resort on Kaua'i in their article published in October 1993.

PRINCEVILLE RESORT

The Princeville Resort is a stunning property. From the moment you enter the spacious lobby you will feel worlds away. While not traditionally Hawaiian, this hotel is classic elegance with a European flare. The use of water throughout the lobby, above the restaurant and in the foyer creates reflecting pools that glimmer and glisten. With a lobby so enormous and opulent, it is surprisingly simple to find a quiet corner. Off to one side is the library lounge, a popular spot for taking afternoon tea, reading a good book, or watching the sun slowly sink from either the veranda or a cozy sofa indoors.

Situated on 23 lush tropical acres, the resort comprises three separate buildings that terrace down Pu'u Poa Ridge, reaching from the top plateau of Princeville to the Beach of Hanalei Bay. The lobby and entrance are located on the 9th floor, the pool and beach are on the first floor. A total of six rooms are available for the physically challenged. There is a freshwater swimming pool and three whirlpool spas plus an exercise room and an in-house cinema showing movies nightly. A thoughtful addition in the guest rooms is a Do Not Disturb light that you can switch on from next to the bed that glows out in the hallway. The bathrooms are divine, filled with oversize bathtubs, marble double vanities, telephones and music speakers. In each bathroom there is a "magic" window which electronically changes to allow for view or opaqueness. It is right up there with the Halekulani on O'ahu, a shower with a view! Tasteful additions, such as the fresh orchids in the vase in the bathroom, add that pampered feeling. The view is one of the amenities here and from every possible angle of the hotel, they've incorporated that picture perfect setting. The resort is beautiful during the day, but perhaps even more spectacular at night. The Living Room Lounge has a very comfortable and homey feel and you can enjoy afternoon tea while you again get an opportunity to appreciate the view.

Cafe Hanalei and Terrace is much more spectacular than its name seems to indicate. In fact, it doesn't have much at all in common with a "cafe." The bay of Hanalei below and the cliffs best known as Bali Hai create a lovely and romantic dining environment for breakfast, lunch, dinner or Sunday brunch. Don't miss splurging on dinner here, or better yet, the Friday seafood buffet. Even if you are not fortunate enough to have the opportunity to stay at this resort, be sure to stop and visit and you are sure to make plans for a stay during another vacation to Kaua'i.

The menu is a blend of American, Oriental, Hawaiian and a touch of Italian for good measure. La Cascata offers Mediterranean cuisine seven nights each week. The Beach Restaurant and Bar serves lunch and snacks daily. The resort also has available a very nice selection of meeting and banquet facilities. Activities include their Hawaiian Cultural program of poi - pounding, Hula and Hawaiian implement demonstrations, Hawaiian story telling and lau hala weaving. Their Keiki Aloha program is for their young guests ages 5 - 12 years and offers special excursions and movie nights, as well as Hawaiian arts and crafts. Program is offered Christmas and summer vacations. Should you feel the need for extra pampering, the Prince Health Club and Spa is located at the Prince Golf and Country Club. *Standard $250; partial ocean $325; o.v. $380; o.f $410; Prince Junior Suite $450. Executive suites are also available. Third person in room is an additional $35 per night.*

PU'U PO'A
5300 Ka Haku Rd., PO Box 899, Princeville, HI 96714. (808) 826-9602. RENT-AL AGENTS: Marc Resorts Hawai'i 1-800-535-0085, toll free FAX 1-800-633-5085, local (808) 922-9700. Kaua'i Paradise Vacations 1-800-826-7782. Ocean-front Realty 1-800-222-5541. Maui & All 1-800-663-696-6962. Hanalei North Shore Properties 1-800-488-3336. Fifty-six units in four story buildings. Pool and tennis court. Units have televisions, washer/dryer, ceiling fans, full kitchens, daily maid service. Units at Kaua'i Vacation Rentals $150-$175 per night for 2 BR units. Units at Maui & All Island $208/179.
2 BR dlx o.v. $229; 2 BR luxury o.v. $259; (max 6)

PRIVATE HOMES

ANINI BEACH VACATION RENTALS
PO Box 1220, Hanalei Bay, HI 96714. 1-800-448-6333, (808) 826-4000, FAX (808) 826-9636. They offer a variety of two, three and four bedroom rental homes on the North Shore. Prices start at $1,200 per week and go upwards to more than $1000 per day. Perhaps you'd like to vacation at Nene Pupule (Crazy Goose) located across from the home of Sly Stallone?

HALE KIPA
5128 Sunset Drive, Princeville. 1-800-866-2539. Hosts Henry and Gloria Drayton This vacation rental is located on the golf course at Princeville. Two story, three bedroom and 3 1/2 bath home has over 3,000 square feet of living area. Four televisions will ensure that each guest has their choice of programming! Pool use at nearby Sunset Drive clubhouse. Discount rate to Princeville golf course. $1,450 per week plus tax. Add $475 for 6 rounds of golf.

HARRINGTON'S PARADISE PROPERTIES
PO Box 1345, Hanalei, HI 96714. (808) 826-9655. FAX (808) 826-7330. A varied selection of homes and cottages around the island.

HOMES AND VILLAS IN PARADISE
150 Hamakua Drive, Suite 719, Kailua, HI 96734. 1-800-282-2736, (808) 236-4143, FAX (808) 235-0828. Several cottages and a number of three, four and five bedroom homes.

KALIHIWAI JUNGLE HOME
Contact: Your Kaua'i Vacation Home, PO Box 717, Kilauea, HI 96754 (808) 828-1626. This 2 bedroom, 1200 square foot vacation home includes hot showers indoors as well as outdoors by the jungle. Situated on one-half acre along the rim of the Kalihiwai Valley jungle, it is located 2 minutes away from 'Anini Beach. Daily, weekly and monthly rates available. Call for current rates.

KILAUEA LAKESIDE ESTATE ★
Contact Cindy and Steve Hunt, 910 The Strand, Hermosa Beach, CA 90254, phone (310) 379-7842. Situated on a 3-acre peninsula surrounded by a 20-acre freshwater lake with 1,000 feet of lake frontage and a white sand beach. You

couldn't get much more private than this! The lake offers boating as well as catfish and bass fishing. The home features 3 large bedrooms and 3 baths, a 2 person spa tub, washer/dryer. High Season rates apply December 15-April 15 and June 15-September 15. Special rates for Christmas holiday.

$1,500 per week low season; $1,800 per week high season. Rates are for up to six guests. Additional guests $100 per week.

MOLOAA KAI
RENTAL AGENT: Prosser Realty 1-800-767-4707. Two bedroom one bath home in Moloaa can sleep up to six persons. *$125 plus $50 cleaning fee.*

NORTH SHORE PROPERTIES
PO Box 607, Hanalei, HI 96714. (808) 826-9622. Condominium rentals, plus many cottages and homes, including Charo's own beachfront villa, equipped with two friendly dogs to play with. *Located on Tunnels Beach, it rents for $2,500-$4,000 per week.*

NA PALI PROPERTIES ★
PO Box 475, Hanalei, HI 96714, (808) 826-7272, FAX (808) 826-7665. Specializes in rental homes on the North Shore. They earn a star for having a wide range of selection and prices. Prices begin at $450 per week and range up to $2,000. Cottages or even 5 BR homes!

THE PAVILIONS AT SEACLIFF
Contact: Estate Manager, PO Box 3500-302, Princeville, HI 96722. (808) 828-1185, FAX (808) 828-1208. RENTAL AGENTS: Anini Beach Vacation Rentals 1-800-448-6333 or (808) 826-4000. Prosser Realty 1-800-767-4707. The property is bordered by the Kilauea Point Wildlife Bird Refuge and Kilauea Lighthouse. The house offers 3 ocean view master suites and 3 1/2 baths. A lap pool with jacuzzi. Washer/dryer, fax machine, plus a complete workout room. Minimum 3 night stay. Rates are for up to 6 guests. 10% monthly discount. $1,000 deposit required. *$600/day, $4,200 per week.*

PROSSER REALTY ★
4379 Rice St., PO Box 367, Lihu'e HI 96766. (808) 245-4711. 1-800-767-4707. Prosser Realty gets special mention for having a very interesting selection of rental homes, they also rent condominiums too!

RETREATS

ISLAND ENCHANTMENT
Humberto Blanco runs this B & B along with another business, Healing Arts Exchange Network, and combines them into Healing Paradise Adventure. Accommodations combined with a 6-8 day tour. Their outdoor adventures are combined with an opportunity to learn and practice the elements of yoga, body/mind techniques, meditation and massage. You can also arrange for a one day custom tour for $75 per person. Call for prices on 6-8 day tours. (808) 823-0705.

KAHILI MOUNTAIN PARK

PO Box 298, Koloa, HI 96756. (808) 742-9921. Owned and operated by the Seventh Day Adventist Church. The camp is 20 minutes from Lihu'e airport and 7 miles from Poi'pu Beach. Located on 197 acres. Cabins, cabinettes and new cabins are available and accommodate up to 6 persons each. The cabinette offers 5 twin beds, 2 that can be made into kings, a kitchenette with a two burner stove and shared bathrooms and showers. $30 double occupancy. The cabin has two twin beds and one double and sleeps up to 4 people. (Two cabins sleep up to 6 persons). Each has 1/2 bath inside and an outdoor private shower. The kitchen includes a two burner stove and small refrigerator. $40 double occupancy. The new cabins have two twin beds and one queen bed, a kitchen with two burner stove. Full indoor bath and shower and screened porch. $50 double occupancy. Each additional person is $6. Laundry on premises. They provide linens (including bedding and towels) dishes, dish soap, cookware.

KAI MANA

Shakti Gawain, author of books including *Creative Visualization, Living in the Light* and *The Path of Transformation: How Healing Ourselves Can Change the World*, now also offers Week-long "Intensives" at her Kaua'i home. Her five-acre estate, *Kai Mana* (which means powerful ocean) is located in Kilauea and overlooks a secluded beach. The week long programs are $100 per person, $2200 per couple and include breakfast and lunch daily. Also included are group sessions, meditation classes and two massages by a licensed practitioner. In addition to the week long retreats, they offer bed and breakfast style accommodations in one of several newly remodeled bedrooms or a cottage located on their property. Select from a queen or king room with full bath is $95 single, $115 double (2 night minimum) or a queen bed (or 2 full beds) and full bath $75 single, $95 double, (2 night minimum). The cottage has a five night minimum and includes a living room, kitchen and bath $125 per night, $750 per week. Master-Card and Visa accepted. Prices do not include tax. Contact Kai Mana, Box 612, Kilauea, HI 96754. Phone (808) 828-1280 or FAX (808) 828-6670.

POINSETTIA

KEAPANA CENTER
5620 Keapana Rd., Kapaʻa, HI 96746. (808) 822-7968, 1-800-822-7968. Located on six acres. Room with shared bath $55 double, $40 single; room with private bath $70 double, $55 single. Rates include continental breakfast, use of jacuzzis. They also offer space for small group retreats. The yurt is a 24' round structure that can accommodate 3 persons. There is a limit of 12 persons in the house. Exclusive use of the house accommodations, 5 BR without breakfast is $300 per night, an extra $60 per night for the yurt.

MAHINA KAI BED & BREAKFAST
Box 699, Anahola, HI 96703. (808) 822-9451. An Asian-Pacific style home located on a terraced hillside overlooking Anahola Bay. The bed and breakfast rooms rent for $95 single, $115 double with breakfast included. Also available is a 2 bedroom apartment that can sleep up to six persons. Rates are $150 for two, $175 for four, and $200 for six. Also on property is a tea house and two large meeting areas, with a capacity for 12-14 persons, this property could be geared for a small retreat. Cost to rent the entire facility is $600 per night. Breakfast would be included and other meals could be served by arrangement. Three night minimum stay is requested.

OLA HOU GUEST RETREAT
332 Aina Loli Place, Kapaʻa, HI 96746. 1-800-772-4567 or (808) 823-0109, FAX (808) 823-0109. In Hawaiian Ola Hou means "to revive." Guests are invited to rejuvenate their mind, body and spirit. Relax "au natural" by the oversized pool, or simmer their stress away in the jacuzzi or stroll through their enclosed 1/2 acre tropical gardens.

Located in the Wailua River Valley, they are adjacent to conservation lands with plenty of unpaved roads and pathways to follow by foot or on mountain bikes. Packages are available for up to 12 persons. They also can conduct guided tours of Kauaʻi to include 1/2 or full day itineraries and a picnic lunch. A masseur on the premises along with a gourmet chef whose services can be arranged by advance reservations. Cottage $90; Large 2 BR suite $125 per night double occupancy (max 4); week rates available. Minimum stay 3 nights. Extra persons $25 per night.

YMCA
The YMCA operates *Camp Naue*. It is located between the 7 and 8 mile markers on the State Hwy. past Haena on Kauaʻi's north shore. Camp Naue is located on four acres on the beach in Haena.

They offer two co-ed bunk houses that will sleep up to 50 people and a bath house with hot/cold showers and restroom facilities. The kitchen seats 60 people. They also have a 2 bedroom/1 bath beach cabin which sleeps up to 6 people. The beach cabin may be rented as part of a group reservation or for individual use. The beach cabin must be rented in order to receive exclusive use of Camp Naue. Because of the capacity of the camp, they only accept reservations for groups of 15 except for the cabin which requires no minimum but a maximum of 6 people.

Camp Naue:
Bunk Houses -- Kaua'i resident $11 per person/non-resident $12 per person.

Tent use -- one person and tent $10 per person
Each additional person in the same tent $7 per person

Cabin -- (renter furnishes own bedding) with group $40 per day, individual rental $60 per day.

Kitchen use: $25 per day and is non-refundable. Kitchen is equipped with most essential utensils.

YWCA
The YWCA operates *Camp Sloggett*. YWCA of Kaua'i, 3094 Elua Street, Lihu'e, HI 96766. (808) 245-5959, FAX (808) 245-5961, camp phone (808) 335-5959.

The YWCA hostel and campground is located in the heart of Koke'e State Park. Henry and Etta Sloggett built the lodge in 1925 as a mountain retreat for their friends and family. Following Henry's death the Sloggett children generously donated the house and grounds to the Kaua'i YWCA and in 1938 YWCA Camp Sloggett was established.

They offer accommodations in Sloggett Lodge which sleeps nine in 2 bedrooms (3 people in each) and 3 in the main room. The kitchen facilities offer commercial double ovens and 6 burner stove, two refrigerators, cookware and table settings for 48 people. A covered lanai space of 800 sq. ft. is suitable for dining, meetings or recreational use. The Weinberg Bunkhouse sleeps 40 people with mixed single and bunk style beds. Two staff rooms sleep 4 each and two common rooms offer space for 16 each. The bathroom has four toilets and showers. In April 1995 they opened additional bathrooms and kitchenettes. Camp rates are $12 per person per night for Kaua'i residents. $15 per person per night for Hawai'i residents. Non-residents are charged $20 per person per night. Children age 5 and under are free. A minimum of 5 people weekdays and eight people weekends. Ten people minimum on weekends during peak season May through September. Tent camping is available to Kaua'i residents for $5 per person per night. Hawai'i Residents $7 per person per night. Non-residents $10 per person per night. A two night minimum on weekends and 3 night minimum over holidays is required. Kitchenette facilities available. Hostel accommodations are in the Weinberg Bunkhouse and tent sites only and include use of bath and recreational facilities. Barbecue, microwave and refrigerator are available on the lanai. No reservations. Individuals accommodated on a space available basis.

CRUISE LINES

One pleasant way to see the Hawaiian islands is aboard one of the *American Hawai'i Cruises* ships, the *Independence* or *Constitution*. These comfortable 682-foot (800 passenger) ships provide accommodations and friendly service during the seven day sail around the islands. In 1993, American Hawai'i Cruises was acquired by The Delta Queen Steamboat Co. and they initiated some interesting new on-board programs. A hands-on Hawaiian museum exhibit, cabins receiving Hawaiian names, traditional Hawaiian church services, menus filled with Hawaiian specialties are among the changes which bring the essence of Hawai'i on board. American Hawai'i has also added on board Kumu (Hawaiian teachers) to teach passengers about the culture and history of Hawaii. A Kumu's Study with historic artifacts will be developed off the central lounge. The Sports Deck Solarium, on the Independence, has been converted into top-of-the-line passenger suites. Direct cellular telephone service is available from each cabin. A major improvement includes the expansion and redesign of the Buffet on the Ohana Deck.

The S. S. Constitution will be entering dry dock the end of June 1995 and will return to duties the end of June in 1996. Complete refurbishment will include the swimming pools, state rooms and public areas.

Both ships depart Honolulu on Saturdays. They travel a seven day route from Honolulu to Kona and Hilo on the Big Island, then to Kahului on Maui and stop at Nawiliwili on Kaua'i.

Also available on both ships are a number of "Theme Cruises" which range from Big Band cruises to one which combines with the island's Aloha Festival. The ships come into port at each of the major islands for a day (or in Maui two) of touring.

Wedding ceremonies can be performed aboard both of American Hawaii's ships with the purchase of a special $595 wedding package. The package includes a minister/judge fee, a Hawaiian lei and haku for the bride and matching lei or boutonniere for the groom, 24 photos in an album, live Hawaiian music and an individual wedding cake for two. Anniversary couples can arrange to renew their vows in a ceremony performed by the Captain himself. See GENERAL INFORMATION chapter for information on tests and licenses.

In 1996 the Independence will visit Kaua'i on Monday and the Constitution on Wednesday of each week.

American Hawai'i has added new shore excursions which include opportunities for passengers to discover the "hidden" Hawaii. Trips include the opportunity to hike through a rain forest to discover a hidden waterfall, or explore the active volcano of Kilauea.

The idea of a cruise is to give you a taste of each of the islands without the time and inconvenience of traveling by plane in-between islands. In fact, it would be impossible to see all the islands in a week in any other fashion.

For additional information contact a professional travel agent or call 1-800-474-9934 for a free brochure.

RENTAL AGENTS:

BED & BREAKFAST

All Island Bed & Breakfast
823 Kainui Drive
Kailua, HI 96734
(808) 263-2342
1-800-542-0344
FAX (808) 263-0308

Bed & Breakfast Kaua'i
6436 Kalama Rd.
Kapa'a, HI 96746
Liz Hey
(808) 822-1177

Bed & Breakfast Hawai'i
PO Box 449
Kapa'a, HI 96746
(808) 822-7771
1-800-733-1632
FAX (808) 822-2723

Pacific-Hawai'i Bed & Breakfast
c/o Neal Realty
602 Kailua Rd., #107C
Kailua, HI 96734
(808) 261-0532
Ask for Karen!
1-800-999-6026
FAX (808) 261-6573
Also vacation homes

CONDOMINIUM AND HOME RENTALS

ASTON HOTELS & RESORTS
22255 Kuhio Ave.
Honolulu, HI 96815
1-800-922-7866
From Hawai'i 1-800-321-2558
FAX (808) 922-8785

Aston Kaua'i Beachboy Hotel
Aston Kaua'i Beach Villas
Kaha Lani

BLUE WATER VACATION RENTALS
1-800-628-5533

Alii Kai
The Cliffs
Kamahana
Pali Ke Kua
Paliuli Cottages
Puamana
Sealodge
Also home rentals

CASTLE RESORTS AND HOTELS
(808) 591-2235
FAX (808) 596-0158
1-800-367-5004

Hanalei Bay Resort and Suites
Po'ipu Shores Condominiums

COLONY RESORTS, INC.
Foster Plaza
680 Anderson Drive
Pittsburg, PA 15220
1-800-448-0302
(412) 920-5700

Po'ipu Kai

GARDEN ISLAND RENTALS
PO Box 57
Koloa, HI 96756
1-800-247-5599
Call 8 am-noon Hawai'i time.

Nihi Kai
Whalers Cove
Waimea by the Sea
Also rental homes
including Stone House

GRANTHAM RESORTS
1-800-325-5701

Nihi Kai Villas
Po'ipu Crater Resort
Po'ipu Kai
Waikomo Stream Villas
Also rental homes and cottages

HANALEI ALOHA RENTAL MANAGEMENT
PO Box 1109
Hanalei, HI 96714
(808) 826-7288

Alii Kai
The Cliffs
Hale Moi
Hanalei Bay Resort
Kamahana
Mauna Kai
Pale Ke Kua
Paniolo
Puamana
Pu'u Po'a
Sealodge
Rental Homes

HARRINGTON'S PARADISE PROPERTIES
PO Box 1345
Hanalei, HI 96714
(808) 826-9655
FAX (808) 826-7330

Rental homes and cottages

KAUAI PARADISE VACATIONS
PO Box 1708
Hanalei, HI 96714
(808) 826-7444
FAX (808) 826-7673
Reservations 1-800-826-7782

Alii Kai I
Alii Kai II
The Cliffs
Hanalei Bay Resort and Suites
Kamahana
Pali Ke Kua
Pu'u Poa
Sandpiper
Also rental homes

KAUA'I VACATION RENTALS
1-800-367-5025
Various cottages and homes
plus a good selection of
condominiums, a few include:

Garden Island Sunset
Hale Awapuhi
Lae Nani
Pali Kai Cottages
Prince Kuhio

MARC RESORTS HAWAI'I
2155 Kalakaua Ave., 7th floor
Honolulu, HI 96815
1-800-535-0085 US/Canada
Toll free FAX (808) 663-5085
Hawai'i (808) 922-9700

Pale Ke Kua
Pono Kai Resort
Pu'u Po'a

MAUI & ALL ISLAND CONDOMINIUMS & CARS
US Mail only
PO Box 947
Lyden, WA 98264
Canadian Mail only
PO Box 1089
Aldergrove, BC V4W 2V1
(604) 856-4190
1-800-663-6962 US & Canada

The Cliffs
Hale Moi
Hanalei Bay Resort and Suites
Islander on the Beach
Kaha Lani
Kapa'a Shore
Kaua'i Beachboy
Kaua'i Beach Villas
Kaua'i Resort Hotel
Kiahuna Plantation
Lae Nani
Makahuena at Po'ipu
Outrigger Kaua'i Beach
Pali Ke Kua
(continued next page)

MAUI & ALL ISLAND
Plantation Hale
Po'ipu Kai
Pono Kai
Pu'u Po'a
Sunset Kahili
Wailua Bay Villas
Whaler's Cove
Also private home rentals

NA PALI PROPERTIES
PO Box 475
Hanalei, HI 96714
(808) 826-7272
FAX (808) 826-7665
Specializes in North Shore
home rentals $400-$2000 wk.

NORTH SHORE PROPERTIES
PO Box 607
Hanalei, HI 96714
(808) 826-9622
1-800-488-3335
FAX (808) 826-1188

Pu'u Poa
Pali Ke Kua
Sealodge
Rental Cottages and homes

OCEANFRONT REALTY
PO BOX 3570
Princeville, HI 96722
1-800-222-5541
Princeville office (808) 626-6585
FAX (808) 626-6478

Alii Kai
The Cliffs
Kamahana
Pali Ke Kua
Paliuli
Puamana
Pu'u Po'a
Sealodge

OUTRIGGER HOTELS HAWAI'I
1-800-733-7777 US & Canada
0014-800-125-642 Australia
FAX 1-800-456-4329

Outrigger Direct 808-926-0679

Outrigger Kaua'i Beach
Plantation Hale

PO'IPU CONNECTION REALTY
PO Box 1022
Koloa, HI 96756
(808) 742-2233
FAX (808) 742-7382

Alihilani Condominiums
Makanui Condominiums
Manualoha Condominiums
Po'ipu Makai
Po'ipu Palms

PROSSER REALTY
4379 Rice St.
PO Box 367
Lih'ue, HI 96766
(808) 245-4711
1-800-767-4707
FAX (808) 245-8115

Banyan Harbor
Kaha Lani
Nihi Kai Villas
Po'ipu Kai
Po'ipu Makai
Prince Kuhio
Puamana
Wailua Bay View
Waimea Plantation Cottages
Also homes and cottages

R&R
Realty & Rentals
1661 Pe'e Road
Po'ipu, HI 96756
(808) 742-7555
1-800-367-8022

Nihi Kai Vilas
Makahuena Resort
Po'ipu Crater Resort
Po'ipu Kai Resort
Po'ipu Palms
Rental homes

RESTAURANTS

The cultural diversity of the Hawaiian islands comes many benefits to visitors and residents alike. Along with the immigrants that have arrived over the years from many varied countries has come their native foods. Some may be familiar, while others will offer an opportunity to sample something new and interesting. The restaurants will be divided into the same three sections of the island as the accommodations. This will simplify looking for that perfect place for breakfast, lunch or dinner based on the location where you find yourself. A little background on some ethnic foods may tempt you to try a few new foods as a part of your dining adventure on Kaua'i.

CHINESE FOODS

Char Siu: roasted pork with spices
Crack Seed: preserved fruits and seeds, some are sweet, others are sour
Egg Roll: a rolled fried pastry with various vegetables, meat or shrimp inside
Okazuya: this is a style of serving where you select dishes from a buffet line
Won Ton: crispy fried dumpling

FILIPINO FOODS

Adobo: chicken or pork cooked with vinegar and spices
Cascaron: a donut made with rice flour and rolled in sugar
Halo Halo: a tropical fruit sundae that is a blend of milk, sugar, fruits and ice
Lumpia: fried pastry filled with vegetables and meats
Pancit: noodles with vegetables or meat

HAWAIIAN FOODS

Haupia: a sweet custard made of coconut milk
Kalua Pig: roast pig cooked in an underground imu oven, very flavorful
Kulolo: a steamed pudding using coconut milk and grated taro root
Lau Lau: pieces of kalua pig, chicken or fish flavored with coconut milk and
          mixed with taro leaves, then steamed inside of ti leaves
Lomi Lomi Salmon: diced and salted salmon with tomatoes and green onions
Long Rice: clear noodles cooked with squid or chicken broth.
Opihi: these salt water limpets are eaten raw and considered a delicacy
Poki: raw fish that has been spiced. A variety of types of fish are used and are
      often mixed with seaweed; for example, tako poki is raw octopus

KOREAN FOODS

Kim Chee: spicy pickled cabbage flavored with ginger and garlic
Kal Bi Ribs: flavored similarly to teriyaki, but with chili pepper, sesame oil and
             green onions
Mandoo: fried dumplings with meat and vegetable fillings

PUERTO RICAN

Pasteles: an exterior of grated green banana that is filled with pork and vegetables

JAPANESE FOODS

Fish Cake: white fish and starch steamed together
Miso Soup: soup of fermented soy beans
Sushi: white rice with various seafood and seaweed
Sashimi: raw fish
Wasabi: very spicy green horseradish root used to dip sushi into

LOCAL FAVORITES

Plate lunches: These combinations might include teriyaki chicken, hamburger with
        gravy or fish, but are always served with rice and a scoop or two of
macaroni salad
Loco Moco: a combination of hamburger, rice, fried egg and gravy
Bento: a box lunch
Saimin: top ramen -- only better!
Shave Ice: flaked ice that can be topped with a variety of flavored syrups,
        sometimes available with ice cream

ISLAND FISH

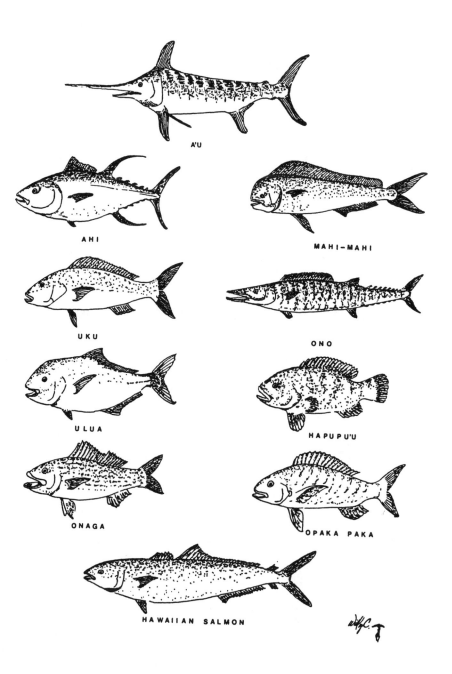

A'U

AHI

MAHI-MAHI

UKU

ONO

ULUA

HAPUPU'U

ONAGA

OPAKA PAKA

HAWAIIAN SALMON

A FEW WORDS ABOUT FISH

Whether cooking fish at your condominium or eating out, the names of the island fish can be confusing. While local shore fishermen catch shallow water fish such as goatfish or papio for their dinner table, commercial fishermen angle for two types. The steakfish are caught by trolling in deep waters and include Ahi, Ono, and Mahi. The more delicate bottom fish include Opakapaka and Onaga which are caught with lines dropped as deep as 1,500 feet to shelves off the island coast lines. Here is some background on what you might find on your dinner plate.

A'U -   The broadbill swordfish averages 250 lbs. in Hawaiian waters. Hard to locate, difficult to hook, and a challenge to land. Considered a steakfish.

AHI -   The yellow fin tuna (Allison tuna) weigh 60-280 pounds and are caught in deep waters off the Kaua'i coast. The pinkish-red meat is firm, yet flaky. This fish is popular for sashimi or seared.

ALBACORE - This smaller version of the Ahi averages 40 - 50 pounds and is lighter in both texture and color.

AKU -   This is the blue fin tuna.

EHU -   Orange snapper

HAPU -   Hawaiian sea bass

KAMAKAMAKA - Island catfish, very tasty, but a little difficult to find.

KAJIKI - Pacific Blue Marlin has a moderate flavor is best sauteed, but also good broiled or poached.

LEHI -   The Silver Mouth is a member of the snapper family with a stronger flavor than Onaga or Opakapaka and a texture resembling Mahi.

MAHI -   Although called the dolphin fish, this is no relation to Flipper or his friends. Caught while trolling and weighing 10-65 lbs., this is a seasonal fish which causes it to command a high price when fresh. *Beware*, while excellent fresh, it is often served in restaurants having arrived from the Philippines frozen and is far less pleasing. A clue as to whether fresh or frozen may be the price tag. If it runs less than $10 it is probably the frozen variety. Fresh Mahi will run $16 - $20 a dinner. This fish has excellent white meat that is moist and light. It is very good sauteed.

MU'U -   We tried this mild white fish at the Makawao Steak House and were told there is no common name for this fish. We've never seen it served elsewhere in restaurants.

ONAGA (ULA) - Caught in holes that are 1,000 feet or deeper, this red snapper has an attractive hot pink exterior with tender, juicy, white meat inside.

ONO -   Also known as Wahoo. ONO means "very good." A member of the Barracuda family, its white meat is firm and more steaklike. It is caught at depths of 25-100 fathoms while trolling and weighs 15 to 65 pounds.

'OPAE - Shrimp

OPAKAPAKA - Otherwise known as pink snapper and one of our favorites. The meat is very light and flaky with a delicate flavor.

PAPIO - A baby Ulua which is caught in shallow waters and weighs 5-25 lbs.

UKU -   The meat of this grey snapper is light, firm and white with a texture that varies with size. It is very popular with local residents. This fish is caught off Kaua'i, usually in the deep paka holes.

ULUA -   Also known as Pompano, this fish is firm and flaky with steaklike, textured white meat. It is caught by trolling, bottom fishing, or speared by divers and weighs between 15 and 110 pounds.

While it is difficult to pick out dining "best bets," we have done our utmost to eat as much as we possibly could to provide you with what we feel is a pretty fair highlight of the most terrific dining options on Kaua'i. If you have some additions to our list, please do write us with your suggestions! After all, each person has their own distinctive tastes, likes and dislikes. We would love to hear yours!

BEST BETS

BEST SMOOTHIES: Fruit smoothies at Banana Joe's Fruit Stand in Kilauea, Mango Mama's in Kilauea, and the People's Market in Puhi, near Lihu'e.

BEST FRENCH TOAST: Wake Up Cafe in Hanalei.

BEST BREAKFAST VALUE: Ma's in Lihu'e.

BEST FINE DINING IN A CASUAL ATMOSPHERE: Roy's, Gaylords and A Pacific Cafe.

BEST DINING VALUE: Eat at one of the local style restaurants!

RESTAURANTS WITH A VIEW: Aldon's has a wonderful view, try it for breakfast. Other views can be enjoyed at the Beach House Restaurant, Bali Hai with a view of Hanalei Bay, and J.J.'s Broiler offering a view of Kalapaki Bay. If you can afford it, Cafe Hanalei at the Princeville Resort wins hands down!

BEST SEAFOOD: House of Seafood has the most varied selection of fresh fish. Keoki's has a good, affordable seafood menu. Fisherman's Galley offers a casual atmosphere and good fish and chips! Generally, seafood is expertly prepared at our three favorite Kaua'i restaurants, Gaylords, Roy's and A Pacific Cafe.

BEST BREAKFAST: Kountry Kitchen, Kalaheo Coffee Shop and the Poipu Bay Resort Grill and Bar.

BEST DINNER BUFFET: Princeville Resort and the Ilima Terrace at the Hyatt.

BEST CHINESE: Hanamaulu Cafe has good food and great ambience. Kaua'i Chop Suey is another winner.

BEST BREAKFAST BUFFET: The Hyatt Regency

BEST SALADS: Warm ahi salad at A Pacific Cafe, a fresh green salad at Kalaheo Coffee House, sauteed scallop salad at Bali Hai, Oriental chicken salad at the Princeville Restaurant or Ilima Terrace at the Hyatt.

BEST SALAD BAR VALUE: Sizzler

BEST PIZZA: Brick Oven pizza, a long time favorite or try the new Tosca for a gourmet pizza from a wood-burning oven. Pau Hana gets points for its variety of unusual toppings!

171

BEST HAWAIIAN: L.C.'s Place in Hanapepe.

BIGGEST RESTAURANT MYSTERY: Black Pot Luau Hut in Hanalei has long been famous for its good Hawaiian food. While you peer through the smeared windows and see fresh flowers in a bowl and serving pieces set on the table, they never seem to be open! Ask locals and the shops nearby and they seem to vaguely remember that it is open once in a while.

BEST MEXICAN: Taqueria (called "The crack"), Sinaloa.

GOOD AND CHEAP: Hamura Saimin, Barbecue Inn and Waipouli Restaurant.

BEST "LOCAL STYLE": Lawai Restaurant.

BEST BAKERY: We can't single out a single one, since there are several that are SO good! Kilauea Bakery, Omoide in Hanapepe, Ohana Bakery in Princeville and the Bread Box in Kalaheo.

BEST HAMBURGERS: Duane's Ono Burgers.

MOST UNUSUAL BURGERS: Buffalo burgers at Ono Family Restaurant.

BEST SHAVE ICE: Halo Halo Shave Ice in Lihu'e.

BEST VEGETARIAN: The Espresso Bar in Hanapepe Bookstore has wonderful gourmet vegetarian dinners.

JANORA BAYOT

RESTAURANT INDEX

173

RESTAURANTS
Alphabetical Index

FOOD TYPE INDEX

AMERICAN
Camp House Grill 200
Jolly Roger 185
Koke'e Lodge 206
Koloa Broiler 206
Kountry Kitchen 188
Ono Family Restaurant 191
Po'ipu Bay Bar & Grill 209
Princeville Restaurant & Bar 219
Rob's Good Times Grill 209
Sideout Bar & Grill 195
Sizzler 195
TomKats Grill & Bar 213
Wailua Marina 198

BAKERIES
Kaua'i Ohana Bakery 218
Kilauea Bakery 218
Lihu'e Bakery & Coffee Shop 189
Michelle's 190
Tip Top Bakery 196

BREAKFAST/BRUNCH
Eggbert's 182
Hanalei Wake Up Cafe 217

BUFFETS
Cafe Hanalei 215
Ilima Terrace 204
Kukui's Restaurant & Bar . . 188
Voyage Room 197

BURGERS AND SANDWICHES
Amelia's 214
Auntie Sophie's Grill
        (Kapa'a) 178
Auntie Sophie's Grill
        (Princeville) 214
Bubba Burgers (Kapa'a) . . . 179
Bubba Burgers (Princeville) . 214
Dairy Queen 181,200
Duane's Ono Burgers 216
Ginger's Grille 183
Hale 'O Java 216
Hanalei Gourmet 217

Joe's Courtside Cafe 205
Kalaheo Coffee Co. & Cafe . 205
Michelle's 190
Mustard's Last Stand 208
Old Hanalei Coffee Company 219
Shipwreck Subs 210
Village Snack Shop 221

CHINESE-THAI-VIETNAMESE KOREAN-PHILIPPINE
Dragon Inn 181
(The) Fortune Cookie 183
Hale Kipa Terrace 183
Cafe Hanalei 215
Ho's Kitchen 184
Kaua'i Chop Suey 186
King & I 187
Korean BBQ 188
Lawai Restaurant 207
Mema Thai Cuisine 189
Olympic Cafe 191
Panda Garden 192
Po's Chinese Kitchen 193
Tammy's Okazu-ya 195
Toi's Thai Kitchen 213
Two Sistahs 196
Violet's Place 196
Wah Kung Chop Suey 197
Waipouli Deli & Restaurant . 198

FAMILY DINING
Aldon's 178
Barbecue Inn 179
Dani's 181
Jolly Roger 185
Keoki's Paradise 206
Koloa Broiler 206
Ma's 189
Mustard's Last Stand 208
Ono Family Restaurant 191
Sizzler 195
Wailua Marina 198

HAWAIIAN/LOCAL STYLE

HAWAIIAN REGIONAL AND PACIFIC RIM CUISINE

HEALTH FOOD

ITALIAN/PIZZA

JAPANESE

MEXICAN

LUAUS

STEAK & SEAFOOD

RESTAURANT INTRODUCTION

What do a green van in Hanalei and A Pacific Cafe (one of Hawai'i's most highly acclaimed restaurants) have in common? They both have earned stars! Tropical Taco has been operating for years out of this landmark vehicle on the North Shore.

The story begins long ago, in a land far, far, (well not really that far) away. When the first paradise guide was released we rated the restaurant by one, two, three or four stars. It was quickly apparent that comparing restaurants as different as Tropical Taco and A Pacific Cafe was a problem. Each was wonderful for what it was, but did Tropical Taco deserve only one or two stars because it has no indoor seating, (no outdoor seating for that matter) and only serves lemonade? Thus evolved the solution of recommending a restaurant on a one-star basis. These are our "favored" restaurants or eateries based on their individuality. In their own way, Tropical Taco and A Pacific Cafe meet particular needs. They both provide very good food for the vacation dollar. So as you read through the restaurant chapter, we've highlighted these special restaurants with our mark of excellence - - a ★ !

The restaurants have been divided into Central/Eastside which will offer dining options for Lihu'e, Kapa'a, Nawiliwili and Wailua. The Southern and Western portion of the island includes Poi'pu-Koloa-Lawa'i-Port Allen-Hanapepe-Waimea-Kekaha-Koke'e. Lastly the section on dining on the North Shore features restaurants (and vans) in the towns of Anahola, Princeville and Hanalei.

We haven't listed the fast food restaurants, McDonald's, Burger King and the like. You'll have no trouble finding them speckled around the island. Just take a breath before you check out the prices.

CENTRAL/EASTSIDE

A PACIFIC CAFE ★ *Pacific Rim/Hawaiian Regional Cuisine*
Kaua'i Village Shopping Center, Kuhio Hwy. in Kapa'a (822-0013) HOURS: 5:30-9:30. SAMPLING: Menu changes daily, but you might start with an appetizer like smoked shrimp lumpia with curry lime dip ($5.75) or Peking duck and shrimp tacos with papaya-ginger salsa ($9.50). Soup might be Thai coconut curry basil with island fish & shrimp or island pumpkin with sweet black Thai rice and sour cream ($5.25) or you might opt for a salad of marinated salmon and ahi with Kaua'i romaine and creamy wasabi dressing ($8.25). Entrees from the wood-burning grill might include grilled moonfish with shrimp polenta and mushroom compote ($21.95) or grilled rack of lamb Hunan style served with cabernet hoison sauce ($22.75). Specialties might feature blackened ono with papaya basil sauce & papaya salsa ($22.95) or seared scallops with caramelized pineapple vinaigrette, taro hash lumpia and lobster oil ($23.25). COMMENTS: This is the one you've heard about. (And so has everyone else, so reservations are a must.) Owner Chef Jean-Marie Josselin has garnered more than his share of accolades and awards since opening in 1990. He is one of the twelve acknowledged Hawaiian Regional Cuisine chefs in Hawai'i and is featured in two cookbooks on the market.

ALDON'S *American*
Kaua'i Sands Hotel, Kapa'a (822-4221) HOURS: Breakfast from 7 am, Dinner from 6 pm. No lunch. SAMPLING: Large selection of hot cakes, waffles, French toast, and egg dishes ($3.95-6.25). Dinners are offered a la carte or complete with soup or salad, beverage, bread, whipped potatoes or rice and vegetable ($7.95-11.50/9.25-12.95). There is spaghetti, roast turkey, chicken stir-fry or leg of lamb. COMMENTS: They serve old-fashioned food at old-fashioned prices. Breakfasts are the best bet, but any time before sunset buys you a great beachfront view. Karaoke five nights a week.

ALOHA DINER *Local*
971-F Kuhio Hwy, Kapa'a, located in the Waipouli Complex (822-3851) HOURS: Tuesday-Saturday, Lunch 10:30 am-3 pm, Dinner 5:30-9 pm. SAMPLING: Local plates for lunch and a few more expensive ones for dinner: Kalua pig or lau lau with lomi salmon and rice or poi ($5.50), with chicken luau, haupia or kulolo and tea or coffee for dinner ($8.50). Other lunches include tripe or beef stew and various combinations ($5.75-7). Dinner with additional items as above and in combination ($9.50-10.50). All specials items available a la carte along with won ton and saimin. COMMENTS: You can try luau food without the show.

AUPAKA TERRACE
Located at the Marriott. Open for breakfast and lunch. An attractive restaurant resembling a large gazebo in a park. The luncheon buffet caters to Japanese tour groups, but they have an a la carte menu as well. Not reviewed before press time.

AUNTIE SOPHIE'S GRILL *Burgers/Sandwiches*
Coconut Marketplace, Kapa'a. (823-0833) HOURS: 11 am-9 pm. SAMPLING: Hamburgers, jumbo hot dogs, and salads ($3.95-8.95). COMMENTS: Owners describe this outlet as more of a "food kiosk" with a more extensive menu at their Princeville location. A hot dog and a beer for $6 seems a bit steep.

BARBECUE INN ★ *American/Japanese*
2982 Kress Street, Lihu'e (245-2921) HOURS: Breakfast 7:30-10:30 am; Lunch 10:30-1:30 pm, Monday-Friday; Dinner 5-8:30 Monday-Thursday, 4:30-8:45 Friday & Saturday. Closed Sunday. SAMPLING: Breakfast - meats and eggs, pancakes ($2.25-7.50) and oriental breakfast of miso soup, teriyaki fish, scrambled egg with green onion, rice and hot tea ($6.95). Lunch - burgers, sandwiches and Japanese dishes plus specials: Reuben sandwich, katsu (chicken cutlet), eggplant parmesan, chicken with broccoli & noodles, breaded mahi mahi or shrimp platter ($3.50-8.95). Dinner - pork chops, teri steak or chicken, spaghetti, lobster, garlic shrimp and specials like prime rib, baked stuffed mahi mahi, hamburger curry, baked salmon and Japanese dinners - teriyaki, tempura, yakitori ($7.25-21.95). COMMENTS: Lunch specials include soup or fruit, drink & dessert; dinner also comes with salad. All sandwiches come on their freshly baked bread; you can buy a loaf to take home! The same family has owned the restaurant since 1940. It was named by the grandfather and although there are now a few token BBQ items on the menu, the BBQ in the name referred to a hibachi or small grill which was just the regular way of cooking. This is a nice family-style restaurant (Keiki menu for both lunch and dinner) with booths and curtains and a light, plantation-style look. Good value, too.

BENTO HOUSE *Japanese/Local*
3122 Kuhio Hwy., Lihu'e (246-9444) HOURS: 6 am-2 pm Monday-Friday. SAMPLING: Takeout box lunches ($3.75-5), daily specials and plate lunches ($4.25-4.75), mini bento ($2.50), cone sushi, spam, teri chicken & teri beef musubi, homemade baked goods & mochi.

BUBBA BURGERS *Burgers*
1384 Kuhio Hwy., Kapa'a (823-0069) HOURS: 10:30 am-6 pm, closed Sundays. SAMPLING: Bubbas, double bubbas, hubba bubbas plus hot dogs, corn dogs, Budweiser beer chili, fish burgers and Italian sausage burgers ($1.50-5.75). Side order of Caesar salad, French fries, onion rings, frings (fries and rings) or chili fries ($1.50-3.50). COMMENTS: With a name like Bubba's, you were expecting maybe escargot? They're fun and funny and serve good, old-fashioned burgers to anyone named Bubba. (That means you!) They used to "cheat tourists and drunks", but had to "cease and desist" after receiving a letter from a San Francisco attorney. So now they also cheat attorneys! They've got another hamburger joint in Hanalei; both locations have take-out and T-Shirts.

BULL SHED ★ *Steak and Seafood*
796 Kuhio Hwy., Waipouli (822-3791) HOURS: Cocktails from 4:30, Dinner 5:30-10 pm. SAMPLING: Prime rib $18.95, garlic tenderloin $16.95, Australian lamb rack $18.95, seafood with steak or chicken combos ($14.50-25.50), catch of the day under $18, usually $15-16. Salad bar is included that offers basic ingredients, but a few unusual items like peas, fresh pineapple and garlic bread. Mud pie for dessert; kids menu of teriyaki chicken $6.95 or fresh fish $7.95. COMMENTS: I expected a dark and dingy steakhouse, but this was light and bright; very open with picture windows and a great ocean view. Arrive early for a view table! The food is consistently good.

BUZZ'S STEAK & LOBSTER   *Steak & Seafood*

Coconut Plantation Marketplace, Kapa'a (822-0041) HOURS: Lunch 11 am-2:30 pm, Dinner 5-10:30 pm. SAMPLING: Lunch offerings include tuna or chicken avocado salad and turkey, mahi mahi, chicken or tuna salad and French dip sandwiches ($4.95-5.95). Appetizers might be mozzarella sticks, calamari, sauteed mushrooms or teriyaki beef sticks ($4.50-7.95). Dinner, naturally, has steak and lobster, alone or in combination with shrimp, scallops, fresh fish, prime rib, baby back ribs, teriyaki chicken, pork chops, spaghetti and seafood linguini ($8.95-17.95). Cheesecake or homemade ice cream pie for dessert ($3.95). COMMENTS: Dinner is served with fresh bread, vegetables, French fries, rice or baked potato, add soup or salad for $2. They no longer have a salad bar.

CAFE PORTOFINO   *Italian*

3501 Rice St., Pacific Ocean Plaza, Nawiliwili (245-2121) HOURS: Lunch Monday-Friday 11 am-2 pm, Dinner nightly 5-10 pm. SAMPLING: Roasted bell peppers and escargot are featured appetizers and with a Hawaiian twist on an Italian favorite, they offer prosciutto with papaya instead of melon ($5.75-7.75). Caesar or warm potato salad ($4.75-6.75) might come next or you might want to go straight to the pastas like lasagna, spaghetti, linguini or fettucine with garlic, cream or gorgonzola ($12.50-13.75). Meat and seafood dishes are served with pasta ($9.50-15.75). Veal comes with basil cream, mushrooms and marsala, tomato and mozzarella, or white wine and chicken with orange and white wine, juniper berry or onions and mushrooms ($12.50-18.75). Specialties include rabbit, Osso Bucco, scampi, sweetbread and eggplant parmigiana ($13.00-19.25). Crepes, profiteroles, caramel custard, and tiramisu are some of the homemade desserts ($3.50-5.50). COMMENTS: It looks like an elegant stucco house with paned windows, beamed ceilings and a patio (a lanai where you can dine al fresco overlooking Kalapaki Beach). Nice bar and lounge areas with live music (usually jazz) on weekends. Food is authentic Italian with ingredients imported from Italy, then made fresh here. Breads, ice creams and desserts made on the premises. Everything made to order; cream sauces are fresh, not from pre-made bases.

CHARLIE'S PLACE   *Mexican/Sandwiches*

1419 Kuhio Hwy., Kapa'a (822-3955) HOURS: Lunch 11 am-3 pm, Dinner 6-10 pm, selected items from 11 am to 10 pm. SAMPLING: burritos, enchiladas, quesadillas, chimichangas, tacos in choice of chicken, beef, chili verde, carnitas, fish or seafood (Lunch $7.25-8.95, Dinner $11.95-13.95). Chicken mole for dinner ($13.95), burgers and sandwiches ($4.50-8.25), Appetizers: Mexican pizza, jalapeno poppers, ono ceviche ($4.50-6.95). Fried bananas or Mexican flan for dessert ($2.95). COMMENTS: Casual, small bar and tables, lunch on the deck. Live entertainment nightly from 9 pm. Owner Charlie Petterson says everything is authentic and made from scratch by Papa & Chino who are from Guadalajara. So why do they have Moussaka ($9.95) and Gyros in Pita ($8.50) on the menu? Charlie's Place used to be a Greek restaurant called Makai and they were held over by popular demand.

DA BOX LUNCH PLACE   *Local*

3204 Kuhio Hwy., Lihu'e (245-5151) HOURS: 5:30 am-1:30 pm (Breakfast 6-10 am) Closed Sundays. SAMPLING: Teriyaki beef, ginger garlic chicken, macaroni or potato salad, golden fried shrimp and more, all boxed to go! Plate lunches $4-7 boxed lunches from $4.25. COMMENTS: A few tables indoors, but you might want to pick up a box to take along to your destination of the day.

DAIRY QUEEN *Local*
Waimea (338-1911) Ele'ele (335-5293 Lihu'e (245-2141)
HOURS: Breakfast from 6:30 am, (Ele'ele from 9 am Monday-Thursday) Dinner after 5 pm. SAMPLING: Eggs, hot cakes and waffles, omelettes, pork chop with gravy, beef or tripe stew for breakfast ($2.50-5.95). Dozens of sandwiches including hot turkey or roast beef, BLT, pastrami, mahi mahi, hot dogs, ham, tuna and chicken salad ($2-4.25). Salads include somen, Oriental chicken and a variety of chef's salads and burgers come with cheese, bacon, teriyaki and BBQ or you can get your burger with fish, chicken, chili or as a tuna or patty melt on rye, ($1.15-3.95). Tacos, burritos, loco moco ($1.25-3) as well as entrees of pork chops, liver and onions, sweet & sour spare ribs, breaded fish, chicken and veal cutlets ($3.75-6.25) are only part of the extensive menu. For dessert, there's all the familiar Dairy Queen treats such as cones, shakes, floats, freezes and a variety of sundaes ($1-3.50) The Lihu'e DQ also has lau lau plate lunches and dinner specials that include prime rib, scampi, rib steak, butterfish and seafood platters- alone or in combinations - are available after 5 ($7.50-14.95). They also offer a variety of specialty submarine sandwiches and French dips ($3.75-4.25). COMMENTS: A lot of food for an ice cream shop; the whole menu is available for take out and they have catering, too.

DANI'S *Local*
4201 Rice St., Lihu'e (245-4991) HOURS: Breakfast 5-11 am; Lunch 11 am-1:30 pm, to 1 pm on Saturdays. Closed Sundays. SAMPLING: Breakfast meats, eggs, omelettes including kalua pig and Dani's special with fish cake, green onion and tomato ($4.20-5.70). Pineapple, banana, papaya hot cakes and sweet bread French toast ($3.20-5.30). Breakfast and lunch specials include combinations of lau lau, kalua pig, beef or tripe stew ($4.70-7.80) and lunch entrees offer steak, pork chops, roast pork, veal, beef or chicken cutlet, fried shrimp, oysters or scallops, plus burgers and sandwiches ($1.70-6). COMMENTS: Popular local coffee shop. Kind of looks like an Elks Lodge Hall without the elk. While Dani's might be a bit brighter (and even cleaner) we recommend driving around the corner to Ma's instead.

DRAGON INN *Chinese*
Waipouli Plaza, 901 Kuhio Hwy. (822-3788) HOURS: 11 am - 2 pm Tuesday-Sunday, 4:30 - 9:30 pm daily. SAMPLING: Soups, appetizers, sizzling platters, hot pots, seafood, cold plate, chicken, duck, beef and pork, egg, vegetable, rice and chow mein ($5.50-18.95). Specials include hot pot kau yuk, almond duck and steamed fish with seasonal vegetables ($6.25-7.95). Dinner specials for 2 to 6 ($19.95-89 - yes that is $89) or dinner plate with egg flower soup, deep fried chicken wing, crisp won ton, ginger and green onion chicken, sweet & sour spareribs, chicken chow mein, and char siu fried rice ($8.25). Lunch buffet offers nine items including soup, appetizer and main course for $5.95. COMMENTS: Banquet room look, but cleaner and brighter. Large portions, good prices.

DUKE'S CANOE CLUB *Hawaiian*
Located in front of the Kaua'i Marriott at Kalapaki Beach. (246-9599) HOURS: Dinner 5-10 pm, cocktails 4 pm-midnight. COMMENTS: The Barefoot Bar is open from 4-11:30 pm. The restaurant, named in honor of Duke Kahanamoku, probably the greatest surfer of all time, features an extensive collection of Duke memorabilia including photos, an impressive 40-foot outrigger canoe, and three of his surfboards. The lava rock waterfall in the center is a focal point, with stairs alongside and a spacious and attractive area upstairs. There is a separate area with a salad bar and wide plantation-like verandas which overlook the ocean. Closed since September 1992, Duke's reopened in early summer 1995 after extensive renovations to retain its original look. The 30-foot waterfall is as spectacular as ever, splashing into a koi pond. The one new change is the addition of koa paneling on the walls. Diners who remember Duke's will be pleased to know that the dining room menu is unchanged. Fresh fish, seafood, steaks, and prime rib are still the most popular offerings with entrees priced under $20. The Barefoot Bar serves cocktails, Hawaiian local favorites, sandwiches, burgers and pupus. Duke's Canoe Club is owned and managed by TS Restaurants which also operates Keoki's Paradise at Poipu and Sharky's Fish Market at Nawiliwili Bay.

EDO MAE *Japanese*
Located at the Marriott, near the lobby overlooking what was the Palace Court. Opening in October/November 1995. Not open in time to review.

EGGBERT'S *Breakfast*
Coconut Marketplace, water wheel side (822-3787) HOURS: Breakfast and lunch, may be open for light dinners. SAMPLING: Three styles of eggs Benedict: veggie, ham and turkey combo and you can choose your own toppings. You can also choose the fillings for your omelette. Banana pancakes, pork and cabbage, steak and eggs, pigs in blankets, smoothies ($3.95-9.95). COMMENTS: This new Eggbert's was due to open in the summer of 1995 as we went to press so some of the vital statistics are still missing. When they were in Lihu'e (before the Hurricane), they were most known for their eggs Benedict and Bloody Marys and were popular with kids for their pigs in blankets and banana pancakes.

FLYING LOBSTER *Seafood*
Kaua'i Coconut Beach Resort, Wailua (822-3455) HOURS: 6-9:30 pm. SAMPLING: Lobster dinners from $14-27; in combination with mahi mahi macadamia, fresh catch, garlic shrimp, pulehu pork ribs or teriyaki top sirloin steak $15.50-22.

KOI

Steak, Hawaiian sampler platter, chicken chassuer, sauteed scallops with shitake mushrooms, seafood, lobster or vegetable stir-fry ($13.50-21.00); seafood salads, burgers or lobster bisque, salad & pupu bar ($6-11). All meals include lobster bisque and salad bar. Signature desserts are the coconut beach Hawaiian sand pie and the Flying Lobster banana coupe. COMMENTS: This is called The Voyage Room at breakfast and lunch and specializes in buffets. The soup, salad and Pupu Bar for $11 adults is a very good deal.

(THE) FORTUNE COOKIE   *Chinese*
4261 Rice St., Lihu'e (246-0855) HOURS: Monday-Friday 9 am-8 pm, Saturday 10:30-3 pm. SAMPLING: Chicken, duck, pork, beef, vegetable and shrimp dishes, also egg fu yung, chow mein ($4.95-10.50). Plate lunches and mini lunches offer lemon, shoyu, spicy or ginger chicken, roast duck, char siu, black bean sauce or sweet & sour spareribs and include rice, sweet & sour cabbage and won ton ($3.95-6.75). Bentos served all day ($4.80-6.45). COMMENTS: Free delivery in Lihu'e with minimum purchase. Opened in 1993.

GINGER'S GRILLE   *American*
Kaua'i Village, Kapa'a (822-5557) HOURS: Soups, salads, sandwiches 11 am-10 pm, Dinner 5-10 pm. SAMPLING: Cobb, chicken, seafood salads; burgers, smoked turkey, club, BLT, chicken and fish sandwiches, shrimp or crab melt ($5.95-9.95). Mozzarella stix, spicy French fries, crispy won ton, calamari or onion rings, wing dings for appetizers ($3.95-6.95) and for dinner NY steak, scampi, mahi mahi and stir-fry - local style - with beef, chicken or shrimp ($12.95-16.95). Shari's island pie is the featured dessert: Oreo cookie crust, Kona coffee ice cream topped with fudge, sliced toasted almonds and whipped cream - $3.50. COMMENTS: Bar/Pub atmosphere. They offer 10% discount for seniors.

HALE KIPA TERRACE   *Chinese/Island style*
Outrigger Kaua'i Beach (245-1955) HOURS: Breakfast, lunch and dinner. SAMPLING: Breakfast: omelettes, eggs Benedict, light or buttermilk pancakes, sweet bread French toast, Belgian waffle ($5.50-11.25). Fitness offerings of fresh fruit frappe, three grain pancake or Kaua'i frittata ($4.75-9.75). Also continental breakfast ($6.95) and buffet ($11). Lunch: French dip, hot turkey, burger, pastrami, mahi mahi, club and ahi salad sandwiches ($8-9.50). Caesar, fruit and Shanghai chicken salad ($9-9.75). Also pupus: potato skins, crispy won ton, Chinese spring rolls, fish platter, nachos, char siu ($4.95-9.95). Dinner features roast beef, huli huli roast chicken, honey glazed pork chop, shrimp tempura, kiawe smoked rack of lamb, fresh fish ($18-27). COMMENTS: They offer two buffets: The prime rib buffet on Saturday ($21) and the seafood buffet every Tuesday and Friday ($36). Several private alcoves with tables and "bamboo booths" that provide a bit of a plantation look accented by coral, blue and lavender colors. Their food is hotel fare and the prices are accordingly inflated.

HAMURA SAIMIN   ★   *Local*
2956 Kress, Lihu'e, just off Rice Street (245-3271) HOURS: Monday-Thursday 10 am-midnight, Friday-Saturday 10 am-1 am, Sunday 10 am-9:30 pm. SAMPLING: No surprise, they serve saimin in small ($2.50), medium ($2.75), large ($3), and extra large ($3.25). Also BBQ, udon, fried noodles ($3) and won ton soup ($4). Most expensive item on the menu is shrimp saimin at $4.25. COMMENTS: A tacky shack that looks like a run-down school room inside. There are

several U shaped formica covered counters surrounded by a variety of unmatched stools. The menu is on the wall and is limited, so ordering and receiving your food is quite speedy. A good thing as during peak meal hours you may have to wait for a vacant stool. You'll find friendly local folks explaining directions to Wailua Falls to a youthful European backpacker and next to them a group with mega numbers of kids sitting with chopsticks in hand eagerly awaiting their steaming bowls of saimin. But don't overlook the chicken and beef sticks. At $1 per they are a deal. The meat is a good size portion, moist and very flavorful. Order at least one to accompany your noodles! Hamura Saimin is not only popular during regular meals, but since so many of the clubs have closed down, it's actually become a late-night hang out. Oh yes, and heed the warning posted, no sticking gum under the counter! They serve shave ice (as Halo Halo Shave Ice) Monday-Friday from 1 pm-4 am.

HANAMAULU CAFE TEA HOUSE & SUSHI BAR ★ *Chinese/Japanese*
Hwy. 56 in Hanamaulu (245-2511) HOURS: Lunch Tuesday-Friday 10 am-1 pm, Dinner Tuesday-Sunday 4:30-9 pm. SAMPLING: Chinese dishes with noodles, pork, beef, chicken and seafood plus steamed fish and lobster. Also soups and appetizers. ($3.75-9) Japanese salads, soups, beef, chicken, pork, seafoods and vegetarian specials. ($4-9.75) Complete dinners: 9-course Chinese or Japanese for 2 or more $14.75 per person. Special tempura platters $12.95, seafood platter $13.50. Plate lunches ($5.50-7) Sunday night Oriental buffet from 5:30-8:30 pm features sushi, sashimi, salads, fish, chicken, crab, teri beef and dessert for $20.95. COMMENTS: The front room is used for lunch, and is decorated in a pleasant Oriental style, but the Japanese Dining Room (where you sit on the "floor") towards the back is a fantasy setting that overlooks a beautiful garden with Koi ponds. Restaurant offers robatayaki cooking grilled in front of you as well as a teppanyaki room and full sushi bar. The food is reliably good. While Hanamaulu seems to be a spot on the road that people drive thru to get somewhere else, consider making it your dining destination. This is one of the best Oriental restaurants on Kaua'i. And if it were located at a "resort" destination, prices would be a lot more!

HANA-YA *Japanese/Sushi Bar*
1394 Kuhio Hwy., Kapa'a (822-3878) HOURS: Lunch 11:30 am-2 pm, Dinner 5:30-9:30 pm. SAMPLING: Dinners include chicken teriyaki, oyako donburi, chicken katsu, shrimp tempura, nabeyaki or tempura soba and assorted sushi platter ($8.95-16.95). Sushi a la carte: spicy hamachi, unagi, salmon skin, spicy scallop, spicy ahi ($4.75-5) and chirashi sushi: assorted pieces of seafood served over a bowl of sushi rice ($14.95). COMMENTS: Very small restaurant, the sushi bar has seating for only 10 and there are only a handful of tables. Currently they don't have a liquor license, so you are welcome to pick something up at the store and bring it along.

HO'S CHINESE KITCHEN *Chinese*
Kukui Grove Shopping Center. (245-5255)

JJ'S BROILER *Steak & Seafood*
4416 Rice Street in Anchor Cove Shopping Center (245-4422) HOURS: Lunch 11 am-5 pm, Dinner 5-9:30 pm, Cocktails 5-11 pm. SAMPLING: Cheeseburgers come with avocado, bacon, mushrooms, pineapple and chili. They are also available

without meat ($6.25-7.75). Salads include Oriental chicken, cobb, Caesar, Italian tortellini, seafood and spinach and there's ocean chowder, onion soup and beef & vegetable soup ($4.25-9.95). Sandwiches of pastrami & swiss, turkey club, mahi mahi, teri chicken or beef, steak, French dip and Reuben are available ($6.25-9.75) as are a surprising number of vegetarian offerings: Kaua'i garden or marinated tofu sandwich and vegetable pizza on a flour tortilla. Before dinner, there's a tableside salad bar, clam bucket, crab legs and ahi carpaccio ($5.75-9.95). Seafood entrees offer broiled scallops with crisp taro, baked lobster tail, coconut shrimp and fresh island fish and char-broiled meats include NY steak, filet mignon, roasted macadamia lamb rack, prime rib, barbeque chicken or pork ribs, spicy wasabi ribeye steak and JJ's signature Slavonic steak ($13.95-21.95). Other specialties are stir-fry, tempura, chicken fettucine, seafood linguini and wok fried lobster ($14.95-25.95). Entrees include the tableside salad bar, vegetables and choice of rice. Key lime pie, JJ's sea of chocolate and double decker ice cream pie are some of the after dinner treats ($3.50-3.95). COMMENTS: Nice outdoor patio and deck for lunch. Dinner is served upstairs with a big picture window overlooking the beach. Their Slavonic steak is a very popular item, the filets of beef are cooked in wine, butter and garlic.

JOLLY ROGER *American*
Just behind Coconut Plantation Marketplace next to The Islander (822-3451) HOURS: Breakfast 6:30 am-noon, Lunch 12-4 pm, Dinner 4-10 pm. SAMPLING: Omelettes, egg dishes, breakfast meats plus apple pancakes, orange bread French toast, waffles with cinnamon apples and macadamia nuts ($3.25-7.95). Burgers, salads, sandwiches including an avocado melt, French dip and Philadelphia steak ($4.95-7.95). Lunch specialties include stuffed quesadilla, fettucini Alfredo with mushrooms and stir-fry ($7.95-9.25) and dinners offer steaks, beef ribs, fresh fish, seafood platters, chicken Polynesian and create-your-own combinations ($11.95-14.95). Then there's sundaes, pies and hot fudge cake or Mauna Kea crunch - a chocolate chip cookie with sundae toppings ($2.25-3.45). COMMENTS: Familiar chain with a traditional menu, though there are a few creative surprises. Specials like steak & all-you-can-eat shrimp ($11.95) and a senior menu with a choice of teriyaki steak or chicken, ground beef, mahi mahi, ono, sirloin steak, spaghetti or hibachi chicken for $7.95 including vegetable, potato or rice, soup or salad and coffee or tea. Food is nothing exotic, but affordably priced with a broad menu offering something for every family member. The breakfast specials are a good value.

JONI HANA *Local*
Located in the Kukui Grove Shopping Center. (245-5213) SAMPLING: Plate lunches with local dishes $4-7.

KALAPAKI GRILL
Located poolside at the Kaua'i Marriott. Grilled burgers, hot dogs, pizza, ice cream and more. Open 10 am - 6 pm daily.

K.C.L. BARBECUE DRIVE INN *Local*
971 Kuhio Hwy. in the Waipouli Complex (823-8168) HOURS: Monday-Saturday 9:30 am-8 pm; Closed Sundays. SAMPLING: Burgers, BBQ chicken or teri beef sandwiches, shrimp burger, hot dog in addition to regular and mini portions of chicken

(lemon, katsu, cutlet, BBQ), beef stew, breaded pork chop, loco moco, teriyaki steak or pork, shrimp curry and specials with two scoops of rice and macaroni salad. Mixed or BBQ mixed plate, seafood combo and seafood platter ($1.25-6.25). COMMENTS: Hard to find a hamburger for $1.25 - or for that matter, mahi mahi fried shrimp and scallops for $6.25, but you can here! It is a kind of funky place, mostly local clientele. An ideal way to stretch your food budget!

KAPA'A FISH & CHOWDER HOUSE *Seafood*
1639 Kuhio Hwy. (822-7488) HOURS: Bar open from 4:30 pm, Dinner from 5:30 pm. SAMPLING: House specialties include a pot of steamed Pacific shrimp, cioppino, fish house or tempura platter, fish & chips, chicken vegetable stir-fry and steak or chicken kabob ($12.95-17.95). A variety of seafood pastas range from $14.95-18.95 and seafood entrees include coconut shrimp, sea scallops, tiger prawns, crab and lobster ($14.95-Market Price). Naturally, they offer chowder (both clam and fish) with or without sherry and there are a few steak and chicken offerings for the landlubber. Tropical and ice cream drinks are a specialty. COMMENTS: A steak and seafood restaurant - hold the steak - that's been around since 1986. The screened Garden Room at the back of the restaurant is airy and full of hanging plants. The children's menu is interesting and more "adult" than most. The chowder is good, but it does seem chintzy that they charge for seconds on bread. The food quality is sporadic and menu items somewhat overpriced.

KAUA'I CHOP SUEY *Chinese*
In Pacific Ocean Plaza at 3501 Rice Street, Nawiliwili (245-8790) HOURS: Lunch Tuesday-Saturday 11 am-2 pm, Dinner Tuesday-Sunday 4:30-9 pm. Closed Monday. SAMPLING: House specials include Kaua'i chop suey with mushrooms, cauliflower and shrimp ($6.75) and hon too mein for 4-6 persons; a lot of food for the price of $24.25. Also chicken, duck, shrimp, scallop, beef, pork, vegetarian, egg, sweet & sour and noodle dishes ($4.05-9.25). Chow mein and other noodle dishes ($5.75-7.95) as well as rice dishes including special fried rice with

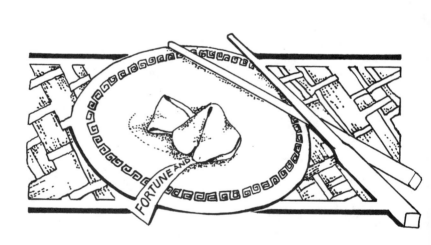

chicken, pork, mushrooms, beans, shrimp and more ($5.50-7.15). Specialty is sizzling rice platters like beef, chicken, scallop or shrimp with lobster sauce with 10 pieces of jumbo shrimp ($6.95-8.55). COMMENTS: Big Chinese banquet room divided into three areas with round archways and red & gold decor. The service is often times slow here. They don't have a liquor license, so it is a bring your own if you so choose. The food is nicely seasoned, and the sizzling platters which arrive crackling and steaming are always fun!

KAUAI KITCHENS   *Local*
In Rice Shopping Center, 4303 Rice Street, Lihu'e (245-4513) HOURS: 7 am-1:30 pm, Saturdays until 2:30, closed Sundays. SAMPLING: sandwiches, plate lunches, bentos, sushi (maki cone) and daily specials: chicken cutlet, fresh corned beef, fish filet, pork adobo, and shoyu butterfish over somen noodles ($1.20-5.95). They also sell Kauai Kookies, baked foods and T-shirts retail from the Kauai Kookie Kompany. COMMENTS: "Quick Tasty Island Style" that you can eat in or take out.

KAUAI SMOKEHOUSE   *Local*
Kaua'i Village, Kapa'a (822-7427) HOURS: 10 am till "whenevah." SAMPLING: Bar-B-Q beef, pork or chicken on an onion roll, grilled hamburger, ribs, combination platters, smoked fish (smoked turkey with one day notice). Local plates, hamburger steak, chicken cutlet, roast pork. Meals served with choice of two: spicy spuds, baked beans, cole slaw, mock-a-roni salad, rice ($4-7). COMMENTS: Opened in 1989. Special spices and Bar-B-Q sauce are used on their menu items. Mostly take out, but a few tables in front.

KIIBO   *Japanese*
2991 Umi St., Lihu'e (245-2650) HOURS: Lunch 11 am-1:30 pm, Dinner 5:30-9 pm. Closed Sunday. SAMPLING: Sushi, tempura, sukiyaki, sashimi, teriyaki chicken, beef and pork, fresh fish, nabe, noodles and special house bentos. COMMENTS: Just off of Rice Street, the decor is very authentic. The food is very traditional Japanese, however, better Japanese fare can be found a little farther down the road at Hanamaulu Cafe Tea House & Sushi Bar.

KING & I *Thai*
Waipouli Plaza, 901 Kuhio Hwy. (822-1642) HOURS: 4:30-9:30 pm, till 10 Friday and Saturday). SAMPLING: Start with the spring rolls with fresh mint and cucumber, ready to wrap in lettuce and dip ($6.25) then try King & I Noodles with beef, pork, chicken or shrimp ($6.50-8.50) and the spicy, tasty Siam eggplant ($6.50). You can choose from red, green or yellow curry ($6.50-8.95), smell the aroma of jasmine rice, and enjoy the Siam fresh basil with chili, garlic, mushroom and oyster sauce $6.50) or Cindy's favorite, sambal with pineapple, bell pepper, carrot, onion, peanut sauce, red chili and coconut milk. You can order it with beef, pork, chicken or tofu ($7.95) or shrimp or fish ($9.95). Thai iced tea or coffee are a must if you've never had them as is the black rice with coconut milk which is the natural color of the herbal rice from Thailand ($2.25) If you don't want to make a decision, they also offer set menus for 2, 3 or 4 ($27.95/38.95/-49.95) which include five items with rice, tea and dessert. COMMENTS: As owners (and sisters) Stephanie and Cindy take turns out front and in the kitchen. (Their brother, Mei, owns Mema Thai Chinese Cuisine down the road a few miles.) The sisters grow their own herbs so when the dish says fresh basil or fresh

mint, it really is. Some of the entrees are excellent, a few are mediocre. The green curry is wonderful, perfectly seasoned and an ideal accompaniment with fresh fish. The fried shrimp, however, proved to be too greasy and were all batter and no shrimp. The portions are a little on the small side, but the prices are affordable. Ask your waiter to offer recommendations on entrees!

KINTARO ★ *Japanese*
370 Kuhio Hwy., Kapa'a (822-3341) HOURS: 5:30-9:30 pm Monday-Saturday. SAMPLING: Tempura, sukiyaki and yakitori dinners, one-pot nabemono, broiled steaks, shrimp, mussels and fish combinations plus complete teppanyaki dinners with appetizer: oysters, chicken or NY steak teriyaki, filet mignon, hibachi shrimp, fish with scallops or lobster tail and tenderloin steak ($10.95-26.95). COMMENTS: Good mussels and steaks; also hand-rolled sushi and soft-shell crab. Stylized, attractive Japanese ambience. They have two serving sections, the general (moderately priced) seating area and second, moderately expensive area with teppanyaki tables where you can enjoy your meal cooked before your eyes. While it is a bit more expensive, it is worth it for the show! Renovated in December '94 including a new aquarium.

KOREAN BBQ *Korean*
356 Kuhio Hwy. in the Kinipopo Shopping Center, Kapa'a (823-6744) HOURS: 10 am-9 pm, closed Tuesday. SAMPLING: Combination plates served with four vegetables and two scoops of rice. Kalbi, teri beef, BBQ chicken, fried or rolled mandoo, fish jun, hamburger steak and fried chicken; also kim chee, miso and kooksoo soup ($4.75-6.95). COMMENTS: They sell vegetables and kimchee and also do catering.

KOUNTRY KITCHEN *American*
1485 Kuhio Hwy., Kapa'a (822-3511) HOURS: Breakfast 6 am-2 pm, Lunch 11 am- 2:30 pm. SAMPLING: Pancakes, French toast, pork chop and eggs, omelettes like Polynesian, garden, sour cream hamburger or tuna served with cornbread or build-your-own and hungryman platter ($3.65-9.25). Lunch fare includes burgers, patty melt, BLT, club, tuna sandwiches and lunch plates (with vegetable, rice or fries and cornbread) with entrees of hamburger steak, grilled pork chop, mahi mahi, sirloin steak or fried chicken ($5.25-7.95). Homemade desserts include blueberry cobbler, Dutch apple pie or cake for ($2.25-2.95). COMMENTS: Looks like an old-fashioned coffee shop of the 50's, but with wood, brick and copper accents. Family-style restaurant, but they do have beer and wine. Good breakfasts!

KUKUI'S RESTAURANT & BAR
Located at the Kaua'i Marriott. HOURS: Breakfast 6:30 am - 11:30 am, Lunch 11:30 am - 5 pm, Dinner 5 pm - 10 pm. They feature a Pacific Rim buffet and a menu with island offerings. Located poolside at the largest swimming pool in the Hawaiian islands. When they opened they offered a $5 discount for early bird diners for their dinner buffet. Breakfast includes macadamia nut pancakes, Portuguese sweet bread French toast and excellent homemade corned beef has with potato and taro. For lunch there is Thai chicken pizza, spring rolls with sundried tomatoes as well as burgers and pasta dishes.

LIHU'E BAKERY & COFFEE SHOP *Filipino*
Rice Shopping Center, 4303 Rice St., Lihu'e (245-7520) HOURS: Monday-Friday 5 am-6 pm, Saturday 5 am-4 pm, Sunday 5-11:30 am. SAMPLING: Unusual Filipino baked goods, also donuts and muffins. Hot Filipino entrees served cafeteria-style from 5 am through lunch.

LIHU'E CAFE *Local*
2978 Umi St., Lihu'e (245-6471) HOURS: Lunch 10:30-1:30 pm, Monday-Friday. SAMPLING: Weekly specials are chicken hekka, chili dog (Monday), meat loaf, chicken curry (Tuesday), roast pork, nishime (Wednesday), hamburger steak, pork tofu (Thursday), beef stew, baked mahi mahi, surprise special (Friday) plus saimin, won ton. Daily specials vary, but might include soft noodles with pork and vegetables, sweet & sour spare ribs, fried chicken and bento lunches ($2.50-5.50). COMMENTS: Rice, potato or tossed salad and kim chee served with all specials, tax included in price.

MA'S *Local/Homestyle*
4277 Halenani Street, Lihu'e (245-3142) HOURS: Monday-Friday 5 am-1:30 pm, Saturday & Sunday to 11:30 am. SAMPLING: Eggs, omelettes, meats and waffles or pancakes come plain or with pineapple, papaya or banana ($5). Lunch entrees include meat loaf, cutlets, fish, fried noodles, tripe stew, curry beef and Hawaiian specials ($3-6). Sandwiches are around $2 with hamburgers at $1.75, roast beef or pork at $2.50. COMMENTS: Ma's opened in the mid 1960's and you can still see Ma cooking on the griddle in back - sort of a forerunner of Roy's open kitchen concept! The breakfasts are a bargain. Try a local variety of spam and eggs for $2. Other breakfasts including omelettes, pancakes or French toast made with Portuguese sweet bread run less than $5. This is definitely a hole-in-the-wall, greasy spoon restaurant, which is what makes it so much fun! The service is friendly with the waitress greeting you with a smile and plunking down a big thermos of coffee so you can serve yourself. (The coffee is free with meals!) Big portions and great prices make it popular with locals and returning visitors. Turn off Rice Street onto Kress Street and another left onto Halenani.

MARGARITAS, A MEXICAN RESTAURANT AND WATERING HOLE
733 Kuhio Hwy., Kapa'a (822-1808) HOURS: 5-9:30 pm, Happy Hour 4-6, SAMPLING: Nachos el deluxe, Mexican pizzas, quesadillas, caliente wings ($5.95-7.50), from the grill: Fajitas, chicken Veracruz, smoked ribs conquistador ($13.95-16.95). Specials include jalapeno poppers, garlic nachos, chicken fajita salad, fish tacos, shrimp enchiladas ($3.95-12.95). COMMENTS: Food is made fresh daily; specials change every few weeks. Contemporary Hawaiian music on Friday and Saturday nights. Good place to watch the sunset during the winter when it goes down between Sleeping Giant Mountain and the coconut grove next door. There is better Mexican food elsewhere on the island, but this is passable middle-of-the-road cuisine. The menu is large and varied and if you choose to eat on the back porch, the donkey and horse in the adjoining coconut grove might stroll over and say "howdy."

MEMA THAI CUISINE ★ *Thai/Chinese*
Wailua Shopping Plaza behind Sizzler, Kapa'a (823-0899) HOURS: Lunch 11 am-2 pm Monday-Friday, Dinner 5-9:30 pm daily. SAMPLING: Appetizers include

shrimp rolls, sa-teh, fish cakes along with some new ones: fried calamari and shrimp on a stick ($5.95-9.25). Salads with beef, calamari or green papaya (eat it with a mint leaf) run $5.95-8.95 and soups (Thai ginger coconut, long rice and spicy lemon grass) are offered at $4.25-6.25. Noodles and rice come in a variety of flavors for $6.25-9.25. Red, yellow and green curry are offered along with house curry and Mema's curry (as a special). They run $6.95-14.95 depending on whether you order them with chicken, beef, pork, fish, shrimp or seafood. Roasted and panans duck are two new entree offerings along with evil jungle prince, garlic with coconut, cashew nut chicken, filet fish with curry, lemon chicken, blackbean sauce stir-fry and fresh basil seafood ($6.25-14.95). There are three pages of vegetarian offerings, including spring rolls, crispy noodles, sa-teh and laab tofu ($4.95-7.25), soups of lemon grass, coconut vegetable or long rice vegetable ($6.25) and entrees like broccoli tofu, garlic coconut mixed vegetables, pad Thai tofu and vegetable curry ($6.50-7.95). Dinners for 2,3, 4 or 6 offer a wide selection and good variety from appetizer to dessert and start at $29.95 for two. COMMENTS: Owner Mei is the brother of Cindy and Stephanie who own King & I. He recently expanded the restaurant to almost twice its size with the addition of the unit next door. The new "annex" has upstairs seating for 25 in traditional Thai style: low tables with cushions to sit on the floor with arm rests to relax while you eat. Some folks think Mema is better than King & I, while others think the reverse is true. The atmosphere of Mema's is more pleasant than the King and I. Plenty of plants interspersed with Thai art and artifacts create a garden-like setting. Mema's also serves some Chinese dishes as well as Thai.

MICHELLE'S CAFE *Bakery/cafe/espresso*
1384 Kuhio Hwy., Kapa'a (823-6608) HOURS: Open Monday-Friday 7 am-5 pm, Saturday 8 am-4 pm, Sunday 8 am-4 pm. SAMPLING: Breakfast includes egg scrambles, Aidell's chicken/apple sausage, oven-roasted breakfast potatoes, Belgian waffles, papayas with yogurt and Anahola granola. Lunches include savory soups, organic green salads, Italian paninis, pastas, island Thai chicken and calzone. Menu items priced $3-8. COMMENTS: Cafe menu specials change daily; full bakery and espresso bar that also offers Chai, a non-caffeinated hot drink of herbs and spices. The cafe atmosphere is pleasant and it is conveniently located in the heart of Kapa'a.

NORBERTO'S EL CAFE *Mexican*
1375 Kuhio Hwy., Kapa'a (822-3362) HOURS: 5:30-9 pm, Closed Sundays. SAMPLING: Specialties include rellenos tampico, enchiladas grande (with beef, chicken or eggplant), burritos rancheros and fajitas made with Kaua'i steak or chicken ($11.50-14.95) or try the taro leaf and chicken enchilada ($12.95). All entrees come with soup, vegetables, rice and beans, corn chips and salsa. Items offered a la carte include tacos, quesadillas, nachos, salads, and burritos ($2.95-7.95). Their homemade desserts have won awards: chocolate cream pie, hula pie and rum cake. COMMENTS: Family operated restaurant since 1977. No lard or animal fat is used in their preparations. Margaritas available by the glass or by the pitcher. People drive from Keka'a for the bean soup. They offer a kids menu. The cantina atmosphere makes for good family dining.

OK BENTO AND SAIMIN *Local*
4100 Rice Street, Lihu'e (245-6554) HOURS: Monday-Wednesday 8:30 am-3 pm, Thursday to 8:30 pm, Friday to 10 pm, Saturday 9:30-2 pm, closed Sunday. Bentos, won ton soup, saimin ($2.45-8.45). COMMENTS: Very small place in former Payless Annex Building. The saimin is good and the place is very busy with lunch time business folks. No credit cards.

OLYMPIC CAFE *Local/Oriental*
1387 Kuhio Hwy., Kapa'a (822-5731) HOURS: Breakfast & Lunch 6 am-2 pm; Dinner 5-9 pm. SAMPLING: Eggs, omelettes and breakfast meats plus local and Japanese items; fried rice, pork chops, hot cakes and waffles ($2.95-9.50). There are burgers, sandwiches and oriental soups for lunch plus entrees like chicken, beef or pork cutlets, liver & onions, beef tomato, fried noodles, chili, shrimp or fish tempura, chicken or pork hekka, long rice or tofu ($2.25-8.25). Dinners feature combinations of steak & fresh fish, teri chicken or shrimp tempura; seafood platter (grilled fish, shrimp tempura, calamari rings) plus larger portions of some lunch items at somewhat higher prices ($5.95-12.50). COMMENTS: Interesting, but deceiving, lavender "Art Deco" building on the outside but looks very basic on the inside - like a small oriental banquet room. The burgers are the homecooked style, no flame broiling here, but as good or even better than Bubba's across the street. We've had saimin better elsewhere. A good value for this side of the island.

ONO FAMILY RESTAURANT ★ *Homecooking*
1292 Kuhio Hwy., Kapa'a (822-1710) HOURS: Breakfast/Lunch 7 am-2 pm; Lunch/Dinner 5:30-9 pm. SAMPLING: Two full pages of egg dishes and omelettes - too numerous to mention - include an unusual variety of meat, cheese and vegetable combinations as well as pancakes (including banana or tropical) and French toast ($2.85-8.75). Sandwiches like cod, veggie, steak, turkey and half turkey & egg salad are offered along with burgers in your choice of beef or buffalo! (A little coarser and meatier, but not at all tough or chewy.) The teri, mushroom, bacon, BBQ, chili, patty melt and pineapple burgers run $3.95-6.95. Salads, fish, stir-fry and chicken burger plus spaghetti and meat balls, beef stroganoff, salisbury steak, meatloaf, buffalo ribs (offered with soup or salad) are $5.95-14.95. Old-fashioned homemade pies have real flavor; there's nothing plastic or artificial tasting in the coconut vanilla, macadamia nut vanilla or chocolate cream or the coconut or macadamia nut custard ($2.50-2.75). COMMENTS: Outstanding service, friendly, attentive and enthusiastic. It's as if they are actually glad to see you and enjoy serving you! (If you're lucky enough, Ginger will be your waitress. When she's not busy taking good care of you, there'll be someone in between to make sure everything's okay and it'll probably be her mother!) This is definitely family style with cute, homey decor: knotty-pine with lots of curtains, knick-knacks and plates on the walls. Dress casual and be comfortable, the workers do. There are no uniforms and sometimes you can't tell the help from the patrons. It's as if you were in someone's home and the guests just get up to help - and the regulars here probably do! To be fair, we have heard disappointed patrons reviewing the restaurant as "oooohnooo" but we found it an "ono" (delicious) and very enjoyable experience.

PACIFIC ROOM AT KAUA'I RESORT   *Pacific Rim*
Kaua'i Resort, (245-3931) HOURS: Breakfast 6:30-10 am, Lunch 11 am-2 pm.
Dinner 6-9 pm. SAMPLING: Lunch and dinner "all day" burgers, saimin, fish &
chips ($6.25-7.50). Daily lunch buffet is available ($9.95 adults/6.95 children). At
dinner choose mahi sauteed with garlic, guava smoked pork loin, seafood fettucini
($14-17.50). Local buffet on Saturday 6-9 pm with roast island pork, poi, sushi,
steamed fish in black bean sauce, grilled Korean chicken and more ($15.95
adults/12.95 children). COMMENTS: They offer an "Early Bird Special" from 5
to 6 pm which includes soup, salad and dessert, coffee/tea and choice of mahi
mahi, chicken, pork loin or 8 oz. rib eye for $9.95. New owners took over in the
spring of 1995 and made some menu changes. The lobby and restaurant have been
spruced up and decorated in Hawaiian theme with pastel shades, very Elvis movie
looking. The breakfast buffet is a little spendy, unless you are a hearty eater. The
dinner buffet is a better value.

PANDA GARDEN   *Chinese*
831 Kuhio Hwy., Kaua'i Village, Kapa'a (822-0922) HOURS: 11 am-2 pm, 4:30-
9:30 pm. SAMPLING: Over 100 offerings of both Cantonese and Szechuan
dishes. Appetizers, soups, chicken & duck, beef and pork, seafood, eggs, sizzling
platters, vegetarian, chow mein and rice - $6.25-12.95. Plate lunch specials offer
a choice of eight entrees with soup, won ton and rice for $5.95 and set dinners for
2 to 10 run $24.95-$179. COMMENTS: They offer both the unusual and the
traditional, but seafood is a particular specialty. Their hot, spicy dishes are marked
with a star. Food is fair to good, but the portions are a bit small.

PAPAYA'S NATURAL FOODS   *Natural/Healthy*
831 Kuhio Hwy. at Kaua'i Village, Kapa'a. (823-0190) HOURS: 8 am-8 pm.
SAMPLING: Rosemary potatoes, egg wrap-ups, tofu scramble, banana pancakes,
granola and quiche to start you off then a variety of sandwiches and entrees for
lunch or dinner: tempeh, garden or tofu burgers, ginger udon noodles, eggplant
basmati rice, spanakopita, Thai curry, chicken enchiladas, chilequillas, lasagna,
hummus, cous cous and excellent Greek vegetable pie ($2.50-6.75). Their honey
sweetened desserts range from white chocolate mango mousse to double chocolate

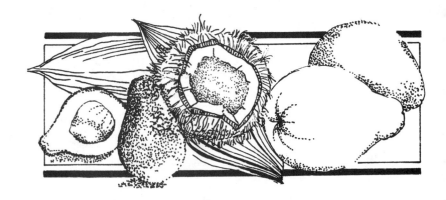

mousse cake and chocolate cheesecake along with a variety of muffins, scones, cookies and brownies. COMMENTS: This is a health food store, one of the few where the patrons actually look fit and healthy! Order at the counter, tables outside. Owner Mary Jackson has been here since 1989 and has quite a following.

PARADISE CHICKEN & RIBS
A kiosk in the Coconut Marketplace serving BBQ chicken and ribs. (822-2505).

PARADISE PIZZA *Take 'N Bake Pizza*
Kaua'i Village, Kapa'a (823-8253) HOURS: 3-8 pm. SAMPLING: Meat, garden and seafood toppings plus specials like Mexican, BBQ chicken, pesto chicken and kim chee ($8.95-18.95). Pistachio delight and tortellini salads ($4.95). Their specialty is a breakfast pizza with eggs and bacon, ham, Italian or vegetarian sausage or onion & bell pepper, or Denver omelette ($7.95-13.95). You can also add additional toppings. Breakfast pizzas are picked up the night before, ready to put in the oven for a hot breakfast the next morning. COMMENTS: This is not a chain; they'll cook small & medium pizzas for you for a charge of $2. The toppings are really loaded on and if you take and bake and don't like the way it is cooked, it is your own fault! They were offering free samples of their peanut butter pizza. Somehow, we don't think this particular creation will catch on.

PLANTERS *Prime Rib & Seafood*
On Hwy. 56 in Hanamaulu (245-1606) HOURS: Lunch 11 am-2 pm, Monday-Friday, Happy Hour 2-5 pm, Early Bird dinners 5-6:30 pm. Dinner 5-9:30 daily. SAMPLING: Salads, burgers, hot roast beef, chicken salad, steak, mahi sandwiches plus lunch entrees of linguini, veggie lasagna, fresh fish and teriyaki chicken ($5.95-9.95). Dinner entrees include several steaks, prime rib or Cajun prime rib, mahi mahi, scampi, fresh catch, Hungarian chicken, stir-fry sesame and shrimp Milano ($12.95-18.95). Appetizers of fresh mushrooms, escargot or shrimp cocktail will start you off at $4.95-6.95 and hula pie, New York style cheesecake and chocolate cake are the toppers for $2.95-3.50. COMMENTS: They make their own bread and offer an early bird special every night from 5-6:30 pm for $9.95-10.95. The decor is reminiscent of the old plantation days with assorted farming paraphernalia as decor, keeping with the historic nature of this building which had a prior life in the plantation industry of Hanamaulu. The restaurant is a little dark, but rather cozy. The food is moderately priced, but don't expect anything beyond the basics.

PO'S CHINESE KITCHEN *Local*
3178-A Kuhio Hwy., Lihu'e (246-8617) HOURS: 6 am-1:30 pm, Monday-Saturday. SAMPLING: Bento and box lunches in three sizes: small/regular/deluxe for $4.25/5.25/6.25. Box lunches include fried chicken, teriyaki meat, egg roll, rice ball, potato salad, luncheon meat, hot dog, side dish and pickled cabbage. Also teriyaki chicken, meat or short ribs plate lunch and hot entree that changes daily. COMMENTS: Tiny place behind the Shell station. Simple and very inexpensive menu. The fried chicken was a wingette, the luncheon meat a piece of spam. All the portions in the small bento were appetizer sized. A la carte items under a dollar. If you want to sample some unusual local food, and not invest more than a pocketful of change, stop by while they fill up your tank.

ROB'S GOOD TIMES GRILL *American*

4303 Rice St., Lihu'e (246-0311) HOURS: 10 am-2 am. SAMPLING: Lots of appetizers/pupus like breaded mushrooms or zucchini, chicken fingers, jalapeno poppers, teri beef, mozzarella sticks, cheese fries, calamari rings ($4-6.95). Cobb, tuna, chef and Pacific catch (shrimp and crab) salads ($3.75-6.95). Pastrami and swiss, chicken melt, club, turkey, French dip and super steak sandwiches ($5.50-6.50). Burgers include mushroom, bacon, teri, blue cheese and chili and entrees feature mahi mahi, fried chicken, fish & chips, stir-fry, chicken tacos and steak ($5.75-8.95). COMMENTS: Rob and Lolly Silverman bought Kay's Pub just prior to the hurricane and opened one week after! They remodeled the walls with pub mirrors and beer signs. They have karaoke every Wednesday and there's satellite tv and a dart board. During football season, they open at 7 am for breakfast - loco moco, omelettes or sweet bread French toast. It is a bit more bar than grill.

ROCCO'S ★ *Italian*

4405 Kukui St. in Pacific House Plaza, Kapa'a (822-4422) HOURS: 11 am-11 pm, to midnight on weekends). SAMPLING: Sauteed or stuffed mushrooms (good mushroom taste and firm texture), white pizza (topped with mozzarella and a side of red sauce), garlic bread, antipasto or caesar salad (made with an exceptionally light tasting olive oil) are the starters for $2.50-6.25. Cheese pizzas run $9-14 plus toppings and pasta offerings of linguini, manicotti, cannelloni and lasagna are $8.95-12.95. Additional entrees include eggplant marsala, scampi or clams and baked or sauteed fresh fish ($11.95-15.95). The fish comes in large portions and the ahi was excellent and surprisingly moist - not an easy thing to do with its tuna texture. Main courses all come with a hot loaf of fresh baked bread and dinner salad. Lunch is a recent addition and offers pasta, sausage or meatball sandwiches (a find on Kaua'i), pizza and pizza sandwiches and seafood and other salads. COMMENTS: This is an upscale, modern version of the old family style pizza restaurants of the 50's and 60's. It's reflected in the ambience with an aquarium and hanging plants and vines in the upper level dining mezzanine. It's also reflected in the prices: complete dinners, large portions and homecooking by the owner, Richard Senkus. The bread is homemade as are the meatballs. Both Hawaiian and contemporary music on the weekends. This is a great find, an excellent value family restaurant with or without a family.

SAMPAGUITA'S/BIG WHEEL DONUT SHOP *Local*

Old Hanamaulu Trading Post (245-5322) HOURS: Donuts from 4 am to 11:30 am. Breakfast 5 am to "whenevah." SAMPLING: Plate lunches $4-5.25; Breakfast: eggs, bacon and hot cakes $3.60. COMMENTS: These are two different places, but in such a small building that it's almost impossible not to list them together. Big Wheel also serves coffee, makes their donuts fresh and frequently has a "Sorry out of Donuts" sign in front. Not surprising, since they start serving them at 4 in the morning!

SEASHELL

This restaurant is scheduled to reopen sometime in late 1995. Tony Isakolk from Pomodoro will be running it. Beachfront location.

SHARKY'S *Steak and Seafood*
Located on the cliffs of Nawiliwili Bay. (246-4470). HOURS: Dinner 5-10 pm, cocktails 4-midnight. A seafood bar is open 4-11 pm. COMMENTS: Closed since September 1992, this oceanview restaurant is scheduled to reopen in the spring of 1996. Reminiscent of an old 1930s Hawaiian fish market, Sharky's features a reasonably priced fresh fish and seafood menu, which changes daily depending on the day's catch. One of the restaurant's highlights is a shark oceanarium with live sharks endlessly circling. Sharky's Fish Market is operated by TS Restaurants. Other TS restaurants on Kaua'i include Keoki's Paradise at Po'ipu and Duke's Canoe Club at Kalapaki Beach, as well as branches on other islands.

SIDEOUT BAR & GRILL *American*
1330 Kuhio Hwy., Kapa'a (822-7330) HOURS: Lunch 11 am-2 pm, Dinner 5-9 pm, Late Menu 10-1 am. SAMPLING: Burger or chicken sandwich with pineapple and teriyaki or chicken with Creole sauce ($6.95) plus roast beef, turkey or veggie sandwich ($5.95). Dinner offerings include Cajun prime rib, mardi gras chicken, catch of the day, seafood or vegetarian pasta and veggie lasagna ($7.95-9.95). COMMENTS: Expect some menu changes, though the style of food will be similar. They have live music Wednesday-Monday from 7 to 1, satellite sports TV and a happy hour from 2-4 pm.

SIZZLER *American*
361 Kuhio Hwy., Wailua Shopping Plaza (822-7404) HOURS: 6 am-10 pm. SAMPLING: Breakfast $2.99 special plus omelettes $6-7, sandwich special $4.99 to steak & shrimp $10, Dinner $7 to $18 for steak & lobster. All-you-can-eat salad, soup, pasta and tostada bar has garlic toast and beverage included for $7.99 (lunch), $8.99 (dinner). COMMENTS: Nicer than a lot of the mainland outlets, but the food is basically the same. Service and food quality vary. Dinners don't include salad bar, which makes a cheap meal rather spendy if you add the price of the salad bar. The salad bar features a taco bar, fruits, soup and pasta, so purchasing it alone proves to offer good diversity, plenty to fill up on and a good value for your vacation dollar.

TAMMY'S OKAZU-YA *Local/Oriental*
4100 Rice St., Lihu'e (246-0460) HOURS: 6:30 am-1:30/2 pm, Mon.-Sat. SAMPLING: Bentos and box lunches, but mostly individual items like chow fun or spare ribs. Most items under $1, up to $3.60. COMMENTS: Go before noon or they are likely to run out.

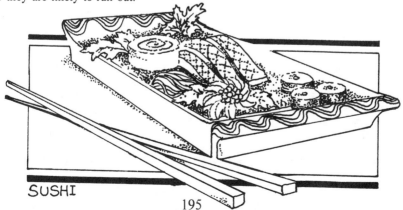

SUSHI

TIP TOP CAFE *Local*
3173 Akahi, Lihu'e (245-2333) HOURS: Breakfast 6:30-11 am, Lunch 11 am-2 pm. SAMPLING: Hot cakes, Kona coffee, sweet bread French toast, mushroom or Portuguese omelette ($4.50-5.25). Burgers, grilled ham and cheese, BLT, tuna sandwiches plus beef stew, saimin and oxtail soup, a popular specialty ($2.95-5.75). COMMENTS: Move over Planet Hollywood, the Tip Top souvenir shop has t-shirts and hats! The bakery closed in December '94, but was bought by the Kilauea Bakery and they continue to make the signature bakery items like macadamia nut cookies and cream puffs. This is an especially popular stop for breakfast and lunch. The pancakes are light and fluffy and the French toast is very good. They've been in business since 1916 and moved to their present location in the early 60's. With no entrees priced at more than $6, you can't go wrong.

TOKYO LOBBY ★ *Japanese/Sushi Bar*
Pacific Ocean Plaza, 3501 Rice Street, Lihu'e (245-8989) HOURS: Dinner 5-9:30 pm, Lunch Monday-Saturday 11 am-2 pm. SAMPLING: Unusual and creative sushi offerings like Kalapaki roll (eel, scallop & nasago), dynamite (scallop & mushroom), Tokyo lobby (tuna & hamachi), spider (soft shell crab), Mayflower (tuna & shrimp in a sashimi boat), caterpillar (eel and sliced curves of avocado draped over the top of the roll) and the bright and colorful Tres Amigos (tuna, yellow tail, salmon) priced $5.50-7.50. Also available are spicy tuna, rainbow roll and garlic tuna sashimi ($5-13). Japanese dinners include nabemono, shabu-shabu, teriyaki, tempura, assorted chicken dishes and combinations ($8.95-24.95). The specialty is the "Love Boat," a choice of three combination dinners in an attractive, artistic Japanese wooden boat at $19.95 for 2. COMMENTS: The tempura was light, crispy and fresh, not mushy or greasy. The sushi was attractively presented in tasty and unusual combinations prepared by Sushi Chef Masa who trained in Japan. They reopened in 1993 and won an award right away. They serve both eat-in and take-out sushi regulars as well as a number of Japanese movie stars and ball players. The restaurant is attractively decorated in fresh colors of pinks and reds. Jack Ho is the owner, but his Mom, Lin Ho, is the manager and sweet, friendly, gracious hostess. "Mom" talks and visits with everyone who comes in and even if the sushi weren't so good, she'd be well worth the star.

TWO SISTAHS *Filipino*
4252A Rice St. in Lihu'e. (246-6033) HOURS: Monday-Friday 10am-8 pm, Saturday 11 am-2 pm. SAMPLING: Very small restaurant serving good Filipino food. Located next to the bakery on Rice Street. Entrees from $5-9.

VIOLET'S PLACE ★ *Local/Filipino*
831 Kuhio Hwy. in Kaua'i Village (822-2456) HOURS: 8 am-2 pm; 4:30-9 pm Monday-Wednesday, till 10 pm Thursday-Sunday. SAMPLING: Moloka'i sweetbread French toast, shrimp or cheese omelette, steak and eggs, homemade pancakes for breakfast ($3.55-7.95). Burgers and sandwiches ($3-4.95) plus Filipino dishes (pork adobo, chicken paria, fish sinigang), Oriental selections (chop suey, won ton mein, saimin), Thai (pork, beef or shrimp Thai) and Hawaiian dishes (kalua pig, akule, lau lau) for lunch and dinner ($3.95-9.50). "Violet's Shrimp" is a favorite ($10.95) and there's also a selection of sushi, salads, steaks and chicken dishes as well as prime rib and fried ice cream for dessert ($3.80-14.95).

COMMENTS: This small restaurant might be easily overlooked. The dishes are pleasantly seasoned and the prices are very reasonable. Everything is freshly prepared and very good. Violet's Place was named after her grandmother and the color is reflected in the lavender walls with irises. At Christmastime the decorations are all purple!

VOYAGE ROOM *Breakfast/Buffets/Lunch*
Kaua'i Coconut Beach Resort, Wailua. (822-3455) HOURS: Breakfast 6:30-10 am, 11 am-1:30 pm. SAMPLING: Breakfast buffet with fruit, pastries, breads, cereals and eggs, breakfast meats and potatoes ($9.50 adults/6.50 children). Also a la carte eggs, omelettes and pancakes ($5.50-10.50). Lunch buffet includes salads, fruits and a somen noodle bar plus three hot entrees with vegetable, potato or rice and soup ($10.50 adults/7.00 children). A la carte sandwiches of turkey, ham, veggie, shrimp salad, BLT and club plus burgers and salads: fruit, garden or Chinese chicken ($3.25-7.50). Island style iced tea is available with cane sugar and pineapple and there are a variety of cakes, pies and ice creams for dessert. COMMENTS: The restaurant stays the same, but the name changes depending on if it is breakfast, lunch or dinner. For dinner this same restaurant transforms into the Flying Lobster. The buffets are a good value if you have a big appetite, otherwise a little expensive for uninspired buffet selections. Some of the hotel packages include the breakfast buffet with your room which is a real bonus.

WAH KUNG CHOP SUEY *Chinese*
Kinipopo Shopping Village, 356 Kuhio Hwy. (822-0560) HOURS: Daily 4:30-8 pm, also 11 am-2 pm Tuesday-Saturday. SAMPLING: Soups, poultry, chop suey, chow mein, gau gee, won ton seafood, beef and pork, egg, vegetables and rice. Lunch specials of three items plus rice $4.75-5.95, Szechwan chicken with rice $6.25, pupu plate with crisp won ton, fried chix, fried shrimp and egg roll $8.25. COMMENTS: Small take-out place with a few tables and chairs. Combination and dinner plates posted on the wall, so you don't have to read, you can just point. While it looks (and it is) pretty dinky, the food is very good and so are the prices! Food is Cantonese style with a few exotic dishes thrown in and the prices make it a good option for filling up those hungry appetites that seem to develop after a day at the beach.

WAILUA MARINA RESTAURANT   *American*
5971 Kuhio Hwy., Wailua River State Park Building B. Located near to Smith's Tropical Plantation in Kapaʻa, (822-4311) HOURS: Lunch 10:30 am-2 pm, snacks and sandwiches 2-4 pm, dinner 5-9 pm. Closed Mondays. SAMPLING: Chef's, Chinese chicken and pineapple boat salads and BLT, tuna, egg, turkey, beef, ham, pastrami, mahi mahi, club, steak, teri chicken or pork sandwiches ($6-8.75). Entree specials like mahi mahi or fried shrimp ($7.95-8.25). Dinner appetizers feature a hot mini lobster salad as well as shrimp cocktail and clam chowder ($2.75-7.25). Char-broiled mahi mahi, ahi stuffed with crab meat, teriyaki steak or filet mignon ($13.75-17.75). Seafood dishes include several combinations of shrimp, lobster and steak as well as calamari, salmon and Chinese style steamed mullet ($10.50-28.75). Fried or baked stuffed chicken with plum sauce, baked stuffed pork chops or cutlet, oxtail stew, prime rib and spaghetti are also on the menu ($9-17.75). Desserts include homestyle cream pie (coconut, macadamia nut or chocolate), ice cream pies (mud, fudge, brownie or spumoni) or lilikoi chiffon pie ($2.25-2.75). COMMENTS: Yonezo and Gladys Arashiro have operated Kauaʻi's only restaurant overlooking the Wailua River for many years now and have been doing such a great job of it that they've outlasted most other Kauaʻi restaurants. Oxtail stew and lilikoi pie are specialties here. (Lilikoi pie is like key lime pie, only better!). Not a typical tropical meal, but try the stuffed pork chops. They are big and thick, but you can cut them without a knife! The fresh fish is always fresh and priced at least a couple of dollars less than it would be anywhere else. With more than three dozen entrees on the dinner menu, you are sure to find something for everyone. There are extra long tables for families or groups, with separate banquet room and cocktail lounge. Seating on the lanaʻi can be more pleasant, however. Wall murals may amuse the younger kids in your family, one across the back wall has 3-D sea turtles, shells and fish. Don't let the tour buses scare you away!

WAIPOULI DELI & RESTAURANT   ★   *American/Local/Oriental*
771 Kuhio Hwy., Kapaʻa (822-9311) HOURS: Breakfast 7-11 am, Lunch 11 am-2:30 pm, Dinner Friday & Saturday 5-9 pm. SAMPLING: Eggs with breakfast meats, pancakes, French toast and homemade corned beef hash ($1.39-5.49). Lunch entrees of shrimp or eggplant tempura, roast pork, chop suey, chow mein, pork tofu, fried chicken, pork or chicken cutlet, beef or chicken hekka, liver with bacon and onions, mixed plate ($2.89-6.49). Burgers and burger platters, sandwiches and saimin ($1.99-5.59). Dinners include fries or rice, salad and iced tea or coffee. Curry or beef stew, egg fu yung, BBQ steak, teriyaki steak, beef tomato and most of the lunch entrees at slightly higher prices ($8.49-12.99). COMMENTS: Small local restaurant. Children's half order portions available on lunch and dinner entrees. When a restaurant is always packed, you know they must be doing something right. Food is good, prices are reasonable.

WILD PALMS BISTRO
Coconut Plantation Marketplace, Kapaʻa (822-1533) Obviously, although we really try, we are not able to eat at every restaurant before the revision of a book. We tried quite a few times to get the owners to send us information, but they were always "too busy." We hope their food is better than their business practices.

YOKOZUNA RAMEN
4444 Rice, Lihuʻe (246-1008). Reopening in 1995 in a new location.

SOUTHSIDE

BEACH HOUSE RESTAURANT *Hawaiian/Asian*
Lawai Beach Road on the way to Spouting Horn (742-1424) HOURS: Breakfast 7-11 am, Lunch 11 am-2 pm, Dinner 5:30-9:30 pm. SAMPLING: Tropical pancakes, egg dishes, pastries along with a choice of healthy alternatives for breakfast ($4.95-8.95). Salads, pastas, burgers and hot specialties like Thai coconut chicken or Szechuan beef stir-fry for lunch ($3.95-9.95). Dinner offers escargot, scallops, shrimp or appetizer stir-fry to start ($5.95-7.95) plus pastas like fettucini coquillage with seafood in a macadamia nut pesto cream and Oriental duck and soba noodles ($17.95-18.95). Entrees include a range of fresh fish, lamb chops, prime rib, chicken and bouillabaisse ($15.95-24.95). COMMENTS: You can't beat the view, you can't beat the free pupus from 4-6 pm and besides that they have a really nifty keiki menu with lots of options for breakfast, lunch and dinner.

BRENNECKE'S *Steak and Seafood*
Po'ipu Beach Park (742-7588) HOURS: Lunch 11:30 am to 4 pm, Dinner 4-10 pm, Happy Hour 2-5 pm (11 am-5 pm on Sundays). SAMPLING: Burgers, sandwiches, soups and salad bar served till 10 pm ($5.75-10.95). Pupus all day, too: ceviche, sashimi, nachos, ribs, mushrooms, Oriental or local style platters ($6.95-12.95). Dinner choices include cioppino, pasta prima vera, ribs, Alaskan king crab legs, shrimp skewers, Oriental chicken stir-fry, Hawaiian spiny lobster, fresh fish or any combination of the above ($14.95-$29.95). COMMENTS: Excellent children's menu and early bird specials starting at $5.95. Salad bar has some interesting items, like whole red skinned potato salad, baby corn, pasta salad and a good choice of dressings. Stir-fry was tasty with big pieces of chicken and the kiawe broiled opakapaka was flavorful. Prices seemed a tad high for such a casual atmosphere, but everything comes with a salad bar and a right-on-the-beach view so it makes it easy to justify. Brennecke's also has T-shirts and a Beach/Activity Center and Beach Deli downstairs. Check your entertainment coupon book for a half price discount on dinner dining.

BRICK OVEN PIZZA *Italian*
2555 Kuhio Hwy., Kalaheo (332-8561) HOURS: 11 am-10 pm Tuesday-Saturday, 3-10 pm Sunday, closed Monday. SAMPLING: Wholewheat or white crust with the usual pizza toppings plus homemade Italian sausage, lean beef & green onions, imported anchovies, smoked ham and pineapple, salami and shrimp. ($8.35-25.60) Pizza breads and hot sandwiches with sausage, seafood, meats and vegetables ($2.65-6.50), salads ($2.15-6.55). Desserts include aloha pie or ice cream sundae cups ($.80-2.55). COMMENTS: Hearth baked pizzas at this family owned operation which has been pleasing residents and visitors alike since they opened in 1977. Good homemade sausage and excellent pizza crust, soft and doughy, but beautifully browned - like a soft pretzel. Couldn't taste the garlic butter on the crust through my cold, but I'm sure it was tasty.

CAMP HOUSE GRILL ★ *American/Home Cooking*

Kaumualii Hwy., Kalaheo (332-9755) HOURS: Breakfast 6:30-10:30 am (to 11 weekends and holidays), Lunch/Dinner 11 am-9 pm (closed for breakfast on Wednesday). SAMPLING: Breakfast quesadilla, pancakes, French toast, biscuits and gravy, omelettes and a variety of breakfast sandwiches - Monte Cristo, BLT, and "Build Your Own" ($3.95-6.95). They have early bird specials ($2.95) before 8 am, but as they say on the menu: After 8:01, No Way! Lunch and dinner offerings include a variety of burgers, salads, several grilled chicken entrees, BBQ pork ribs, sirloin steak Polynesian, fresh catch and kalbi ribs and come with two side orders ($4.25-7.95). They're known for their homemade pies, so if you don't save room for dessert, you'll just have to buy a whole one from the glass case on your way out. Pineapple cream cheese macadamia or chewy chocolate chip macadamia nut sound good enough to eat (and they are!) and so do the cream pies of coconut, banana, and chocolate. COMMENTS: The burgers are good, but the ribs are outrageously good! This looks like a funky neighborhood diner, but it is bright, spacious and naturally, it's comfortable and casual. It's home cooking all the way and home-baking as far as the pies are concerned. There's a children's menu and it is no secret this is a family place - available for lunch and dinner.

DAIRY QUEEN *Local*

Three locations: Waimea (338-1911) Ele'ele (335-5293) Lihu'e (245-2141) HOURS: Breakfast from 6:30 am, (Ele'ele from 9 am Monday-Thursday) Dinner after 5 pm. SAMPLING: Eggs, hot cakes and waffles, omelettes, pork chop with gravy, beef or tripe stew for breakfast ($2.50-5.95). Dozens of sandwiches including hot turkey or roast beef, BLT, pastrami, mahi mahi, hot dogs, ham, tuna and chicken salad ($2-4.25), salads include somen, Oriental chicken and a variety of chef's salads and burgers come with cheese, bacon, teriyaki and BBQ or you can get your burger with fish, chicken, chili or as a tuna or patty melt on rye, ($1.15-3.95). Tacos, burritos, loco moco ($1.25-3) as well as entrees of pork chops, liver and onions, sweet & sour spare ribs, breaded fish, chicken and veal cutlets ($3.75-6.25) are only part of the extensive menu. For dessert, there's all the familiar Dairy Queen treats like cones, shakes, floats, freezes and a variety of sundaes ($1-3.50) The Lihu'e DQ also has lau lau plate lunches and dinner specials that include prime rib, scampi, rib steak, butterfish and seafood platters-alone or in combinations - are available after 5 ($7.50-14.95). They also offer a variety of specialty submarine sandwiches and French dips ($3.75-4.25). COMMENTS: A lot of food for an ice cream shop; the whole menu is available for take out and they have catering, too. I remember the Waimea outlet from years ago - it's almost as much a landmark as the canyon!

DONDERO'S *Italian*

Hyatt Regency Kaua'i, Po'ipu (742-1234) HOURS: 6-10 pm. SAMPLING: Antipasto consists of porcini mushroom crepes, beef carpaccio prosciutto with melon, pasta squares in broth or minestrone soup and several salads including one tossed with gorgonzola, walnuts and apple ($4.75-9.50). Ribbon pasta is sauteed with scallops, Italian bacon, shitake mushrooms, asparagus and red peppers; netted open ravioli comes with seafood, spinach pasta is covered with sauteed shrimp and lemon, porcini mushroom pasta is served with chicken and spinach and Dondero's special risotto combines different ingredients every day ($9.25-14). Veal dishes include saltimbocca, scallopini and osso bucco, sauteed chicken breast comes with marsala and grapes, sauteed shrimp is served on bow tie pasta with asparagus and champagne sauce and there's rack of lamb, cioppino and several hearty lasagna and spaghetti dishes ($23-28). Hyatt also offers healthy, natural cuisine offerings like Sicilian bean and artichoke salad ($7.75) and whole wheat pasta primavera ($20) and lists the calories and nutrition percentages. Moving right along to desserts, however, (where they don't list the calories) there is tiramisu, berries with zabaglione, creme brulee, hazelnut chocolate flambe crepes or semifreddo frozen parfait with warm fruit sauce ($5.50-6). Or drink your dessert and have a Dondero's cappuccino with Bailey's, Grand Marnier and macadamia nut liqueur ($6.50). COMMENTS: Decor is an upscale Italian version of a Mexican cantina: tiled floors with "hand-painted" stucco walls and "real" three-dimensional seashells stuck on over painted-on shells. There's a colorful mural at the back and outside dining is on a villa patio. The color scheme is dark green and white and somehow it all worked - it was fun, yet fancy, about the closest thing to fine dining that there is in Kaua'i. Both appetizers and desserts can be ordered in sampler plates, a real plus when there are so many good things to try. The food is Italian with a difference that should appeal to purists as well as the more adventurous Italian food lover. While dining is casual on the garden isle, they do request men wear shirts with collars. Reservations suggested.

FISHERMAN'S GALLEY ★ *Seafood*
1850 Kaumualii, Puhi (246-4700) HOURS: 10 am-9 pm, Fridays till 10; Saturday and Sunday until 8. SAMPLING: Ono chowder, smoked fish salad with feta cheese, seafood salad, sashimi ($3.50-12.50). Fish 'n chips is the specialty: deep fried marlin or cod served with seasoned fries (5.95-8.95). Also seafood melt, Hawaiian fish or lobster platter, fish 'n shrimp, NY steak, Bruno burger (named after a friend), broiled fish sandwich, BBQ ribs and several combination platters ($6.95-$22.95). Specials include lasagna, shrimp bisque and bouillabaisse. Beer and wine are available. Grandma Lois makes all the desserts such as cheesecake, tropical carrot cake and raspberry brownies ($3.50). COMMENTS: This is a small restaurant with wooden booths (like a captain's galley), nautical decor and, of course, lots of pictures of fishermen with their respective catches of the day. I don't usually like fish 'n chips, but I sure liked these! The fish was fresh and moist, the batter light and crispy and the chips were seasoned and tasty. The creamy ono chowder is made from stock and fresh fish and the Italian dressing is made from scratch. The coleslaw is homemade, vinegar style, and several dishes

offer creamy, homemade scalloped potatoes. Leslie and Bo Jordan opened in June of 1994. They also own Gent-Lee Fishing so the fish is freshly caught off their own boats. If a boat catches ahi, they'll have a great sashimi special that night, e.g. $6 a plate. And by the time you read this, they should be open for breakfast (6 am) and serving pancakes, silver dollar potatoes and smoked fish omelettes. The location was formerly Sireno's Sausage Factory and they plan to use the facilities to make sausage again for breakfast, lasagna and other items.

GAYLORD'S RESTAURANT ★ *American*

At Kilohana Plantation just outside of Lihu'e (245-5608) HOURS: Lunch Monday-Saturday 11 am-3 pm, Sunday brunch 9:30 am-3 pm, Dinner daily from 5 pm. SAMPLING: Lunch salads include Mrs. Wallace's Delight with a sampling of three salads; ahi, turkey and shrimp, peppered ahi or chicken Caesar, spinach and citrus, nuts and greens, Oriental chicken and southern cobb ($7.95-9.95). Sandwiches come with soup or salad and fries or rice: Wally's Reuben, sliced turkey, open-faced crab melt or chicken parmesan, hot pastrami, bay shrimp and avocado and hot teriyaki chicken croissant ($7.95-9.95). Signature lunch dishes range from baby back ribs to seafood quesadilla ($8.95-11.95). Dinners feature appetizers of blackened prawns, pot stickers, honey baked brie and spicy seafood won ton ($6.94-9.95) and entrees of steak, rack of lamb, prime rib (regular or blackened) veal piccata, barbecued prawns, shrimp scampi, seafood rhapsody, lobster tail, duck, cornish game hen, chicken roulade, pasta with sauteed prawns, chicken and rosemary and baby back ribs ($14.95-26.95). Extensive dessert list with linzertorte, Kilohana mud pie, tropical mousse, lemon tart with blueberry coulis, French silk and homemade banana-coconut cream pie ($3.95-4.95). COMMENTS: The atmosphere and recreation of the old rooms of the plantation living and dining areas makes this a special place to dine. Unfortunately, the dining area is along the courtyard and on a cool, or rainy afternoon or evening they drop the canvas walls with plastic windows. While this helps keep the elements out, it does detract a bit from the ambience. Sort of gourmet dining in a tent. The food is excellent, however, and while some of the wait staff are young and not highly skilled, they are friendly, eager and attentive. Dining here is certainly worthy of a recommendation, but preferably on a warm and sunny afternoon or evening. Gaylord's salad was wonderful and the seafood fettucini offered an ample portion of prawns, scallops, and mussels. Unlike some fettucini which has a thick, heavy cream sauce, this was lighter and flavored perfectly with lemon grass. A wonderful taste combination. The fresh fish is generally highly recommended, but may also be sold out if you are a late diner. Except for the fresh fish, most dinner entrees are fairly priced and good portions. The banana-coconut cream pie was a delight, nothing fancy or exotic, just one of those wonderful comfort foods! Although we have had readers report inconsistency in food and service, we would still recommend it!

GREEN GARDEN ★ *Local plus*

Hanapepe Town (335-5422) HOURS: Breakfast 8:30 am-2 pm (from 8 am on Saturday and 7:30 am Sunday), Lunch 10:30-2 pm, Dinner 5-9 pm. Closed all day Tuesday. SAMPLING: Breakfast of eggs, breakfast meats, waffles, hot cakes and French toast ($3.65-4.95). Lunch sandwiches include salad or fries and beverage and include hot roast beef or pork sandwiches, mahi melt, tuna tomato club and burgers ($3.95-6.25). Entrees also include vegetables and feature chicken chow mein, shrimp tempura, sweet & sour spare ribs and BBQ chicken ($5.45-7.35) and specials like seafood curry, ono saute or Hawaiian platter. Dinner appetizers include a choice of escargot, shrimp cocktail, mussels, sashimi or mushrooms for $6.95. They offer some of the same lunch entrees at only slightly higher prices as well as kiawe broiled pork chops, steaks, kabobs, chicken peppercorn and lobster ($6.50-26.95). Posted specials, too, like spaghetti & fried chicken, mussel cioppino and lemon-pineapple breast of chicken ($8.25-11.25). They also offer a salad bar for $2 additional, $5-7 a la carte. They're known for their "mile-high" pies like coconut or macadamia cream, chocolate and especially the lilikoi ($2). COMMENTS: This family owned restaurant has been here since 1948 serving an eclectic mix of local, homestyle and gourmet meals in large portions for small prices. Good selection of children's choices. The salad bar, given the inflated prices of fresh produce on Kaua'i, is a real value! Very casual with the spacious garden look of a large greenhouse. The long family-style tables are popular with tour bus groups and perhaps negates an intimate dining experience. But the portions are generous, the menu is broad, the atmosphere pleasant, the prices reasonable and the pies fabulous!

GROVE DINING ROOM   *Multi-cultural*
9600 Kamualii Hwy. at Waimea Garden Cottages (338-5422) HOURS: Lunch Tuesday-Friday 11:30-2 pm, Dinner Tuesday-Thursday 5:30-9 pm, till 10 Friday and Saturday. Sunday Brunch 10 am-2 pm. SAMPLING: Plate lunches along with burgers, prime rib sandwich, kalua pork on a bun and salads like Caesar, chop chop, garden greens and fresh fruit ($3.25-8.25). Dinner appetizers include Asian crab cakes, scampi and sashimi ($6.75-8.95) and entrees range from Hawaiian seafood stir-fry to prime rib, from chicken tempura to kalbi ribs or vegetarian lasagna ($12.95-18.95). Kikiaola sand pie (coffee and vanilla ice cream atop a macadamia nut-butter crust with whipped cream topping) is the specialty for dessert ($3.95). On Friday and Saturday they serve a Hawaiian plate special with several salads, entrees and dessert for $19.95. The luau dinner is accompanied by live Hawaiian music. Sunday brunch offers carved prime rib, an omelette station, ham, eggs Florentine, banana French toast, breakfast meats and fruit, potatoes, salads, vegetables, assorted muffins and cheesecake with juices and champagne for $16.95 ($14.95 seniors, $8.95 keikis). COMMENTS: Attractive plantation look with tall ceilings and wrap around lanais that have a nice view of the Hawaiian-style cottages and grounds. A surprisingly romantic atmosphere. The weekend luau dinner has become very popular. A great way to enjoy Hawaiian food plus entertainment at a cost far less than a luau. Good food and friendly service make this a good dining option.

HANAPEPE ESPRESSO BAR   ★ *Gourmet Vegetarian*
Located in the Hanapepe Bookstore at 3830 Hanapepe Road, (335-5011/335-8544) HOURS: Breakfast Wednesday-Sunday 8 am-11 am, Lunch 11 am-2 pm. Dinner served Thursday-Sunday 6-9 pm. SAMPLING: Breakfast naturally begins with espresso and other coffee drinks and there are multi-grain waffles and pancakes, vegetable home fries and baked fritattas ($3.75-7.75). Lunch includes soups and salads, healthnut sandwich, pasta and garden burgers with various combinations of pesto, sundried tomatoes, sauteed mushrooms or spinach spread ($4.25-7). Dinners change weekly and might include an appetizer of roasted leeks, red pepper, capers and feta cheese wrapped in phyllo dough and served with eggplant & Maui onion relish ($6.25) or entrees like pasta primavera with broccoli, tomatoes and marinated mushrooms on farfalle with a fire-roasted bell

pepper butter sauce or shallot white wine vinaigrette; lasagna with seared tomatoes and fresh spinach with a fresh basil pesto cream sauce; or oven roasted vegetables, fresh spinach and smoked mozzarella in puff pastry ($16.95-17.95). Desserts include creme brulee and chocolate mousse. COMMENTS: Bookstores are always a great place to grab a cup of coffee or a pastry, but owners Larry Reisor and Chris Ayers went a step further adding a trendy dining counter and seats and full restaurant area with tables and chairs, then hiring former Tamarind chef Greg Forker to make the gourmet vegetarian dinners that even meat eaters like. They're made with an Italian flair and with such fresh, flavorful vegetables that most don't know anything's "missing." Live music on dinner nights with regular or Hawaiian slack key guitar. Reservations recommended.

HOUSE OF SEAFOOD ★ *Fish/Seafood*
1941 Po'ipu Road at Po'ipu Kai Resort (742-5255) HOURS: 5:30-9:15 pm. SAMPLING: Crab linguini, braised mussels, steamed clams, oysters Rockefeller, and scampi provencal are a few of the appetizers ($6.50-10) or you can try clam, French onion, seafood gazpacho or Wailua taro clam chowder ($4-6). Entrees feature an abundance of fresh fish as well as shrimp luau, scallops Poipu, lobster saffron, crab stuffed prawns, Coquilles St. Jacques, abalone, paella, cioppino and bouillabaisse ($18.50-38). Meat lovers aren't left out, several steaks are offered alone or in seafood combinations ($21-34). Several adult-style steak and seafood offerings are available on the keiki menu and desserts might include baked Alaska, Grand Marnier souffle, chocolate-dipped kiwi or flambe specialties like cherries jubilee, bananas Foster or crepes Suzette. COMMENTS: As they say "Our name says it all" and they do offer quite an extensive seafood menu with both traditional and creative new preparations of their entrees and soups. Long-room dining area with beautiful wood floors and large open windows which allows the evening breeze to come in. Chances are they will have something on the menu that you haven't ever tried before. However, given that the meals are a la carte, when you add soup and/or salad to your bill at about $5 each, your meal is going to climb upwards. The atmosphere is very pleasant and if you love fresh seafood, this is the place to come.

ILIMA TERRACE   *Island style*
Hyatt Regency Kaua'i, Po'ipu (742-1234) HOURS: Breakfast 6-11 am, Lunch 11 am-2:30 pm, Dinner 5-9 pm. SAMPLING: Assorted cereals, fruits, pancakes and waffles plus strawberry or vegetable crepes and banana French toast ($3.75-9) Eggs, omelettes or breakfast meats (4.25-9.75) and a daily breakfast buffet ($16.50) or Sunday Brunch ($19.75). Lunch starts with quesadillas, buffalo wings, Thai spring rolls or a variety of salads: cobb, fruit, nicoise, ahi Caesar or lemon-barbecued chicken ($3.75-9.75). Burgers, pizza, pasta, or entree specialties like stir-fry chicken and noodles or tempura along with healthy offerings such as red lentil chili, grilled salmon salad, chicken burger or vegetable club are also available ($5-15). Dinners feature the same light fare as lunch along with grilled fish or filet mignon and roast chicken ($19-23) or a nightly buffet that includes salad bar, breads, fruits and cheeses, pastries and hot food depending on the night: Sunday, Pacific rim; Monday/Thursday, prime rib Tuesday/Friday, island-style; and Wednesday/Saturday, barbecue ($23.95). COMMENTS: Dinner buffets are an affordable way to experience the luxury of dining at the Hyatt. Their healthy,

natural cuisine options are a plus. The breakfast buffets are a little spendy, but the dinner buffets are a better value. Reservations suggested.

JOE'S COURTSIDE CAFE *Salads/Burgers/Sandwiches*
Located at Kiahuna Tennis Club, Po'ipu (742-6363) HOURS: Breakfast 7-11 am, Lunch 11 am-2 pm. SAMPLING: Pastries, breads and healthy fruits, along with eggs Benedict, loco moco, huevos rancheros, tofu scramble, French toast and pancakes are the breakfast options or you can create your own omelette from a list of ingredients. For lunch, choose your ingredients for a personalized salad or opt for a Caesar with grilled chicken breast or fresh fruit and yogurt ($5.50-7.50). Sandwiches include a turkey melt, hot ham & cheese or vegetarian or try a burger, hot dog or chicken avocado with jack cheese hot off the grill ($4.95-6.75). They recently added a South Shore steak sandwich (like a Philly) and a fresh fish entree. COMMENTS: This open air restaurant, which overlooks the tennis courts, opened December '94 with the bar opening the following spring. "Eat at Joe's" on Aloha Fridays when they are open till 7 pm and have free happy hour pupus.

KALAHEO COFFEE CO. & CAFE ★ *Sandwiches & Salads*
2436 Kaumualii Hwy., Kalaheo (332-5858) HOURS: Monday-Saturday 6 am-5 pm; Sundays 7 am-2 pm. SAMPLING: Breakfast offers Anahola granola, scrambled egg sandwich, assorted pastries, pancakes, Belgian waffles and build-your-own omelettes. Lunch till closing. You can have Kaua'i grown salads, deli sandwiches, soup and grilled sandwiches like hot pastrami, tuna melt, or grilled herb chicken, fresh vegetable or turkey burger. Ice cream desserts and pastries including cheesecake, brownies, muffins, carrot, chocolate and coffee cakes. And of course they have plenty of coffees and teas. COMMENTS: Owners Kristina and John Ferguson (former chef at The Grove restaurant in Waimea) opened in May of 1994 and already have a quite a following. The fresh salads are excellent and the sandwiches are piled high. A good place to stop after a visit to the Canyon for a late lunch and/or leisurely cup of coffee, or pick up some lunch to eat up at Kukuiolono Park! They also offer periodic dinners and cooking classes.

KALAHEO STEAK HOUSE *Steak/Seafood*
4444 Papalina Road (332-9780) HOURS: 5:30-9:30 pm. SAMPLING: Clams by the bucket, artichokes, mushrooms and teriyaki steak stix will start you off ($3.25-5.95) and they're followed by dinners of steak, pork, poultry, prime rib, seafood or combinations you can choose ($11.95-24.95). Cornish game hen, teriyaki pork tenderloin and Kalaheo shrimp are some of the more unusual offerings and all come with salad, fresh rolls (from The Bread Box bakery across the street) and baked potato or rice. For dessert, there's rum cake and/or ice cream. COMMENTS: Nice wood decor with hanging plants. Located in a quiet, residential neighborhood. The portions are ample and a good value.

KANA'S *Local*
4505 Puolo, next to the original Lappert's in Hanapepe (335-0400) HOURS: Breakfast, 6-10:30 am; 10:30 am-2:30 pm for lunch and take out. SAMPLING: Local style breakfasts plus plate lunches: teriyaki beef or chicken, loco moco, chicken katsu, fried saimin ($3.50-5.25) along with burgers ($1.50-2.25). They also offer daily specials and Friday Hawaiian plate specials. COMMENTS: Locally owned by the Kanahele Family; they have good local food served with family-style aloha.

KEOKI'S PARADISE   *Steak & Seafood*
Po'ipu Shopping Village (742-7534) HOURS: Dinner 5:30-10 pm; seafood and taco Bar 4:30-11:30 pm. SAMPLING: Sashimi, Thai shrimp sticks, fisherman's chowder and summer rolls to start ($3.95-8.95) and entrees of fresh fish (with several preparations), pesto shrimp macadamia, Pacific Rim rigatoni (with seafood), prime rib, steaks, Koloa pork ribs, Balinese chicken (in garlic and lemon grass) and vegetarian lasagna ($10.95-19.95). Ice cream, triple chocolate cake and "The Original Hula Pie" from Kimo's (which is still the best!) ($2.95-4.95). The taco bar offers appetizers and local plates from the regular menu plus burgers, salads and Mexican dinners like fish, beef or chicken tacos, cheese or chicken enchiladas and chicken quesadilla ($3.95-6.95). COMMENTS: This is one of the popular TS restaurant chain that also owns Kimos's on Maui, Duke's Canoe Club in Waikiki and the recently reopened Duke's and soon-to-be reopened Sharky's here on Kaua'i. As with our description of Kimo's on Maui, the TS restaurants seem to have a love/hate relationship with folks. We enjoy them, but we don't go expecting "A Pacific Cafe" cuisine. The food is generally a good value, but quality does seem to be a bit sporadic. So, perhaps we have just been the lucky ones! However, the atmosphere at Keoki's is very pleasant with plenty of family appeal. The lagoons with koi, waterfalls, and plenty of lush greenery in this open air, multi-level restaurant create a setting reminiscent of Disney's Jungle Land (albeit without any mechanical elephants or alligators.) The kids will love the tropical atmosphere. Arrive between 5 and 6 pm for a selection of early bird specials. During low season they may not be busy, but you might want to call ahead for reservations just to be sure.

KIAHUNA GOLF CLUB RESTAURANT
Located at the Kiahuna Golf Course in Po'ipu. (742-6055) HOURS: Currently only serving sandwiches. Full service is expected to resume in the future, but no projected date was given.

KOKEE LODGE   *American*
3600 Kokee Road, Waimea (335-6061) HOURS: 9 am-3:30 pm. SAMPLING: Continental and light breakfasts, quiche, cornbread, muffins ($2.25-4.95). Lunch sandwiches on 12-grain bread ($5.75 and up) plus Kokee Lodge specialties like chili, Portuguese bean soup, cornbread and lilikoi pie ($2.95-4.95). COMMENTS: Rustic atmosphere and good place to stop on the way to Waimea Canyon. Considering you are what seems to be in the middle of the Hawaiian wilderness, the food is remarkably good. Nothing like a bowl of bean soup with a side of cornbread followed by their outrageous fudge cake to warm you up on a cool afternoon adventure in upcountry Kaua'i.

KOLOA BROILER   *Broil-Your-Own*
Old Koloa Town Center, (742-9122) HOURS: 11 am - 10 pm. SAMPLING: Appetizers are Germaine's roadhouse chili, chile con queso dip and chips, teriyaki beef sticks, sashimi ($3-7). Entrees are all "Broil Your Own" top sirloin, baby back pork ribs, beef kabob, mahi mahi, BBQ chicken, beef burger and fresh fish and come with salad bar, baked beans and sourdough bread ($6-14.95). COMMENTS: One of the last of the broil-your-own which can lead to some serious socializing at the grill. So if that's your thing, this is your place! (Personally when we go out to eat it is to avoid cooking!) We hear they have good mai tais, too. At least you can't complain if the food isn't "perfectly" cooked!

KUPONO CAFE   *Health food*
1571 Poʻipu Rd., at the Hyatt Regency. HOURS: 9 am - 1 pm. SAMPLING: Breads and muffins, fruits, and cereals along with fresh fruit juices and smoothies $2-$4.50. Red lentil chili with yogurt and baked corn chips, garden burger, salad $4-6.50. COMMENTS: Located at the Spa of the Hyatt Regency. Enjoy a healthy breakfast or lunch after indulging in a facial or massage, or working out in their fitness room or swimming laps in their 25 yard lap pool.

LC'S PLACE   *Local style*
3771 Hanapepe Rd., (335-3991) HOURS: Breakfast and lunch 7 am-2 pm. Dinner 6-9 pm, Monday - Friday and until 11 pm on Saturday. COMMENTS: Located in old Hanapepe, LC's place has local grinds, saimin etc. They cook their kalua pig in a real imu. A good choice if you'd like to sample some local dishes.

LA GRIGLIA   *Italian*
Poʻipu Shopping Village (742-2147) HOURS: 11 am-10 pm. SAMPLING: Distinctive salads (blackened chicken celery, chop chop and Caesar with blackened chicken or bay shrimp). Sample unusual burgers such as blackened, Italian sausage, eggplant parmigiana, meatball and chicken Florentina with spinach and cheese ($5.95-7.95). Appetizers include focaccia bread, shrimp crostini and stuffed mushrooms ($3.95-6.95). In addition, they offer pastas with lemon chicken sauce, puttanesca (tomato, garlic, capers, olives) and white cheese sauce, there are specials like pasta with vodka cream sauce, gnocchi verdi, chicken cacciatore and seafood linguini ($9.95-12.95). Panini "sandwiches" are a specialty: grilled bread is covered with combinations of meat and vegetables like salami, provolone, roasted peppers, eggplant, blackened chicken, artichoke hearts or marinated, grilled sirloin tip ($6.95). COMMENTS: Opened in December '94 in the old Venturi's location. Looks like a take-out place, but the food is definitely restaurant-worthy. Homemade sauces and pastas; the breads, focaccia and panini are all baked on the premises. You can order at the counter or be served at one of the outside tables. Children's menu; espressos and coffees available. No liquor license, but beer & wine available at Whaler's Store.

LAWAI RESTAURANT   *Local/Oriental*
3687 Kaumualii Hwy., Lawai (332-9550) HOURS: 9 am-9 pm. SAMPLING: Extensive menu of local and Oriental dishes: soup, pork, beef, poultry, seafood, chop suey, eggs, vegetarian, noodles and appetizers, noodles in soup salad, Chinese plates, NY steak combos, Filipino specials, curries, Japanese dishes plus sandwiches, steaks and seafood. Chinese sausage, crispy duck with plum sauce, baked crab claws, ham & egg fu yung, duck noodles with vegetables, chicken papaya, sukiyaki don, shrimp tempura, fish teriyaki and 8 & 9 course dinners offered for two or more ($4-16.75). COMMENTS: This small eatery, which opened in 1985, is particularly popular with local residents. There are three pages full of dishes on their printed menu and even more on blackboard.

LINDA'S RESTAURANT   *Local*
3840 Hanapepe Road, Hanapepe (335-5152) HOURS: Monday-Friday; Breakfast 7:30-10:30 am, Lunch 10:30 am-1:30 pm, Dinner Monday-Saturday, 5:30-9 pm. SAMPLING: Breakfast offers eggs, spam, corned beef hash, beef stew bowl, saimin, miso soup ($2.85-4.50). Lunch selections include burgers, sandwiches, fried saimin, plate specials ($2.50-5.75). Dinners feature plate specials, salads and

saimin ($2.95). Medium and large pizzas including Hawaiian, Mexican and ultimate ($9.99-19.99). COMMENTS: Small coffee shop. Pizzas have homemade crust brushed with garlic butter.

MUSTARD'S LAST STAND / CAPT'N HELMS *Burgers/Hot Dogs*
Corner of Hwy. 50 & Koloa Road (332-7245) HOURS: 9 am-sunset. SAMPLING: Charbroiled hamburgers, hot dogs and sausages spicy chicken sandwich, Capt'n Helms fish 'n chips, Lappert's ice cream ($5-8). Daily specials. COMMENTS: Twelve different hot dogs that you build yourself from a condiment bar that includes cheeses, onions, guacamole, salsa, mushrooms, mustards, sauerkraut and chili. Looks like a tourist stop in the middle of the desert - that or a Disneyland ride. Good place to stop with the family.

PANCHO & LEFTY'S *Mexican*
Old Koloa Town Center (742-7377) HOURS: Breakfast 8 am-12 noon, lunch and dinner 11 am-9:30 pm. SAMPLING: Breakfast omelettes, waffles, pancakes and Mexican egg, burrito and chorizo (they make their own) specialties ($4.95-9.95). The same menu for lunch and dinner offers the Mexican food basics plus seafood enchiladas, Mexican burger, tamale dinner (they make their own), carnitas (Perez family recipe from Mexico) ($6.95-15.95). They also have two original creations: pechugas pollo relleno (chicken breast stuffed with jack cheese and chiles, dipped in egg batter and pan-fried - $12.95) and a hot, sexy appetizer, Vesos Calientes or The "Hot Kiss" which is an order of whole jalapeno peppers stuffed with shrimp and cheese, then wrapped in bacon and charbroiled ($5.95). Smack! COMMENTS: Owners Penny & Terry Wigzell moved Pancho & Lefty's from Maui in 1990 and opened a Kona outlet two years later. They still have a lot of former Maui customers come in especially to order the burrito verde. They have a prime rib special on weekends.

PIZZA BELLA *Pizza/Italian*
Po'ipu Shopping Village (742-9671) HOURS: 7:30 am-9 pm (Sunday breakfast to noon). SAMPLING: They have breakfasts of omelettes, loco moco, corned beef hash, pancake sandwich, banana or blueberry pancakes and Hawaiian sweet bread French toast ($2.50-5.95). Sandwiches include burgers, Italian sausage or meatball, hero, pepper steak, chicken salad and eggplant or chicken parmesan ($4.95-6.95). Salads include Caesar, chef, cobb and pasta ($3-8.95). Pasta dishes include lasagna and linguini with a variety of sauces ($5.25-8.95) and the pizza toppings include BBQ chicken or pork, seafood, Cajun shrimp, as well as Mexican or vegetarian combos. They also feature New York style pizza with a variety of traditional toppings, small to large from $8.75-21.50. COMMENTS: Delivery hours from 5:30-8:45 pm for $1.50 charge. Nothing memorable.

PIZZA HUT *Italian*
Kukui Grove Shopping Center area at 3-3171 Kuhio Hwy. (245-9531) HOURS: 11 am-11 pm weekdays, weekends open until midnight. SAMPLING: This is a popular chain on the mainland, and remains so here. The pizza is not extraordinary, but having a salad bar along with it is a treat in Hawai'i. One trip through the salad bar is $2.07, $3.64 for unlimited. Lunch buffet is $5.99 and includes all the pizza you can eat, plus salad bar. Dinner buffet is $7.99.

PLANTATION GARDENS
Located at Kiahuna Plantations. No information available as we prepare for press.

PO'IPU BAY BAR & GRILL *American with Island Touches*
Just past the Hyatt on the golf course at Po'ipu Bay Resort (742-8888) HOURS:
Breakfast 7-11 am, Sandwich bar 11-2, Lunch 11 am-5:30 pm. SAMPLING:
variety of breakfast meats and egg dishes plus omelettes, tropical or strawberry
pancakes and colossal cinnamon rolls ($2.95-9.95). Early bird special for $4.95.
Lunch offers burgers, hot dogs, chicken and fish sandwiches ($5.25-9.95) and
dinner entrees like shrimp curry and Szechuan pasta primavera at reduced prices
($11.95-12.95). They also feature a sandwich and salad bar with a good variety
of deli meats, cheeses, breads and cold salads for $8.95. Dinners might start with
macadamia nut brie, smoked chicken quesadilla, roasted garlic or spring rolls
($4.95-9.95) followed by entrees like coconut shrimp, scampi, pork ribs, rasta
pasta chicken (with garlic wine and sun-dried tomatoes), prime rib, filet mignon
and meat and seafood combinations ($14.95-21.95) as well as lighter sandwiches
and burgers under $10. Specials might offer seafood crepes, fresh fish or seafood
mixed grill ($18.95-21.95). Dessert options include black mountain sundae, apples
torry (sauteed with cinnamon schnapps over vanilla ice cream) and a sweet
homage to the Beatles: "Lennon Poppy Seed Poundcake" and "Strawberry Fields
Poundcake" ($3.95-5.95). COMMENTS: Windows all around with views of the
golf course. Looks like an old fashioned hotel dining room or dining room of a
country club. Good reviews on the breakfast for quality and price, especially the
eggs Benedict and home fries. Sandwich bar is a novel idea and good for golfers
on the run.

POMODORO ★ *Italian*
Rainbow Plaza in Kalaheo (332-5945) HOURS: 5:30-10 pm. SAMPLING:
Antipasti of calamari fritti, mozzarella marinara or prosciutto and melon ($5.95-
7.95), a variety of pastas - spaghetti, ravioli, cannelloni, manicotti, baked penne
and lasagna, the house special ($8.95-14.95) and Pomodoro specialties like veal
parmigiana, pizzaiola, piccata or scaloppini; eggplant or calamari parmigiana,
scampi, chicken cacciatore and chicken saltimbocca, an unusual change from veal
($14.95-18.95). Italian desserts like zabaliogne, tiramisu, spumoni are featured.
COMMENTS: This location was previously Casa d'Italiana. Surprisingly attractive
tables and settings for nondescript shopping plaza location. Separate cocktail
lounge. Their food is fresh and flavorful, although entrees are a la carte, prices
remain moderate. Plenty of items on the menu for the children to enjoy.

ROY'S PO'IPU BAR & GRILL ★ *Euro-Asian*
Po'ipu Shopping Village (742-5000) HOURS: 5:30-9:30 pm. SAMPLING: Dim
sum and appetizers include potstickers, shrimp on a stick, escargot cassoulet,
lemon grass crusted fish satay and ravioli of shitake & spinach ($5.95-7.95).
Grilled Chinese chicken, crisp calamari or Maui onion are a few of the salads
($4.25-6.95). Their imu baked pizzas feature mesquite grilled chicken, puna goat
cheese & shitake mushroom, eggplant or keiki style ($4.95-7.50). Roy's entrees
offer Thai stuffed chicken, Northern Chinese roasted duck, charbroiled garlic
mustard short ribs, and oven roasted pot roast ($14.95-17.95). There are also
nightly specials in every category: Okinawan sweet potato soup, caramelized
onion pizza, kiawe grilled rack of lamb and macadamia nut crusted shutome
($4.25-23.95). Roy's signature dessert is the dark chocolate souffle, literally

swimming in rich chocolate plus the apple-blueberry-mango cobbler, guava sherbet lilikoi float and strawberry brulee ($5.50-6.50). COMMENTS: This is the newest restaurant owned by trendsetter and chef Roy Yamaguchi who first gained accolades and the attention of food critics and celebrities at his Hawaii Kai location. He opened a successful second location in Kahana, Maui, along with a sister restaurant, Nicolina, that he named after his daughter. Executive Chef Mark "Mako" Segawa-Gonzales holds the culinary reins at this new Po'ipu location. Apparently they learned something from their Kahana, Maui location and have enclosed the kitchen behind huge glass windows. You can still enjoy watching the chefs prepare your meal, without having to be overwhelmed by the noise. They offer one set menu while a second menu offers nightly specials. A rust and green theme is carried throughout and when the weather allows, the side panels are opened up to make it a bit more open air. No view here, the food is the main attraction. The sesame seared kajiki salad with lemon ginger vinaigrette ($7.25) was outstanding, and we would have been happy enlarging the portion and making a meal on that. This was one of the daily specials which are designed around the best and freshest ingredients each day. Kajiki is a type of marlin and the searing really sealed in the moisture and flavor. One entree we sampled was the ginger seared mahi mahi with tamarind coconut sauce and mint oil ($21.95). The combination of ingredients in this sauce might be a good one, but the only flavor that came through was the ginger and it was so strong that it overpowered the mahi. The seafood pasta, an item on the regular menu, had a good portion of seafood and a pleasant red sauce that enhanced the seafood. Cream of broccoli was the soup of the day and was good but not especially noteworthy. The apple-blueberry-mango cobbler required 20 minutes advance preparation and was delightfully served in the shape of an apple. The food was very good, but perhaps it was just our choice of entrees, and the fact that the night before we'd had a world class meal at A Pacific Cafe that made it a tough comparison. In any case, based on this most recent experience, A Pacific Cafe squeaks by with a little bigger thumbs up, but it is a very close call. While service at Roy's was unrushed, it was maybe just a bit too attentive. A couple we'd interviewed had the same complaint, that after each bite the wait staff was checking in to make sure it was okay. With the new glassed-in kitchen, if you are a lip reader, you might enjoy figuring out what those chefs are really saying!

SHIPWRECK SUBS *Sandwiches*
Po'ipu Shopping Village (742-7467) HOURS: 11 am-3 pm. SAMPLING: Create your own 6" or 13" subs on white or wheat with turkey, roast beef, ham, pastrami, salami, tuna, egg, veggies, chili plus choice of Swiss, provolone, cheddar or jack cheese and condiments. With 1 meat ($4.25-5.99), 2 meats ($4.50-6.25), or 3 meats ($4.75-6.50). COMMENTS: They have a kid's special for ages 12 and under: peanut butter and jelly with chips and a small soda for $3.

SI CISCO'S *Mexican*
Located in the Kukui Grove Shopping Center. (246-1563) HOURS: Lunch 11 am - 4 pm, dinner 4 pm - 9 pm. SAMPLING: A la carte entrees ($5-9) or full dinners (less than $15) are available. COMMENTS: This is another love it or leave it restaurant. The food quality and service seem to be inconsistent. While the food was considered authentic, spicy, and very good by some, others found it less appealing. The service can be very friendly or inattentive and slow. They also have menus for gringos and children.

SINALOA ★ *Mexican*

3959 Kamualii Hwy., Hanapepe (335-0006) HOURS: Lunch 11 am-3 pm, Dinner 5-9 pm, closed Wednesdays. SAMPLING: Good selection of burritos and chimichangas plus a variety of nachos, quesadillas and tacos (Taco de Pescado has grilled mahi mahi and shrimp) as well as combinations with enchiladas, chile relleno, fajitas and tacos ($2.95-10.95). COMMENTS: Almost all dishes have a vegetarian offering. Tortillas are made daily at the restaurant site and come in "flour" or "wheat." The restaurant is painted in bright colors and there is live music several nights a week. They are planning to expand and start a happy hour very soon if they haven't already.

SUEOKA'S ★ *Local*

Koloa. (742-1112) HOURS: Sunday - Friday 10 am-3 pm, Saturday 10 am-4 pm. Located in Koloa next to Seouki's Grocery Store. SAMPLING: Plate lunches, sandwiches and burgers, local foods. COMMENTS: What a delight to still find a local walk-up restaurant. Much like the old Azeka's Market on Maui, this small, unobtrusive structure on the side of the grocery store not only has REALLY cheap food, but it is REALLY good too. A chance to sample some local dishes, they serve a variety of plate lunches with specials that change daily. The specials are listed on papers stuck on the window and as they sell out of that item, they pull the paper off. You'll see plenty of local folks picking up their lunch during their break. Hamburgers begin at 95 cents, grilled cheese $1.50, fishburger $1.60 or saimin at $1.40. The teriyaki sandwich seemed like a splurge costing a whopping $2.50. It was not a huge sandwich, but very tender and flavorful, and at this price you could order two! Plate lunches like fried chicken, tripe stew, teriyaki run $3.25-4.15. No place to sit and eat, but we recommend you take your order over to the beach and enjoy a bargain meal with oceanfront dining.

TACO DUDE *Mexican*

Located at the Coconut Marketplace (822-1919). HOURS: Lunch and dinner. SAMPLING: Fairly good food, moderately priced $3-6.

TAISHO *Japanese*

Old Koloa Town (826-6277) HOURS: 5:30-9:30 pm. SAMPLING: Appetizers include tofu, spring rolls, pot stickers and won ton ($4-8.95) Entrees of tempura, stir-fry, teriyaki or calamari ($8.95-12.95) Combination dinners with a variety of teriyaki, tempura, katsu and soft shell crab ($10.95-14.95). Taisho Bento with California roll or sashimi, shrimp tempura and steak ($19.95) and Japanese Bento with California roll or sashimi, shrimp & vegetable tempura, teri beef or chicken ($18.95). COMMENTS: Small sushi bar in rear. Early Bird specials before 6:45, full dinners with sushi and teriyaki chicken ($9.95-10.50). Taisho is owned by the Ishii family who also own Sumo.

TAQUERIA NORTENOS ★ *Mexican*

Located in Po'ipu Plaza. (742-7222) HOURS: 11 am-11 pm Monday thru Saturday, closes Wednesdays at 5:30 pm. SAMPLING: Mexican fare, nothing much over $6, with most items priced $2-4. COMMENTS: Burritos and the works. This is the epitome of a hole-in-the-wall restaurant. The few tables in a small room behind the walk-up counter is a joke, resembling a large closet that they converted. But don't be mislead. This place has really great food! The prices appear average, but wait until you see the portions!! You can fill up and then some for $6 or less. So the ambience isn't much, grab some food to go and head to one of Kaua'i's beautiful parks or beaches.

TIDEPOOLS ★ *Seafood & Steak*

Hyatt Regency Kaua'i, Po'ipu (742-1234) HOURS: 6-10 pm. SAMPLING: The menu changes frequently, but an example would be: For starters there's papaya coconut sea scallops, beer battered coconut chicken or shrimp, beef or chicken satay, steamed cherry stone clams ($7-9.50) or you can create your own combination pupu platter for $9.50 per person. Then follow up with Kaua'i onion soup or clam chowder and Kaua'i onion and tomato, Caesar or green salad ($5-7.50). Then enjoy selection of entrees: beef shabu shabu, sukiyaki or nabeyaki are the Japanese dinners offered ($29-34) and healthy choices include pan-seared swordfish or tenderloin beef tips ($23-26). Fresh Hawaiian fish is prepared several ways or there's prime rib, lamb kebab, and steaks in addition to specialties like charred ahi sashimi, seafood mixed grill, shrimp scampi, vegetarian lau lau or wok fried tofu ($19-28). A variety of meat & seafood combination plates are offered for $32. Desserts range from warm apple tart to mud pie to banana cream pie to chocolate macadamia nut pie to coconut cream pie ($5-5.50). COMMENTS: They offer contemporary Hawaiian cuisine featuring Kaua'i grown products like onions and sweet corn plus vegetables and herbs from an Omao farm, Chinese noodles from Kaua'i Noodle Factory, island-grown fruit and Hawaiian fish. The build-your-own pupu platter and choice of entree combinations is a great way to taste and sample. A diverse selection of menu items can make dining an experience! Selected entrees are available for the kids in your family at half price, making this rather expensive dining choice a more affordable one. While the children in your traveling party will enjoy the Robinson Crusoe atmosphere, the adults will enjoy fine dining in a romantic setting. The restaurant is built like a series of grass-thatched Polynesian huts over a tranquil lagoon - it definitely puts you in the mood for fish! It kind of looks like Humuhumunukunukupa'a Restaurant at the Grand Wailea on Maui, but thank goodness this one is easier to pronounce! Call ahead for reservations.

TOI'S THAI KITCHEN *Thai*

Ele'ele Shopping Center, near Hanapepe (335-3111) Hours: Lunch 10:30 am-2:30 pm, Dinner 5:30-9 pm. Closed for lunch on Sunday. SAMPLING: Lunch fare includes burgers, sandwiches, and soups (such as tom yum, long rice, tofu, saimin). Appetizers include spring rolls, mee krob and deep fried tofu plus salads with beef, pork or chicken; shrimp, mahi mahi or calamari and beef, chicken or pork laab ($3.95-12.95). Entrees include green papaya salad, choice of rice and dessert: jub chai, buttered garlic nua, satay, ginger sauce nua, nua krob and cashew chicken or shrimp ($9.95-13.95).

COMMENTS: Located inside the Port Allen Bar. They don't accept credit cards. These types of restaurants simply drive the computer spell checker nuts!

TOMKATS GRILLE AND BAR *American*

Old Koloa Town Center (752-8887) HOURS: 11 am-10 pm, Happy Hour 4-6 pm. SAMPLING: Nibblers like fried onion rings, mushrooms, mozzarella sticks, chicken fingers, calamari rings and buffalo wings ($4.75-7.50). Several salads, choice of burgers and sandwich traditions like a patty melt, Reuben, French dip or ham and cheese ($4.50-8.25). Also seafood or steak ka-bobs and roast chicken and nightly specials like steak, scampi, fish or prime rib ($6.50-12.75).

COMMENTS: Opened January, 1995. The name of the restaurant is derived from the first names of owners, Tom and Kathy Podlashes, and Katnip is behind the bar. Very good desserts and Tom makes the carrot cake! They provide a special menu for kittens 12 and under. Wood decks in a rustic garden setting.

WAIMEA PIZZA AND DELI *Pizza/Sandwiches*

Kamualii Hwy., Waimea (338-0009) HOURS: Monday-Saturday 11 am-9 pm, Sunday till 8. SAMPLING: Pizzas include barbeque chicken, Italian vegetarian, Ami special (with salami, zucchini, red onions, mushrooms, garlic and Feta cheese) and Tony special (pepperoni, sausage, Canadian bacon, salami, bell peppers, onion, tomato, zucchini, eggplant, mushroom, olives & garlic) (S-M-L $8-25). There's a pizza sandwich, tuna with jalapenos, French dip, deli meats and the Southwestern: turkey, avocado, zesty salsa mixture, lettuce & tomato - great on their fresh baked sourdough, the salsa really perks up the turkey and avocado and brings out the flavor! ($4-5.75) They also offer rotini, lasagna and several salads plus smoothies, espresso and cappucino with cake and cookie options for dessert.

COMMENTS: This used to be C&K Cafe; they're set back slightly from the main highway but are easy to find. Everything is homemade: the pizza sauce and crust, breads, pastas and smoothies.

NORTH SHORE

AMELIA'S   *Sandwiches/Snacks*
At Princeville Airport, 3541 Kuhio Hwy. (826-9561) HOURS: 10 am-6:30 pm Sunday-Thursday, open later for later flights in the summer, bar only (with music) till midnight on weekends). SAMPLING: Turkey or tuna sandwich $6, hot dogs, chili, nachos ($3.50-5). COMMENTS: More character than most bars with interesting Amelia Earhart decor and great view.

AUNTIE SOPHIE'S GRILL   *American*
Princeville Center (826-1202) HOURS: Lunch 11 am-4 pm, Dinner 4-9 pm. SAMPLING: Gourmet hamburgers (bacon, chili, teriyaki, mushroom, BBQ, peppercorn, Mexican plus turkey and vegetarian) and sandwiches like steak, patty melt, French dip, veggie, teriyaki chicken and turkey Reuben ($5.75-7.95). Also available are Caesar, Mandarin, taco and chopped salads. Hot dogs with cheese, bacon, chili or sauerkraut ($3.75-7.95). Garlic peppercorn NY steak is a dinner specialty or there is fresh fish, baby back ribs, teriyaki steak and fried chicken ($10.95-14.95). COMMENTS: Casual white wood plantation look with ceiling fans and tropical fabric tablecloths and seatcovers.

BALI HAI RESTAURANT   ★ *Traditional with Pacific Rim touches*
Located at the Hanalei Bay Resort, 5380 Honoiki Road (826-6522). HOURS: Breakfast 7-11 am, Lunch 11:30 am-2 pm, Dinner 5:30-10 pm. SAMPLING: Unusual island-style items for breakfast like sliced bananas with coconut cream, macadamia nut waffles or the taro patch breakfast with two eggs, Portuguese sausage, poi pancakes and taro hash browns ($3.75-12.50). Lunch offers Kaua'i onion soup, smoked tofu salad, quiche, island papillotte (fresh fish steamed in a banana leaf), chicken Hanalei (breaded with peanuts and panko) and a good selection of sandwiches: Monte Cristo, Reuben, or Bali Hai burger ($4-12.75). Dinner appetizers include sesame crusted chicken served with a tangy lilikoi pineapple marmalade ($8), or sample an excellent salad entree of sauteed scallops in hot bacon dressing over organic greens - with edible flowers! ($13.50). The house specialty, salmon Bali Hai, is salmon with spinach cream cheese duxelle in puff pastry ($22.50). Entrees include a choice of soup or salad and there are children size portions on selected items. COMMENTS: Whatever you order, it comes with a stunning, panoramic view of the Bay and Hamolokama Mountain and Waterfall. Halau O'Hanalei entertains with a hula revue every Sunday at 7.

BLACK POT LUAU HUT   *Hawaiian*
Aku Road in Hanalei. (826-9871) A family owned business, with Hawaiian fare and a local favorite for more than ten years. This very small restaurant wins for the biggest mystery. With Christmas lights glowing in the window and fresh flowers on the table it would appear they are in business, but for the last year or more, no one seems to know for sure and we have never been able to get an answer on the phone. We like mysteries, so if you EVER see it open or get a chance to eat there, please let us know!

BUBBA BURGERS   *Burgers*
Hanalei Center on Kuhio Hwy. (826-7839) HOURS: 10:30 am-6 pm daily. SAMPLING: Bubbas, double bubbas, hubba bubbas plus hot dogs, corn dogs, Budweiser beer chili, fish burgers and Italian sausage burgers ($1.50-5.75). Side

orders of Caesar salad, French fries, onion rings, frings (fries and onion rings) or chili fries ($1.50-3.50). COMMENTS: With a name like Bubba's, you were expecting maybe escargot? They're fun and funny and serve good, old-fashioned burgers to anyone named Bubba. (That means you!) They used to "cheat tourists and drunks", but had to "cease and desist" after receiving a letter from a San Francisco attorney. So now they also cheat attorneys! Both this and their Kapa'a location offer take-out and T-Shirts. If you purchase a hat or shirt and wear it when you order your burger, you'll get a free drink! The teriyaki burger was pitiful, in our opinion. Some really rave about Bubba's, but we think the drive back to Anahola is worth a bettah burger at Duane's.

CAFE HANALEI ★ *American with Thai*
Princeville Resort (826-2760) HOURS: Breakfast, Lunch, Dinner 6:30 am-9 pm; Breakfast Buffet to 10:30 am (9:30 Sundays), Sunday Brunch 10 am-2 pm. SAMPLING: Breakfast buffet offers crepes, pastries, fruits, omelettes, pancakes and breakfast meats ($19.50). Salads for lunch include soba noodle, cobb, chilled shrimp, and Caesar. Sample burgers, broiled chicken, roast beef, club, fresh fish and marinated tofu ($8.95-16.50). Dinner appetizers have a Thai accent starting with the chicken and beef satay with spicy peanut sauce ($10.95) or Thai spring rolls with Thai sweet chili sauce ($9.95) and the corn and clam chowder which has Thai curry and coconut milk ($5.50). Entrees feature Japanese specialties like tempura udon (hot), tenzaru udon (cold) and oyakodon (chicken and onion in broth) along with broiled fresh fish with caramelized onion, grilled rib steak with eggplant or stir fried tofu ($10.50-18.25). Desserts are more tropical with pineapple macadamia nut crunch, Kona espresso mousse and minted mango creme brulee. There's also tapioca with lemon curd and fresh berries as well as the resort's signature chocolate cheesecake ($5.25). Sunday Brunch again features a lot of Thai dishes along with salads, fresh seafood, chicken entrees, pastas, hot breakfast entrees, carved roast beef, an omelette bar, fruit crepe bar and waffle bar and plenty of desserts. It's offered with or without champagne ($29.95/33.50). COMMENTS: Nestled deep down below the opulent lobby at the foot of two elegant staircases, this restaurant has the perfect view of Hanalei Bay with the perfect full-length picture windows to gaze and glory in it unencumbered. The Seafood Buffet on Fridays 6-9 pm is a pricey $39.95, but well worth the splurge. An entire buffet of hot seafood dishes range from seafood lasagna to crab bisque, fish cakes to bouillabaisse or escargot in puff pastry. A least a dozen choices before moving to the cold seafood display filled with sashimi, huge prawns on ice, and seafood salad selections from tako poki to bay shrimp with cilantro and avocado. Save room for the barbecue, where a chef will cook your fresh fish to order. We had a selection of fresh ono or salmon or a skewer of scallops and prawns. Oh, did we mention dessert?

CHARO'S RESTAURANT & BAR *Mexican*
Kuhio Hwy. next to Hanalei Colony Resort in Haena (826-6422) HOURS: 11:30 am-9 pm daily. SAMPLING: Quesadilla platters, fajitas, nachos ($5-11.95). Shrimp specialties: cocktail, fajitas, enchiladas and fried in macadamia nuts ($8.95-20.95) and gringo items like burgers, chicken fingers, NY steak and fresh fish sandwich ($5-20). COMMENTS: Splendid location right on the beach, too bad the food doesn't live up to the view. Live entertainment nightly from 6:30 to 8:30 and Happy Hour from 3 to 5 featuring tropical flavored margaritas. Recently remodeled and has an open kitchen.

CHUCK'S STEAK HOUSE   *Steak and Seafood*

Princeville Shopping Center (826-6211) HOURS: Lunch 11:30 am -2 pm, Dinner 6-10 pm. SAMPLING: Lunch offers a good selection of burgers and salads plus several hot and cold sandwiches and sides. ($3.50-12.25). Dinner entrees include a salad bar with bread and rice. Fish, shrimp, crab, lobster plus prime rib, top sirloin, barbequed beef ribs and several steak and seafood combinations ($15.95-23.95, crab or lobster from $33.95-60). COMMENTS: It's called Chuck's Steak House and they have that and seafood, too. They also have a children's menu. Casual, rustic look with a lot of wood.

DUANE'S ONO BURGERS   ★   *Burgers*

On the highway in Anahola (822-8191) HOURS: Monday-Saturday 10 am-6 pm, from 11 am on Sunday. SAMPLING: The teriyaki burger is the biggest seller here, but there are lots to choose from: BBQ, blue cheese, avocado, mushroom and combos like "Duane's Special" (1,000 island, grilled onions, pickles, sprouts, cheddar & Swiss) or the "Local Girl" (teriyaki, Swiss cheese, pineapple). Burgers are priced from $3.90-6.20 and there are sandwiches, too. Fish, chicken, patty melt, tuna and grilled cheese ($2.75-6.75) and side orders of fries, onion rings or salad are $1.80-3.10. They have keiki burgers and sandwiches as well as some great shakes including marionberry - not the mayor of DC, but a yummy combination of boysenberry and blackberry ($2.95). COMMENTS: Burgers are piled high with lots of "stuff," like a Dagwood burger. Try the fries with the special seasoning they have on the counter - ono! The outdoor tables have a great mountain view! These burgers are worth the drive, from whatever side of the island you visit. The teriyaki isn't strong and salty, but...just right! You'll know you are in Anahola when you see the line outside the little red building! (By the way, don't go looking for Duane; the Cords and the Jacobsens own it now and you'll probably see one of them working behind the counter.)

HALE O'JAVA   *Sandwiches/Salads*

Princeville Center (826-7255) HOURS: 6:30 am-9 pm. SAMPLING: Sandwiches include an assortment of panini style selections on focaccia bread: mozzarella, tomatoes and fresh pesto; Black Forest ham, artichoke hearts, tomato, fontina cheese; Italian salami, roasted peppers, provolone cheese; bresaola meat, arugula, mild goat cheese. Also pizzas!. Deli selection include an array of colorful chilled salads (curry pea, wild rice & snow peas, artichoke & fennel) or hot soups (corn chowder, fresh tomato, potato & prosciutto). If you have room, top it off with a dessert (banana split cake, tiramisu, mud slide, tropical carrot cake). Breakfast options include pastries and muffins ($3.95-7.95). The usual hot coffee drinks as well as Italian coffee, icy fruit or coffee granitas, Italian sodas and fresh juices. COMMENTS: Opened in December, '94, they are currently offering live jazz every Wednesday from 5:30-8:30 pm. The espresso is served in huge Italian style cups and it is perfectly wonderful sitting in the courtyard with a steaming mug and one of their tasty sandwiches or salads. Salads are good and freshly made. Seating is limited. No table service, you order at the counter and serve yourself.

HANALEI DOLPHIN   ★   *Steak and Seafood*

Hanalei (826-6113) HOURS: 5:30-10 pm. SAMPLING: Appetizers include ceviche, seafood chowder, artichoke and stuffed mushrooms ($5-6); seafood entrees of fresh fish, calamari, scallops, shrimp and crab ($14-18). Chicken, steak and "surf and turf" combinations ($15-24) and light dinners offer a broccoli casserole, seafood chowder or salad and bread ($8-10). Homemade desserts change daily. COMMENTS: Almost all the entrees are under $20 and come with salad, fries or rice and bread. Menehune (kid size) portions available on several dishes. Pretty reliable food, but nothing exotic or Pacific Rim! They don't take reservations and unless you arrive early, you will probably have a wait. Put in your name and spend your time browsing through the adjoining gift and clothing stores. The food is hearty, some of the sauces are a bit on the heavy side, but the salads are a very pleasant surprise. Served family style in a bowl the mixed greens are accompanied by homemade garlic croutons and an assortment of dressings you can add yourself. They have a fish market, too, open from 11 am-6 pm.

HANALEI GOURMET ★ *Sandwiches/Salads*
5161 Kuhio Hwy. Old School Building at Hanalei Center (826-2524) HOURS: 8 am-10:30 pm. SAMPLING: Basic sandwiches like turkey, roast beef, corned beef, chicken salad and tuna with "the works" ($4.95-6.25). More gourmet varieties ($6.95-7.50) include Oregon bay shrimp (open-faced with melted jack cheese and remoulade sauce) and roasted eggplant sandwich with roasted bell peppers, provolone cheese and a sour cream-lime-cilantro sauce with sweet red onions. Salads include antipasto, chicken boat and ahi pasta with lemon, sweet relish, sweet red onions and sour cream - another tasty choice ($4.75-8.95). Pupus include boiled shrimp, cheese board, smoked salmon, Hawaiian seafood sampler and artichoke dip ($4.75-18.95) and breakfast offerings include muesli, fruit, bagels, eggs and a selection of gourmet pastries ($1.50-7.50). They also serve gourmet dinners from 5:30-9:30. Fish tacos, Mandarin scallop crepes and fettucini carbonara are a few of the possibilities. COMMENTS: The roasted eggplant sandwich was excellent, fresh, unusual and full of flavor. In fact, just about everything on the menu is good! The place is generally busy, from first thing in the morning with people at the bar by 9 am with others enjoying piping hot coffee and pastries at the lanai tables. Specials are written on the blackboard left over from when it was a schoolroom. Didn't try any of the bakery selections, but the lunch fare was very good and word is that the dinners are, too.

HANALEI WAKE UP CAFE ★ *Hawaiian/Mexican*
Aku Road, (826-5551) HOURS: Breakfast 5:30-11:30 am, to 1:30 pm on Sundays; Lunch 11:30 am-3 pm; Dinner 5:30-9 pm. SAMPLING: For breakfast, there's the Hanalei quesadilla, veggie tofu, custard French toast topped with pineapple, homemade granola or you can build your own omelette ($4.25-6.85). Later in the day there are grilled Hawaiian favorites like stir-fry, huli huli, mesquite smoked chicken and BBQ chicken or ahi with teri glaze ($7.95-11.45). Sandwiches include burgers, teri chicken, veggie burger and grilled ahi ($6.50-7.95) and dinners feature Mexican food like burritos, tostadas, quesadillas, Mexican pizza, tacos or enchilada plate with choice of chicken, vegetables, cheese or ahi ($6.50-8.95). Nachos, potato skins and taco are also available for $6.50-7. Macadamia or Kona coffee mud pie are available for dessert ($3). COMMENTS: Small coffee shop type restaurant, family-owned and operated by Brando, Kaula, Keoki and Lani. The motif here is "surf" from the photos and trophies to the video playing on the television. The custard French toast is to die for, and while it appears to be a small portion, it is plenty filling, really more custard than toast. The breakfast quesadillas are good-sized portions that should appease those hearty morning appetites. The Mexican meals are flavorful, not too heavily spiced, and

served in ample sized portions. The atmosphere is VERY casual, most folks look like they just walked in from the beach and left their surfboards on the front stoop.

KAUAI OHANA BAKERY ★ *Baked Goods/Breads*

Princeville Center (826-7711) HOURS: Monday-Friday 6 am-6 pm, Saturday 6 am-4 pm, Sunday 8 am-3 pm. SAMPLING: Focaccia bread pizza, "pizza" bialys, handmade bagels and brioche, taro rolls, banana macadamia nut bread (made with fruit juice), bread pudding, chocolate dipped strawberries and strawberry fleurons - like an open cream puff. Breads include sundried tomato & garlic or taro. COMMENTS: Free coffee with any danish or breakfast pastry and the offer is good all day. Owner Denis Johnston was the pastry chef at Hanalei Bay and the Westin Kauai. Don't be surprised if there is a line out the door!

KILAUEA BAKERY & PAU HANA PIZZA ★ *Bakery/Pizzeria*

Kong Lung Center on the road to the Lighthouse. (828-2020) HOURS: 6:30 am-9 pm, pizza from 11 am. Closed Sundays. SAMPLING: Pastries and breads baked daily. Try the island-style pastries (macadamia nut sticky bun, tropical fruit filled Danish) and unusual breads like limu sourdough with sea algae, sun-dried tomato and fresh basil, poi bread, feta cheese and sweet red bell pepper, Hawaiian sourdough (from a guava starter) and Na Pali brown bread made with fennel, caraway, orange rind and cocoa. Pizzas are just as innovative with a lot of unusual toppings and combinations: "Great Gonzo" (roasted eggplant, red onion, goat cheese and roasted garlic), "Classic Scampi" (tiger prawns, tomato, roasted garlic, capers, asiago and mozzarella cheeses) and "Billie Holiday" smoked ono, swiss chard, roasted onions, gorgonzola rosemary sauce and mozzarella cheese) priced $10.95/18.25/25.75. Regular pizzas are priced by size and toppings and run from $7.25 to $16.25 plus toppings. They also have an Abrezone, an open-faced vegetable calzone on a baguette, and have recently added a BBQ chicken - island style pizza. COMMENTS: Pizza crust is extra crispy and the staff, from manager Steve to pizzamaker Oli to hostess Lani are extra nice. Owners Tom and Katie Pickett started the bakery in their home, expanded, then added pizza. If you don't have a big appetite or a family, you can order pizza by the slice! They recently salvaged the old Tip Top Bakery and are baking their own goods and some old favorites (eclairs and the famous macadamia nut cookie) for Tip Top fans.

LA CASCATA *Italian*

Princeville Resort (826-2761) HOURS: 6-9:30 pm. SAMPLING: Antipasto beginnings include ahi or beef carpaccio, pan roasted potatoes and grilled mushrooms, salad of cannellini beans, avocado, radicchio with steamed shrimp and clams, or a combination antipasto plate ($5.50-13.95). Pastas and rice come in appetizer or entree sizes: spinach ravioli with fresh scallops in a shitake mushroom ragout; penne pasta with lobster and clams, or pancetta, or fresh mozzarella; linguini with chicken breast, sun-dried tomatoes and wild mushrooms, risotto with shrimp and asparagus or cannelloni with ricotta and macadamia nuts baked with light tomato veloute ($9.95-27.95). Baked salmon, grilled veal chop, roast lamb, grilled swordfish, broiled Hawaiian snapper, seared pepper ahi, beef tenderloin, and broiled Kona lobster are the entrees prepared with an Italian accent ($26.95-35.95). The desserts vary from warm sour cherry tart to lilikoi creme brulee to hazelnut/pistachio semi-freddo or tiramisu to chocolate cappucino crepe with cinnamon anglaise ($5.75). If you can't make up your mind, there is a sampler plate with flourless chocolate cake, mini fruit tart and nougat semi-freddo for $6.75. COMMENTS: Dinners begin with focaccia bread squares and olive oil or tomato & garlic tochu sauce to dip them in. A complete three course dinner is available with your choice of appetizer or soup or salad, main entree and dessert for $40.25 per person. They have an extensive selection of wines, by the glass and by the bottle. The food is very good, but you'll pay the price.

OLD HANALEI COFFEE COMPANY *Coffee/Pastries & Light Lunches*
5183 Kuhio Hwy. in the Hanalei Center (826-6717) HOURS: 7 am-5 pm Monday-Saturday, 8 am-4 pm Sundays. SAMPLING: In addition to flavored coffees, they offer espresso, lattes, cappucinos, frosted or hot mochas, teas and smoothies as well as "Sin-a-Buns," muffins, brownies, cookies and carrot cake baked fresh daily. Also Kaua'i waffles with butter & syrup, fruit or "The Works." Lunchier offerings include black bean veggie or black bean egg quesadilla, Kaua'i green salad, Italian panini sandwiches and homemade soups. Price range from $1.25 for coffee to $5.75 for the waffle with the works. COMMENTS: The menu offerings are very limited, but what they have is good. Casual and pleasant atmosphere especially if you like jazz and old records with your coffee or light meal. Owner Bill Farley has a serious collection that he plays throughout the day.

PIZZA HANALEI *Pizza*
Ching Young Village (826-9494) HOURS: 11 am-9 pm, By the slice for lunch only, to 4 pm. SAMPLING: Combinations or choose your toppings from pepperoni, homemade sausage, Canadian bacon, pineapple, bell pepper, tofu, onion, mushroom, jalapeno, fresh garlic, zucchini, pesto and more. Small, medium or large from $8.25-33.80. Also spinach lasagna, pizzarito (pizza ingredients rolled up in a pizza shell like a burrito), salad and garlic bread ($3.95-6.95). COMMENTS: Pizza Hanalei has been here for twelve years. Their pizzas are all hand made to order. Sauce is homemade as are the crusts: whole wheat with sesame seeds or white. Well, it sounds good doesn't it? It even looks good. However, we tried the pesto pizza and could have sworn there was fish on it. The sesame coated crust looked wonderful, but it was dry as a board. One bite was enough! Hop in the car and head back to Kilauea for pizza. Others report they have enjoyed the pizza here.

PRINCEVILLE RESTAURANT & BAR ★ *American/Tropical*
Just before Princeville at the Princeville Golf Course. (826-5055) HOURS: Breakfast 8-11 am, Lunch 11:30 am-3 pm. SAMPLING: Breakfast sandwich, loco moco, Belgian waffle, or a banana ball which is three pancakes and an egg with choice of bacon or sausage ($5.25-6). For lunch they have a burger, fresh catch or vegetarian sandwich, local style plate (sukiyaki for example), fried saimin and variety of Chef's Specials ($7-9.50). The Oriental chicken salad is one of those specials, but it is so popular (rightly so) that they promise to put it on the permanent menu. The salad was fresh and crisp, so big it covered the entire plate and the wasabi sesame dressing was fantastic! Other specials might include a teriyaki chicken sandwich or ahi seared salad. All the portions are really big. COMMENTS: This is the restaurant formerly known as Prince . . . they've changed the name to avoid any confusion, but it remains confusing in other areas, like in how to describe it. Is it an elegant snack bar? A luxurious coffeeshop? Or an economical country club? The floors are marble, but the plates are paper, so what's the story? It's mainly that they cater to golfers who just want a quick bite

before golf and hotel employees who don't have a lot of time either. Since they don't have a lot of visitors who seek it out, they cut down on the cost of operations (such as the use of real plates). So, don't worry about the image, just seek and find good food in the marble and glass ambience of a beautiful building that looks like a mini version of the Princeville Resort. You'll find it downstairs in a cool atrium with palm trees and ceiling fans, garden furniture in pink and green and a gorgeous view of the golf course. An even better value with the use of a half price coupon from the Entertainment book.

TAHITI NUI *American/Hawaiian*
Kuhio Hwy., Hanalei (826-6277) HOURS: Breakfast 7-11:30 am, Lunch 11:30 am-2 pm, Dinner 5-10 pm. Luau Wednesday and Friday at 6:30 pm (separate entrance and admission). SAMPLING: Breakfast egg dishes including "Huevos Nui" with beans, eggs and cheese on a flour tortilla ($5.95), loco moco, a local favorite of hamburger, gravy, egg and rice ($5.95) and Haena omelette with Portuguese sausage and kim chee ($6.95). Plate lunches of hamburger, chicken or fried rice ($5.95-6.25), sandwiches, burgers and salads ($5.95-8.95) and home-made ice cream pie for dessert ($3.25). Dinners start with pupus like Tahitian poisson cru, sashimi, shrimp cocktail or whole artichoke ($3.95-7.95). Calamari provencale is a signature dish ($16.95) and they also have scampi, curry, chicken teriyaki, fresh fish, NY steak and prime rib ($13.95-18.95). Entrees are served with a salad, vegetable and rice or potatoes. There's also a children's menu. COMMENTS: There's an old-fashioned (50's style) Polynesian Bar; decor is South Seas with bamboo walls and ceiling fans. The lanai out front facing the highway is a great place to people watch - it seems to be a national pastime with North shore locals! The food is good, but equally good and slightly cheaper breakfasts next door at the Hanalei Wake Up Cafe. Tahiti Nui also offers a twice weekly luau. See section on Luaus at the end of this restaurant chapter.

TOSCA ★ *Italian*
The Hanalei Center, Kuhio Hwy. (826-1222) HOURS: Lunch Tuesday thru Friday 11:30-2 pm., Dinner 5:30-10 pm, pizza available until 11 pm. No longer serving Sunday Brunch. SAMPLING: Gourmet pizzas are cooked in a wood-burning oven using kiawe, guava and ironwood ($7.50-9.25). Wood roasted chicken with gorgonzola cheese, basil pesto and bell peppers was light, but tasty - each bite had a different combination of flavors. Appetizers were creative like the taro onion torta made from Kaua'i taro and Maui onion ($7) and the crostini verdura: olive pesto and fresh vegetables on toast ($4). Pastas like seafood farfalle (shrimp and scallops in a light anchovy and roasted garlic sauce with crispy calamari) come in appetizer and main course portions: $7.50/9.25-11.50/18.50. Main courses are served with vegetables and bread-in-a-bag (Really! The French bread is served in a paper sack!) and offer unique preparations of lamb, veal, striploin, and fresh fish for $17.70-$22.50. Desserts are Kona coffee cheesecake or marble cake layered with mousse and they recently added an espresso machine. COMMENTS: The wood tables and stucco walls give the indoor restaurant an Italian bistro feel or you can eat in the courtyard nestled in a "sunken" wood patio. The atmosphere, like the food, is familiar and comfortable, but just unusual enough to make it interesting. Chef Guy Higa came from the Coco Palms via Inn on the Cliffs and has put his particular expertise in Italian cuisine and seafood to its best use. Tosca opened in February, 1995 which is how long owner Claudi Swenson has had a winner.

TROPICAL TACO ★ *Mexican*

What's green and has no address? The Tropical Taco van! This is like the truck and the stop in one. They're parked in front of Hanalei Dolphin every day but Monday, open from 11 am to 3 pm. Owner Roger Kennedy has been serving Mexican food from his van since 1978. SAMPLING: Everything made fresh daily: Tacos, burritos, fat jack burritos, piece of fresh fish from $1 per piece. If you are thirsty, it is lemonade or nothing. Cash only!

VILLAGE SNACK SHOP & BAKERY, DELI & COFFEE SHOP

Ching Lung Village, Hanalei (826-6841) HOURS: Breakfast 6 -11 am, Lunch 11 am-6 pm. SAMPLING: Eggs, pancakes, rice, spam. Side orders from $1, full breakfast $2.75-3.50. Plate meals $5.95. Sandwiches $4, burgers, hot dogs, chicken sandwich ($2.95-5.95). Beach lunch to go includes sandwich, soda, fruit or salad ($5.95). The bakery serves haupia cake, Boston cream pie, cobblers and breads.

WINDS OF BEAMREACH *American*

Located at Pali Ke Kua, Princeville (826-6143) HOURS: 5:30-9:30 pm. SAMPLING: Appetizers include teriyaki meat sticks, mussels marinara, fresh steamed clams ($5.95-8.95). Entrees are served with soup or salad & roasted potato or rice: medallions of pork tenderloin with peppercorn sauce, chicken Florentine or teriyaki, shrimp scampi, NY steak, filet mignon, stir-fry vegetables ($14.95-22.95). Dessert offers Tahitian lime pie, cheesecake, guava chiffon pie and hula pie ($3.75-4.50). COMMENTS: Fresh fish steamed Hawaiian style with fresh ginger, garlic & green onion is a specialty. The teriyaki steak is also popular. Owner Diane Anakalea makes all the desserts, salad dressings and a lot of the soups. Her husband tends bar and their three children serve as wait and bus help. A real family establishment! No ocean view here, but they do overlook the pool so at least there's water and there is a nice view of the mountains. Our ultimate test of a meal is the fish and the coffee. Both were average. The fish was fresh, but the seasoning was flat. The poi rolls were yummy and the salad was a pleasant mix of leaf lettuce with homemade dressings. The Tahitian lime pie was a disappointment, resembling lime sherbet with walnuts on it.

J·BAYOT

ZELO'S CAFE ★   *Asian/Italian*

Princeville Center (826-9700) HOURS: 7:30 am-9:30 pm, Breakfast to 11 am, Dinners from 5 pm. SAMPLING: Omelettes, Hawaiian-style French toast, pancakes, veggie fritatta, biscuits & gravy, granola ($3.95-7.25). Pupus include fried mozzarella or stuffed baked potato. They feature an interesting variety of fries! Enjoy them cajun and loaded with cheese, bacon and ranch dressing or waffle style ($1.95-5.95). Caesar, Mediterranean, Cajun chicken and Chinese chicken ($3.95-10.95) are some of the salad varieties. Burgers can be enjoyed with cheddar, Cajun cheese, sour cream mushroom, blue cheese, teriyaki, plus chicken, turkey and ahi choices ($5.75-7.95). The sandwiches are served on freshly baked bread and include club, ham and cheese, marinated artichoke & pesto cream cheese ($4.75-7.45). Specials encompass soft shell fish taco, jumbo raviolis, spinach lasagna and chicken ratatouille ($8.95-13.95). Dinner offerings feature several preparations of ahi, seafood ratatouille, chicken or shrimp pesto tortellini, chicken parmesan or eggplant lasagna ($13.95-17.95). Beer and wine are available as are specialty coffees. COMMENTS: The menu is diverse. Just how do you classify a restaurant that serves Cajun burgers, veggie frittatas and Chinese chicken salad? The homemade soups are good and the salads tasty. The sandwiches are thick and hearty. The kids will enjoy the fruit smoothies and the grownups can cool their whistle on a chocolate espresso shake. They've been here for a few years so they certainly must be doing something right! The white wood and casual "porch" location out back makes for a pleasant atmosphere.

LUAUS

KAUA'I COCONUT BEACH RESORT LUAU   ★

(808) 822-3455 extension 651. Received the "Kahili" Award from the Hawaii Visitors Bureau for it's "Keep it Hawaii" program. This luau features only the dances, legends and lore of Kaua'i. It also provides the visitor with the opportunity to witness "kahiko" hula, one of the most ancient forms of this cultural dance. The dancers are beautifully dressed and make some very speedy costume changes. They put the pig in the imu at 10:30 in the morning, so if it works out with your schedule, stop by the Luau Halau Pavilion and see how it is done. The luau begins at 6:30 pm with the blowing of the conch horns and a shell lei greeting. Seating is family style, however, a little too crowded to make it comfortable to get in and out of your seat. Haupia and fresh pineapple are on the table when you arrive. The buffet is a pleasant mix with fried rice, mahi, kalua pork, lomi lomi salmon, baked taro, teriyaki beef and tropical chicken combined with assorted salads. The kalua pork was wonderful and the teriyaki beef was surprisingly moist and flavorful. The chicken was in a sweet and sour sauce that seemed just too sweet. Dessert options were coconut cake or a pasty flavorless rice pudding. Arrive early and wait in line for the better seats. They do have smoking and non-smoking sections. Family night each Saturday evening, one child accompanied by an adult paying full price attends free. For additional children, cost is regular child rate. The cost is $45.00 for adults, children 6 to 17 are $27.24, and children under 6 are free. This luau is held on Tues., Thurs., Sat. and Sun.; on Saturdays one child is free with each adult. Advance reservations are needed. (808) 822-3455.

SMITH'S TROPICAL PARADISE
174 Wailua Rd., Kapaʻa, HI 96742 (808) 822-4654
Smith's provides a luau with dances and songs from the South Pacific. Featured are Tahiti, China, Japan, the Philippines, New Zealand and Samoa, in addition to Hawaii. The luau grounds are located on their 30 acre botanical and cultural garden. The luau is held Monday, Wednesday and Friday and the cost is $43.75 per adult (age 14 and up), youth ages 7-13 years runs $26, children 4-6 years runs $17. The luau is held in their gardens under a covered area. The luau begins at 6 pm, but the gates open an hour early for touring of the grounds. They have an open bar which opens at 6:10 and closes at 7:30, serving beer, wine, and mai tai. The buffet serves beef, chicken, pork, fish, salads and dessert. Reservations are required.

TAHITI NUI
(808) 826-6277
This North Shore luau is currently held only once a week on Wednesday at 6:30 pm. Held in the back room of the Tahiti Nui restaurant, long room with long tables and a stage at the end. Tahitian and Hawaiian buffet. The food is authentic - no glitz or glamour. It's a family-style luau and there are always lots of kids. Food is served in Tupperware-like dishes; it's as if you went to someone's home for a luau dinner and the guests took turns getting up to perform. This is a small luau room (as luaus go), and, again, it is indoors. The advantage is that from most any table you have a good view of the stage and the tables are not so packed together that it is difficult to get in and out of your seat. (Important when you want to hit that buffet line!) A more intimate and local luau with a friendly atmosphere. They cook the pig in an imu out in back, not a very attractive pit, but then it is authentic imu cooking. The menu is an all-you-can-eat buffet that includes one alcoholic drink. Buffet items include kalua pig, baked fish, Hawaiian chicken, sweet potatoes, poi, lomi salmon, green salad, potato salad, fresh fruits, garlic bread, haupia, Tahitian rice pudding, pineapple upside down cake, chocolate cake, fruit punch and coffee. Admission is $38 adults with children half price for the dinner and show. Show only is $15.

NIGHTLIFE

Gilligan's at the Outrigger offers perhaps the island's most diverse evening entertainment. It varies each night and includes stand-up comedy nights and Wednesday movie night. The free Wednesday movie features a film that was at least partially filmed in Hawaii. (245-1955)

Hap's Hideaway on Rice St. in Lihu'e is a sports bar.

Happy Talk Lounge in the Hanalei Bay Resort.

Kuhio's Night Club at the Hyatt (742-1234). This elegant nightclub has dancing with a cover charge. Dress code includes shorts and shoes.

The Princeville Resort Library Lounge has evening entertainment.

Rob's Good Time Grill in Lihu'e offers karaoke.

Stevenson's Library at Hyatt is a quiet retreat with a large aquarium, chess tables, and bookcases filled with volumes.

Zelo's at Princeville sometimes has jazz entertainment in the evenings.

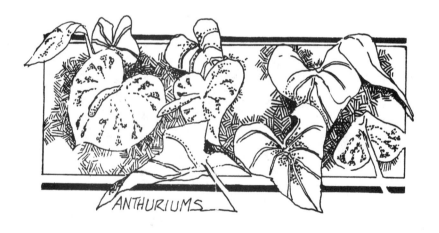

ANTHURIUMS

BEACHES

INTRODUCTION

Kaua'i, being the oldest of the major Hawaiian islands has beaches that have been worn with time. Because of this, you will not find exotic dark sand beaches, but rather those of golden sand that has been gently polished over millions of years. Another interesting fact is that Kaua'i has more miles of sand beaches than any other of the major Hawaiian islands. If you are the active beach-goer, who likes to snorkel or swim, or the type that prefers to find a quiet shady beachfront spot, Kaua'i offers a diverse selection.

We have not given a full description of every beach on the island but focused on those that were either the most beautiful or offered the best activities. Wherever possible, we have used the true Hawaiian names for the beaches, while including the local names as an aside. For more information on Kaua'i's beaches, the ultimate book is *Beaches of Kaua'i and Ni'ihau* by John R.K. Clark, published by University of Hawai'i Press. This reference will provide you with everything you want to know and perhaps a little bit more!

To the best of our calculations, there are 43 white sand beaches. Most are accessible by foot; three are accessible by water only and six are by water or by trail. Fifteen of the beaches have public facilities. Kaua'i has more linear miles of sandy shore line than any of the other islands, approximately 113 miles.

Following is a two page map of Kaua'i which depicts the location of the most popular beaches around the island. For further directions, refer to the enlarged area maps located in the Where to Stay - What to See section of this guide.

As with all of the Hawaiian islands, the beaches of Kaua'i are publicly owned and most have right-of-way access; however, the access is sometimes tricky to find and parking may be a problem! Parking areas are provided at most developed beaches, but they are often small. Some have lifeguards on duty.

In any parking lot, but even to a greater degree in the undeveloped areas where you will have to wedge your vehicle along the roadside, it is vital that you leave nothing of importance in your car as the occurrence of theft, especially at some of the more remote locations, is high.

At the larger, developed beaches, a variety of facilities are provided. Many have convenient rinse-off showers, drinking water, restrooms and picnic areas. A few have children's play or swim areas. The beaches near the major resorts often have rental equipment available for snorkeling, sailing, and boogie boarding, and some even rent underwater cameras. These beaches are generally clean and well maintained.

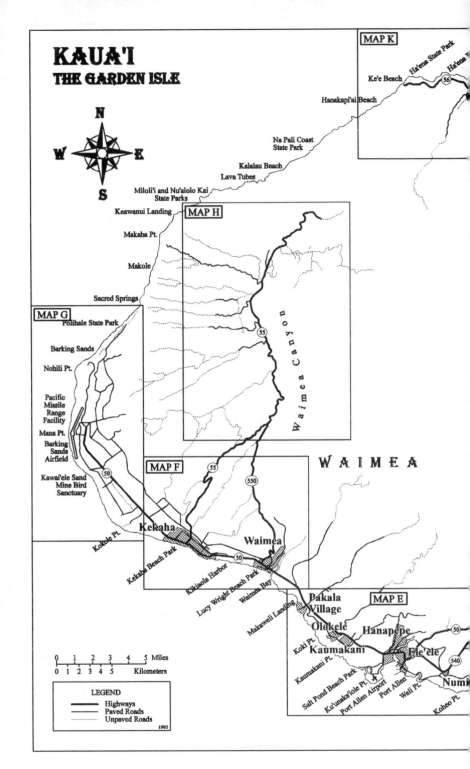

KAUA'I
THE GARDEN ISLE

MAP K

Ha'ena State Park
Ha'ena

Ke'e Beach

56

Hanakapi'ai Beach

N
W E
S

Na Pali Coast
State Park

Kalalau Beach

Lava Tubes

Miloli'i and Nu'alolo Kai
State Parks

Keawanui Landing

MAP H

Makaha Pt.

Makole

Waimea Canyon

Sacred Springs

MAP G

Polihale State Park

55

Barking Sands

Nohili Pt.

Pacific
Missile
Range
Facility

Mana Pt.

Barking
Sands
Airfield

WAIMEA

Kawai'ele Sand
Mine Bird
Sanctuary

MAP F

55

550

50

Kekaha

Waimea

Kokole Pt.

Kekaha Beach Park

Kiķiaola Harbor

50

Lucy Wright Beach Park

Waimea Bay

Makaweli Landing

Pakala
Village

MAP E

Olokele

Hanapepe

Koki Pt.

Kaumakani

Ele'ele

50

540

Numi

Kaumakani Pt.

Salt Pond Beach Park

Ku'maka'iole Pt.

Port Allen Airport

Port Allen

Weli Pt.

Koheo Pt.

| 0 | 1 | 2 | 3 | 4 | 5 | Miles |
| 0 | 1 | 2 | 3 | 4 | 5 | Kilometers |

LEGEND
—— Highways
—— Paved Roads
.... Unpaved Roads

1995

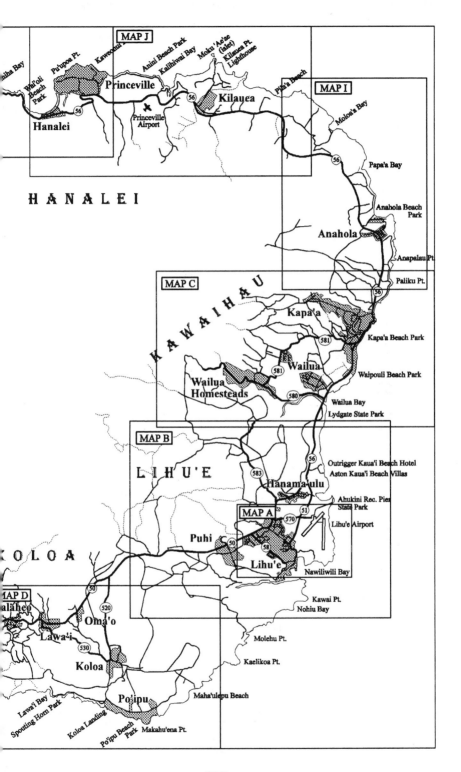

MAP J

Waioli Bay
Wai'oli Beach Park
Pu'upoa Pt.
Kaweonui Pt.
Anini Beach Park
Kalihiwai Bay
Moku 'Ae'ae (islet)
Kilauea Pt.
Lighthouse
Pila'a Beach

Princeville
Hanalei
Princeville Airport

Kilauea

56

MAP I

HANALEI

Moloa'a Bay

56

Papa'a Bay

Anahola Beach Park

Anahola

Anapalau Pt.

Paliku Pt.

MAP C

56

K A W A I H A U

Kapa'a

581

Kapa'a Beach Park

Wailua

581

Waipouli Beach Park

Wailua Homesteads

580

Wailua Bay
Lydgate State Park

MAP B

L I H U ' E

56

Outrigger Kaua'i Beach Hotel
Aston Kaua'i Beach Villas

583

Hanama'ulu

Ahukini Rec. Pier
State Park

MAP A

570

51

Lihu'e Airport

Puhi

50

Lihu'e

58

Nawiliwili Bay

K O L O A

Kawai Pt.
Nohiu Bay

MAP D

50

520

Oma'o

'alaheo

Molehu Pt.

Lawa'i

530

Kaelikoa Pt.

Koloa

Lawa'i Bay
Spouting Horn Park

Po'ipu

Maha'ulepu Beach

Koloa Landing
Po'ipu Beach Park
Makahu'ena Pt.

227

Kaua'i's most gentle beaches in the winter are found on the Southern coastline. While the Princeville/Hanalei region receives the brunt of most of the tropical weather, storms can affect the condition of the beaches all around the island. Seasonally, there is also a great change in the island's beaches. While any beach you visit may be calm and idyllic in the summer, there may be high and treacherous surf during the winter months. Unlike Maui, whose southern and western beaches form part of a protected area sheltered by the islands of Kahoolawe and Lana'i, Kaua'i has beaches which are more exposed.

The North shore of Kaua'i has higher surf during the months of October through May. On the East coast, high surf from the east and north is also more frequent during the same months. The south shore also receives high surf from the west and east and heavier rain during the winter months of October through May, and high surf from the south can occur April through September. High surf from the north and west will affect the west shore beaches during October through May and the summer southern swell will affect the west side during April through September. Even on a very calm day, there can be an unexpected wave surge. Many of the beaches have changed dramatically as a result of Hurricane Iniki. Some will never be the same again. Lydgate and Salt Pond Beaches have two sea pools which are protected from the surf and ideal for young children. You'll find lifeguards on duty at Lydgate Park, Po'ipu Beach, Salt Pond, Ke'e and Hanalei Pavilion. Other beaches may be manned with life guards during the busier summer months or on busy weekends.

Seasonal conditions can also affect the beach itself. Sand is eroded away from some beaches during winter to be re-deposited during the spring and summer.

Here are some basic water safety tips and terms. Most of the north and west shore beaches of Kaua'i do not have the coral reefs or other barriers which are found on the south and eastern shores. These wide expansive beaches pose greater risks for swimmers with strong currents and dangerous shorebreaks. You may see swimmers or surfers at some of the beaches where we recommend that you enjoy the view and stay out of the water. Keep in mind that just because there is someone else in the water, it doesn't mean it is safe. Some of these surfers are experts in Hawaiian surf, and we advise that you do not take undue risks. Others might be visitors just like you, but not as well informed!

A *shorebreak* is the place where the waves break directly on the shore, or very near to it. Smaller shorebreaks may not be a problem, but waves that are more than a foot or two high may create hazardous conditions. Most drownings on Kaua'i happen at the shorebreak. Conditions are generally worse in the winter months. Even venturing too close to a shorebreak could be hazardous, as standing on the beachfront you may encounter a stronger, higher wave that could catch you off guard and sweep you into the water.

A *rip current* can often be seen from the shore. They are fast moving river-like currents that sometimes can be seen carrying sand or sediment. A rip current can pull an unsuspecting swimmer quickly out to sea and swimming against a strong rip current may be impossible. Unfortunately, these currents are another leading cause of drownings in Kaua'i.

Undertows happen when a rip current runs into incoming surf. This accounts for the feeling that you are being pulled. They are more common on beaches which have steep slopes.

We don't want to be alarmists, but we'd prefer to report the beaches conservatively. Always, always use good judgement.

Kona winds generated by southern hemisphere storms cause southerly swells that affect Po'ipu and the southern coastline. This usually happens in the summer and will last for several days. This condition can cause unusually high summer surf.

Northerly swells caused by winter storms northeast of the island are not common, but can cause large surf, particularly on the northern beaches at 'Anini Beach Park, Kauapea Beach, Kaka'anui Beach and the beaches at Princeville and Hanalei.

Based on drowning records from 1970 through 1988, according to The Kaua'i Guide to Beaches by Pat Durkin, the five most dangerous beaches, listed in order of drownings are Hanakapi'ai, Lumaha'i, Wailua, Hanalei and Waipouli. Other beaches with high incidents of drownings are Polihale, 'Anini, Kalalau and Kealia. Pat Durkin notes that "drowning statistics are also a reflection of a beach's popularity. For instance, if Wainiha and First Ditch [Kekaha] were as popular as Lumaha'i or Polihale, they would probably have higher drowning rates, as conditions are similar." (Kauai Guide to Beaches is published by Magic Fishes Press, PO Box 3243, Lihu'e, HI 96766.)

Kaua'i's ocean playgrounds are among the most benign in the world. There are only a few ocean creatures that you should be aware of. *We will attempt to include some basic first aid tips should you encounter one of these. Since some people might have a resulting allergic reaction, we suggest you contact a local physician or medical center should you have an unplanned encounter with one of them.*

Only once, and that was on Maui, have we seen Portuguese Man-of-War. These very small creatures are related to the jellyfish and are propelled by the wind. The one time we encountered these beautiful sea creatures, they had been blown in by an unusual wind and covered the beach with glistening crystal orbs filled with deep blue filament. If they are on the beach, assume they are in the water, so stay out. On rare occasions they will be seen drifting in the ocean during a sea excursion and the staff will change snorkeling destinations if this is the case. The sting is unpleasant, so don't touch! If you are stung you can use vinegar to help neutralize the venom. Diluted ammonia or baking soda is said to provide a similar effect, or try out the local remedy which is urine.

In the water avoid touching sea urchins, the pricking of one of the spines can be painful. You will need to check carefully to be sure all of the spine has been removed.

Coral is made up of many tiny living organisms. Coral cuts require thorough disinfecting and can take a long time to heal.
Cone shells look harmless enough, they are conical and in colors of brown or black. The snail which inhabit the shells have a defense which they use to protect themselves and also to kill their prey. Their stinger does have venom and it is suggested that you just enjoy looking at them. Cleaning the wound and soaking it in hot water for 30-90 minutes will provide relief.

Eels live among the coral and are generally not aggressive. You may have heard of divers who have "trained" an eel to come out, greet them and then take some food from their hands. We don't recommend you make an eel for a pal. While usually non aggressive, their jaws are extremely powerful and their teeth are sharp. And as divers know, sea animals could mistake any approach or movement as an aggressive or provoking act. Just keep a comfortable distance, for you and the eel. Also, should you poke around with your hands in the coral, they might inadvertently think your finger is some food. This is one of the many reasons you should not handle the coral. Eels are generally not out of their home during the day, but a close examination of the coral might reveal a head of one of these fellows sticking out and watching you! At night, during low tide, at beaches with a protective reef, you might try taking a flashlight and scanning the water. A chance look at one of these enormous creatures out searching for its dinner is most impressive.

Sharks? Yes, there are many varied types of sharks. However, there are more shark attacks off the Oregon coastline than in Hawai'i. In the many years of snorkeling and diving, we have only seen one small reef shark, and it was happy to get out of our way. If you should see one, don't move quickly, but rather swim slowly away while you keep an eye on it! If there is any area of murky water, such as the Waimea River, you might want to avoid swimming in that area.

Always exercise good judgement and reasonable caution when at the beach. Unfortunately, it is a too common occurrence when a person stretches their limits, or forgets their common sense and the Kaua'i papers must report yet another drowning victim. Even a calm sea might have strong currents.

Here are some additional *beach safety tips*:

1. "Never turn your back to the sea" is an old Hawaiian saying. Don't be caught off guard, waves come in sets with spells of calm in between.

2. Use the buddy system, never swim or snorkel alone.

3. If you are unsure of your abilities, use floatation devices attached to your body, such as a life vest or inflatable vest. Never rely on an air mattress or similar device from which you may become separated.

4. Study the ocean before you enter; look for rocks, shorebreak and rip current.

5. Duck or dive beneath breaking waves before they reach you.

6. Never swim against a strong current, swim across it.

7. Know your limits.

8. Small children should be allowed to play near or in the surf ONLY with close supervision and should wear flotation devices. And even then, only under extremely calm conditions. The protected pools at Lydgate and Salt Pond are safer alternatives.

9. When exploring tidal pools or reefs, always wear protective footwear and keep an eye on the ocean. Also, protect your hands.

10. When swimming around coral, be careful where you put your hands and feet. Urchin stings can be painful and coral cuts can be dangerous and you can also damage or injure the coral

11. Respect the yellow and red flag warnings when placed on the developed beaches. They are there to advise you of unsafe conditions.

12. Avoid swimming in the mouth of rivers or streams or in other areas of murky water.

Paradise Publications and the authors of this guide have endeavored to provide current and accurate information on Kauaʻi's beautiful beaches. However, remember that nature is unpredictable and weather, beach and current conditions can change. Enjoy your day at the beach, but utilize good judgment. Paradise Publications and the authors cannot be held responsible for accidents or injuries incurred.

Surface water temperature varies little with a mean temperature of 73.0 degrees fahrenheit in January and 80.2 degrees in August. Minimum and maximum range from 68 to 84 degrees. This is an almost ideal temperature (refreshing, but not cold) for swimming and you will find most resort pools cooler than the ocean.

BEST BETS:

We would really like to be able to give you the definitive list of the best beaches on Kaua'i. Unfortunately, that is not possible. It will depend on seasons and ocean conditions. Remembering that the south shore has better beach conditions, generally, in the summer and the north shore has better conditions, generally, in the winter, here is a list of our recommended best bets:

BEST SNORKELING:
Beginners - Po'ipu Beach
Intermediate - Tunnels

BEST WINDSURFING:
Beginners - 'Anini
Intermediate - Tunnels or Maha'ulepu

BEST FOR CHILDREN:
Lydgate Beach Park and Salt Ponds

BEST FOR SWIMMING:
Po'ipu, Hanalei Bay and Salt Ponds

BEST FOR SUNSETS:
Ke'e Beach, Pakala Beach

BEST FOR SUNRISES:
Lydgate or Maha'ulepu

BEST FOR TIDEPOOLS:
Kealia Beach

BEST FOR BEACHCOMBING:
Wainiha, Nukole, Ka'aka'aniu, Waialkalua Iki, Kauapea, 'Anini, Kealia.

The following beach index refers to a variety of beaches and beach parks. Some of them are not true beaches. For example, Spouting Horn is a beautiful beach location, but only for viewing and not for any aquatic activities. Be sure to read all the descriptions of the beaches, even those with which have no recreational activities, yet are accessible and beautiful Kaua'i destinations.

The stars ★ indicate beaches which are recommended for family activities. They are more protected and have lifeguards on duty.

BEACH INDEX

WESTERN SHORE

Waimea, Kekaha, and Polihale

POLIHALE BEACH / BARKING SANDS BEACH

The Polihale State Park extends for five miles along the eastern shore and encompasses 140 acres. Large dunes are formed along the back of the beach that can reach up to 100 feet high. You'll know you have arrived at Barking Sands when you see the military installation. The Pacific Missile Range is operated by the Navy, but there are no state signs posted.

The Polihale State Park marks the southern end of the Na Pali. Dangerous surf conditions preclude swimming, etc.

More than 100 years ago, the sand from this area was studied at the California Academy of Sciences and it was discovered that it had small holes or "blind cavities." The resulting vibration of these unusual sand grains causes a sound that is said to be that of barking or singing when rubbed between the hands. Hence the name for this beach area.

We couldn't make it bark! What do you think? A similar anomaly occurs on one beach on O'ahu and another on Ni'ihau. A few other places in the world have sand with this remarkable skill. After you've tried making the sand bark, you might try searching the shoreline for the extremely small shells used in making the necklaces of Ni'ihau. The same currents that bring them ashore on Ni'ihau, also bring some to this stretch of coastline.

In the middle of the beach park, about 3 1/2 miles along the cane road, is an area cleared of coral. Named the Queens Pond or the Queens Bath it is reportedly named for Leilani, the Queen of Kaua'i who bathed here. The legend has it that when a chief from O'ahu asked for her hand, a battle ensued between the O'ahu chief and the chief of Kaua'i. After the battle, Leilani was so distraught that she poisoned herself and turned into a seabird. They say you can still here the groans of pain from this battle in the sand.

While you may see locals driving along the beach, this is not advisable. Not only will the rental car companies not be pleased should you become stuck, but there is also a plant unique to this area that is threatened by beach driving. The Ohai is an endangered beach plant found only in Hawai'i. On Kaua'i, the only place these 30 foot shrubs grow is at Polihale and officials fear that the damage caused by beach traffic is further endangering the survival of this species.

The Poli-hale heiau is a four terraced temple found on the slopes above the beach, almost indistinguishable after the centuries of erosion. This heiau was sacred to Miru, the God of Po. It was said that the oceans below Polihale was the land of the dead. You can see the sculptured cliffs at the end of the beach.

234

In the early days the grass houses on this side of the island were all small and made of grass. There was one large living room and two doors on opposite sides. Eric Knudsen, an early pioneer on Kaua'i, recalled that his father was curious as to why all the houses were built with their gable-ends east and west and doors facing toward the mountains and towards the sea. The obvious reason might be for tradewinds to create cool breezes through the home, or perhaps for those wonderful ocean and mountain visits. However, when he questioned a fellow he was told, "Why, you know that Po, the abode of the dead, lies under the ocean just outside Polihale, where the cliffs and the ocean meet and the spirits of the dead must go there. As the spirits wander along on their way to Po, they will go around the gable-end of a house but if the house stood facing the other way, the spirits would walk straight through and it would be very disagreeable to have a spirit walk past you as you were eating your meal. In fact we can always tell when a battle has been fought by the number of spirits passing at the same time." And be sure to bring some shade with you, because you won't find much here!

Recommended for: An opportunity to experience the vast barking sands, picnics, a glimpse at the south end of the Na Pali and a nice long drive!
Facilities: Picnic pavilions, showers, restrooms
Access: Follow the Kaumuali'i Highway at Mana to the end and then follow signs along the cane roads approximately five miles. There are no state signs posted, but some smaller, difficult to read signs might be noted along the way.
Camping: Camping is allowed, but permits from the state are required.

KEKAHA BEACH
This is a 15 mile stretch of coastline reaching from Kekaha to Polihale located on the western end of the town of Kekaha and along the Kaumuali'i Highway. Along the roadside the beachpark is attractive and includes facilities nearby. Several decades ago, this shoreline had severe erosion problems. In 1980 a seawall was constructed along the roadway. Strong rip currents are generated here during high surf that is particularly dangerous during winter and spring months. Surfers occasionally enjoy the surf at a couple of locations along this beachfront. If the wind is blowing up at Polihale, chances are you might find enjoy your picnic lunch with less sand in your sandwich here at Kekaha. Shorebreak and rip currents all year make this a dangerous beach for water activities. However, an excellent beach for sunsets or a picnic lunch.

Recommended for: Picnics, beach play and sunsets
Facilities: Picnic pavilions, showers, restrooms
Access: Follow the Kaumuali'i Highway past Kekaha
Camping: No camping

LUCY WRIGHT BEACH PARK
Lucy Kapahu Aukai Wright was born August 20, 1873 in Anahola. She was a well-loved school teacher in Waimea for thirty five years until her death in 1931. This beach is dedicated to her memory. An earlier very notable visitor arrived at this beach site. Captain James Cook landed here on his arrival to the Sandwich Islands in January 1778. Because of the location of this beach on the west side near the mouth of the Waimea River, the beach collects assorted debris and the water is murky. It is not popular for sunbathers or swimmers, but you might see surfers offshore.

Facilities: Restrooms, showers, parking area, picnic tables at Waimea Pier
Access: On the Waimea side of the bridge over Waimea River, turn mauka on Lawai Rd. off Kaumuali'i Hwy. and follow to the park
Camping: By county permit on grassy area

RUSSIAN FORT ELIZABETH HISTORICAL PARK
On the east bank of the Waimea River is another of the Russian Forts built by Georg Anton Scheffer during the years of Russian trading on Kaua'i. However, Georg had his sights set on conquering the islands of Hawai'i in the name of Russia, but when the Kamehameha learned of this he was quickly expelled in 1817. This 17 acre site is now the Russian Fort Elizabeth State Historical Park.

Facilities: Restrooms and a pavilion with historical information

PAKALA BEACH
Great offshore waves make this a popular summer surfing spot. You might enjoy watching the surfers demonstrate their skills. A wonderful location to enjoy a Hawaiian sunset.

SALT POND BEACH PARK
The natural flats along this beach have been used by Hawaiians for generations. Today, this site continues to be used for traditional salt making. In late spring the wells or puna are cleaned and the salt making process runs through the summer months. Mother nature has been kind enough to create a ridge of rock between the two rocky points at Salt Pond Beach, resulting in a large lagoon area that is fairly well protected, except during times of high surf. Popular for surfing and wind-surfing as well. This park is popular, because of its protected swimming area, for families and children. A lifeguard is generally on duty.

Recommendedfor: Swimming and snorkeling most of the year, except during high surf. Popular for surfing and windsurfing as well
Access: From the Hwy. turn onto Lele Road, past the cemetery, turn right onto Lokokai St. From the Hwy. Lele Rd is marked Hwy. 543. You can also follow the signs to the animal shelter, which will get you almost to the beach.
Facilities: Picnic areas, restrooms, rinse off showers, lifeguard
Parking: Paved parking area
Camping: With county permit

HANAPEPE BEACH PARK
The Hanapepe Beach Park has a picnic area, restrooms, showers and parking, but not recommended for beach activities.

PORT ALLEN
Port Allen has restroom facilities and boat launching. Hanapepe Bay is the second largest port on Kaua'i. Port Allen has little to offer in the way of a beach or beach activities. However you might enjoy stopping in at the Red Dirt Shirt Factory near the harbor. Also in the harbor are Target Drones warning that all stay away.

Access: In Ele'ele turn mauka off Kaumuali'i Hwy on Waialo Rd., follow it to parking area at the boat launching area

SOUTHERN SHORE

Po'ipu, Koloa, Lawa'i and Kalaheo

SPOUTING HORN
There are a number of places around the Hawaiian islands that have the perfect conditions to form a blow hole. The best displays at Spouting Horn are during high surf when the water and air rushing together make a fine display. The geyser can reach heights of 60 feet. As you'll note by the many cars, tour buses and vendors booths, this is a popular visitor destination. There is no access to the ocean. Do Not Enter signs post the danger of being on the rocks should you attempt to descend down. The obvious danger is that you could be hit by a wave and pulled down. There is a legend about a sea monster which once lived in the area. Listening the groaning sounds made by the water as it courses underneath the rocky ledge, you can imagine that there truly must be a dragon or other mythical creature sighing and moaning. The sound effect happens even without the hole blowing. Many years ago it was noted that the salt spray was damaging to the crops. So during one night, we were told, an unscrupulous fellow was sent to blow the hole, widening it so that the force of the spray would be lessened.

Recommended for: Enjoying one of nature's wonders, a blow hole!
Facilities: Restrooms, vendors selling their wares
Access: Enter from Hwy 520, the road forks into Poipu Road on one side, Lawai Road on the other. From Lawai Road (also known as Spouting Horn Road) it is two miles and located along the roadside
Parking: Large paved parking area

BEACH HOUSE PARK
Located along side the road, this narrow beach is primarily usable only during low tide. Swimming and snorkeling can be good during low surf. The reef makes good snorkeling for even the beginner. This is a very, very small beachfront located right off the road, tucked between hotels and the restaurant with plenty of traffic going past. Not a very scenic or picturesque beach location.

Recommended for: Swimming and snorkeling during calm surf
Facilities: Restrooms, showers and paved parking area across the road from the beach.
Access: Enter from Hwy. 520, the road forks into Poipu Road on one side and Lawai Road on the other (also known as Spouting Horn Road). It is not as far down as Spouting Horn and is located across from the Lawai Beach Resort

PRINCE KUHIO PARK
This beach park is dedicated to Prince Jonah Kuhio Kalaniana'ole. He was born in 1871 and in 1902 was elected to be a delegate to Congress, where he served until his death on January 7, 1922. He was known as the "People's Prince" because of his achievements for his Hawaiian people. You can see the foundation of Kuhio's parent's home, royal fishpond, shrine, Hoai Heiau where the kahuna (priests) meditated and lived and a sitting bench that faced the grounds.
Prince Kuhio Park is located on Lawa'i Beach Road. Prince Kuhio was the youngest son of Kaua'i's chief David Kahalepouli Piikoli and the grandson of Kaumuali'i, the last King of Kaua'i. His aunt was Kapiolani and Prince Kuhio was adopted by Queen Kapiolani and grew up in the royal household in Honolulu. The monument at this parks marks his birth site.

Recommended for: Swimming, snorkeling and sunning during low tide and calm seas. During high tide it becomes just a park, with no beach!
Facilities: Public restrooms
Parking: Paved parking area

KOLOA LANDING
In the height of the early plantation days, Koloa Landing was the departure and arriving port for passenger and cargo vessels as well as whaling ships. Today Koloa Landing is a remnant of history, this old boat launch is now used as a departure for beach scuba dives. No facilities.

PO'IPU BEACH   ★
This is the beach in front of the Kiahuna Plantation. Several nearby hotel resorts are still awaiting their future, three years following Iniki. This beach suffered heavily from Hurricane Iniki and still has not returned to its finest form. Still, it is good snorkeling as a result of the offshore reef. Boogie boarding is popular here and you might see surfers riding the waves farther out. Windsurfers enjoy this site as well. Dangerous water conditions during high surf.

Recommended for: Snorkeling and swimming during calm seas, stay inside the reef area
Access: The east end of Ho'onani Road
Facilities: Only a rinse off shower, lifeguards sometimes on duty

WAI'OHAI BEACH
This beach was the site of the Kundsen home until construction began on the Wai'ohai Resort in 1962. Vlademar Knudsen was the son of the premier of Norway, who first went to California and made a fortune in the gold rush before relocating to Kaua'i and making a second fortune as founder of Kekaha Sugar Company.

Anne Sinclair was the daughter of Elizabeth Sinclair, none other than the same lady who purchased the island of Niʻihau in 1864. Anne Sinclair and Vlademar Knudsen married in later years. The site on Waiʻohai was selected by Anne Knudsen for her beach house. This is actually a part of Poʻipu Beach.

Recommended for: This sandy beach is good for surfing, swimming and snorkeling during calm seas. High surf generates dangerous conditions
Access: No real access until the old Stouffer's reopens. Can be reached from adjoining beach
Facilities: Only those found at nearby Poʻipu Beach Park
Parking: Dirt parking lot next to Brennecke's

POʻIPU BEACH PARK ★
Here you will find another one of Hawaiʻi's eight tombolos. Without knowing it was something special, you probably wouldn't have noticed it at all. This is a strip of sand which connects two pieces of land. There are only eight tombolos in all of Hawaiʻi. Snorkeling around the right side of Nukumoi Point is very good. The beach is protected by Nukumoi Point and a shorebreak on the east. Bodyboarders are attracted to the waves offshore. High surf can occur April through September. The county has lifeguards on duty here.

Recommended for: Swimming and snorkeling during calm seas
Access: Turn mauka off Poʻipu Rd. then west onto Hoʻowili Rd
Facilities: Restrooms, rinse off showers, lifeguard, playground
Parking: Paved parking area

BRENNECKE BEACH
Hurricane Iwa in 1982 changed the configuration of this beach and Iniki did further damage. The shorebreak onto the rocks with little beachfront remaining can be hazardous to the boogie boarder. At one time this beach was so popular for sunbathing that it was called Bikini Beach and it offered what was considered by many to be the best body surfing on Kauaʻi. In an effort to give mother nature a little hand in the restoration of this beach, Kauaʻi residents have obtained a county permit to dump sand on the beach above the high water mark. It is hoped that this will help the beach to begin the slow restoration process a bit more quickly. Resort and community groups have begun donating funds toward the purchase of sand. Brennecke's Beach Center rents beach equipment.

KEONELOA BEACH (SHIPWRECK BEACH)
This sandy shore fronts the Hyatt Regency. Keoneloa and Mahaʻulepu are a part of the same beach. It is commonly referred to as Shipwreck Beach for the long-gone ship that years ago ran aground. Hurricane Iwa took away the remains of the wreck, but the motor may still be occasionally visible. A good spot to watch surfers and windsurfers, but swimming, even during calm seas, may not be advised. The Hyatt does erect flags to indicate the condition of the surf, but still use your own good judgment.

Recommended for: Sunning, watching the windsurfers and surfers
Access: A road runs between the Poʻipu Bay Resort Golf Course and the Hyatt
Facilities: Public restrooms, shower facilities for Hyatt guests
Parking: Paved parking area at bottom

MAHA'ULEPU BEACH

It was here that King Kamehameha I made his attempt to conquer the island of Kaua'i in 1796. Unfortunately, a storm forced a retreat, but the advance forces of Kamehameha's troops arrived on the island unaware of the order to retreat and were quickly killed.

This is the beach site where George C. Scott portrayed Ernest Hemingway in the movie "Islands in the Stream." Maha'ulepu Beach is actually a collection of smaller beaches. They offer a diverse assortment of aquatic activities including fishing, surfing, bodyboarding, body surfing, kayaking, windsurfing, snorkeling and swimming.

The three areas along this beachfront are Gillin's Beach, Kawailoa Bay and Ha'ula Beach. Gillin's was named for the supervisor of Grove Farm Company, Elbert Gillin, who arrived in the islands in 1912 and relocated to Kaua'i in 1925 and built his home here. He was the supervisor of the Ha'upu Range Tunnel. Following two hurricanes, all that remains is Gillin's chimney. Several feet below this beach are the Rainbow Petroglyphs. Discovered in January of 1980 when a severe storm took out as much as six feet of beachfront, the petroglyphs were suddenly exposed. Working in reverse, the sea soon chose to cover them up once again. Currents at Kawailoa Bay make it unsafe for swimming or snorkeling. To reach Ha'ula Beach you may park on the east side of Pa'o'o Point and travel to the shore by trail. This area is the south shore's most dangerous beach.

Recommended for: The first beach, Gillin's, on occasion may be good for the experienced snorkeler during calm surf. Ha'ula Beach, since it requires a bit more effort to reach this may be the perfect place to sit and enjoy a beach by yourself
Access: A little tricky since access is over public land. You must pass a guard house and sign a release, but to get to the guard house you need a release from the McBryde Sugar Company. You can pick one up at their main office Mon.-Fri. 3-10 pm, Sat. and Sun. 7 am-10 pm. The information number for McBryde sugar is (808) 335-5111. You can also call and request that they mail you a form. Be sure to do so a month prior to your arrival. Then you'll need to stop at the guard house to sign a release with the Grove Farm at the guard house. Since access could be denied at any time, it is requested that you take all your litter with you and be respectful of the right to use these gorgeous beaches of Kaua'i. From Weliweli Rd. in Koa it connects with a dirt road by the sugar mill, follow it mauka. Or, take the dirt road at the end of Po'ipu Rd. and turn right at the cane road. Be aware of cane hauling trucks.
Facilities: None
Parking: On the side of the road

EASTERN SHORE

Nawiliwili, Lihu'e, Wailua, Kapa'a

KALAPAKI BEACH

This site is of historic significance in surfing history as the location where ancient Hawaiians practiced the skill of bodysurfing. The wave conditions continue to attract surfers and body surfers and the gentle off-shore slope makes it a good option for swimmers during calm seas. During periods of high surf, surfers come out in droves. However, we advise that you leave the high surf for the experienced surfers.

William Harrison Rice and Mary Sophia Rice, arrived on Kaua'i as missionaries in 1841. Their son William Hyde Rice purchased the land around this beach from Princess Ruth Ke'elikolani and here he built his home. Later, the Kaua'i Surf Hotel was built on this wonderful beachfront. In 1987 Amfac sold 175 acres and leased an additional 208 acres to Hemmeter-VMS Kaua'i Company. The result was the Westin Kaua'i Resort with an architectural style that some found outrageous, but most thought was garish. Hurricane Iniki virtually destroyed the resort and while the resort's lagoons opened the next year, the hotel sat empty for more than two years. Marriott picked up the option and in 1994 began renovating the property into a blend of hotel and timeshare condominiums. With the large town of Lihu'e nearby and the close proximity to the Marriott Hotel, you are likely to find this beach more populated than most. This beach is better protected than some, except during east swells, but caution is advised at all times.

Recommended for: Swimming, snorkeling, windsurfing and bodyboarding during low surf conditions
Access: Beach access is at the left side of the bay or through the Nawiliwili Park public access on the right.
Parking: Public parking area at the west end next to the stream which enters this bay
Facilities: Nearby Nawiliwili Park has restrooms. Facilities provided by the Marriott are for hotel guests only.

NININI BEACH

There are two beaches located here. Both can be affected by high surf and Kona storms. Snorkeling at the larger sandy stretch can be good when the ocean is calm. During high surf enjoy the bodysurfers. Sometimes it is referred to as Running Waters Beach because of the irrigation runoff that once occurred here. Nearby you'll see the Nawiliwili Light Station located at the point. This area is popular with shore fishermen catching reef fish.

Recommended for: Snorkeling on calm days only for the experienced
Access: Turn at Ahukini Rd. follow the dirt road 2.6 miles to Ninini Point
Parking: No parking

NUKOLE

Nukole means beach of the kole fish, and is the proper Hawaiian name. This beach stretches from Hanama'ulu Bay to Lydgate Park for approximately two miles. It is often referred to as Nukolii, after a dairy that once had cattle grazing in the area and archeological events suggests that prior to that there was a Hawaiian settlement. The Outrigger Kaua'i, located on this beachfront, maintains the public beach park pavilion and adjoining bathrooms. You may see local residents trying their hand at fishing, surfing and even diving on this beachfront. Swimming and snorkeling are not recommended at any time of the year.

Recommended for: Sunbathing, beachcombing and sunrises
Access: Turn mauka on Kaua'i Beach Drive, which leads to the Outrigger Hotel to reach the southern portion of the beach
Parking: Parking area for about five cars
Facilities: A county park with the pavilion, rinse off showers and restrooms maintained by the Outrigger Hotel

LYDGATE BEACH ★

This forty acre "state" park is dedicated to Reverend John Lydgate who more than a century ago founded the Lihu'e Union Church and was a force in the establishment of public parks and historic sites on Kaua'i. Wailua was once the home of the island's royalty. The banks of the Wailua River were a sacred area in ancient Hawaii and a favored dwelling place reserved for the kings and high chiefs of Kaua'i. Near the mouth of the river in Lydgate Park are remains of a heiau that was a place of refuge for those who had broken a taboo. Two large pieces of smooth stone where women of royal blood or high chiefly rank gave birth are located on the river's north shore. Nearby is Holoholoku Heiau, believed to be the oldest heiau on Kaua'i. About 25 years ago the breakwater was added which created two protected pools, ideal for swimming. The pools have a sandy bottom. Plan on bringing along some bread to feed the fish. Generally there is a lifeguard on duty. You may see windsurfers at this beach during south or Kona winds. While this is called a state park, it is actually maintained by the county.

Recommended for: Swimming for adults and children within the protected pools. Not advised beyond the pools. Good location for beginning snorkelers to try out their skills.
Access: South of the Wailua River turn mauka on Leho Drive, then continue mauka on Nalu Rd. If you are heading North, the turn off is easy to spot, heading south there is no marked entrance. Heading north it is just past the Wailua Golf Course, heading south, if you get to the golf course, you've missed it! It is located below the Aston Kaua'i Resort
Parking: Large Parking area
Facilities: Restrooms, rinse off showers, picnic pavilions, wonderful playground for kids!
Camping: Permits for camping available from the county

WAILUA BEACH
A half-mile stretch of beach from the Wailua River north. It is located across the Highway from the Coco Palms Resort (which in 1995 had still not reopened since Iniki) and is the beach which fronts the Lae Nani condominiums. *The Beaches of Kaua'i* by John R.K. Clark explains that the surfers shorebreak is called Horners, named after Albert Horner a pineapple industry pioneer. His mansion was built on this beachfront in 1929 and was later moved by new owners Mel and Pauline Venture to an inland location in Wailua. Dangerous currents much of the year make this beach advisable only for walking and sunning. There are lots of resorts located along here and Aldon's restaurant has a nice oceanview location. There is one small protected pool at Alakukui Point, which during calm surf is safe for wading. Also at Alakukui Point are some remnants of an old heiau.

Recommended for: Beachcombing, walking, sunning
Access: All along from Lydgate to River to Kapaa
Parking: Parking area near Wailua Bridge and limited parking on Papaloa Rd.
Facilities: None

WAIPOULI BEACH
This narrow strip of beach runs from the Coconut Plantation Resort to the Waika'ea Canal in Kapa'a. The Kaua'i Coconut Beach Resort is located on this beachfront. While the pedestrian trail among the ironwood trees above the shoreline is popular for joggers or walkers, the beachfront is covered by beach-rock and very strong offshore currents make it unsafe for swimming year round. Some marginal swimming might be pursued at the southern end of the beach, but even then, only under very calm surf conditions. A popular fishing location.

Recommended for: Swimming is marginal in the summer months
Facilities: Only for hotel guests

KAPA'A BEACH PARK
With its location nearer civilization and the adjoining canal used as a boat launch, you are likely to find this beach more populated. This beach has encountered severe shoreline erosion over the last 30 years. You'll note that some human measures have been made to stop the erosion, such as jetties at the mouth of the canal. In the evening you might want to stroll down the beach (on a moonless night) and perhaps you'll be lucky enough to see fishermen practicing lamalama (torch fishing).

Recommended for: A few areas of the beach offer adequate swimming when the surf is calm, but not especially recommended. Shore fishing is popular here. Great sunrises!
Access: Turn toward the ocean off Kuhio Hwy. at Niu Street, near the Kapa'a ballpark
Parking: Parking area
Facilities: Restrooms, rinse off showers, public swimming pool

KEALIA BEACH

Once the town of Kealia was a thriving plantation town, complete with a train depot and at the nearby landing an inter-island steamer would stop for passengers. Today it is not much more than a stretch along the highway. The word Kealia means "salt encrusted." Interesting to note that almost every Hawaiian island has a beach named Kealia!

Recommended for: Tidepools during low tide, strong rip currents make it unsafe for water activities, particularly dangerous during high surf.
Access: Hwy. 56 at milemarker 10
Parking: Parking along the roadside
Facilities: None
Camping: No

DONKEY BEACH

This is one of the few beaches for which we could find no Hawaiian name. Apparently before the advent of machinery, mules were used to haul cane seed to the fields. Some say that there were only mules and no donkeys at all, but whichever the case, the name Donkey Beach stuck. Located 1 1/2 miles from Kealia Beach, it is a very pastoral setting. Here you will find a popular body and board surfing location, however high surf in winter and spring months create dangerous rip currents and shorebreaks. There is no public access to this beach, but beachgoers, oblivious to the no trespassing sign continue to find this beach. Its inaccessibility has made this beach the site for nude sunbathing. Nude sunbathing is not legal in Hawai'i and periodic arrests are made.

Recommended for: Fishing
Access: There is no public access
Parking: Only along the road at mile marker 11
Facilities: None

ANAHOLA BEACH and 'ALIOMANU BEACH

This beach is located on the corner of Anahola Bay. It is a popular park during the summer for local residents. There is a reef and pockets of sand create pools that are pleasant for the kids. Anahola Stream is found at the north end of the beach. 'Aliomanu Beach is at the north side of Anahola Beach. It is widely used by fishermen and limu kohu, a popular seaweed is harvested here.

NORTHERN SHORE

Hanalei, Kilauea, and Princeville

KA'AKA'ANIU BEACH (LARSEN'S BEACH)

L. David Larsen, a Swedish born plant pathologist, arrived in Hawaii in 1908 and later managed the Kilauea Sugar Plantation. This beach was named for the site upon which he built his home. Dangerous rip currents and a shallow rocky shore make this unappealing for swimmers. The offshore reef is a popular location for the harvesting of limu kohu, a type of seaweed. During times of low tide you may see the harvesters at work or net throwers catching fish. The county access, purchased in 1979, was sold under the condition that the access not continue all the way to the beach. In hopes of making the beach less attractive and therefore less populated, it will take a little bit of effort to reach this sandy crescent. Once you reach the head of the path, it will take you less than 10 minutes to walk down to the beachfront.

Recommended for: Beachcombing, watching seaweed being harvested, fishing
Access: 1.2 miles from the north intersection of Ko'olau Rd and Kuhio Hwy. there is a public access. A trail will require a 5-10 minute hike to reach the shoreline

WAIALKALUA IKI BEACH

Dangerous rip currents at Waialkalua Iki make it a lovely spot to visit, and a popular fishing location, but inadvisable for water activities. In 1911 on the hill overlooking the ocean, a heiau was discovered. There is a trail from the valley up to this archeological site. The twin beach, Waiakalua Nui is just slightly east and is covered with beach rock.

Recommended for: Beachcombing
Access: Near the end of North Waiakalua Rd. is a public access to the shoreline down a steep trail that requires a 5-10 minute walk
Parking: This is a private beach so there is no public parking area
Facilities: This is a private beach so there are no facilities

KILAUEA POINT NATIONAL WILDLIFE REFUGE
The Kilauea Point National Wildlife Refuge was established in 1974. The acquisition of land has continued ever since and this sanctuary now encompasses 203 acres. The refuge was struck hard by Hurricane Iniki. Not only was there much damage to the birdlife and vegetation, but the famous lighthouse was also seriously affected. At Kilauea Point, they reported that about 80% of the native plants suffered damage. On Crater Hill, at least 25% were lost and an additional 50% damaged. Mokolea Point vegetation suffered little damage. Kilauea Point lost the most birds and suffered the worst damage to the habitat. The Kaua'i Natural Wildlife Refuge complex lost 12 of their 20 buildings. There was also damage to the lighthouse visitor center and bookstore, storage buildings, fences, and the water delivery system.

A tombolo is not an unusual musical instrument or an Italian sausage, but rather an unusual beach condition. There are only eight tombolo within the Hawaiian islands and one example may be found here at Kilauea Point. A tombolo is a sandbar that connects the shoreline to an island. This is a strip of sand which connects two pieces of land. There are only eight tombolos in all of Hawai'i. You can view it at the base of Makapili Rock where it connects the rock to the shoreline. Construction began on the 52 foot lighthouse in 1912 and it was not until 1976 that it was put out of commission.

KPNHA is a non-profit corporation dedicated to environmental interpretation, education, protection and enhancement. Information on membership can be obtained by writing: KPNHA, PO Box 87, Kilauea, HI 96754.

Visitor Information Phone: (808) 828-1413
Access: Turnoff Kuhio Hwy. where the large sign indicates Kilauea Lighthouse
Facilities: Bookstore, restrooms, visitor center, charge for admission
Parking: Large paved parking area

KAUAPEA BEACH
This 3,000 foot long beach lies between Kalihiwai Bay and Kilauea Point. It's access is a little tricky given that you cannot see the beach from the highway and the access is not clearly marked. The beautiful people of the 1960's referred to it as Secret Beach, and it is still called this today. Dangerous water conditions due to winter and spring high surf make water activities during these times ill advised. During calmer summer months, you may find a wide variety of beach activities including surfing, bodysurfing and bodyboarding. Again, possibly because of inaccessibility, you should be advised that nude sunbathing does occur at this beach site. Remember that nude sunbathing is not legal in Hawai'i and periodic arrests are made. From this beach you can see Moku'ae'ae Island, a bird sanctuary and part of the Kilauea Refuge.

Recommended for: Beachcombing, bodysurfing or bodyboarding during summer periods of low surf.
Access: 0.4 miles west of the town of Kilauea, an unmarked dirt road intersects the Kuhio Highway. From the end of the dirt road you'll find a trail leading to the beach. The trail down to the beach requires a 10 minute hike.
Facilities: None
Parking: Along the roadside

KALIHIWAI BEACH

This crescent of white sand is fringed with ironwood trees. You'll see board-surfing in the summer. During the winter, stay out of the water and watch the surfers. Stay away from the mouth of the river, where rip currents may occur. Kayaking up the river can be done except during heavy rains or flooding.

Recommended for: Calm summer days only for body surfing, swimming and snorkeling.
Access: Take the Kalihiwai Road (eastern exit)
Facilities: None
Parking: At the beach under the ironwood trees

'ANINI BEACH PARK

Apparently this beach was called Wanini, but sometime during the years, it was abbreviated. (One story tells that the "W" just fell off the sign, so they changed the name of the beach rather than repairing the beach sign.) With a two mile offshore reef, this beach is popular for varied types of fishing (pole, spearing, throw-net) and also seaweed harvesting. Snorkeling, windsurfing, beachcombing, reef walking and boating are also to be found here. Water conditions are very dangerous during high surf which causes strong rip currents. Many drownings and near drownings have occurred here over the years. This beachfront was the location for several scenes in Honeymoon in Vegas.

Recommended for: Windsurfing, swimming only during very calm summer surf, stay away from the west end of the beach where there is a channel. Snorkeling can be good here during the summer. Stay inside the reef.
Access: Follow Kuhio Highway to Kalihiwai Road and take Anini Road to the beach
Facilities: Picnic facilities, showers, restrooms
Parking: Long stretch of grass for parking with an open area next to it for boats and trailers
Camping: With county permit

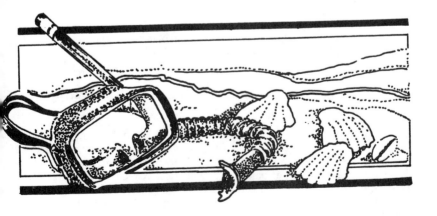

PRINCEVILLE
Princeville is a 2,000 acre tract of land lying between Hanalei Bay and 'Anini Beach. The resort development began in 1968 and is composed of condominiums, private homes and several hotels. Most of the development sits along the bluffs with only three small beaches. One is located below the Sealodge condominiums, another below the Pali Ke Kua condominiums (sometimes called Hideaways), while the third is at the base of the Princeville Resort. There are several accesses to the Princeville shoreline. Seven accesses are available through the Hanalei Bay Resort. None of these beaches are safe for winter time water activities. The Princeville resort is located on the hill called Pu'u Poa. Below is the Pu'u Poa Beach which runs about 1,200 ft. between the resort and the mouth of the Hanalei River. Only during calm summer surf will you find an opportunity to snorkel amid the reef. Pu'u Poa is the best of the three Princeville beaches. Kayaks can be rented at the Beach Activities Center at the Princeville Resort to explore the river.

Recommended for: Swimming and snorkeling only during calm summer months at Pu'u Poa Beach. Limited swimming and snorkeling at Kenomene and Kaweonui Beaches during calm surf in summer months.

Access to Kenomene Beach (at Sealodge condominiums): A trail at the end of Kamehameha Road. A hike of 10-15 minutes down a very steep goat-like trail is required to reach the shoreline.

Access to Kaweonui Beach (at Pali Ke Kua condominiums): Just before the gate at the Princeville Hotel there is a path down to the beach. It will take a 5-10 minute walk down the stairs and trail to reach. Guests of Pali Ke Kua have a private trail.

Pu'u Poa Beach (Princeville Resort): Access through Princeville Resort
Facilities (Kenomene Beach): None
Facilities (Kaweonui Beach): None
Facilities (Pu'u Poa Beach): None

HANALEI BAY
The Hanalei Bay begins its two mile sandy stretch at Pu'u Poa and ends at the Makahoa Point toward the west. A small number of beaches and beach parks line this area, including Black Pot Beach, Hanalei Beach Park, Waikoko Beach, and Wai'oli Beach Park. There are three parking areas. The Pier located here was condemned before Hurricane Iniki and has since been rebuilt.

Access: Turn right on Aku road and another right turn on Weke Road

BLACK POT BEACH
Another one of the few Kaua'i beaches with no true Hawaiian name, this site was dubbed "Black Pot" for the huge cooking pot that was shared by picnickers and fishermen. Black Pot Beach Park is located where the Hanalei River meets the ocean on the eastern end of the bay. A popular site for local residents to gather, their furor was raised when in late 1967 it was announced by new owners of the property that they planed to build a condominium. In 1973 they finally sold the land to the county.

Recommended for: Swimming, bodyboarding, surfing, windsurfing, kayaking during calm summer surf
Parking: Parking only along the bay on Weke Road
Facilities: Restrooms, showers, lifeguard on duty seasonally
Camping: With county permits

HANALEI BEACH PARK

Hanalei means "lei shaped." The Hanalei Pier, is a scenic location, and one you'll no doubt remember if you saw the movie South Pacific. The wooden pier was constructed in 1892 and then 30 years later was reinforced with concrete. It was used by the local farmers for shipping their rice crops to market until it was closed in 1933. In 1979 the pier joined other landmarks in the National Register of Historic Places. A lifeguard is sometimes on duty at Hanalei Beach Park during busy weekends. The beach can be calm and serene during low summer surf, but extremely treacherous during winter and spring high surf.

Recommended for: Picnics anytime, summer time swimming
Access: Turn right on Aku Road, and a second right onto Weke Road
Facilities: Picnic tables and restrooms. Lifeguard at the Hanalei Bay Beach.
Parking: Areas of compacted sand are located for parking at various intervals along the beach

WAIKOKO

Waikiko, which means "blood waters," is the last of the beaches along Hanalei Bay. It offers an offshore reef, making this narrow beach a good place for children to swim. The offshore water is very shallow, in fact, too shallow for most adults.

Recommended for: Snorkeling during calm seas and good swimming for children in the shallow, reef protected ocean. During times of high surf you can enjoy watching surfers on the outer edge of the Waikoko Reef.
Access: Located along Highway 56, a half mile past mile marker 4
Facilities: None
Parking: Along side the road

LUMAHA'I BEACH

This beach is tucked beneath some lush cliffs and became famous for a well known scene in the 1957 film South Pacific. Actually, it was the eastern end of this beach, which has a separate name, Kahalahala (which means pandanus trees), where Mitzi Gaynor filmed her famous "wash that man right out of her hair" scene. A more scenic stretch of beach is hard to imagine, but unfortunately that is about all you should do at this one. The width of Lamaha'i Beach is said to vary as much as 360 feet with the seasonal movement of the sand from one end to the other. With the steep shore comes the danger of high surf, dangerous shorebreak and strong currents. There is no protective reef, so the ocean drops off very quickly. The nearby Lumaha'i River may rise dramatically as a result of flash floods, so even wading along the shore is not advisable. You may see body or boardsurfers enjoying this beach, but when the surf becomes even slightly rough, you'll see that even the experts stay out of the waters. With the danger of rogue waves, most common during high surf, again, even wading is not recommended.

You may have heard of oʻopu, a unique freshwater fish which spends its first few months in the sea before returning to the freshwater stream. They have adapted well to their existence by using their lower front fins as a suction cup to hold onto rocks, even those extremely steep rock walls which form waterfalls. Using its tail to propel themselves, the oʻopu travels slowly upstream. The adults come down the Lumahaʻi stream (and others on Kauaʻi) in late summer and fall, spawn and then send their young for their ocean experience. The young (larvae) mature into juveniles called hinana and return to their freshwater origins and migrate upstream. These interesting marine creatures are found no where beyond Hawaii and are highly valued for their meat.

Recommended for: Enjoying the view, and an outstanding photo opportunity at the 5 mile marker post or at several other small pullouts along the road. Swimming is safe at Kahalahala only on the calmest of summer days.
Access: Along the Highway at the 4 mile marker before the bridge and parking along the 6 mile marker nearer the river
Facilities: None
Parking: Very limited along the roadside

WAINIHA BEACH PARK
The term Wainiha means "unfriendly." This wide beach has no reef, so it is completely unprotected from the open ocean. High surf, therefore, creates very dangerous conditions as a result of rip currents and shorebreaks. Numerous drownings and near drownings have been reported here. The water is murky as a result of the Wainiha stream and not recommended for any water activities. The stream cuts back into the valley reaching into the Waiʻaleʻale Crater. Given the heavy rainfall that comes down from the crater, unexpected flash floods can and do occur in the stream. Hence, swimming here is not advisable. Since there is no protecting reef, beachcombing on the dry sandy shore can be good!

A few miles beyond is Powerhouse Road, the turn off to climb inland through the valley. The road travels through some beautiful, not-to-be missed scenery and ends at the Powerhouse. Built in 1906 it served to provide irrigation for the McBryde Sugar Company. Where the road ends the trail begins there is a hiking trail known as the Powerhouse Trail.

Recommended for: Beachcombing
Facilities: No facilities
Parking: Off road parking only, near mile marker #7

KEPUHI BEACH
You may perhaps be thinking you are seeing double. Yes, there is a Kepuhi Beach on the south shore. This north shore stretch of beach is actually three beaches: *Wainiha Kuʻau Beach*, *Kaonohi Beach*, and *Kanaha Beach*. There is a series of reefs which make this area popular for throw netting. The beach point at Kaonohi is the location of the YMCA Camp Naue. These beaches frequently have strong currents that are especially dangerous during high surf. Not recommended for water activities except on very calm days. Again, the high surf and dangerous currents have caused many drownings and near-drownings over the years.

Recommended for: Summertime swimming on days of calm surf
Access: Along highway 56 there is access on Alamoʻo Road and Alealea Road, just before mile marker #8
Facilities: None
Parking: Parking off road among the ironwood trees

MAKUA BEACH

Since you are not likely to find most people referring to this stretch of beach by its Hawaiian name, you should also know it is known as "Tunnels Beach." It was named for the underwater caves located here. Located on Haʻena Point it is one of the more popular beach sites on the northern shore of Kauaʻi. While the shoreline has much beachrock making it less attractive to swimmers, the offshore reef offers good snorkeling during calm surf.

During the spring and winter time high surf there are very strong rip currents at Makua Beach. Even during low surf, the current offshore can be treacherous. During this high surf, it is a popular surfing spot, but only for the expert. The surf break on the outer reef is often referred to as Tunnels.

You may also see fishermen using spears or nets along the reef. Divers named this beach tunnels for the many tunnels found around the lagoon that is created by the reef. You may recognize this beach as the major location for the television mini-series "The Thorn Birds."

Recommended for: Watching windsurfing, swimming and snorkeling during periods of low and calm sea, and beachcombing during high seas. Very dangerous during winter months.
Access: Two public accesses, one at the east side of Haʻena Point, the other to the west. You'll find the first at .3 miles past mile marker 8 on Hwy. 560 and the second 1/2 mile past the same marker.
Facilities: None
Parking: Limited parking off Kuhio Hwy.

HAʻENA BEACH PARK

This is a five acre park maintained by the County of Kauaʻi. Hukilau translated means to fish with seine, or pull ropes. You may be familiar with the Hukilau song and hula being performed at a luau you've attended. Today this style of fishing is never done. But in past times this beach was a hukilau site when fishermen would come to this site, then called Maniniolo (meaning traveling manini fish) and throwing their nets, out into the sea and then pull their catch onto shore. This is different than net fishing which you might see done by a single fisherman. The foreshore here is steep. The resulting shorebreak is dangerous and make it unsafe for swimming or bodysurfing. Although you may see some body-surfing done here, it is not for the novice. Across the road from Haena Beach Park is Maninolo Dry Cave. This lava tube was a sea cave in earlier centuries when the sea was higher. You can follow the tube several hundred yards and emerge at the other end. We were told that the cave was larger before it was filled in with sand by the tsunami that hit the island in 1957.

Following another 2/10 of a mile past Haena State Park and just beyond Limahuli Steam are the **Waikapala'e Wet Caves,** accessible by a short hike up and behind the gravel parking area. One of the caves has a fresh water pool and a unique phenomena. The Waikapala'e (the modern translation means water of the lace fern) Wet Cave has a cool shady cave known as the blue room. It requires a venture into the chilly waters and, depending on the water height, possibly an underwater swim through a submerged tunnel. This is one adventure we have yet to try, but we are told it is an inspiring experience. Apparently the reflection of the light through the tunnel causes the incredible blue effect on the cavern walls.

Ha'ena Beach Park Recommended for: Swimming and snorkeling in the summer with calm surf, particularly dangerous during winter months.
Access: Located on the Wainiha side of Ha'ena
Facilities: Restrooms, showers, picnic pavilions
Camping: Permits available from the county
Parking: Along the roadside

HA'ENA STATE PARK and KE'E BEACH
Highway 56 goes as far as this beach before it ends. This is the beginning of the Na Pali Coast and Na Pali Coast State Park, which is only accessible by boat or by hiking trail. The 230 acres of Ha'ena State Park includes a number of ancient archeological sites. Remnants of ancient Hawaiian villages and the Kaulu o Laka Heiau can be found here. This sacred altar is set along a series of tiers on the cliffs of Na Pali and was built for Laka, the goddess of hula. It is one of the dramatic sites on the island with views of the cliffs and ocean. The heiau is still used today by hula halaus.

The John Clark guide to beaches of Kaua'i tells the story of the Taylor Camp, which was populated by over 100 flower children during the 1960's and 1970's. Howard Taylor, who happens to be the brother of Elizabeth Taylor, offered refuge at his seven acre property for their "hippie" community when they were evicted from a public beach park and threatened with jail time. Apparently the commune members shared a communal shower and one open air toilet. If you're over 40 years old, you may remember the puka shell fad. Apparently these hippies began with shells gathered on the beach, holes made in the center (puka meaning hole) and strung to make a necklace. Elizabeth Taylor donning one of these necklaces, a gift from her brother, created a craze which virtually wiped out shells on all the beaches in Hawaii. Great story, eh! Comb the beach for your own shells and you'll have a little piece of this legend. Now back to the hippies, who continued to run free and naked, pile trash (to the point of seriously polluting the ocean) and then turned to the cultivation of marijuana for their income -- well, it was a happy ending for the beach. Howard Taylor left, turning the land deed over to the state in 1974 and after several years the hippies were finally evicted and the state took over the park in 1977. Swimming is only advisable during very calms conditions.

At the very end of the beach park is Ke'e Beach and is best visited during the week when the crowds aren't as large. There can be good swimming and snorkeling, but again (are you tired of hearing this?) only if the surf conditions are calm. Stay inside the lagoon as the area beyond the reef can have strong currents. If the parking lot is full (and it often is on weekends) follow the dirt road that veers to the right. There has been a lifeguard on duty here, but as we go to press there is talk of cuts which would eliminate the lifeguard at this beach. Ke'e may look familiar to you for it is where the final scene of Body Heat was filmed starring Kathleen Turner.

Recommended for: Good swimming and snorkeling at Ke'e in the summer with very calm surf, great sunsets
Facilities: Restrooms, showers
Access: Located at the trail head to the Na Pali Coast
Parking: Parking areas near the end of Kuhio Highway. If the lot at Ke'e is full, continue on the dirt road and there is more parking beyond the restrooms.

NA PALI COAST STATE PARK
"Na pali" means the cliffs, so remember in using this term don't say The Na Pali Cliffs, for that would mean, "The cliffs cliffs." This 6,500 acre state park is composed of dramatic cliffs, dense rainforests and lush coastal valleys. There is 15 miles of shoreline between Ke'e Beach and Polihale Beach on Kaua'i's eastern shore.

There are a total of five major beaches within this state park: Hanakapi'ai, Kalalau, Honopu, Nu'alolo Kai and Miloli'i. The Hanakapi'ai Beach can be reached in a day's hike. It is a distance of two miles from Ke'e and may take 1/2 - 2 hours to reach. Remember to pack plenty of drinkable water, and include sunscreen lotion and a hat, along with comfortable shoes. It might be recommended to also include a small first aid kit with an ace support bandage. You may find remnants of a fishing village and a farming community which once resided here. Due to the remoteness of this coastline, beach lovers need to use extra caution. Sadly, it is perhaps at the Kalalau Beach that more drownings occur, per visitor, than anywhere else on the island of Kaua'i. As mentioned before, this is a remote wilderness area and help would be a long time in reaching you should you become ill or injured.

KIHIKIHI   JBayot

253

As with other of the north shore beaches, surf and currents are extremely hazardous. A hike to this beach is recommended for summer when the trail has had time to dry out from spring rains and the ocean is calmer. A hike which travels another two miles inland from the beach will take you to the Hanakapi'ai waterfall. The falls flow down for about 300 feet to the pool below. Avoid swimming beneath the falls, and resist the urge to drink the water (all fresh water in Hawai'i should be purified before drinking). It is also advisable that you bring along some mosquito repellent!

There is an 11-mile trek along the steep cliffs of the Kalalau Trail to Kalalau Beach. Due to the rugged terrain and steep elevations, it may well take an entire day to reach the beach. The Kalalau Valley was called the Valley of Healing Light by the ancient Hawaiians. Remember to treat any heiaus with respect.

Again, the summer months are most advisable. The area was inhabited until 1919. In the late 1960's and early 1970's the area was again populated, once again by hippies. With serious sanitation problems the state implemented a program which limited access to the area by restricting the number of camping permits. Boat and helicopter landings also came under restrictions. Camping is allowed only at the shoreline at Kalalau and water is available for cooking and drinking following purification, i.e. boiling. With no fronting reef and strong currents, it is dangerous to swim here at any time of the year.

The remaining three of Na Pali's beaches are only accessible by boat. Camping is permitted in areas of the state park. Permits are not required for day hikes.

HANAKAPI'AI
We recommend you simply stay out of the ocean here. This north shore beach is particularly dangerous, and the #1 beach for drownings during the 1970-1988 period. This combined with the remoteness of this shoreline means that beach lovers need to use extra caution. As mentioned before, this is a remote wilderness area and help would be a long time in reaching you should you become ill or injured.

The Hanakapi'ai Stream flows into the ocean at this sandy beachfront. The rivermouth has dangerous rip currents. Summer trades can cause the current to be especially hazardous. Conditions are even more dangerous during winter months.

There are some ponds along the stream for a quick dip, but keep an eye out above the valley as rain in the uplands can result in flash flooding of the streams. Even the Department of Land and Natural Resources recommends you avoid the ocean. A reminder, as with any freshwater on the island, it needs to be boiled or otherwise treated before drinking. Also see the recreation section of this book under camping for more information on this beach area.

Recommended for: Scenic beauty only
Facilities: Toilets
Access: A two mile trek from the trail head at Ke'e Beach, at the NW end of Kuhio Hwy. It is not recommended that you park and leave your car overnight. Several companies can arrange to drop you off and pick you up.
Camping: By permit with the state

KALALAU BEACH

The trail from the Hanakapi'ai Valley to the Kalalau Valley is a difficult one and should not be attempted as a day trip. An 11 mile hike from the trail head at Ke'e Beach, it traverses along scenic ocean cliffs with significant elevation changes (meaning a lot of up and down!). The beach is long and narrow during the summer, but with close shorebreak, it is unsafe at all times of the year. During the winter, the beach disappears. No water activities can be recommended for this location. This is one of Kaua'i's five most dangerous beaches, based on incidents of drowning. As with other valley beaches, the Kalalau Stream mouth area is subject to rip currents. As we write this text the Kaua'i daily newspaper reports another death by drowning on this beach. A 30-year old man lost his balance playing in the waves and was pulled out by the rip current. Also, be alert to the possibility of flash floods during rainfall in the upper region. This is the last beach accessible by foot along the Na Pali Coast. The remaining beaches are accessible only by boat. Also see the recreation section of this book under camping for more information on this beach area.

Recommended for: Scenic beauty only
Facilities: Toilets
Access: Eleven strenuous miles on foot along Na Pali Coastline from the trail head at Ke'e Beach at the NW end of Kuhio Hwy. It is not recommended that you park and leave your car overnight. Several companies can arrange to drop you off and pick you up.

HONAPU and NUALOLO KAI BEACHES

Accessible only by boat, Honapu has no facilities and camping is not allowed. Nualolo is a popular summer destination for the charter boats that depart out of Na Pali. The snorkeling can be excellent along the reef that fans out from shore. Several charter boat companies have state permission to land at this beach, others must anchor offshore. Snorkelers need to stay clear of the shallow reefs due to the danger of surges.

Recommended for: Snorkeling at Nualolo Kai during calm summer months
Facilities: Toilets and picnic tables
Access: Charter boats during the summer months, especially Nualolo Kai

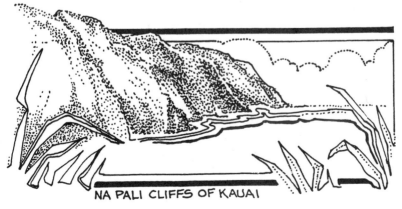

NA PALI CLIFFS OF KAUAI

RECREATION AND TOURS

INTRODUCTION

Kaua'i, The Garden Isle, has much to interest the outdoorsman or outdoorswoman. Whether it is the land, the air or the ocean that beckons, there are a variety of activities to tempt even the die-hard lounge chair athlete.

There are a number of agencies on Kaua'i that can assist you with booking the recreational activity of your choice. Kaua'i 800, for example, can be contacted by phone in advance of your arrival. Phone 1-800-443-9180. They promise to get the best rental car rates on the island.

BEST BETS

For great snorkeling try Lydgate or Poi'pu Beach on the South Shore or Makua Beach (also known as Tunnels) on the North Shore.

Take a helicopter tour and get a spectacular view of Kaua'i.

The golf aficionado will delight in the Prince Course in Princeville. Rated as the Number 1 course by Golf Digest, it is well deserved. Excellent play and outstanding scenery!

Take a tour to Ni'ihau by air and spend an afternoon sunning, napping, snorkeling and lunching on one of their beaches.

If the whales are in residence, take advantage of a whale watching excursion to view these beautiful mammals a bit more closely.

For an underwater thrill consider an introductory scuba adventure, no experience necessary.

For an eye-popping, spectacular aquatic adventure, take a zodiac tour of the Na Pali coast.

Take a self-guided tour up Wailua River by kayak to the Fern Grotto.

View the Waimea Canyon, one of the most spectacular of Mother Nature's creations.

Hike along the Kalalau Trail: this 11 mile trek along the rugged Na Pali coastline is not for the novice hiker.

Enjoy a hiking excursion in the summer months with an interpretative guide from the Koke'e Natural History Museum.

Spend a day, or part of one, at one of Kaua'i's wonderful health spas.

Take a bottle of something bubbly and watch a romantic sunset at Ke'e Beach or Pakala Beach.

Take advantage of an incredible golfing value on a picturesque course, the 9 hole Kukuilono Golf Course. Start your play about 3 pm, miss the crowds, and if you don't finish you won't feel bad. Greens fee is a bargain at only $6.

The horticulturist or amateur gardener will not want to miss visiting one or all of the lovely tropical gardens.

Here is an outline of some of the activities that might be enjoyed on the island of Kaua'i, along with the price you might expect to pay. Remember to always check the local brochures for coupons, and don't be afraid to ask if they are running a special offer!

Helicopter tour (55-60 minutes)	from $150
Na Pali coast ocean excursion (zodiac or catamaran)	from $ 75
Sunset sail along the coastline	from $ 45
Deep sea fishing (1/2 day trip)	from $ 75
Fresh water fishing (1/2 day trip)	from $100
River kayak (1/2 day guided)	from $ 50
Scuba diving (2 tank w/equipment)	from $ 90
Hawaiian luau	from $ 45
Horseback riding (1-2 hour)	from $ 40
Land tours (around the island guided bus tours)	from $ 50
Golf (nine holes)	from $ 6
Golf (eighteen holes)	from $ 18-145

SCUBA DIVING

BICYCLING

Bicycle John's - Their outlets in Lihu'e and Kapa'a have road bike rentals. Free delivery, free pick-up, free map, free car rack. Daily price is $25-30, or as low as $13 per day at a weekly rate. (808) 245-7579.

Kaua'i Downhill - Coast 12 miles down hill along Waimea Canyon Rd. (808) 245-1774. 1-800-234-1774. Open seasonally.

Outfitters Kaua'i - Offer mountain bike rentals for your own exploration along with car racks, kid's seats, helmets and plenty of directions. Their Koke'e Mountain Bike Ecotour travels into the areas above Waimea Canyon with a guide. This interpretative nature ride follows secluded fire roads. 2827A Po'ipu Rd., Po'ipu Beach, HI 96756. (808) 742-9667, FAX (808) 742-9667.

BOAT TRIPS

As opposed to sea excursions, these are boat trips on non-ocean going vessels:

South Sea Tours - They offer hourly tours of the 40 acres of waterways at Kaua'i Lagoons aboard Italian crafted motor launches. The captain gives an interesting narration of thee many exotic animals, from kangaroos to monkeys, that inhabit the different man-made islands. Cost of the tour is $12 for adults, $6 for children 12 and under. Canoe rides which include a stop at one of the islands are also available. South Sea also handles fishing, helicopter and other tours and recreational activities. (808) 245-2222 or 1-800-367-2914.

Smith's Tropical Paradise cruises up the Wailua river to the famous Fern Grotto. Trips operate every day, every half hour starting at 9 am. Trip duration is 1 hour and 20 minutes. Current schedule is departures at 9 am 10:30 am, 1 pm, 2 pm and 2:30 pm with later departures on Mon., Wed. and Fri. Adults $10, children under 12 $5. (808) 822-4111.

BOWLING

Lihu'e Lanes - 28 lanes open daily at 4303 Rice St., in the Rice Shopping Center, $2.75 per game, plus $1.25 shoe rental. Check flyers for coupon specials! The snack bar has hula pie for $2, and Roy Rogers or Shirley Temples for the kids to drink. Open 9 am - midnight Monday through Saturday, Sundays noon to midnight. (808) 245-5263.

CAMPING

When planning your camping vacation on Kaua'i, remember that space is very limited at the most popular campsites, so make arrangements well in advance. See the section on hiking for more information on some of this areas.

In early 1995 the State of Hawai'i announced budget cutbacks which would seriously curtail use of state parks and camping activities at them. We will keep you posted in our Update newsletters!

STATE PARKS

Camping permits are available from the State of Hawai'i at (808) 241-3444 or by writing 3060 Eiwa Street, Lihu'e, HI. These permits are free of charge. All campgrounds, except the parks along the Na Pali Coast, are equipped with restrooms, showers, drinking water, fireplaces and picnic tables. Camping is restricted to five consecutive night at each of their parks. The exception is the Na Pali Coast Park/Kalalau Trail where a maximum of five consecutive nights are allowed on the entire trail. During peak season (May through September) applications must be received at least six months in advance and will be issued pending space available. Permits may be obtained through correspondence, however, you must submit xeroxed copies of your identification (passport, driver's license, etc.) for each adult (age 18 or older) and the names and ages of minors in your group. Permits are issued Monday through Friday (except Holidays), 8 am to 4 pm only at the Lihu'e office.

Note that it is unsafe to leave cars at the trail head when hiking into the Na Pali coast area. Hanalei Sea Tours is one operation that can provide camper and hiker drop off service (May through September). Contact them at (808) 826-7254.

These uninhabited valleys on the northern coastline were once the home for hundreds, if not thousands, of Hawaiians. Residents inhabited some of these valleys until the early 1900's and several archaeological studies have been conducted in this region.

Hanakapi'ai
The end of the road on the Northern Coastline is at Na Pali State Park. From there is the launching site for two of Kaua'i's incredible hikes. Be sure to wear good sturdy hiking boots, or if you wear tennis shoes, bring old ones as the dirt and mud will cause permanent staining to your footwear. The trip to Hanakapi'ai Beach can be reached in a day. It is a distance of two miles from Ke'e and may take 1 1/2 to 2 hours to reach. You may find remnants of a fishing village and a farming community which once resided here. Due to the remoteness of this coastline, beach lovers need to use extra caution. Sadly, it is perhaps at the Kalalau Beach that more drownings occur, per visitor, than anywhere else on the island of Kaua'i. As mentioned before, this is a remote wilderness area and help would be a long time in reaching you should you become endangered. As with other north shore beaches, surf and currents are extremely hazardous. Even the Department of Land and Natural Resources recommends you avoid the ocean. A hike to this beach is better in summer when the trail has had time to dry out from spring rains and the ocean is calmer. The trip to the beach will reward the hiker with outstanding coastline vistas. A side trip is to follow the Hanakoa Valley along an unmaintained trail for another two miles to the Hanakapi'ai waterfall. The falls flow down for about 300 feet to the pool below. Avoid swimming beneath the falls, and resist the urge to drink the water (all fresh water in Hawai'i should be purified before drinking). The upper half of this trail is more difficult, with boulders and fallen trees to negotiate and should be hiked only in good weather to avoid the danger of flash floods. It is also advisable that you bring along plenty of mosquito repellent! Contact the State Parks Department for overnight camping permits.

Kalalau State Park

It is an 11 mile trek along the steep cliffs of the Kalalau Trail to Kalalau Beach. Due to the rugged terrain and steep elevations, it may well take an entire day to reach the beach. As you leave Hanakapi'ai Valley, the hiking becomes more strenuous, climbing 800 feet in elevation. After passing through the Ho'olulu and Waiahuakua Valleys you enter the Hanakoa Valley which is home to many native lowland forest plants. Camping is available near the Hanakoa Stream. You may see some coffee plants still growing here. In the late 1800's there were terraces of coffee plants grown here and these cleared areas are now the campsites. There is an unmarked 1/3 mile trail to Hanakoa Falls, but with eroded sections on this unmaintained trail, hiking can be hazardous. The next five miles along the trail is in a region which offers little protection from the sun. Crossing the Kalalau Stream near the mouth of the valley will reward the weary hiker with a small waterfall. Camping is allowed only by this sand beach. During the summer, sea caves just beyond the waterfall can be used as shelter, but during winter and high surf, they are filled with water. An easy two mile trail follows the Kalalau Valley ending at a pool in the stream. The Kalalau Valley was called the Valley of Healing Light by the ancient Hawaiians. Remember to treat all heiaus with respect. The area was inhabited until 1919 and taro was grown. Now the valley is filled with wild Java plum, guava and a mango tree or two. In the late 1960's and early 1970's the area was again populated, this time by hippies. With serious sanitation problems the state implemented a program which limited access to the area by restricting the number of camping permits. Boat and helicopter landings also came under restrictions. Camping is allowed only at the shoreline at Kalalau and water is available for cooking and drinking following purification, i.e. boiling. With no fronting reef and strong currents, it is dangerous to swim here at any time of the year. Hiking is best during the summer months, but it is also more difficult to obtain a permit.

Miloli'i State Park

A part of the Na Pali Coast State Park. Forty acres with restroom picnic, camping and small boat access. Located on Kaua'i's eastern shore. Access only by boat, weather permitting.

Nualolo-kai

No camping until further notice and day use permit is required. It is accessible by small boat only, weather permitting. Many tour boat operators use this oceanfront for snorkeling trips as a part of their Na Pali boat tours. In the late 1950's, Dr. Kenneth Emory working on behalf of the Bishop Museum, began a project to study the Nualolo Kai area. The valley contained all the materials to sustain a substantial population. The bark of the hau tree was used for making twine and this very soft wood was well suited for canoe outriggers and fires. The streams offered fresh water shrimp and along the shore were opiis (limpets) and pipipis (Black shellfish). Salt was gathered from the seas and the kukui tree was useful for a variety of needs of the early Hawaiian. Canoe hulls could be made from the wood of the Kukui and the nuts, high in oil, were strung together made an imperfect, but adequate candle. The bark was also used to dye fishing nets. The pandanus trees leaves (lauhala) were woven into mats. Another tree, the noni, has medicinal properties that were valuable for the early Hawaiians. Robert Krauss, during a trip to visit Dr. Emory in the valley while excavating wrote in his book

Here's Hawai'i the following... the "gnarled tree with the lumpy fruit is the noni. It has medicinal properties. The Hawaiians tied noni leaves over boils for drawing out infection. The green juice from the crushed pulp of a young noni apple, used as a gargle, is good for sore throat. Taken internally it will cure fish poisoning." It is unknown why the Hawaiians left this valley, but Emory speculated it may have been influenced by the arrival of the early missionaries who preferred to have their congregations more centralized.

Polihale State Park
Where the Na Pali meets the west side of Kaua'i is where you'll find Polihale. It is a desert like climate and there are pavilions which offer some shade from the hot rays of sun. Showers, restrooms and barbecues.

Koke'e State Park
The cooler climate of upcountry Kaua'i will give you a very different camping experience compared to the beachfront facilities. Many nearby trails throughout the park offer varied daytime excursions. Hikes range from a .1 mile walk to an overlook of Waimea Canyon to a 3.5 mile trail through forested terrain. Trails into the neighboring forest reserves include Nualolo, Awaawapuhi, Honopu, Pihea and Alakai Swamp Trails.

During June and continuing through September the Koke'e Natural History Museum offers a series of guided hikes in the scenic uplands of West Kaua'i. Hikes (each Sunday and Wednesday), are led by one of the trained volunteers of the Koke'e Natural History Museum's. The hikes vary in length and in difficulty and since space is limited. They ask that you call ahead to reserve your spot. A $2 donation is requested. Tours include a hike along Cliff and Canyon trails to Waipo'o Falls, hikes along the fairly strenuous Pihea Trail or a family hike along Berry Flats Trail. Along the way your interpretative guide will explain about the flora and fauna discovered along your hike.

For information on cabin rentals at Koke'e, contact Koke'e Ventures, PO Box 819, Waimea, HI 96796, (808) 335-6061.

Information on the trails in Koke'e Park can be obtained from the Division of Forestry, Department of Land and Natural Resources, 3060 Eiwa Street, Lihu'e, HI 96766 or write PO Box 1671, Lihu'e, HI 96766. (808) 241-3433.

COUNTY PARKS

Send for an application for camping permit from Kaua'i County (808) 241-6660 or write Parks Permit Section, Department of Public Works, Division of Parks and Recreation, 4193 Hardy Street, Portable #5, Lihu'e, HI 96766. The cost is $3 per adult per night. Children under 18 are free. Upon receipt of your application, your requests will be logged in their reservation book. Permits will be issued one month prior to the first camp date. Thereafter, permits may be obtained when you arrive on Kaua'i. Open 7:45 am - 4:30 pm, Monday through Friday, except holidays. Permits can also be issued by the Park Ranger, at the campsite, for a charge of $5 per adult, per night. Persons wishing to obtain permits after normal business hours should go to the Kaua'i Police Department, 3060 Umi Street, Lihu'e, HI 96766. Permits will be issued at the rate of $3 per adult per night.

Ha'ena Beach Park
Camping is permitted across Ha'ena dry cave, under the trees. The 4.7 acre park has pavilions, toilets, showers, tables, and barbecue grills. Swimming is unsafe here.

Hanalei Beach Park
2.47 acres, toilets, tables, barbecue grill, and swimming. May only be open Fridays, Saturdays and holidays.

'Anini Beach Park
Easy access to campsites makes this a good choice for families. Facilities include a pavilion, restrooms, showers, barbecues and picnic tables.

Hanama'ulu Beach Park
Located 1/2 mile from Hanama'ulu Town. Facilities include tables, toilets, pavilion, barbecue, and showers in this 6.5 acre park. Camping is permitted under the trees in self-contained mobile campers or tents.

Niumalu Beach Park
Located two miles from Lihu'e. Currently closed.

Lucy Wright Park
Campsites can be seen from the main highway on your left. 4.48 acres, toilets, showers.

Salt Pond Beach Park
6 acre park, pavilion, tables, toilets, showers. This campground was closed for a time. Call to see if they are open and allowing campers.

Camping Equipment: Pedal and Paddle Hanalei (808) 826-9069 or Kapa'a (808) 822-2005.

ECO TOURS

Na Pali (Eco) Adventures ★ is dedicating to the understanding and protection of our eco system. Their guided trip along the Na Pali coast is led by a trained naturalist. They use motor-powered, hard-body catamarans that provide a smoother and dryer ride than on the inflatables or rafts, but still plenty of thrills! They have sight seeing cruises only or sightseeing combined with a one hour snorkeling experience at one of several protected bays along the coastline. Snorkel gear and light refreshments are included on this later cruise. The operators are genuinely concerned with the welfare of whales and other aquatic life, and it shows in the way they run their cruise. If the whales are out there, they'll find them. An underwater microphone allows you to hear the whales' musical conversation. In addition to whales (in season), you might also be treated to a pod of dolphins swimming along your boat, green sea turtles floating like huge army helmets upon the water or if you look quickly, you may spot a flying fish. We were fortunate during our excursion to be greeted by Kaua'i's most rare aquatic animal. The monk seal on first sighting appeared to be lounging in the water, however, on the return trip he appeared in another bay, giving us what appeared to be a smile! Realizing that there is estimated to be only three seals living in the waters around Kaua'i, our captain felt that we had seen the same seal twice and that they rarely see them more than a couple times of year. Ours was a lucky trip indeed. Cost is $80 adults, $60 children for snorkel and tour. Sunset tour $60 adults, $40 children. Mini morning sightseeing $60 adults, $40 children. PO Box 1017, Hanalei, HI 96714. (808) 826-6804. FAX (808) 826-7073. 1-800-659-6804.

FISHING

FRESH WATER

Kaua'i offers some diverse fishing options. In addition to ocean excursions you anglers will delight to learn that Kaua'i offers some outstanding freshwater fishing! Area reservoirs are home to several varieties of bass including the peacock bass (otherwise found only in Columbia and Venezuela). Since there is no restocking program, your outfitter will release all fish that are caught.

Several areas are stocked with rainbow trout, although trout season is limited to the first 18 days of August and then only on weekends and holidays through September.

Cast & Catch - They offer fresh water bass guided trips. A 5-hour trip aboard their 17 1/2 foot boat to catch large-mouth bass, peacock bass and small-mouth bass. Beverages and tackle supplied. Hotel and airport pick-up available. A five hour trip is $105 for the first person, $175 for two. (808) 332-9707.

JJ's Big Bass Tour - Sample bass fishing at one of the various reservoirs of Kaua'i. They supply tackle and refreshments along with hotel pick-up. The 17 foot monarch bass boat accommodates up to three people. A half day trip for 1 person is $100, full day $150, 2 persons $150 half day, $200 full day, three persons half day $175, full day $225. PO Box 248, Kalaheo, HI 96742 or (808) 332-9219, pager phone number on Kaua'i 654-4153.

Check with the Division of Aquatic Resources, Department of Land and Natural Resources (808) 241-3400 regarding licensing for freshwater fishing. Also inquire about seasonal trout fishing at Koke'e.

FISHING SUPPLIES:

Lihu'e Fishing Supply (808) 245-4930

Stan's Fishing and Liquor Supplies (808) 335-5212

FISHING

OCEAN

On ocean-going fishing trips, unlike some parts of the country, the captain keeps the fish you catch. Although they will often cut enough for you and your family to enjoy for dinner. You might wish to check with your boat captain/crew before the trip to determine their policy. The cost of a half day trip will run $75-$90.

'Anini Fishing Charters - They charge $75 per person for shared charter for a 1/2 day, $90 for 3/4 day and an eight-hour fishing excursion runs $115. They have 7 trolling lines and bottom fishing available aboard their 30 ft. twin diesel boat. Bob Kutkowski is the owner/operator of Sea Breeze IV. (808) 828-1285

Gent-Lee - They offer 4-6 hour ocean fishing charters aboard their 32' and 36' Sportfisher. Spectators and children under 11 are half price. $90 for 4 hours, $120 for 6 hours. PO Box 1691, Lihu'e, HI 96766. (808) 245-7504, FAX (808) 245-1853.

Liko Kaua'i Cruises - Operates on the northwest side of Kaua'i and offers a mix of fishing combined with sightseeing and snorkeling. (808) 338-0333,

Robert McReynolds Fishing Charters - They offer shared and exclusive charters on their 30' Na Pali style Wilson fishing boat named Ho'omaika'i, which means to make good or thanksgiving. A half day trip is 4-6 hours and runs $85. A full day is $130. Exclusive use is $400 half day, $500 all day. Children under 12 are $65 half day, $110 all day. (808) 828-1379.

Sport Fishing Kaua'i - Operate a 28' Vida Del mar II and 38' Kauai Kai. Half day trip is $90, 3/4 day trip is $120. (808) 742-7013.

True Blue Charters and Ocean Sports - They operate on the east shore (808) 246-6333.

FITNESS CENTERS

Also see "Retreats" in Accommodations section.

Anara Health and Fitness Spa - Located at the Hyatt has a full range of services offered daily between 6 am and 8 pm. Massage, skin care, body care, and fitness facilities. Daily spa facility use for hotel guests is $10 and includes Turkish steam room, Finnish sauna, Swiss shower, open air lava rock shower garden, outdoor whirlpool and jacuzzi, weight room, lap pool, lock room, and fitness activities. (Non-guests charge is $18). The spa facility includes full nail and hair salon along with the Kupono Cafe which features light dining for breakfast and lunch. (808) 742-1234.

Kaua'i Athletic Club - They offer aerobics, racquetball, handball, freeweights, swimming pool, jacuzzi, pro shop, child care and deli. Hours Mon.-Fri. 6 am-10 pm, Sat. and Sun. 8 am - 6 pm. Single day visit $12. One week unlimited use $40, 2 weeks unlimited use $55. One month unlimited use $80. (808) 245-5381.

Prince Health Club and Spa - Located at the Prince Golf and Country Club, on the Northern Shore in Princeville, provides massages and aromatherapy treatments along with their complete health and fitness facility. Passes start at $12 per day; weekly and monthly passes are also available. (808) 826-5030.

FLIGHT SEEING

HELICOPTERS

A helicopter tour will cost $90-130 for a 40-50 minute tour and $140-168 for a 50-65 minute flying experience. We suggest that you wait until mid-way in your island vacation, if not even a little longer, before experiencing the island by helicopter. It is much more interesting to see the island's landmarks by air after first having had a close hand look at them on land.

A helicopter altitude regulation took effect in late October of 1994. While safety was the chief concern for these new guidelines, tour operators voiced their fears that without the close-up experience which visitors have enjoyed for years from a helicopter tour, the industry will be crippled. It was noted that the normal cloud ceiling is about 2,000 feet over the mountainous regions of Hawaii. The regulations require pilots to stay 500 feet below the clouds and 1,500 feet away from valley walls which will eliminate more than 50% of the areas previously visited by helicopter tours. Within a few days of the new regulations, a Papillion helicopter with two passengers lost power at an elevation of 800 feet and made a rough landing to the valley floor of Haleakala on Maui. Only minor injuries were reported by the pilot and passengers. In late November, the Hawaiian Helicopter Operators Association claimed that the Federal Aviation Administration had violated its own rules and they subsequently filed a lawsuit charging that the new regulations had been imposed without first having public input. The FAA's response was that in an emergency situation, no public input is required.

The Helicopter Association projects annual losses to total as much as $50 million. Our Update newsletters will keep you posted as to the final outcome of this legal action.

Helicopters fly around Kaua'i in a clockwise direction, so seating on the right side of the craft offers the best viewing. However, the seat assignment is based on weight and yes, they generally have you step on a scale to make sure you are honest.

Some helicopter companies are owner-operated. Most brochures talk about the owner's flying experience. In some cases, this may not be the person piloting your helicopter tour. In other cases you'll find that it is indeed the owner that operates each and every tour.

Air Kaua'i Helicopter Tours - The brochure for this company states that you'll fly with Chuck DiPiazza the owner. Chuck flies air conditioned A-Stars with custom bubble windows providing exceptional visibility and a two way intercom. Also reported to be the only tour helicopter on Kaua'i equipped with a compact disc player and a special noise cancelling system. Tours begin at a minimum 40 minute flight, which may give you a sample without crimping the pocket book quite as much. (808) 246-4666 1-800-972-4666.

Bali Hai Helicopter Tours - Departs from Port Allen Airport. PO Box 1052, Kalaheo, HI 96741. (808) 335-3166, 1-800-325-TOUR.

Island Helicopters - Flies A-Star helicopters that depart from Lihu'e. PO Box 831, Lihu'e, HI 96766. (808) 245-8588, 1-800-829-5999.

Jack Harter Helicopters - Flies Bell Jet Ranger. Jack originated helicopter tours on Kaua'i. (808) 245-3774.

Na Pali Helicopters - (808) 245-6959

Ni'ihau Helicopters - flies Augusta helicopter, departs from Hanapepe. Cost runs about $235 for a ninety minute flight which circles Ni'ihau and lands briefly on one of the beaches. The Hyatt offers a helicopter tour of Ni'ihau that includes lunch and five hours to enjoy one of the beaches. (NOTE: They don't fly unless they have a full 4 passenger manifest). PO Box 370, Makaweli, HI 96769. (808) 335-3500. FAX (808) 338-1463.

Ohana Helicopter Tours - Flies A-Star and Bell Jet Ranger, departs Lihu'e. 1-800-222-6989 or (808) 245-3996.

Pacific Island Helicopters - Owner/operator Herbert Hood offers a 40 minute island tour, a thirty minute canyon/coast tour or a 60 minute deluxe tour. Their A-Star and Hughes 500D helicopters are equipped with stereo entertainment, intercom and you receive a video of your trip. 1-800-359-3057, (808) 335-3115, FAX (808) 335-5610.

Papillon Helicopters - departs from Lihu'e and Princeville Airports. They fly A-Star helicopters. PO Box 339, Hanalei, HI 96714. (808) 826-6591; 1-800-367-7095, FAX (808) 246-0528. Toll free from neighbor islands 1-800-606-5661.

Safari Helicopters - departs from Lihu'e. Flies A-Star, departs Lihu'e. Preston Myers, owner and pilot, has over 30 years of flying experience. Their three-camera video/sound system with two way intercom captures your actual tour along with your pilot's narration. PO Box 1941, Lihu'e, HI 96766. (808) 246-0136,

South Seas - departs Lihu'e, flies Bell Jet ranger. (808) 245-7781.

Will Squyres Helicopter Tours - Will Squyres began his company in 1984 with twenty-two years of flying experience. He uses a Bell 206B four passenger helicopter with windows that go from the top of your head to your knees and offer great visibility and ventilation. During their 60-65 minute tour you will visit the Waimea Canyon, the Na Pali Coastline, Wai'ale'ale Crater, the famous Jurassic Park waterfall as well as settings used in many other films made on Kaua'i. Cost is $150. They have three pilots. (808) 245-8881 or (808) 245-7541.

AIRPLANE TOURS

Fly Kaua'i - scenic airplane tour in a 5-passenger Cessna 206. They also offer Ni'ihau tours, and charter tours statewide in their nine-passenger Cessna 402. (808) 246-9123.

GOLF

KAUA'I LAGOONS GOLF CLUB
Facilities include a driving range, pro shop, putting green, restaurant and bar. PO Box 3330 Kalapaki Beach, Lihu'e, HI 96766. (808) 241-6000 or 1-800-634-6400.

Kiele Course
This 18-hole, par 72 course is 7,070 yards and was designed by Jack Nicklaus. The course features deep ravines, ocean cliffs and a wedding chapel. Each hole is named for an animal and a white marble statue of the animal adorns each tee. Golf Digest rated this course #3 in Hawai'i and #88 in the United States. With the nearby Kaua'i Lagoons Chapel by the Sea, perhaps this might be the perfect course for the groom-to-be to combine a few holes of golf before or after the ceremony! $145 includes golf cart, on-cart beverages, spa admission and same-day practice facility.

Lagoons Course
Designed by Jack Nicklaus, this 18-hole course, par 72 has 6,942 yards of play. This course is less demanding than Kiele, but the Scottish links style course is popular with the recreational golfer. It has a forgiving layout with wide fairways and four tees for all skill levels. Greens fee $100.

KIAHUNA GOLF CLUB
Located in Poʻipu. Robert Trent Jones, Jr. designed this 18-hole, par 70 course. Kiahuna features ocean and mountain views, as well as some surprises which include lava rock walls, a huge lava tube, a Blind Eye Spider cave and Hawaiian archaeological sites. Championship 6,353 yards. Facilities include driving range, pro shop, putting green, snack shop and bar. $50 per person, $95 for two including cart. 2545 Kiahuna Plantation Drive, Koloa, HI 96756. (808) 742-9595.

KUKUIOLONO GOLF COURSE ★
Located in Kalaheo. This public course is situated on top of Kukuiolono Park and the fourth and fifth holes have spectacular views. This course features ample fairways, a Japanese garden and ancient Hawaiian rock structures. Play is on a first-come basis, no reservations. The 9 holes are a par 36, with 2,981 yards of play. Facilities include a driving range, pro shop, putting green and snack shop. Golf club rentals available. At $6 per nine holes, it is hard to go wrong. This course is usually very crowded. We suggest you tee off about 3 pm: you get through a fair part of the course (and see that spectacular view at the 4th and 5th hole) and for the price it doesn't matter if you don't finish. (808) 335-9940.

MAKAI COURSE
Princeville Resort. Designed by Robert Trent Jones, Jr., this is actually three courses rolled into 27 holes: The Lakes, The Ocean and The Woods are each nine holes, par 36. Facilities include driving range, pro shop, putting green and snackbar. This course is currently rated the #7 course in Hawaiʻi by Golf Digest. $110 regular rate, $90 for Princeville Resort Guests, $80 for hotel guests. PO Box 3040, Princeville, HI 96722. (808) 826-3580.

POʻIPU BAY RESORT GOLF COURSE
Located adjacent to the Hyatt Regency Kauaʻi. This 18-hole, Scottish links style course, with a par 72 was designed by Robert Trent Jones, Jr. It has been described as the "Pebble Beach of the South Pacific." This course boasts an archeological site that has been incorporated into the course and some outstanding

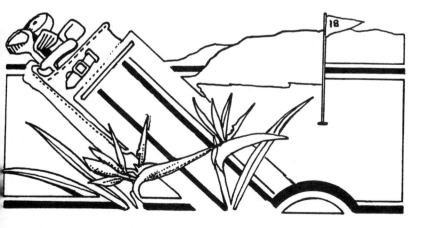

ocean vistas. During winter, golfers can even catch glimpses of the whales as they pass off-shore. Facilities include a driving range, pro shop, clubhouse, putting green and practice sand bunkers. Hyatt Regency guests $85; others $120. Includes golf cart and range balls. Club rental $20. 2250 Ainako St., Koloa, HI 96756. (808) 742-8711.

PRINCE COURSE ★
Princeville Resort. The Prince Golf Course opened in 1990, designed by Robert Trent Jones Jr. The 18-holes are a par 72 with 7,309 yards of play. Scenic vistas include the rugged cliffsides and the famous "Bali Hai" location. The course fits snugly along the cliffsides of Kaua'i's North Shore. With one hole featuring a waterfall as a backdrop. With a USGA course rating of 75.3, this course is ranked as the most challenging in the state. However, multiple tees on each hole accommodate the casual golfer as well. Driving range, pro shop, putting greens, restaurant and bar are available. Golf Digest currently rates this course #1 in the state of Hawai'i and #43 in the United States. The Makai Course runs $100 standard, $90 if you are a guest at a property at Princeville, $80 if you are a guest at the Princeville Hotel. The Prince Course charges $140 standard, $95 for Princeville area guests and $85 for Princeville Hotel guests. PO Box 3040, Princeville, HI 96722. (808) 826-3580, 1-800-826-4400.

WAILUA MUNICIPAL GOLF COURSE
18-holes, 440 yards, par 72. Considered by some to be the best municipal course in the state, it is located on the eastern shore in Kapa'a. With shaded ponds, Pacific ocean views and a very low greens fee, this may be a great option for the budget traveler. Facilities include a driving range, pro shop, putting green, restaurant and bar. $25 weekday, $35 on weekends, and $14 for the cart. Write: 3-5351 Kuhio Hwy., Lihu'e, HI 96766. (808) 241-6666.

HANG GLIDING

Birds in Paradise is an opportunity to experience hang glider ultralight flying. Tandem instructional tours are offered in these powered ultralights and a wing mounted video is available of your flight. (808) 822-5309. (808) 639-1067.

HAWAIIAN CANOE ADVENTURES

Hanalei Beach Boys - They offer an adventure in Hanalei River and Bay. The two hour tour includes legends and folklore history of the area as well as scenic points of interest. Morning, afternoon and sunset tours available. Call (808) 826-9000.

HIKING

Also see section on Camping in this chapter for detailed information on several hiking trails.

The Hawaii State Department of Land and Natural Resources, Division of Forestry, has free trail and wildlife maps. You will need to send a self-addressed stamped envelope with your request and a small fee for handling. Call or write for requirements to the Department of Land and Natural Resources, Division of

Forestry and Wildlife, 3060 Eiwa St., #306, Lihu'e, HI 96766. (808) 241-344. Contact them about the Na Pali Coast Trail at the same address or phone (808) 241-3445.

Kayak Kaua'i Outfitters - They have fully outfitted hiking and camping tours. Hiking trips are a combination of hiking and/or kayaking and/or biking and last a single day or up to six days. The botanical ramble is a one day Natural History tour. It includes day packs, rain gear, lunch and refreshments. About a five hour trek with fairly easy hiking, a chance to swim, so pack a suit $75. Secret Falls is also a one day tour, this one to the Wailua River and waterfall. This is five hours of easy hiking and paddling and suitable for all ages at a cost of $75. The ancient Na Pali Quest is a guided six day paddling, camping and hiking expedition, offered only May through September at $175 per person per day; Madame Pele's Sojourn is a six day guided hike of the Na Pali coast available all year. Suitable only for those persons in very good shape. $150 per person per day. Kapa'a (808) 822-9179, Hanalei (808) 826-9844, toll free 1-800-437-3507.

Humberto Blanco runs a Bed & Breakfast along with another business called Healing Arts Exchange Network. He has combined the two into Healing Paradise Adventures. Accommodations combined with a 6-8 day tour. Their outdoor adventures are combined with an opportunity to learn and practice the elements of yoga, body/mind techniques, meditation and massage. You can also arrange for a one-day custom tour for $75 per person. (808) 823-0705.

The Sierra Club also publishes a quarterly newsletter, the Malama, available by subscription for $7 per year at the above Sierra Club address. Visitors can write to the Kaua'i group a couple of months prior to their arrival and request a schedule by sending a self addressed stamped envelope and a $1 fee. Bob Nishek on Kaua'i (808) 822-9238, has offered to provide our readers with the latest hiking information. Advance registration is necessary for all outings in the event of last minute changes due to inclement weather. They suggest a $3 donation for each person participating in the outings.

Several excellent references are available for the interested hiker. See ordering information at the back of this guide. Craig Chisholm is the author of *Kaua'i Hiking Trails, Hawaiian Hiking Trails* and *Hawai'i: The Big Island Hiking Trails*. His guides provide excellent topographical maps, good directions and detailed information including the number of calories you can expect to burn, time required to travel the trail round trip and elevation.

During June and continuing through September the Koke'e Natural History Museum offers a series of guided hikes in the scenic uplands of West Kaua'i. Hikes, each Sunday and Wednesday, will be led by one of the trained volunteers of the Koke'e Natural History Museum's. The hikes vary in length and in difficulty and since space is limited, call ahead to reserve your spot. A $2 donation is requested. Tours include a hike along cliff and canyon trails to Waipo'o Falls, hikes along the fairly strenuous Pihea trail or a family hike along Berry Flats Trail. Along the way your interpretative guide will explain about the flora and fauna discovered along your hike.

Since the most exercise Dona is willing to do is to turn over in the sun, she sent her friend, Gary Thurman, out to hike the Kalalau Trail. Then after 13 miles, she made him write about it! Here is the review!

Kalalau Trail
This time-worn trail of eleven miles starts next to Ke'e Beach at the end of Hwy. 56. There you will find parking, bathrooms and showers. A sign at the beginning of the trail will provide you with all the pertinent information you will need for your hike. (Maps, permits, mileage, restrictions, etc.) The first two miles/one hour to Hanakapi'ai and additional 1.8 miles/45 minutes to Hanakapi'ai Falls is as far as most people go. Though this hike is relatively short, it is strenuous so it is advisable to bring your own drinking water and snacks. The first half of the Kalalau Trail is more lush with many native plants interspersed with wild orchids and ginger along with papaya and mango trees. Ancient terraced rock walls used for taro-growing are visible and in surprisingly good shape. Then further along this pristine coast, there are prehistoric valleys of green velvet, cascading waterfalls, ancient Hawaiian heiaus, turquoise water and ominous sea cliffs. During whale season, these magnificent creatures can be spotted from the trail as they breech out of the water. All along the coast there are beautiful vistas from many promontories all the way into Kalalau. This final destination has a refreshing waterfall for bathing. Hikers venturing on from Hanakapi'ai will need overnight camping permits which you can get from the State Parks Office.

Following is the Awaawapuhi Trail, one of twenty-nine trails in *Kaua'i Hiking Trails*, reprinted here with permission. Author Craig Chisholm comments that this trail is a bit more effort than some, but "it is well-marked and the view at its end is, in my opinion, the most impressive in Hawai'i." This trail is located in the Koke'e area. The trail is 2 1/4 hours up and 1 1/2 hours down. The round trip on this trail will travel 6.5 miles. Highest point is 4100 feet, lowest point 2560 feet. While this trail may be a bit rugged for the family travel with younger children, there are many other trails outlined in Chisholm's that are less strenuous and of shorter duration.

Awaawaphui

Awesome views of the Na Pali Coast and its isolated, hanging valleys make this trail one of the best for photography in Hawai'i. The trail descends 1500 feet through native dryland forests to twin viewpoints above the sheer cliffs dropping into the remote Awaawapuhi and Nualolo Valleys. The floors of these rarely visited valleys are accessible only by water and then only after difficult climbing from the sea. However, the viewpoints provide good vantage points of the valleys and the great fluted walls enclosing them. The sight is memorable, especially, if you sit at the viewpoints and watch the sunlight and shadows play on the cliffs and sea near dawn. Every morning helicopters flutter like dragonflies in and out of the steep-cliffed valleys below. The Division of Forestry and Wildlife has marked many endemic plants along the route and has published an interpretive guide to them available at the divisions's office in Lihu'e or the Kokee Museum.

Route: From Koke'e State Park Headquarters go 1.6 miles up Highway 550 toward the Kalalau Lookout. The trail-head is on the left, in the Na Pali-Kona Forest Reserve, across from a dirt road and just before the 17-mile mark on the Highway. At first the broad trail leads north and goes up a little. It them descends switchbacks, generally in a northwesterly direction. Along the way there are many numbered and labelled endemic bushes and trees. At approximately 3 miles form the start, the Nualolo Cliff Trail, which is a connector from the Nualolo Trail, leads in from the left (south). Soon after this junction, the Awaawapuhi Trail ends at the metal-railed viewpoints overlooking the sea, great cliffs, white-trailed tropic birds, and the inevitable 8 a.m. helicopters. Do not go close to the rims of the canyons. The small stones covering the hard surfaces on the eroded areas, like ball bearings on concrete, provide treacherous footing. The drop to the valley floor on either side is between 1500 and 3000 feet, depending on the bounce. The plants in the native dryland forest are rare and the danger of fires extreme; thus, neither overnight camping nor fires are permitted. Water is unavailable.

For a small fee, The Sierra Club, Hawaii Chapter, will send you an information packet describing state trails and trip-planning information. The current cost for their *"Hiking Softly in Hawai'i"* brochure is $4. Write them at their O'ahu address, Sierra Club, Hawai'i Chapter, PO Box 2577, Honolulu, HI 96803. The Honolulu phone number is (808) 538-6616. You can write to their local chapter at PO Box 3412, Lihu'e, HI 96766.

HORSEBACK RIDING

Horseback riders are afforded the opportunity to enjoy some of Kaua'i's most breathtaking scenery. On the north shore, you can take a four-hour ride to a mountain waterfall. Near Waimea, visitors can enjoy the island's only oceanrides while watching the sun sinking slowly over the island of Ni'ihau. At Po'ipu Beach, a three hour breakfast trail ride encompasses scenic views of the ocean beaches and mountains.

C.J.M. Country Stables - Owner Jimmy Miranda and his crew will take you into hidden valley ranch land, past secluded beaches and bays to discover the picturesque beauty of Hawai'i on horseback. Rides are suited for the beginning as well as the more experienced rider. Restricts include a weight limit of 250 pounds, an age limit of over 7 years and enclosed shoes are required. A three-hour ride with breakfast runs $68. A two-hour hidden beach ride departs at 10 am and lasts approximately 2 hours. Afternoon rides also offered. On Sundays they have a 10 am rodeo offered once a month and its free!   Po'ipu (808) 742-6096. $40-$65

Po'oku Stables - A maximum of six riders. Minimum age is 8 years. Their waterfall picnic ride lasts approximately four hours. Lunch is included. Guests can swim in the waterfall pond if they'd like. The outing includes a short steep hike (without the horse) down to the base of the falls. All riders must be in good physical condition. Weight limit restrictions, 180 lbs. for women, 220 pounds for men. $95 per person plus tax. Their Hawaiian country ride is a 1 1/2 hour trip across ranch land with views of the Hanalei Mountains, the taro fields of the Hanalei Valley and Pacific vistas. Cost is $50 per person plus tax. PO Box 888, Hanalei, HI 96714. (808) 826-6777.

HUNTING

For hunting on Kaua'i contact the Department of Land & Natural Resources, Division of Wildlife 241-3446 regarding procedures to be licensed and hunting guidelines.

The Travel Company on Kaua'i can assist you with organizing a hunting trip to any of the islands. (808) 246-2644.

Ni'ihau Safari, Ltd. Exclusive full day hunting of wild boar and feral sheep on the privately owned island of Ni'ihau. (808) 335-3500. FAX (808) 338-1463.

WILD BOAR

JET SKIING

This water recreational activity is not permitted on Kaua'i.

KAYAKING

With its many navigable rivers, Kaua'i is a jewel for the kayaker. You can choose an adventure on your own, take a guided tour, or go with a group expedition. There are sea kayaking adventures to be enjoyed, but they are recommended for the experienced kayaker or with a guided excursion group.

If you should have the question on your next game of trivial pursuit, "How many rivers are there on Kaua'i?" you could answer five, six, seven or nine and probably be correct. After exhaustive research and pure conjecture, we decided that it depends on the weather and who you ask. The problem seems to be the determination of just what is a stream and what is a river. A river is usually considered larger than a stream, but how much larger? After a heavy rain, a stream may certainly look river-like. The Hawai'i Visitors Bureau, Parks and Recreation Department and various maps and guidebooks all have their own answer. The Hawaii Visitors Bureau goes with seven. It seems there are five that can be agreed upon as being "rivers" by most of these sources: Waimea, Hanapepe, Wailua, Hanalei and Wainiha. The others are more often called streams: Lumaha'i, Huleia, Kalihiwai and Makaweli. However, the Huleia and Kalihiwai are referred to by some as rivers.

In any case, there are several streams/rivers perfect for kayaking: The Waimea, Hanapepe, Huleia, Wailua, Kalihiwai and Hanalei. Each can be navigated for only about three miles. The Waimea River, Kaua'i's longest, can be accessed in Waimea at the Lucy Wright Park. This is the location where Captain James Cook first set foot in the islands in 1778. Each river has its own personality and differing picturesque scenery. The Huleia River passes the Haupu Ridge with views of the Hoar Head mountains, as well as passing by the "Menehune" Fish Pond and the Huleia National Wildlife Refuge. The Kalihiwai River/Stream, with its mouth at Kalihiwai Bay near Princeville, travels through lowland areas of Kaua'i. The Hanalei River twists through the valley past fields of taro. The Wailua River is accessible from Wailua State Park and you can reach and enjoy Fern Grotto State Park along the banks.

Depending on the seasons and surf, sea kayaking locations will vary. In the summer months, the north shore may often be calm and perfect for various skill levels of kayakers. The Na Pali coast trip is a 16-mile kayak adventure and can be accomplished in one day or more, depending on weather conditions and camping permit availability. In the winter, the southern shore offers many options.

For more information, pick up a copy of *Paddling Hawaii* by Audrey Sutherland at local bookstores.

KAYAK RENTALS AND KAYAK GUIDED TOURS

You may choose to enjoy a kayak guided tour, or rent equipment and explor one of Kaua'i's beautiful rivers at your own pace.

Hawayaking - They offer Hanalei River guided tour runs twice daily with a party of six maximum for each trip. Departs at 9:30 am and 12:30 pm. (808) 826-9195.

Island Adventure: Kaua'i by Kayak - They have two and one-half hour guided tours down the Huleia River past the Menehune Fishponds. Trips begin near the Nawiliwili small boat harbor and run Monday through Friday at 8:45 am and 12:45 pm. $42 per person. Snacks and refreshments included. PO Box 3370, Lihu'e, HI 96766. (808) 245-9662.

Kaua'i Water Ski and Surf - Kayaks are among the variety of equipment available for rent. Located at a concession at the Wailua River State Park. Self-guided tours up the Wailua River to Fern Grotto are available. Single or two-person kayaks rentals (808) 822-3574.

Kayak Kaua'i Outfitters - Their one day or multiple day guided tours are available year round. They can be geared for the active adventurer or for the whole family. Sea kayaking year round, 3 hour guided tour of the Hanalei River National Wildlife Refuge & Bay snorkel $45; bicycle beach cruise $45; one day botanical ramble or Secret Falls trip, a hiking and/or paddling tour $75; summer Na Pali sea kayak voyage $125; Kipu Kai, one-day sea kayaking and whale watching $100; rent and paddle your own canoe to Fern Grotto $48 per couple. For the more dedicated, there is the six day sea kayak and highland trek, offered October through April. This adventure is $175 per person per day and only for the trekker in good physical condition. Kapa'a (808) 822-9179, Hanalei (808) 826-9844, toll free 1-800-437-3507.

Outfitters Kaua'i - Owners Rick and Julie Haviland have one and two person kayaks, sea kayaks, river kayaks, surf kayaks, and even dive kayaks. Information and maps on kayaking locations are provided. Novice kayakers are directed to river locations, experienced kayakers can rent kayaks for ocean trips. Guided tours can be half or full day outings. Na Pali tours are offered only during the summer. Po'ipu. 2827A Po'ipu Rd., Po'ipu Beach, HI 96756. (808) 742-966. FAX (808) 742-9667.

Paradise River Rentals - They are located at the Kilohana Planation in Lihu'e. They offer self-guided tours of Kaua'i's six top kayaking rivers. Kayak rentals also include safety equipment, maps, a cooler, picnic tarp. One or two person kayaks available. (808) 245-9580.

Pedal and Paddle - They offer summertime guided trips of Na Pali. River trips are self-guided. Daily rentals of single and two-person kayaks available. Hanalei (808) 826-9069 or Kapa'a (808) 822-2005.

LAND TOURS

Grayline - Four trips available for sightseeing on Kauaʻi. A full day canyon and river tour, Waimea Canyon and Kalalau Valley Lookout tour, Wailua River/Fern Grotto tour, and a tour of Hanalei. (808) 245-3344.

Kauaʻi Mountain Tours - These mountain van tours travel in a 4 X 4. Half day adult tour $55, child $38. Full day tour including lunch runs $78 adults, $55 children. Daily tours include a picnic lunch. Tours will take you beyond the normal land excursions in their twelve passenger air-conditioned buses. PO Box 3069, Lihuʻe, HI 96766. (808) 245-7224. 1-800-452-1113.

Kauaʻi Paradise Tours - Island sightseeing in 6 passenger van to Waimea/Kalalau or the North Shore. $62 includes a six hour tour and picnic. Narration available in English or German with owner/tour guide Max Dereyl. PO Box 3927, Lihuʻe, HI 96766. (808) 246-3999, FAX (808) 245-2499.

Robert's Hawaii - This company uses vans and full size buses for sightseeing around the island. (808) 245-9558 or 1-800-767-7551.

Trans Hawaiian - Three trips available: 1) Hanalei and Haena Tour visits the Wailua River and its ancient temples, Opaekaa Falls, Kilauea Lighthouse and Refuge, Lumahai Beach, Hanalei Bay, the wet and dry caves at Haena and Keʻe Beach $29-46.25. 2) Waimea Canyon Tour which tours Nawiliwili Harbor, the Menehune Fishponds, Russian Fort Elizabeth, Waimea Town, Waimea Canyon, Kalalau Valley Lookout and Spouting Horn $36.25-61.25. 3) Waimea Canyon/Wailua River Tour is a full day trip that circles the island from the Eastern shore to the Northern $55.50-68.75. Prices quoted vary depending on pick-up location. Ask about children and senior citizen discounts. (808) 245-5108.

LUAUS See chapter on Restaurants.

CHRIST MEMORIAL CHURCH, KILAUEA

MOVIES/MOVIE RENTALS

The Coconut Plantation Cinemas in Wailua is a dual theater. (808) 822-9391.

Gilligan's at the Outrigger has free movies each Wednesday that were filmed on or are associated with Kaua'i. Phone (808) 245-1955.

Kaua'i Film Festival: call the County Information office at (808) 245-2313 for upcoming schedule.

Kukui Grove Cinemas has two screens in their theater adjoining the Kukui Grove Shopping Center. Phone (808) 245-5055 to hear a recording.

The Princeville Hotel has complimentary movies for hotel guests shown four times daily in their small, private cinema.

If you have a VCR at your accommodation, there are plenty of options for renting movies. If you don't have a machine you can rent one of those as well. Block Buster videos is the biggest chain on the island. They have their main outlet at 4-771 Kuhio Hwy. at Waipouli Town Center in the mall next to Foodland. Their rentals are for three days and they do have drop off boxes at other places around the island. It is about $5 for a three-day rental. Waipouli Town Center location (808) 822-7744. Other video stores are scattered around the island including Shaka Video in Waimea, Hanalei Video and Music in Hanalei, Jack Wada Electronics in Lih'ue and Kaua'i Video in Lihu'e, Kalaheo and Waimea. About the least expensive rentals we found were at Safeway in Kapa'a.

MUSEUMS/GARDEN TOURS/CULTURAL TOURS

Kaua'i offers some of the finest garden and cultural tours in the Hawaiian chain. Be sure to find time to take in at least one of the following varied options.

The *National Tropical Botanical Garden* ★ is a nationally-chartered non-profit organization that is actually made up of five separate gardens. Three are on Kaua'i, one is on Maui and another is located in Florida. Each of the gardens has an individual name, however they are sometimes incorrectly referred to as simply the "National Tropical Botanical Garden."

The Lawa'i Garden (National Tropical Botanical Garden Headquarters Garden) is located on Kaua'i's southern shore in the lush Lawa'i Valley, and was the first garden site to be acquired by the National Tropical Botanical Garden. The NTBG headquarter facilities are located adjacent to the Lawa'i Garden. The headquarters complex includes a scientific laboratory, a herbarium housing nearly 30,000 specimens of tropical plants, an 8,000 volume research library, a computer records center, an educational center, and offices for staff and visiting scientists.

Lawa'i Garden is a research and educational garden that comprises 186 acres. The garden's extensive collections include tropical plants of the world that are of particular significance for research conservation, or cultural purposes. Special emphasis is given to rare and endangered Hawaiian species and to economic

278

plants of the tropical world. Three Springs is at the interior of the Lawaʻi Garden (located makai or toward the mountains). This 120 acre area was acquired as a bequest to the Garden. As yet undeveloped, *Three Springs* will eventually be designed as an additional garden section, emphasizing the beautiful natural land and water features. PO Box 340 Lawaʻi, Kauaʻi, HI 96765. Phone (808) 332-7324. FAX (808) 332-9765.

The nearby *Allerton Garden* is located oceanfront at Lawaʻi-Kai, adjacent to the Lawaʻi Garden. This was formerly a private 100 acre estate. The beautifully designed garden is managed by the National Tropical Botanical Garden pursuant to an agreement with the Allerton Estate Trust. In the 1870's Queen Emma, the widow of Hawaiian King Kamehameha IV, began the garden during her visit to Kauaʻi. The gardens were lovingly developed and expanded over a period of 50 years by Robert Allerton and his son John. Robert Allerton, a millionaire from Chicago, purchased the McBryde Estate at Lawaʻi Kai in 1937. He and his son John Gregg Allerton converted the lower valley into expansive gardens. The sculpted gardens contain numerous plants of interest, outstanding examples of garden design and water features, as well as Queen Emma's original summer cottage. The cottage was severely damaged by Hurricane Iniki and plans for restoration are underway.

Reservations are required for tours of the Lawaʻi and Allerton Gardens. Tour fee is currently $25. The tour is primarily of the Allerton Gardens, but a little of the Lawaʻi Gardens is also included in the two and one-half hour tour. They are developing different tours and prices. For information on scheduled tours and reservations, call (808) 332-7361. PO Box 340 Lawaʻi, HI 96765.

Grove Farm Homestead ★ in Lihuʻe is an example of the old style of plantation living. This was the plantation home of George N. Wilcox until 1978. A fascinating two and one half hour tour is given. This is, in our opinion, the best cultural tour on the island. Tours by advance reservation only. Admission $5. Currently tours are offered Monday, Wednesday, and Thursday 10 am and 1:10 pm. Call to verify schedule. (808) 245-3202.

There are 480 acres of guava orchards under commercial cultivation at the *Guava Kai Plantation* in Kilauea, which is considered the Guava Capitol of the world. Visit the plantation's visitor center and discover how guava is grown and processed into a variety of treats. Guava has fewer calories and more vitamin C than oranges, and it is also a good source of vitamin A, potassium and phosphorus. Guava is actually not a citrus, it is a berry with a fleshy seed cavity and a thick skin. The guava can survive in dry or very tropical conditions. The Kilauea orchards receive 100 inches of rainfall each year with a temperate 65-80 degree weather that is very agreeable to this crop. During dry months each tree receives up to 75 gallons of water per day. The seedlings were planted in this orchard in 1977 and began producing fruit in 1979. The first commercial yield was in January of 1980 with a 2,000 pounds per acre harvested. Today the yield is 5,000 pounds per acre or about 400 pounds of fruit per tree per harvest cycle. The fruit at this plantation is hand-picked and harvested year round on a full-scale crop cycling system. The fruit meat can vary from white or yellow to orange or pink.

The variety grown at the Guava Kai Plantation is a hybrid developed by the University of Hawai'i's College of Tropical Agriculture and has bright pink flesh and an edible rind. The color in your glass of juice is all natural. The guava was a native of South America and it was introduced islands in 1791 by the Spaniard Don Francisco de Paula Marin, who was an advisor to Kamehameha I. The guava flourished and many now grow wild in Hawaii. There is a self guided tour that includes a view of the orchard and the processing plants as well as an informative eight minute video. There is a man-made fish pond and an assortment of native Hawaiian plants to enjoy as your stroll the grounds. The snack bar, open only in the summer months, sells ice cream, juice, breads and other bakery items made with guava. There are free samples of guava juice, jams, jellies and coffee. Since they are owned by Maunaloa, they also sell their products at slightly lower rates than retail outlets. Guava Kai Plantation is open 9 am - 5 pm. (808) 828-6121.

The family owned and operated business, **Kamokila Hawaiian Village** in Wailua, sustained serious damage from Hurricane Iniki. They have been busy recreating the original site of Kamokila and you can visit ruins and petroglphys. Nineteen huts were destroyed and they have been rebuilt. All are different and have a different cultural significance. For instance, there is the medicine huts, assistant chief's, canoe, etc. Visitors can watch them make poi or try samples, make haku leis and watch salt making (like that done at the salt ponds.) The taro fields have been refurbished and there are fifteen peacocks on the grounds along with a new road to the village and a boat shuttle. Located opposite Opaekaa Falls, the Kaumo'o Road entrance is just past the Wailua Bridge. Admission is $5 adults, $3 children.

The **Kaua'i Museum** is located in downtown Lihu'e. Through murals, artifacts and artwork, discover how the islands have changed since Captain Cook's arrival at Waimea in 1778. The Museum Shop specializes in Hawaiian Island memorabilia, Hawaiian books, and local crafts. They also have rotating exhibits so there will be something new and different every time you visit. Open weekdays 9 am - 4:30 pm, Saturday 9 - 1 pm, closed Sunday. The first Saturday of the month is free admission day and it features special family events and activities. Admission $5, children under 17 are free, senior admission $4.00 (808) 245-6931.

The **Kaua'i Historical Society Museum** at the Coco Palms Resort remains closed as the resort hotel has not been re-opened since Hurricane Iniki.

Kiahuna Plantation offers free self-guided tours of their **Moir Gardens** or guided tours. Call for current day and time this tour is given. Phone (808) 742-6411.

Kilohana is reminiscent of the grandeur and elegance of an earlier age. At the time when sugar was king on the island and prosperity reigned, plantation owners would build luxurious homes. One of the grandest on Kaua'i was the home of Gaylord Parke Wilcox and is known as Kilohana. Built in 1935, it was designed by a British architect named Mark Potter. The grounds were carefully landscaped and inside furniture arrived from the exclusive and expensive Gump's in San Francisco. In addition to the gift shops, galleries, and Gaylord's Courtyard Restaurant you'll find several tour options for this 35 acre estate. The Canefield Tour is a step back into the history of sugar cane on Kaua'i. A horsedrawn wagon helps return you in time to 1835. The Carriage Ride is a romantic excursion around the grounds. They are offered daily 11 am - 6:30 pm. Horse drawn Sugar Cane Tours are set up by advance reservations, 246-9529. Admission to Kilohana and the beautiful grounds is free, carriage rides are $7 adults, $4 children. Sugar Cane Tours are $18 adults, $10 children and are offered at 11 am and 2 pm, Tuesday, Thursday and Saturday. (Check the entertainment book for a Cane Tour discount coupon). Kilohana and the shops open daily at 9:30 am. Gaylord's serves brunch Saturday and Sunday 9:30 am - 3 pm, lunch Mon.-Friday 11 am - 3 pm and dinner from 5 pm. Located just outside Lihu'e, travel east along Kaumualii Highway, Route 50. Kilohana is on your left just before the town of Lihu'e. If you are arriving from the north or east, travel Kuhio Hwy., Route 56 south and west through Lihu'e. Bear right at the traffic light at the end of Kuhio Hwy. Kilohana will be 1.4 miles down Kaumualii Highway on your right.

Koke'e Natural History Museum contains geographic maps of Kaua'i along with exhibits of native plant and bird species. Admission is free, but donations are accepted. (808) 335-9975.

The *Limahuli Gardens*, in Haena, on Kaua'i's north shore is an area of overwhelming natural beauty. Located one-half mile past the nine-mile marker on Kuhio Highway #560, this is another branch of the National Tropical Botanical Garden (NTBG). The NTBG is a privately funded, non-profit organization. It is the nation's only tropical botanical garden chartered by the U.S. Congress. Headquartered on Kaua'i, its principal mission is research, conservation and education relating to the world's tropical plants. The NTBG consists of five distinct gardens in the Hawaiian Islands and in Florida. Three gardens are on Kaua'i, Lawa'i, Allerton and Limahuli, and one is on Maui. This lush garden offers a walking tour that leads you uphill through a 15-acre garden and forest to a beautiful viewpoint overlooking the ocean. You will see ancient taro terraces, many of the plants introduced to Hawai'i by the early Polynesians, as well as

KILOHANA

plantings of native Hawaiian species and the pristine Limahuli Stream. Their guided tours are 1 1/2 - 2 hours long. A self-guided tour is available and you also need to allow a couple of hours. Advanced reservations are required for all tours and they request that visitors meet promptly for their tours. If you must cancel your reservation, they request a phone call at least two hours in advance of your scheduled tour. All visitors are met by the National Tropical Botanical Garden staff at the garden's entrance. Parking area and restroom facilities are available. Picnic lunches are not allowed on the grounds. Guided tours are offered Tuesday at 1 pm and Sundays at 10 am at a cost of $15. Self-guided tours are available for $10 per person on Tuesdays at 10 am, Wednesdays at 10 am and 1 pm, Thursdays at 10 am and 1 pm, and Sundays at 1 pm. Phone 826-1053 for information.

Olu Pua Gardens and Plantation Estate is located in on the way to Waimea Canyon, one mile past Kalaheo. This plantation estate was once the residence for the Alexander family back in the 1930's and designed by Hawai'i's foremost architect, C.W. Dickey. The Alexander family ancestors first arrived in the islands as missionaries, later founding Kaua'i's largest pineapple plantation. The estate is located on twelve acres. Admission is $10. Their one hour tour is offered daily, every hour between 9:30 and 2:30.

Wai'oli Mission House was the home of island missionaries Abner and Lucy Wilcox. This 19th century New England-style home was shipped in pieces from Boston around Cape Horn to Kaua'i. The home features beautiful koa wood furniture and other items from the period. Open to the public Tuesday, Thursday and Saturday from 9 am - 3 pm. Wai'oli Mission House Museum in Hanalei was built of coral limestone blocks in 1837. Guided tours are available at no charge. Donations Accepted. PO Box 1631, Lihu'e, HI 96766. (808) 245-3202.

POLO

Polo season begins in late April and runs through September. Mathces are held each Sunday at the 'Anini Polo Field, 3 pm. The field is located across the road from 'Anini Beach.

RIVER EXCURSIONS

Also see section on Kayaking. Small motor boats available for rent from Paradise River Rentals (808) 245-9580.

Smith's Tropical Paradise cruises up the Wailua river to the famous Fern Grotto. Trips operate every day, every half hour starting at 9 am. Last boat departs at 2:30 pm or 3:30 pm, depending on the day of the week. Trip duration is 1 hour and 20 minutes. Current schedule is departures at 9 am, 10:30 am, 1 pm, 2 pm and 2:30 pm. On Monday, Wednesday and Friday a later 3:30 departure is offered. $10, children under 12 $5. (808) 822-4111.

RUNNING

Kaua'i has no official running organization, but if you're interested in joining a Sunday morning jogging group or would like to find a jogging partner, call Dave Walker at 338-1475. If you'd like to know more about marathons or running events, see the EVENTS section of this guide or try calling the Kaua'i Athletic Club, Footlockers or Dan's Sports as they usually have entry forms for any current running events.

SCUBA DIVING

Scuba divers can explore the General Store, a 65-80 foot deep reef with a variety of marine life and a 19th century steamship, or the Sheraton Caves which has interesting lava formations and plenty of green sea turtles. At Koloa Landing, divers might discover bottles or fittings from old whaling ships and parts of the train track that once ran between Koloa and the area's sugar mill. On the North Shore there are underwater lava tubes and archways. While on the eastern shore divers can explore the wreck of the Lukenbach, a German freighter that sank 40 years ago. Off Ni'ihau are 130 foot deep reef walls with abundant marine life, considered by some to be the best diving in Hawai'i.

Popular shore diving beaches include Makua Beach (Tunnels) on the North Shore, and on the southern shore Koloa Landing and Prince Kuhio Park in Poi'pu.

If you'd like to do an introductory scuba dive, a boat dive on Kaua'i will run you $70-90. Shore dives are available from several dive companies. Dive Certification takes several days and some offer PADI while others NAUI. The cost of certification on Kaua'i runs $295-$425. You can do some of your basic PADI and NAUI certification before you leave home, and then arrive on Kaua'i for final dive and certification. Check with the dive shops regarding their policy on this. A few dive companies offer prescription masks. Most of them offer a 3 tank dive to Ni'ihau, a little steep, but quite an adventure to a reef wall, $175-$215. One dive shop suggested that visitors with limited time do "PADI" dive preparation on the mainland and they can then be certified on Kaua'i in just two days. Classes are generally no more than 6 persons, or if you prefer private lessons, they run slightly more. The following dive companies (except for Sunrise) rent gear for the day. $30-$65.

Adventures West - The west side's only diving facility is located at 9633 Kaumualii Highway, Waimea, HI 96796. (808) 338-1662 or FAX (808) 338-0838. Excursions are available for half day, full day, night dives or snorkeling trips. They dive along the leeward and northwest coasts of the island.

Aquatic Adventures - Boat and shore dives, introductory, retail sales. (808) 822-1434.

Bay Island - offers NAUI and PADI scuba certification. They have daily guided snorkel and scuba tours as well as rentals. Located on the beach at the Princeville Hotel, they conduct their dives from the shore. (808) 826-7509.

Bubbles Below - offers scuba charters that specialize in marine biology. Their 35 ft. vessel, Kaimanu, takes out only 6 divers at a time. They do a variety of dives including a multi-level drift dive. Also available are night dives. They do Ni'ihau dives but warn that the rougher channel conditions make this trip only for the hardy and the 20 mile open ocean crossing usually takes an hour to go across and an hour and a half to come back. This includes three tanks at three different locations. This trip is only available Saturdays, April - October. If you are interested in underwater photography, they have a professional camera system and they charge $50 for a roll of 24 photos with negatives included. Night/Twilight dives are 2 tank dives for $85. Morning or afternoon dives are four hour trips and are a 2 tank dive at two locations. Rental equipment is available for rent: wetsuit $5, regulator $5, buoyancy compensator $5, mask/fins/snorkel/boots $5, complete package $15. The all day Ni'ihau trip is $200. Owners Linda and Ken Bail have years of experience. Linda began her scuba diving experience at age six and has instructed divers since 1977 as a NAUI course director and PADI master scuba diver trainer. Ken has been a NAUI instructor and PADI master scuba diver trainer since 1982. They share their love for the marine environment and include the marine ecosystem in their briefing. 6251 Hauaala Rd., Kapa'a, HI 96746. (808) 822-3483.

Dive Kaua'i Scuba Center - dive tours, boat charters, equipment rentals, introductory dives and PADI certification. Scuba tours $65-80; intro to scuba $80; PADI certification $195-250. Rental equipment $6 per day or $26 per week. (808) 822-0452.

Fathom Five Divers ★ full service dive store and PADI certification. Introductory dives from one of their two 26' dive boats. They visit more than 20 dive locations ranging from 30 to 90 feet. Some dive sites include Sheraton Caverns, General Store, Ice Box, Brennecke's Ledge, Turtle Bluffs, and Zack's Pocket (named after their Hawaiian boat captain who discovered this site.) Their dive sites are only 10-15 minutes from the harbor, which makes a two tank boat dive a half day trip and provides adventures for the experienced and beginning divers. Maximum of 6 divers. Introductory 2 tank boat dive, no experience necessary $120 includes class, dives and gear. Introductory shore dive with one tank $79. For those who wish to join the boat trip, but don't wish to scuba, a $60 fee includes snorkel gear. (Half price if on standby) Their 4 or 5 day course for PADI certification includes lectures, diving each day and two boat dives on the last day. $359 includes it all. PADI, NAUI SSI open water check out dives are also available. (808) 742-6991

Mana Divers Scuba - They operate a 33 foot custom cabin cruiser with a maximum of 6 passengers. Their large swim platform offers easy water access and their hot fresh water shower is a real treat. They specialize in PADI instruction and do snorkeling and sunset tours as well. They offer half day two tank dives twice daily for $85 plus tax, or $100 with full gear outfit. One tank guided night dives are available for $65 plus tax, $80 with full gear. Weather permitting, they offer three tank trips to Mana Crack, and Ni'ihau Island. The Mana Kai is family owned and operated by Ken Lewis and Chan Airhart. (808) 742-9849.

Ocean Odyssey - (808) 245-8681

Seasport Divers - excursions depart aboard their six passenger boat from the Kukuiula small boat harbor. With 26 different dive sites to choose from, they can address all levels of diving enthusiasts. They offer a morning (8:30 am-12:30 pm) or afternoon (1 pm-4 pm) two tank, two location dive or an evening 6 pm-8:30 pm 1 tank night dive. Underwater videos will be filmed by the divemaster and are available for $39.95. They also offer 35 mm camera rentals. Two tank dives including equipment run $90, 2 tank dives without equipment $75, 1 tank night dive with equipment $70, 1 tank night dive with no equipment $65. Introductory boat dive with previous pool lesson $125. Snorkeler or rider $45. Shore dives for non-certified divers run $105 for a 2 tank resort dive, $75 for a 1 tank resort dive or refresher dive. Open water certification takes 3-4 days and runs $350. Advanced open water takes 2-3 days and runs $250. They offer complimentary pool lessons daily. Call for the scheduled lesson nearest to your location. They can arrange Ni'ihau Island dives as well. Also available are watersport equipment rentals including snorkel gear, boogie boards, beach chairs and scuba gear. PO Box 638, Kolo'a, HI 96756. (808) 742-9303 or (808) 742-7288 or FAX (808) 742-6636.

Sunrise Diving - No swimming skills are required for this diving experience. They do shore dives and outfit you in shallow water where the scuba gear becomes weightless. They conduct all dives from a calm beach and keep the group size down to six divers. (808) 822-7333

SEA EXCURSIONS

Sea excursions on Kaua'i have more limited options than on some of the other islands, but what makes it special on the garden island are the intimacies of the trips. Most use small boats with as few as 6 or a maximum of 25, so that the experience is much more personal.

Depending on the time of year, the roughness of the water can vary greatly. If you are concerned about motion sickness there are several over-the-counter medications that you could discuss with your doctor. Dramamine has been used my millions of people for years, however those folks that we have met that have

HUMUHUMUNUKUNUKUAPUAA

used this for motion difficulties have been so significantly affected by the sleepiness (which is a side effect for some individuals) that they can virtually sleep away the entire trip. While this might be an option for avoiding discomfort, they can't be having nearly as much fun as those of us who are alert! Bonine is another motion medication that can be purchased over-the-counter that for some people has less of a drowsiness effect. Ginger, which can be purchased in capsules at health food stores is recommended as a preventative for motion sickness as well. Check with your physician as to what options might work for you and with your health conditions and with other medications you may already be taking. Using simple techniques such as keeping your eye on the land and avoiding a heavy, greasy meal before a boat trip are the only precautions most people need to use!

Bluewater Sailing - Half day (4-hour) snorkeling trips aboard their 42' Piersen ketch. Snorkeling/sailing with light meal $75 adults. Evening 2 hour sunset sail with snacks and sodas $45. In the winter they sail from Port Allen to south shore locations. In the summer they sail along the northern coastline with snorkeling at Hanalei Bay. PO Box 1318, Hanalei, HI 96714. (808) 822-0525.

One of our readers, HJP of Deerfield, IL writes about their experience:

Sail Away to a Secluded Bay is an exclusive sail for 8 passengers. The four hour sail departs from Hanalei Bay at 11 am and returns at 3 pm. A gourmet deli lunch is provided. Cost is $100 per person and Blue Water Sailing is the tour operator. The boat is a 42' sail boat that will put up its sail once out of Hanalei Bay. It sails toward the Na Pali coastline where, if the sea is not too rough, guests can snorkel, swim and have lunch when Captain Rick drops anchor. The other area that is used is Honey Lagoon where it is very calm and great for snorkeling. Captain Rick will tell about the whales and sea animals that inhabit our ocean. He will also narrate stories of Kaua'i as he has lived there for over 20 years and sailed for over 10. An Exceptional Trip!

Captain Andy's Sailing Adventures - Sail aboard the 46' catamaran "Akialoa." Seasonal whale watching. Half day sailing, snorkeling, sightseeing and swimming plus deli lunch. Departs from Poi'pu. This is one of our two companies that we could find that does a Sunset Sail. Two hours of sailing fun with pupus. Cost for this evening sail is $46.87 adults, $31.25 children, including tax. Their four hour tour and picnic from Poi'pu to Kipu Kai is $78.12 adults and $62.50 children. (808) 822-7833.

Captain Sundown - Message on machine said not currently operating (808) 245-6117

Capt. Zodiac ★ Raft trips along the Na Pali coast during the summer months. During the winter they offer south shore excursions (December - April) that include 2 1/2 hour adventures to Kipukai for snorkeling or swimming. They offer sunrise trips, sunset trips, day trips and seasonal whale watching. A three-hour sunrise trip runs $65, some day trips also include a picnic and a hike. (808) 826-9371 or 1-800-422-7824. A brief review of a zodiac excursion follows:

The trip along the Na Pali coast is nothing short of incredible. Simply calling it a "majestic coastline," sounds too cliche for such spectacular scenery. The ride is thrilling and invigorating, yet it is difficult not to be in awe of the incredible western shore of Kaua'i. One minute you'll be "oohing" and "ahhing" over the scenery and the next you may be "eeking" with roller-coaster delight over the ride! The five hour trip stops for a picnic lunch along a secluded beach. Lunch includes deli sandwiches, pasta salad, sodas and cookies for dessert. There is time to eat and then snorkel (if sea conditions permit), explore around the beach and nearby forested area, or simply sit and soak up the beauty of the island.

Catamaran Kahanu - Tours of the Na Pali coastline in this power catamaran. Maximum 20 passengers. Covered area and private restroom. There are power engines on this catamaran to cruise near the coastline. A full buffet style lunch is included along with snorkel equipment. Cost is $85 adult, $65 child. Whale tours offered seasonally. (808) 826-4596. FAX 826-9371.

Hanalei Sea Tours - Cruise down Na Pali through sea caves to Nualolo Kai Beach. Snorkel gear and lunch provided for this 5 1/2 hour trip. Half day Na Pali coast tour includes snorkeling, 4 hours. Na Pali Coast Mini Tour includes seasonal whale watching and a good opportunity for sightseers and photographers to take in the beauty. This is one of the few companies that offer winter tours through Na Pali. A good opportunity to see the whales and dolphins as well as the incredible scenery. PO Box 1437 Hanalei, HI 96714. 1-800-733-7997 or (808) 826-PALI.

A nice alternative to a zodiac boat trip is a powered catamaran with their comfortable seats and a smoother, drier ride! Almost immediately after leaving Hanalei Bay, we were treated to a show from the playful Hawaiian spinner dolphins. A little further out, a pod of humpback whales swam by. With the majestic Na Pali Coast in the background, that was a magnificent sight. Although we could not actually go in (the winter waves were a bit high), the captain treated us with an up-close look at several splendid sea caves. One had a waterfall at the opening and he teased us by getting extremely close to it. Those of us in the back had put on our slickers and told him to go for it; we were ready! As we headed down the coast to Nualolo Kai Beach for snorkeling, sodas and snacks, we passed a large lava tube and the promontory dividing Kaua'i's most secluded and romantic beach, Honopu. (It was the backdrop for movies like King Kong and Jurassic Park.) There was plenty of time for snorkeling and just relaxing before heading back for another look at the scenic beauty of the waters and cliffs of Na Pali.

Liko Kaua'i Cruises - A 38 foot cabin cruiser with the luxury of a freshwater shower. Deli lunch provided. They cruise the Na Pali coastline. They depart from Kikiaola Harbor in Kekaha. $85 adults, $65 children, a 4 1/2 hour trip leaves at 8:30 am. (808) 338-0333.

Na Pali (Eco) Adventures - ★ is dedicating to the understanding and protection of our eco system. Their guided trip along the Na Pali coast is led by a trained naturalist. They use motor-powered, hard-body catamarans that provide a smoother and drier ride than on the inflatables or rafts, but still plenty of thrills! They have sightseeing cruises only or sightseeing combined with a one hour snorkeling experience at one of several protected bays along the coastline. Snorkel gear and light refreshments are included on this later cruise. The operators are genuinely concerned with the welfare of whales and other aquatic life, and it shows in the way they run their cruise. If the whales are out there, they'll find them. An underwater microphone allows you to hear the whales' musical conversation. In addition to whales (in season), you might also be treated to a pod of dolphins swimming along your boat, green sea turtles floating like huge army helmets upon the water or if you look quickly, you may spot a flying fish. We were fortunate during our excursion to be greeted by Kaua'i's most rare aquatic animal. The monk seal on first sighting appeared to be lounging in the water, however, on the return trip he appeared in another bay, giving us what appeared to be a smile! Realizing that there is estimated to be only three seals living in the waters around Kaua'i, our captain felt that we had seen the same seal twice and that they rarely see them more than a couple times of year. Ours was a lucky trip indeed. Cost is $80 adults, $60 children for snorkel and tour. Sunset tour $60 adults, $40 children. Mini morning sightseeing $60 adults, $40 children. PO Box 1017, Hanalei, HI 96714. (808) 826-6804. FAX (808) 826-7073. 1-800-659-6804.

Sundancer Cruises - Whaling watching, Na Pali excursions, snorkeling trips, private charters and helicopter/boat packages. Sundancer Cruises operates a Power Catamaran. 2 1/2 hour wet & wonderful sails $59, $49 for 12 and under. Na Pali Quest is $84 adults, $69 for youths 12 and under and includes a deli buffet. PO Box 148, Eleele, HI 96705. (808) 335-0110, FAX (808) 335-5610.

SKATING

Rollerblade every Sunday from 4 pm to 6 pm there is free at GIFT In-Line Skating Club at Kukui Grove West Village, behind the driving range and bumper boats. Full safety gear required. Free lessons on how to skate, stop, turn and go backwards. Mini races too! For information call Sunday Murch at 245-5381.

SNORKELING

Since weather conditions and ocean conditions cause very dramatic differences in the snorkeling conditions from day to day, a dive shop is a great place to find the tip for the best spot of the day. The staff is friendly and they are eager to ensure you have a great snorkeling experience. If weather conditions are just right, Tunnels on the North Shore is a wonderful snorkel spot. Poi'pu Beach on the South shore will be of interest to the novice and intermediate snorkeler.

You can purchase a disposable underwater camera. You'll get some interesting souvenir photos, but the quality isn't nearly as good as the real thing. One trick we discovered was to use vaseline on the mustache to help seal the mask. Several areas around the island have fish that are accustomed to being feed. In fact, they almost expect it! They enjoy bread or try the dried packages of noodles. One source in days gone by recommended that we try peas. Thinking it would be healthier for the fish than white bread, we gave them a try. The fish were not too interested and then we learned that the uneaten peas would wash up on the shore making a squishy, smelly mess. We were also told that the fish have trouble digesting the outer coating of the pea. A number of dive shops, and Safeway, carry a little package of smelly fish food pellets. The price tag is a couple of dollars for two tubes of food. You can cut off one end of the plastic tube-bag and slowly shake out the pellets.

Kids will take to snorkeling with little effort. The only difficulty might be in their excitement when they spot the fish for the first time. They may forget they have a snorkel in their mouth when they try and shout out their glee. Our son became very adept at talking with his snorkel in his mouth, and hearing his words come out the top of his snorkel is a constant source of amusement. For the child which lacks confidence, use water wings for extra buoyancy. A life jacket, of course, is even more security. An adult may find taking a paddle board out and positioning themselves over the top of it (face in the water on one side and feet in the water on the other) a way to get over their initial jitters. Rest assured that snorkeling is much, much easier than swimming. Even easier than walking! All you have to do is float and breathe!

Lydgate is a fine beach for the novice child snorkeler. It has a very sheltered area which will inspire confidence. Perhaps the most difficulty for a beginning snorkeler is just getting into the water. Waves make this a more difficult task. Once you're in the water and enjoying the sights, you'll wonder why you never tried it before. Poʻipu Beach is generally good for beginning snorkeling as well. For intermediate snorkelers Keʻe, Hideaways or Tunnels can be good during calm summer surf. The dive shops can advise you which locations are best at the time of your visit.

Rental equipment is available at a number of locations around the island. With snorkel gear you will get what you pay for. Prices range from $4-5 a day and up. Silicon gear is preferred, but you won't find that at the economy prices. If you plan on adding snorkeling to your list of regular recreational activities, you may find it worthwhile to bite the bullet and invest in your own set of gear. You can pickup an inexpensive set of fins, mask and snorkel for a child at Long's drugstore, Costco, Kmart or Walmart.

REEF DWELLERS

J. BAYOT

289

Also refer to the Sea Excursions section for snorkeling trips which are available from various departures around the island. Also see the scuba section which has information on beach rental equipment.

Bay Island Water Sports - Offers snorkel tours from the beach in Princeville. (808) 862-7509.

Brennecke's Beach Center - Rents cheap equipment, but it is cheap. (808) 742-6570.

Fathom Five - Half day boat trips are available to secluded snorkeling sites off the South side (808) 742-691.

Hanalei Surf Company - Offers a range of rental equipment: mask, fins and snorkel, $20 per week; boogie board, $30 per week; wet suits, $4 per day. Located on Kuhio Hwy #560 across from the Ching-Yung Village. (808) 826-9000

Kaua'i Snorkel Rental - Rental snorkel equipment runs $4 a day, $10 a week, located in the Coconut Market Place (808) 823-8300.

Mana Divers Scuba - They operate a 33-foot custom cabin cruiser with a maximum of 6 passengers. Their large swim platform offers easy water access and their hot fresh water shower is a real treat. They specialize in PADI instruction, but also do snorkeling and sunset tours as well. 742-9849.

Pedal and Paddle Hanalei - They rent snorkeling equipment at two locations. In Hanalei (808) 826-9069 or Kapa'a (808) 822-2005.

Po'ipu Surf & Sport (808) 742-1132

SeaFun Kaua'i - Walk in from shore 1/2 day snorkel adventures at many varied beaches. They provide pick up, equipment, snorkel instruction and guided tour of the reef, snacks and drinks. In the summer they snorkel at 'Anini or Tunnels in the winter at Lawa'i or Po'ipu Cost is $50 adults, $37.50 children under 13. Winter tour to south coast, summer tour to north shore. $50 adults, $37 children. PO Box 3002, Lihu'e, HI 96766 (808) 245-6400.

Snorkel Bob's has two shops at Ahukini Rd. in Lihu'e and Po'ipu Shopping Village and several others opening soon. $15-40 per week for snorkel/fins/mask.

SNUBA

Snuba Tours of Kaua'i - Snuba, as it sounds, is a blend of snorkeling and scuba. The air source is contained within a floatation raft that follows you as you move beneath the ocean. The guided underwater tour includes personalized instruction, fish food and equipment, $49 per person. Hourly Monday through Saturday beginning at 9:30 am with the last dive at 1:30 pm. They dive from Lawa'i Beach. (808) 823-8912.

SURFING

Hanalei Surf Company rents boards fiberglass surfboards for $15 per day, $65 per week. Soft surfboards $12 per day, $50 per week. Boogie board $5 per day, $30 per week. Located on Kuhio Hwy. across from the Ching-Young Village. (808) 826-9000.

Margo Oberg's Surfing School. Located at the Kiahuna Plantation Resort (808) 742-6411, FAX (808) 742-1750. Lessons run $40 per person per hour.

Kayak Kaua'i Outfitters offers Hawaiian surf boarding lessons, $25 per hour. Kapa'a (808) 822-9179; Hanalei (808) 826-9844; 1-800-437-3507.

Windsurf Kaua'i offers surfing instruction and rental equipment. PO Box 323 Hanalei, 96714. (808) 828-6838.

TENNIS

Kaua'i County has eight municipal public tennis courts. Hanapepe courts were damaged by Iniki and are no longer open. Available courts are in Waimea, Kekaha, Koloa, Kalaheo, Lihu'e, Wailua Homesteads, Wailua Houselots and Kapa'a New Park. Many hotels have courts available for guest use.

The Hyatt Regency has a tennis center with plexi-pave courts. Open 7 am - 6 pm, court fees are $20 per hour. Daily instructional clinics (9:30-10:30 am) run $12 per person per hour, discounts for "juniors" ages 15 and under. Private lessons available. They also offer club memberships. (808) 742-6251

Kaua'i Lagoons Racquet Club (808) 241-6000

Po'ipu Kai Tennis Complex (808) 742-1144

Princeville Resort Tennis Complex (808) 826-3620

THEATER

The Kaua'i Community Players does several productions annually. Check the local newspaper for upcoming performances. Call 822-1099 for more information.

The Kaua'i Community College of Performing Arts is anticipating that their new $12 million theater will open in the Fall of 1995. The theater complex was almost complete when Hurricane Iniki destroyed it. The new hall will have seats for 550 persons and will add an exciting new dimension to theater possibilities on Kaua'i.

WATERSKIING

Kaua'i Water Ski - Rates run $85 per hour, $45 per 1/2 hour, $25 single ride. They travel up the Wailua River in a Master Craft. Mondays through Fridays 9 am - 5 pm. (808) 822-3574.

WHALE WATCHING

Whale watching is seasonal, generally late November through March, although stragglers may linger into April and some anxious for those warm waters of the Hawaiian islands may arrive a bit ahead of schedule. The best vantage points for whale watching are from one of the boats that make excursions out in search of these magnificent mammals. You can also view them from above during a helicopter tour. As for a best bet, we would recommend one of the condos above the bluff at Princeville or the Northern most point of the island at the Kilauea lighthouse.

WILDLIFE REFUGES

As you pass the Princeville Center you are at mile marker 28 on Hwy. 56, which now switches to mile marker 0 as you suddenly change to highway 560. Just past this on the left is the scenic lookout for the *Hanalei Wildlife Refuge*. The Hanalei Wildlife Refuge was established on 917 acres in 1972 and is located in the Hanalei Valley. Unique to many refuges, taro is allowed to be commercially farmed on a portion of the property and one permit is granted for cattle grazing. Administered by the U.S. Fish and Wildlife Service as a unit of the National Wildlife Refuge System, they actively manage habitat to provide wetlands for endangered Hawaiian waterbirds. Historic farming (taro) and grazing practices are compatible with the refuges objectives and thus permitted to a limited degree. There are 49 species of birds, including the endangered Hawaiian black-necked stilt, gallinule, coot, and duck that make their home here. Of the 49 species, 18 are introduced. There are no native mammals, reptiles or amphibians, except possibly the Hawaiian bat. The refuge is not open to the public, but an interpretive overlook on the state highway just north of the refuge allows an excellent photo opportunity. Hurricane Iniki caused major damage to the facilities and habitat of this refuge and recovery continues.

Located along the Huleia River is the *Huleia National Wildlife Refuge*, which is home to the endangered koloa duck. In 1973, 241 acres were purchased to provide water bird habitat. The lands, once taro and rice fields, are now breeding and feeding grounds for a variety of waterfowl. the refuge is located in a relatively flat valley along the Huleia River which is bordered by a steep wooded hillside. There are 31 species of migratory birds which inhabit the area and 18 of these species were introduced. A special permit is issued annually to a commercial kayaking

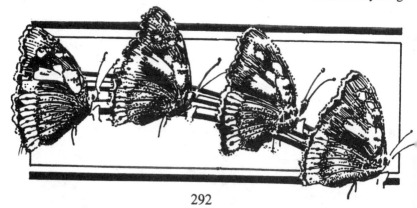

business for access through an upland portion of the refuge. The refuge, adjacent to the menehune fish ponds, is not open to the public, however, a view of it from the Menehune overlook along the road is possible.

The *Kilauea Point National Wildlife Refuge* was established in 1974 and is recognized as Hawai'i's largest seabird sanctuary, a place that is home to more than 5,000 seabirds. This refuge is a nesting site for the red-footed booby, wedge-tailed shearwater, Laysan albatross and many other species of Hawaiian seabirds. The acquisition of land at Kilauea Wildlife Refuge has continued ever since with this sanctuary now encompassing 203 acres. The refuge was struck hard by Hurricane Iniki. Not only was there much damage to the birdlife and vegetation, but the famous lighthouse was also seriously affected. At Kilauea Point, they reported that about 80% of the native plants suffered damage. On Crater Hill, at least 25% were lost and an additional 50% damaged. Mokolea Point vegetation suffered little damage. Kilauea Point lost the most birds and suffered the worst damage to the habitat. The Kaua'i Natural Wildlife Refuge complex lost 12 of their 20 buildings. There was also damage to the lighthouse visitor center and bookstore, storage buildings, fences, and the water delivery system.

WINDSURFING

Once again, weather conditions will determine where this activity is best suited. 'Anini is the best for beginners. Located near Princeville it offers a lagoon with protected waters and steadily blowing winds that make it ideal for the beginning or intermediate windsurfer. Advanced windsurfers enjoy Tunnels on the North Shore or what they refer to as the YMCA Beach located 1/4 mile past Charo's and Mahaulepu on the South Shore.

'Anini Beach Windsurfing - Windsurfing lessons offered for $25 for the first hour, $20 an hour after that. It includes all equipment and instruction. Rental of equipment includes racks and runs $50 for 24 hours. (808) 826-9463.

Windsurf Kaua'i - Located on the North Shore with instruction at 'Anini lagoon. Celeste Harvel is a master instructor who offers state-of-the-art beginning windsurf boards. These boards are a foot shorter, 11' feet as opposed to the conventional 12' board, which allows for easier maneuvering. The boards are also just slightly wider. 'Anini lagoon has a maximum depth of seven feet and 10-20 knot winds year round. Half of the lagoon is designated for windsurfers, the other half for swimming and snorkeling. Lessons for first timers run $75 for a three hour class with a maximum of 6 people in the class. This phase of instruction includes learning how to steer, sail and come back to shore. The second level class is the same price and length, but completes certification. This three hour instruction includes learning how to jibe, beach start and rigging. The new equipment makes windsurfing easy for everyone. For the less athletic individual she utilizes a 15 square foot sail with a 4 1/2 foot boom which is very manage-able. She has custom equipment for children and can teach anyone five years and up. She also offers extensive windsurf equipment rental. Rental equipment is $50 all day or $20 per hour. In the winter, spring and fall Celeste also offers surfing lessons at Hanalei Bay. Using a long board with a soft foam deck, the one and one half hour instruction plus use of the board for the rest of the day runs $50. PO Box 323 Hanalei, HI 96714. (808) 828-6838.

RECOMMENDED READING

Aikin, Ross R. Kilauea Point Lighthouse: The Landfall Beacon on the Orient Run. Kialauea Point Natural History Association. 1988.

Alexander, Arthur C. Koloa Plantation, 1835-1935, a history of the oldest Hawaiian sugar plantation. Honolulu: Honolulu Star Bulletin. 1937.

Anderson, Mary E. Scenes in the Hawaiian Islands. Boston: Cornill Press. 1865.

Anderson, Isabel Weld Perkins. The Spell of the Hawaiian Islands and the Philippines. Boston: The Colonial Press. 1916.

Barrhre, Dorothy. Hula, historical perspectives. Honolulu: Bishop Museum. 1980.

Beekman, Allan. The Niihau incident: the true story of the Japanese fighter pilot. Honolulu: Heritage Press of Pacific. 1982.

Begley, Bryan. Taro in Hawaii. Honolulu: The Oriental Publishing Co. 1979.

Bennett, Wendall Clark. Archaeology of Kauai. Honolulu: Bernice P. Bishop Museum Bulletin. Kraus Reprint Co. 1971.

Bird, Isabella. Six Months in the Sandwich Islands. Tokyo: Tuttle. 1988

Boom, Bob and Christensen, Chris. Important Hawaiian Place Names. Hawaii: Bob Boom Books. 1978.

Borg, Jim. Hurricane Iniki. Honolulu: Mutual Publishing. 1992.

Chisholm, Craig. Hawaiian Hiking Trails. Lake Oswego, OR.: Fernglen Press. 1994.

Chisholm, Craig. Kaua'i Hiking Trails. Lake Oswego, OR.: Fernglen Press. 1991.

Clark, John R. K. Beaches of Kaua'i and Ni'ihau. Honolulu: University of Hawaii Press, 1990.

Day, A. Grove. Hawai'i and its People. New York: Duall, Sloan, Pearce. 1955

Ellis, William. Journal of William Ellis (1794-1872). Honolulu: Advertiser Publishing Co. Originally published in 1917. Reprinted in 1963.

Fielding, Ann. Hawaiian Reefs and Tidepools. Hawaii: Oriental Pub. Co.

Forbes, David. Queen Emma and Lawai. Kauai Historical Society. 1970.

Forander, Abraham. Hawaiian Antiquities and Folk-Lore. Honolulu: Bishop Museum Press. 1919.

Franck, Harry A. Roaming in Hawaii: A Narrative of Months of Wandering Among the Glamours Islands That May Become or 49th State. New York: Grosset & Dunlap. 1937.

Gay, Lawrence Kainoahou. Tales of the Forbidden Island of Niʻihau. Topgallant Publishing Co. 1981.

Gay, Roland Lalana Kapahukaniolono. Hawaii, Tales of Yesteryear, a collection of Legends and Stories. R. Gay Co. 1977.

Golf Hawaii: the complete guide. Windward Promotions. 1991.

Haldey, Thelma H. Road guide to Kokeʻe and Waimea Canyon State Parks. Honolulu: Bess Press. 1993.

Haraguchi, Paul. Weather in Hawaiian Waters. 1983.

Harrison, Craig S. Seabirds of Hawaii: Natural History and Conservation. NY: Comstock Publishing. 1990.

Hawaii Audubon Society. Hawaii's birds. Honolulu: The Society. 1993.

Hazama, Dorothy. The Ancient Hawaiians. Honolulu: Hogarth Press.

Hoverson, Martha ed. Historic Koloa: A guide. Koloa: Friends of Koloa. 1988.

Hume, Kathryn Cavarly. Robert Allerton Story, 1873-1964. John Greegg Allerton. 1979.

Hurricane Iwa Hits Hawaii. Lubbock, TX: C.F. Boone. 1982.

The Kauaʻi Papers. Kauai: Kauai Historical Society. 1991.

Joesting, Edward. Kauai: The Separate Kingdom. Honolulu: University of Hawaii Press. 1984.

Judd, Gerrit. Hawaii, an Informal History. New York: Collier Books. 1961.

Kauai Bicentennial Committee. Waimea, Island of Kauai 1778-1978. Kauai Bicentennial Committee. 1977.

Kauai Historical Society. The Kauaʻi Papers. Kauaʻi. 1991.

Kelly, Marion. Pele and Hiʻiaka visit the sites at Keʻe, Haʻena, Island of Kauaʻi. Honolulu: Bernice P. Bishop Museum Press, 1984.

Klass, Tim. World War II on Kauaʻi Historical Research by Tim Klass. Kauaʻi Historical Society. 1970.

Knudsen, Eric Alfred. Kanuka of Kauai. Tongg. 1944.

Kndusen, Eric. Teller of Tales. Honolulu: Mutual Publishing. 1946.

Knudsen, Valdemar. Koolau, outlaw: a story about the Na Pali Coast. Koloa: V. Knudsen. 1976.

Kramer, Raymond J. Hawaiian Land Mammals. VT: C.E. Tuttle Co. 1971.

Krauss, Bob. Grove Farm Plantation: the biography of a Hawaiian sugar plantation. Palo Alto, CA: Pacific Books. 1984.

Krauss, Robert. Here's Hawaii. New York: Coward-McAnn, Inc. 1960.

London, Jack. Stories of Hawaii. Honolulu: Mutual Publishing. 1965.

Ludwig, Myles. Kauai in the eye of Iniki. Hanalei Bay, Kauai: Inter-Pacific Media. 1992.

McSpadden, J. Walker. Beautiful Hawaii. New York: Thomas Y. Crowell, 1939.

Morey, Kathy. Kauai Trails: Walks, Strolls, and Treks on the Garden Island. Berkely, CA: Wilderness Press, 1991.

Moriarty, Linda. Ni'ihau shell leis. Honolulu: University of Hawaii Press. 1986.

O'Malley, Anne E. Miracle of Iniki: stories of aloha from the heart of Kaua'i. Honolulu: Bess Press. 1993.

Pukui, Mary and Korn, Alfons. Echos of Our Song. Honolulu: University of Hawaii Press. 1973

Pukui, Mary K. et al. The Pocket Hawaiian Dictionary. Honolulu: The University of Hawaii Press. 1975.

Pukui, Mary Kawena. Tales of the Menehune. Honolulu: Kamehameha Schools Press. 1985.

Pratt, Douglas. Enjoying birds in Hawaii. Honolulu: Mutual Publishing. 1993.

Rice, William Hyde. Hawaiian Legends. Honolulu: Bishop Museum Press. 1977.

Smith, Robert. Hiking Kauai. Long Beach, CA: Hawaiian Outdoor Adventures. 1989.

Smith, Robert. Hawai'i's Best Hiking Trails. CA: Hawaiian Outdoor Adventures. 1991.

Smith, Walter James. Legends of Wailua. Kauai Printers. 1955.

Stepien, Edward R. Niihau, A Brief History. Published by the Center for Pacific Island tudies, 1988.

Stevenson, Robert Louis. Travels in Hawaii. Honolulu: University of Hawaii Press. 1973.

Tabrah, Ruth. Kaua'i, The Unconquerable Island. Las Vegas. K.C. Publications. 1988.

Tabrah, Ruth. Ni'ihau, the last Hawaiian Island. Kailua, HI: Press Pacific. 1987.

Tanimoto, Charles Katsumu. Return to Mahaulepu Personal Sketches. C.K. Tanimoto. 1982.

Tava, Rerioterai. <u>Niihau: the traditions of a Hawaiian island.</u> Honolulu: Mutual Publishing. 1989.

Titcomb, M. <u>Native Use of Fish in Hawaii.</u> Honolulu: University of Hawaii Press. 1952.

Valier, Kathy. <u>On the Na Pali Coast</u>. Honolulu: University of Hawaii Press. 1988.

VanHolt, Ida Elizabeth Knudsen. <u>Stories of Long Ago: Niihau, Kauai, Oahu.</u> Daughters of Hawaii. 1985.

Westervelt, W.D. <u>Myths and Legends of Hawaii.</u> Honolulu: Mutual Publishing Co. 1987.

Wichman, Juliet Rice. <u>A Chronicle and Flora of Niihau</u>. Kaua'i: National Tropical Botanical Garden. 1990.

Wichman, Frederick. <u>Kauai Tales.</u> Honolulu: Bamboo Ridge Press. 1985.

Wichman, Frederick. <u>Polihale and other Kaua'i legends.</u> Honolulu: Bamboo Ridge Press. 1991.

Wisniewski, Richard A. <u>The Rise and Fall of the Hawaiian Kingdom.</u> Honolulu: Pacific Basin Enterprises. 1979.

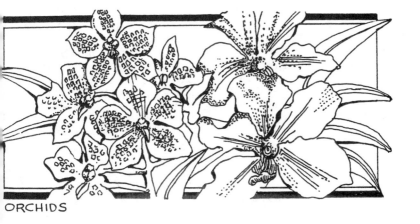

ORCHIDS

ENJOY ALL OUR PARADISE FAMILY GUIDES TO HAWAII

Hawaiian guides for every budget and every member of the family! Designed for travelers who want to set their own pace with complete vacation control. These are THE guides to have. Complemented by quarterly newsletters which update the changes in the islands between guidebook revisions. Plenty of "insider" information from authors who really know the islands! These Hawaiian titles and videos may be ordered direct from Paradise Publications.

MAUI, A PARADISE FAMILY GUIDE

(Including the Island of Lanaʻi) by Greg & Christie Stilson. The island of Maui is one of Hawaiʻi's most popular. This guide is packed with information on over 150 condos & hotels, 200 restaurants, 50 great beaches, sights to see and travel tips for the valley island. All new! The island of Lanaʻi, as a part of the County of Maui, has been added to this popular guide. Lanaʻi recently joined the tourist industry with the opening of two fabulous new resorts. There is fine dining, local eateries, remote beaches, wonderful hikes and an enchantment unlike any other island. *"A down-to-earth, nuts-and-bolts companion with answers to most any question."* L.A.Times. 360 pgs, multi-indexed, maps, illustrations, $12.95. 6th ed. 7th edition due out late 1996, projected price $14.95.

KAUAʻI, A PARADISE FAMILY GUIDE

by Dona Early & Christie Stilson. Completely revised and rewritten since Hurricane Iniki, this information packed guide describes island accommodations, restaurants, secluded beaches, plus recreation and tour options. "If you need a 'how to do it' book to guide your next to Kauaʻi, here's the one.". 300 pages, multi-indexed, maps, illustrations, $14.95. Fourth edition.

HAWAIʻI: THE BIG ISLAND, A PARADISE FAMILY GUIDE

by John Penisten. Outstanding for its completeness, this well-organized guide provides useful information for people of every budget and lifestyle. Each chapter features the author's personal recommendations and "best bets." Comprehensive information on more than 70 island accommodations and 150 restaurants. Sights to see, recreational activities, beaches, and helpful travel tips. 284 pages. Maps and illustrations. $12.95. 4th ed.

UPDATE NEWSLETTERS! *THE MAUI UPDATE, THE KAUAʻI UPDATE,* and *HAWAIʻI: THE BIG ISLAND UPDATE* are quarterly newsletters published by Paradise Publications that highlight the most current island events. Each features late breaking tips on the newest restaurants, island activities or special, not-to-be missed events. Each newsletter available at the single issue price of $2.50 or a yearly subscription (four issues) rate of $10. Canada $12 per year.

FREE! A complimentary copy of Paradise Publication's quarterly newsletter, **THE MAUI UPDATE,** is available (at no charge) by writing Paradise Publications (Attention: Newsletter Dept.) 8110 S.W. Wareham, Suite 304, Portland, OR 97223, and enclosing a self-addressed, stamped, #10 size envelope.

We know you have a wonderful visit to Maui. Since this book expresses primarily the author's opinion on accommodations, restaurants, and recreation, we would sincerely appreciate hearing of your experiences. Any updates or changes would also be welcomed.

ORDERING INFORMATION

Available from Paradise Publications are books and videos to enhance your travel library and assist with your travel plans, or provide a special gift for someone who is planning a trip! For a full listing of current titles send request to Paradise Publications. Prices are subject to change without notice.

BOOKS

MAUI, THE ROMANTIC ISLAND, and *KAUA'I, THE UNCONQUERABLE* by K.C. Publications. These two books present full color photographs depicting the most magnificent sights on each island. Brief descriptive text adds perspective. Highly recommended. 9 x 12, 48 pages, $6.95 each, paperback. Also available from K.C. Publications: *HALEAKALA* and *HAWAII VOLCANOES* Each of these fascinating and informative book is filled with vivid photographs depicting these natural volcanic wonders. A great gift or memento. 9 x 12, $6.95 each.

DIVERS GUIDE TO MAUI by Chuck Thorne. This easy-to-use guide will give you all the information you need to choose the perfect dive site. $9.95.

HAWAII GOLF GUIDE, published by TeeBox, features every island course. Information is comprehensive covering the basics, such as course location, number of holes and phone number, as well as in-depth information on golf course features and course strategy. 165 pages, published in 1994. $12.95.

HAWAIIAN HIKING TRAILS by Craig Chisholm. This very attractive and accurate guide details 49 of Hawaii's best hiking trails. Includes photography, topographical maps, and detailed directions. An excellent book for the out-of-doors person! 152 pgs., $15.95. 1994.

KAUAI HIKING TRAILS by Craig Chisholm. Also from Fernglen Press this 160 page book features color photographs, topographical maps and detailed directions to Kaua'i's best hiking trails. A quality publication. $12.95. 1991.

HIKING MAUI by Robert Smith. Discover 27 hiking areas all around Maui. 5 x 8 paperback, 160 pages. $10.95. Also by Robert Smith. *HIKING KAUA'I*, over 40 hiking trails throughout Kaua'i. 116 pages, $10.95. *HIKING HAWAII (The Big Island)*, 157 pages, $10.95. Black & white photographs and maps. Compact and easy-to-use.

COOKING WITH ALOHA by Elvira Monroe and Irish Margah. Discover the flavors and smells of the Hawaiian islands in your own kitchen with this easy-to-follow cookbook. appetizers to desserts are covered. A great and inexpensive guide to cooking your favorite Hawaiian foods. 9 x 12, paperback, 184 pages, $9.95.

MAPS!

By popular request, we now carry the excellent series of full-color topographical maps by cartographer James A. Bier. Map are available for $2.95 each for the islands of O'ahu, Maui, Kaua'i and the Big Island of Hawai'i.

VIDEOS   *(All Videos are VHS format)*

***NEW!!* HAWAII ON FOOT** -- Robert Smith recently completed this video which explores the best dayhikes and backpacks on the four major islands -- Kaua'i, Maui, Hawai'i, and O'ahu. This video contains narratives on Hawaii's unique flora, fauna, geology, folklore and Hawaiian culture. It also contains safety information and equipment needs for your hiking or backpacking experience on Kaua'i. Robert Smith is the author of *Hiking Maui, Hiking Kaua'i, Hiking Hawaii, Hawaiian Hiking Trails* and *Hiking O'ahu* and has sold thousands of these guidebooks since they were first published. 40 minutes $19.95.

FOREVER HAWAII -- This 60 minute, video portrait features all six major Hawaiian islands. (Note: Does not include coverage of the resorts on Lana'i.) It includes breathtaking views from the snowcapped peaks of Mauna Kea to the bustling city of Waikiki, from the magnificent Waimea Canyon to the spectacular Halakeala Crater. A lasting memento. 1992. $24.95

FOREVER MAUI -- An in-depth visit to Maui with scenic shots and interesting stories about the Valley Isle. An excellent video for the first time, or even the returning Maui visitor. 30 minutes. 1992. $22.95

FLIGHT OF THE CANYON BIRD -- An inspired view of the Garden Island of Kaua'i from a bird's eye perspective; an outstanding 30 minute piece of cinematography. This short feature presentation explores the lush tropical rain-forests surrounding Waialeale (the wettest spot on earth), the awesome Waimea Canyon and the Napili Coastline. The narration explores the geologic and historic beginnings of the island. A lasting memento or gift! $22.95.

EXPLORE HAWAII: A TRAVEL GUIDE -- The scenes are similar to that of Forever Hawai'i, but this is a very fast paced 30-minute tour of all six islands. One helpful feature of this tape is the way place names of the areas being viewed are displayed on the screen. $14.95.

KUMU HULUA: KEEPERS OF A CULTURE -- This 85-minute tape was funded by the Hawaii State Foundation on Culture and Arts. This beautifully filmed work includes hulas from various troupes on various islands, attired in their brilliantly colored costumes and explores the unique qualities of hula as well as explaining the history. $29.95.

HULA - LESSONS ONE AND TWO -- "Lovely Hula Hands" and "Little Brown Gal" are the two featured hulas taught by Carol "Kalola" Lorenzo who explains the basic steps of the hula. A fun and interesting video for the whole family. 30 minutes. $29.95.

SHIPPING: In the Continental U.S.-- Please add $4 for 1 to 4 items (books or videos). Each additional item over 4, please add $1. Orders shipped promptly by US First class mail If you'd prefer items shipped bookrate mail, we'll be happy to quote you shipping costs. Canadian Orders -- Please add $4 for the first book and $1 each additional book/tape. Orders shipped U.S. small parcel airmail. Federal Express or overnight mail services are available.

Include your check or money order/Visa or Mastercard information and send to:
PARADISE PUBLICATIONS, 8110 S.W. Wareham, Suite 305
Portland, Oregon 97223   Phone or FAX (503) 246-1555